Lecture Notes in Computer Science 12287

More information about this series at http://www.springer.com/series/7410

Jonathan Anderson · Frank Stajano ·
Bruce Christianson · Vashek Matyáš (Eds.)

Security
Protocols XXVII

27th International Workshop
Cambridge, UK, April 10–12, 2019
Revised Selected Papers

 Springer

Editors
Jonathan Anderson ⓘ
Memorial University
St. John's, NL, Canada

Bruce Christianson ⓘ
University of Hertfordshire
Hatfield, UK

Frank Stajano ⓘ
Computer Laboratory
University of Cambridge
Cambridge, UK

Vashek Matyáš ⓘ
Masaryk University
Brno, Czech Republic

ISSN 0302-9743   ISSN 1611-3349 (electronic)
Lecture Notes in Computer Science
ISBN 978-3-030-57042-2   ISBN 978-3-030-57043-9 (eBook)
https://doi.org/10.1007/978-3-030-57043-9

LNCS Sublibrary: SL4 – Security and Cryptology

This Springer imprint is published by the registered company Springer Nature Switzerland AG
The registered company address is: Gewerbestrasse 11, 6330 Cham, Switzerland

Preface

This volume contains the revised proceedings of the 27th International Workshop on Security Protocols, held at Trinity College, Cambridge, UK, during April 10–12, 2019. The theme of this year's workshop was "security protocols for humans." Getting protocol details right is critical in the presence of a malicious adversary, but so is understanding the context in which a protocol is deployed: protocols are components of larger systems that human beings put their trust in. How can we design protocols to expose meaningful information about state and functionality to their users? What are the consequences when we don't? How can we bridge the gap between technical definitions of protocol correctness and users' security expectations?

As with previous workshops in this series, participation in the 2019 workshop was by invitation only, following submission of a position paper. The format of the workshop is intended to encourage vibrant discussions; the papers in this volume have been revised by their authors to incorporate ideas that emerged from this discussion. The discussion itself is also represented in this volume by a curated transcript that accompanies each paper.

Three awards were presented at the 2019 workshop, based on votes submitted by workshop participants. The Roger Needham Award for the paper eliciting the most interesting discussion award was awarded to Diana A. Vasile for her presentation, "Ghost Trace on the Wire? Using key evidence for informed decisions." The Best Presentation Award went to Mansoor Ahmed for his presentation, "Snitches Get Stitches: On the Difficulty of Whistleblowing." Finally, the Most Interesting Questions Award went to Fabio Massacci.

Our thanks go to all authors who participated in revising their position papers and transcripts of discussions. Two papers, unfortunately, are not included in this volume due to a lack of participation in the editorial process. Special thanks are also extended to Brett Gutstein, Michael Dodson, and Harry Jones who assisted in the smooth running of the workshop, including the recording of workshop audio to aid the transcription process.

We hope that reading these proceedings will encourage you to join in the debate, and perhaps even to send us a position paper for the next workshop.

July 2020

Jonathan Anderson
Program Chair

Frank Stajano
General Chair

Bruce Christianson
Vashek Matyáš

Previous Proceedings in this Series

The proceedings of previous International Security Protocols Workshops are also published by Springer as *Lecture Notes in Computer Science,* and are occasionally referred to in the text:

No published proceedings exist for the first three workshops.

Contents

Human Limitations in Security

Secure Sharing and Collaboration

Is the Future Finally Arriving?

Evidence of Humans Behaving Badly

Warnings

Designing for Humans

Transparency Enhancing Technologies to Make Security Protocols Work for Humans

Alexander Hicks and Steven J. Murdoch[✉]

University College London, London, UK
{alexander.hicks,s.murdoch}@ucl.ac.uk

Abstract. As computer systems are increasingly relied on to make decisions that will have significant consequences, it has also become important to provide not only standard security guarantees for the computer system but also ways of explaining the output of the system in case of possible errors and disputes. This translates to new security requirements in terms of human needs rather than technical properties. For some context, we look at prior disputes regarding banking security and the ongoing litigation concerning the Post Office's Horizon system, discussing the difficulty in achieving meaningful transparency and how to better evaluate available evidence.

1 Introduction

The theme of this year's workshop, security protocols for humans, highlights the importance of understanding the human context in which protocols are deployed. In particular, as computer systems are increasingly used to make decisions which will have significant consequences for the people involved, it is important to understand the interplay between the meaning of security for those that execute the protocol and those that are subject to the decisions of the protocol.

One important aspect of this is how failures of a system affect different parties. The fact that failure does not always affect the party responsible for the failure is unfortunate but has already been discussed in the context of security economics [1]. Last year we also broadly discussed the related role of incentives in security protocols [2]. The takeaway from this work is that of course incentives matter, but implementing them is hard. In particular, it is important to provide a way of enabling them: evidence.

Producing evidence in the context of computer systems has already been covered to some extent in the context of banking security, specifically the EMV (EuroPay-Mastercard-Visa) protocol now used for smart card payments worldwide [8]. The idea presented in that paper is to reveal some information about the state of the system and the execution of a protocol, creating evidence can be produced that can help resolve disputes. Cryptographic tools can also ensure that the evidence is "correct".

© Springer Nature Switzerland AG 2020
J. Anderson et al. (Eds.): Security Protocols 2019, LNCS 12287, pp. 3–10, 2020.
https://doi.org/10.1007/978-3-030-57043-9_1

But evaluating evidence is not as straightforward as simply making sure that it is correct in the cryptographic sense. Looking at the legal notion of evidence, many complexities arise.

2   Resolving Civil Disputes

A scenario in which security protocols play a central role in a legal case is disputed card transactions. Here, a customer denies responsibility for a card transaction by claiming it was unauthorised and therefore is entitled to a refund under the Payment Services Directive 2 (PSD2). The bank instead claims that the customer either indeed authorised the transaction or was grossly negligent – and therefore is responsible for the transaction. A central component of the bank's evidence in such disputes is the outcome of the EMV protocol run between the card issued to the customer and the terminal operated by the merchant.

As this is a civil dispute, to resolve the dispute in their favour, a party need not show what has actually happened or even that any explanations reach a particular probability of occurring. All that is required is that a party demonstrate that, given the evidence presented, the explanations in which they are not liable are together more likely than those in which they are liable. For this purpose, the odds form of Bayes' theorem – Eq. (1) – is appropriate. If the posterior odds are less than one, then the party is found to be not liable. This is simply a re-statement of Bayes' theorem, taking the ratio of the standard form of the theorem for $P(liable|evidence)$ and $P(\neg liable|evidence)$.

$$\underbrace{\frac{P(liable|evidence)}{P(\neg liable|evidence)}}_{\text{posterior odds}} = \underbrace{\frac{P(liable)}{P(\neg liable)}}_{\text{prior odds}} \cdot \underbrace{\frac{P(evidence|liable)}{P(evidence|\neg liable)}}_{\text{likelihood ratio}} \tag{1}$$

In practice, however, directly applying Bayes's theorem in a court setting is far from straightforward, and attempts to do so have been controversial [9]. Many relevant probabilities would not be known numerically, and so there is the risk that such factors would be given less weight than those which were known numerically. Furthermore, in the case of a jury trial how likelihoods are combined are at the discretion of the jury members. Nevertheless, Jaynes has shown that Bayes' theorem naturally follows from a logical application of intuitive principles [4], so considering the implications of Bayes' theorem can be instructive for understanding the result of intuitive decision making.

To compute the overall posterior odds, Eq. (1) could be applied once, taking into account all evidence available, but due to the large number of items of evidence, this approach could be unwieldy. An alternative approach is to apply the formula sequentially for each item of evidence to find the posterior odds, which then becomes the prior odds for the application of the formula on the next item of evidence. Sequentially updating the posterior odds with new evidence in this way is the same as considering all of the evidence in one go, if we assume that evidence is conditionally independent given that a party is liable (or not).

Denoting $P(liable|e_n)_{e_{n-1},...,e_1}$ as the posterior probability of the party being liable given evidence e_n after having evaluated it for evidence $e_{n-1}, \ldots, e_1$ and using our assumption of conditional independence given the liability of the party, we can then obtain the result stated in Eq. 2. An argument for this is given in Appendix A.

$$\left\{ \frac{P(liable|e_n)}{P(\neg liable|e_n)} \right\}_{e_{n-1},...,e_1} = \frac{P(liable|e_1, \ldots, e_n)}{P(\neg liable|e_1, \ldots, e_n)} \tag{2}$$

If there is a dispute, then there will be evidence consistent with the party (*e.g.* a bank customer) being liable, because otherwise, the dispute would not have occurred in the first place. To evaluate the likelihood ratio, we also need to know the likelihood of such evidence appearing should the party not be liable. Such an event would occur if and only if there is some fault in the system or the processes around the system, and so, in turn, we need to know the probability of a system fault. The system operator would claim this to be low, through arguing that past disputes were overwhelmingly decided in its favour.

This way of resolving disputes is effectively a sequential application of Bayes' theorem, but where the prior odds include the result of previous disputes. The sequential approach will reach the same answer but critically depends on the posterior odds being transferred to be the prior odds of the next application. However, the result of a dispute is a binary liable or not-liable decision whereas the posterior odds is a real number. Even if a previous dispute was resolved by the narrowest margin, the odds would naturally be amplified when carried over to the next dispute as a certainty that the system worked properly.

This amplification property, combined with the fact that the system operator will settle disputes out-of-court if the evidence does show that the system has failed, leads to unfairness for customers. When there is no definitive evidence showing that the customer is not liable, the amplification effect of sequential disputes creates a presumption that the system is operating correctly. Each dispute that is resolved in the system operator's favour will reinforce its position, even without any evidence that the system is operating correctly.

To illustrate the above, consider cases for which the bank claims that the customer is liable. Their records will presumably show that the EMV protocol exchange completed successfully. The bank would then argue their records shows that the genuine card was used. Indeed, we have a high degree of confidence in the security of the underlying cryptography of EMV (RSA and 3DES), and while formal methods have failed to identify some flaws in the protocols, subsequent studies have increased confidence that within the abstraction set out, the EMV protocol does what it is supposed to.

When the outcome of a case hinges mainly on the prejudices of the adjudicator resulting from previous disputes, and not on the evidence produced by the system explicitly designed to resolve such disputes, apparently something has gone wrong with the way we design security protocols and the dispute resolution systems around them. The focus on rigorously analysing a small part of the system – the abstract security protocol between card and terminal – then arguing each dispute separately, is destined to fail.

By relaxing the level of proof required, we can dramatically expand the parts of the system we can analyse. In the words of John Tukey, "far better an approximate answer to the right question, which is often vague, than an exact answer to the wrong question, which can always be made precise" [10]. Rather than making a formal-methods based argument on the protocol alone to change the likelihood ratio, we can make a statistical argument about the system as a whole to change the prior odds.

Furthermore, the problem introduced by sequentially deciding individual cases can be addressed by examining a collection of cases simultaneously. While the likelihood that any single customer is negligent or complicit is significant, the likelihood that every customer disputing a transaction is considerably less. By dealing with multiple cases at the same time, this sort of argument becomes possible and has the potential to overrule the presumption that the system is operating correct that has resulted from previous disputes.

3   Post Office and the Horizon Accounting System

Banking disputes of the type discussed above rarely make it to court because the risk to the customer of having to pay a bank's costs is prohibitive. In cases where banks consider that they likely must disclose potentially sensitive information, they are quick to settle, and so the broader issues we have raised do not get resolved. However, an important case in the High Court of England & Wales which has the potential to change the situation is the Group Litigation against the government-owned company – Post Office Limited.

This case concerns disputes between the Post Office and subpostmasters who operate some Post Office branches on their behalf, offering not just postal services but also savings accounts, payment facilities, identity verification, professional accreditation and lottery services. These subpostmasters have been held liable for losses that the Horizon accounting system, operated by the Post Office, reports being present. The position of the Post Office is that subpostmasters are contractually obligated to compensate the Post Office for such losses. The subpostmasters claim that these losses are not the result of errors or fraud on their behalf but instead are due to malfunction or malicious access to Horizon.

So far one of the three trials is finished, with a judgement expected in January 2019. This trial focuses on the legal relationship between the subpostmasters and Post Office Limited, and the consequences of this on the validity of the contract terms holding subpostmasters liable for purported losses. The next trial, expected to start in March 2019, will deal with the Horizon system itself, but we have already learned much from the first trial in the Group Litigation, as well as previous legal proceedings dating back to 2009. For example, the Post Office has now disclosed that there have been accounting errors in Horizon, and their

staff have the ability to remotely modify accounts without the subpostmaster's
authorisation, both contrary to their previous statements[1].

Although this case has not attracted much media attention, its importance
to future cases of disputes relating to computer evidence should not be underes-
timated. The Post Office has described the case as an "existential threat", and
the losses of subpostmasters have been in the tens of thousands of pounds [6,7] –
leading to bankruptcy, illness and even criminal prosecution. Unlike the handful
of previous individual bank disputes, this trial has seen significant investment in
both legal and technical expertise (total costs exceeding £10 m before the trial
had begun) and so it is reasonable to expect the Post Office's claims will be subject to close scrutiny. Much of the pre-trial activity was relating disputes between
claimants requesting that certain documents and data be disclosed to them, and
the Post Office who claimed that they had no duty to so. Such expense is only
possible because a Group Litigation[2] allows resources of the 500+ claimants to
be pooled, who are also supported by an investment fund that presumably will
pay the costs of the Post Office should the claim fail.

The Group Litigation also allows a collection of cases to be examined in
parallel and so has the potential to avoid the limitations of evidence raised
in Sect. 2 and the risk of applying a what is effectively a cyclic argument in
consecutive individual cases when computer error, negligence or fraud are all
fully consistent with the evidence. The case will also examine whether it is
fair or not to require users of a computer system to be bound by its results
when their capacity to influence the incentive-design of the system or scrutinise
its operation is limited. As expressed by McCormack on the subject of Seema
Misra's case [7], it is striking that "a subpostmaster could be held responsible
for losses they incurred as a direct result of a failing to notice an error in a
sophisticated computer system over which they had no control".

4   Conclusion and Discussion

We do not yet fully know what evidence the Post Office will present to support
their case that the purported losses are genuine, but we can use this example to
discuss what would be adequate evidence resulting from the security protocols
supporting Horizon. Prior work has proposed systems improving transparency
surrounding the transaction in dispute, which is indeed a good approach. For
the reasons outlined in Sect. 2 we would propose augmenting these requirements
to also include transparency of transactions that are the subject of other disputes (that perhaps the institution conceded) or non-disputed transactions. Such
evidence could be used to make a statistical argument whether the behaviour

---

[1] Further details can be found through the crowd-funded coverage by journalist Nick
Wallis at http://www.postofficetrial.com/.
[2] This sounds like a US Class Action, but is quite different. Claimants participating
in a Group Litigation Order must opt-in, are still liable for the other party's costs
if they lose, and each case is still treated individually albeit with issues that are
common to all.

regarding the dispute is indeed an exception or whether this case is just one anomaly out of many.

This approach creates both legal and practical difficulties. While the rules for admissibility of evidence vary, they do usually require that evidence is relevant and a case would have to be made to justify the additional effort of extracting information for transactions that are apparently unrelated. Rules for admissibility may also include restrictions for the purposes of benefit to society, such as prohibiting evidence relating to the bad character of an individual in order to help the rehabilitation of offenders. Evidence relating to the previous behaviour of an individual in dispute could fall foul of such restrictions.

The justice system is facing similar challenges in cases where cause and effect can be argued statistically on a population but not necessarily in every single case. For example, it is known that increases in air pollution will result in increased deaths from respiratory disorders. Statistical arguments could even, with high confidence, predict the expected number of deaths that would not have occurred were levels of pollution decreased. However, linking any one death to pollution is difficult since the most likely explanation may well be that it would have occurred regardless of the level of pollution. Similarly, damage from any one storm cannot be definitively be linked to climate change even though we can know with confidence that climate change will increase the number of storms.

Practically, disclosing information on individuals who are not a party to the dispute could violate their privacy. Here, privacy-preserving transparency approaches like VAMS [3] could usefully be applied. The current iteration of Horizon is effectively centralised following an upgrade that took place to make the system more efficient, so this would have to be changed back to a more distributed model where subpostmasters have control over their local system.

According to Ian Henderson of Second Sight, a company charged with independently investigating the Horizon system and subsequently fired by Post Office, Horizon had around 12000 communication failures every year and software defects at 76 Post Office branches as well as unreliable hardware [5]. Issues with software and hardware lessen the gain of a transparency overlay on top of the system, as that would provide integrity for information that is logged, but would only show inconsistencies if events fail to be logged properly across the system. One way of resolving this would be to design the system so that subpostmasters can get some assurance that local processes were correctly executed, for example, by using trusted hardware[3].

Some problems are however, out of control of the protocol and system designer. One is how to provide incentives to organizations commissioning systems to produce better evidence. When parties are evenly matched, this could be included in a contract but when there is a disparity, like the Post Office vs. subpostmasters or banks vs. their customers, policy interventions are needed. A potential requirement might be that evidence from a system that indicates

---

[3] This is not unlike how safety-critical systems like traffic lights operate. The complex system is mediated by a much simpler high assurance unit that ensures certain invariants, like there being only one green light active at a junction.

that someone is liable is only acceptable if the system operator can demonstrate that the system would be able to clear someone who is innocent. Courts may play some role, but they are restricted in what they can do – as the Post Office barrister reminded the judge in his closing statement, the court must apply the law, not common-sense.

Acknowledgments. The authors would like to the attendees of the workshop, Peter Sommer, and Stephen Mason for interesting discussions. Alexander Hicks is supported by OneSpan (https://www.onespan.com/) and UCL through an EPSRC Research Studentship, and Steven Murdoch is supported by The Royal Society [grant number UF160505].

A   Sequential Application of Bayes' Theorem and Conditional Independence

Assuming conditional independence of the pieces of evidence given the liability (or not) of a party, we can obtain Eq. 2 for multiple pieces of evidence evaluated sequentially from the following calculation.

$$
\begin{aligned}
\left\{ \frac{P(liable|e_n)}{P(\neg liable|e_n)} \right\}_{e_{n-1},\dots,e_1}
&= \left\{ \frac{P(liable)}{P(\neg liable)} \right\}_{e_{n-2},\dots,e_1} \cdot \frac{P(e_n|liable)}{P(e_n|\neg liable)} \\
&= \frac{P(liable)}{P(\neg liable)} \cdot \prod_{i=1}^{n} \frac{P(e_i|liable)}{P(e_i|\neg liable)} \\
&= \frac{P(liable)}{P(\neg liable)} \cdot \frac{P(e_1,\dots,e_n|liable)}{P(e_1,\dots,e_n|\neg liable)} \\
&= \frac{P(liable|e_1,\dots,e_n)}{P(\neg liable|e_1,\dots,e_n)}
\end{aligned}
\tag{3}
$$

The assumption of conditional independence given that the party is liable (or not) allows us to go from $\prod_{i=1}^{n} P(e_i|liable)$ to $P(e_1,\dots,e_n|liable)$. This means that if we know that a party is liable, then knowing a piece of evidence e_i does not yield additional knowledge about another piece of evidence $e_{j\neq i}$ *i.e.* $P(e_j|e_i, liable) = P(e_j|liable)$. Similarly, we also use the assumption that pieces of evidence are conditionally independent given that the party is not liable to go from $\prod_{i=1}^{n} P(e_i|\neg liable)$ to $P(e_1,\dots,e_n|\neg liable)$. (Note that we are not concerned with whether or not the liability of different parties is dependent, but rather whether different pieces of evidence are conditionally independent given the liability of a party).

We argue that assuming conditional independence of the items of evidence given the liability (or not) of a party is reasonable because the effect that a piece of evidence might have on another is through its effect on the belief that the party is liable (or not). When the liability (or not) of the party is given, then it may no longer have a noticeable effect, and thus the pieces of evidence can be assumed to be conditionally independent given the liability (or not) of a party.

References

1. Anderson, R.: Why information security is hard-an economic perspective. In: Proceedings of the 17th Annual Computer Security Applications Conference, ACSAC 2001, Washington, DC, USA, p. 358. IEEE Computer Society (2001). http://dl. acm.org/citation.cfm?id=872016.872155
2. Azouvi, S., Hicks, A., Murdoch, S.J.: Incentives in security protocols. In: Matyáš, V., Švenda, P., Stajano, F., Christianson, B., Anderson, J. (eds.) Security Protocols 2018. LNCS, vol. 11286, pp. 132–141. Springer, Cham (2018). https://doi.org/10. 1007/978-3-030-03251-7_15
3. Hicks, A., Mavroudis, V., Al-Bassam, M., Meiklejohn, S., Murdoch, S.J.: VAMS: verifiable auditing of access to confidential data. CoRR abs/1805.04772 (2018). http://arxiv.org/abs/1805.04772
4. Jaynes, E.T.: Probability Theory: The Logic of Science. Cambridge University Press, Cambridge (2003)
5. Jee, C.: Computer World UK: Post Office obstructing Horizon probe, investigator claims, February 2015. https://www.computerworlduk.com/infrastructure/ post-office-obstructing-horizon-probe-investigator-claims-3596589/
6. Mason, S.: Case transcript: England & Wales-Regina v Seema Misra. Digit. Evid. Electron. Signat. Law Rev. **12**, 45–55 (2015)
7. McCormack, T.: The post office horizon system and Seema Misra. Digit. Evid. Electron. Signat. Law Rev. **13**, 133–138 (2016)
8. Murdoch, S.J., Anderson, R.: Security protocols and evidence: where many payment systems fail. In: Christin, N., Safavi-Naini, R. (eds.) FC 2014. LNCS, vol. 8437, pp. 21–32. Springer, Heidelberg (2014). https://doi.org/10.1007/978-3-662-45472-5_2
9. Steventon, B.: Statistical evidence and the courts—recent developments. J. Crim. Law **62**(2), 176–184 (1998)
10. Tukey, J.W.: The future of data analysis. Ann. Math. Stat. **33**(1), 1–67 (1962)

Transparency Enhancing Technologies to Make Security Protocols Work for Humans (Transcript of Discussion)

Steven J. Murdoch[✉]

University College London, London, UK
s.murdoch@ucl.ac.uk

If you've heard some of my talks before then most of the time I've been banging on about Chip & PIN. I'm not, in this talk – this is about another dispute, another court case, and this is Bates and Others vs. Post Office Ltd. And in my first five minutes I'm hoping to tell you why this is interesting.

So if you've used a post office, or you've seen a post office, one thing that you might not actually realise is that relatively few of these places are actually owned by Post Office Ltd. A large number of them are owned and run by people called sub-postmasters or sub-postmistresses. They are self-employed, they are legally classed as agents and they run this post office on behalf of Post Office Ltd.

The actual products that they sell are from the Post Office or Royal Mail. The rules that they follow, again, are set by Post Office Ltd. They've got a limited amount of discretion, but the key thing that I'm going to talk about is the computer system, which is dictated by Post Office Ltd. and it's called Horizon.

And Horizon is very important if you're a sub-postmaster because whatever Horizon says is judged by your contract to be the truth. And in particular, if there is a shortfall between what money you have or what products you have and what Horizon thinks you have, then you, as a sub-postmaster, are personally liable for this.

And you think, post offices, they sell stamps, that's fair enough, you lose a few stamps and that's bad. But post offices do foreign exchange, they do banking services, so these shortfalls are easily in the tens, sometimes hundreds or thousands of pounds. And this is a problem if you're in one of these situations. Many sub-postmasters have had bad experiences and they blame Horizon. They think that because of bugs, or because of inappropriate access to Horizon, someone has caused them to run a shortfall and therefore they have lost a lot of money.

So I guess none of you are sub-postmasters and I don't think you're going to become a sub-postmaster, at least by the end of the talk I'm pretty sure you do not want to be a sub-postmaster, but why do I actually care? One aspect that I do think about is the human cost of the problems in Horizon.

The disputes been running since 2000, roughly, and people have been bankrupted, people have been jailed because there's also allegations of criminal behaviour. People have died while being under investigation, allegedly driven to

© Springer Nature Switzerland AG 2020
J. Anderson et al. (Eds.): Security Protocols 2019, LNCS 12287, pp. 11–19, 2020.
https://doi.org/10.1007/978-3-030-57043-9_2

an early grave as a result of the investigations that they've been put through as a result of what they say are bugs in Horizon.

So that's important. But this is a computing conference, so I'm going to mainly focus on what lessons we can learn from this case that apply to the design of other security systems. And most of the time when something goes wrong, certainly in the Chip & PIN cases, we don't find out what went wrong. And one reason we don't find out what went wrong is because the dispute in Chip & PIN are maybe a few hundreds of pounds, maybe a few thousands of pounds – the legal investment in this is maybe a few thousand, sometimes a little bit more. But you cannot get to the bottom of a bug in a complex distributed system involving thousands of people, and millions of lines of code, by investing a few thousand pounds. Whereas, in the Post Office case here, the budgets are much, much higher. And so we might actually start to get to the bottom of some of these technical and legal issues.

So why is there so much money available? Well, one is that the Post Office has deep pockets. They are, what's termed as a "arm's-length government body" which is kind of like the quantum-computing hack of government. It's a super-position of both, part of government and not part of government. So when the Post Office does something the government likes, then the government can cause them to keep on doing more of that. When the Post Office does something that the government doesn't like, or the public is angry about, like closing post offices in places where people don't have access to banking, then the government can say, "Oh, we're not in control, this is a commercial consideration".

But ultimately, when I say that they have deep pockets, I mean your pockets, because they are owned by the government, they have shareholders, but there's only one of them and that's the government – and so when they spend money they're spending your money. So thank you for your contribution to this talk.

On the other hand you have the sub-postmasters. Now, they are not rich, certainly the ones who have lost all their money are not going to be very rich, but they're backed by investment funds. And this is quite an interesting way of getting justice. So this investment fund has got roughly a billion dollars, and they are spending it, they are investing it in this dispute in the hope that the sub-postmasters will win, and then the investment funds will get a return on their investment by taking a proportion of the damages. So if you're interested in this sort of thing they're called "Therium".

So I say, "adequately resourced". What does "adequately resourced" mean? The trial's going on, it's been going on roughly a decade now. Before the trial even started both sides have spent a combined total of 10 million pounds. There was a recent hearing which cost about half a million pounds for one day.

Each side has multiple QCs. QCs are a very senior type of barrister in the UK. Most recently this chap, who's called Lord Grabiner, he is also the master of Clare College, not very far away from where we are here in Trinity, and when he charges for his service, it's about 3,000 pounds per hour, so a nice job if you can get it. If you compare these sorts of resources in terms of legal expertise, and there's also plenty of technical expertise, then you get quite a different story than for the types of issues that are going on with Chip & PIN.

So I mentioned four trials, running for a decade, very detailed, complicated technical and legal aspects. But ultimately they are going to make a fairly simple decision. What is more likely, given the evidence, are the sub-postmasters liable for the costs that they have been allocated? Or are they not liable?

And we have laws of probability for reasoning about these sorts of questions, one of which is Bayes' rule, what this slide shows is just a reinterpretation of Bayes' rule – it doesn't look like the standard one that you're used to seeing, but it's exactly the same, it's just reordered a little bit. And rather than looking at individual probabilities, what it looks at is the ratio between the probabilities of two different scenarios. Because this is a civil case, (there have been criminal aspects – I'm not going to talk about those) civil cases are dealt with on balance of probabilities, so what is the most likely explanation for this particular evidence? And that's called the "posterior odds".

So over here, you can see the posterior odds. Actually computing this directly is a bit hard, so what Bayes' rule allows you to do is compute two different things, multiply them together, and that gives you the answer. The first thing that you use is called "prior odds" and this is, "before you saw the evidence, what do you think the likelihood is?" This is so you can take into consideration how much fraud is going to happen, for example, you can take into account the honesty of the Post Office.

But you also have pages and pages of evidence and what Bayes' rule asks you to do is compute the likelihood of getting a particular bit of evidence given a particular scenario.

Jonathan Anderson: Is this something that the judges are explicitly aware of? This seems a bit numerical.

Reply: Yes, so, Bayes' rule as typically stated is numerical. And judges don't think about that sort of thing. There have been times in the past where people have been asked to do this sort of thing: it hasn't worked out very well. What they do think about is, "what is more likely?" which is why I've used the odds version of Bayes' rule.

And there's a book which is cited in the paper by ET Jaynes, which shows that whenever you start with a set of internally consistent probability rules, you end up with this. So, they are almost certainly not thinking about this equation, but this is what they will come to intuitively if they're thinking any sort of logical way. And it kind of makes sense.

People have an initial expectation of what they think is the case, and then they allow themselves to be judged based on the evidence that they've presented, and what they are looking at is whether the evidence is consistent with this particular scenario. And that's exactly what this equation is.

I'm not actually going to talk mostly about the numerical topic, because most of these things, you cannot sensibly allocate numbers, but I think this is likely compatible with what they're thinking. Thanks for the question.

So this is about making a single decision, but one question is, "How do you actually come up with these prior odds?" And another question is, when you have multiple decisions to make, "How do you think about these sorts of decisions?" And you use the same equation.

You make a decision based on the evidence you've seen, and then the posterior odds for the first decision then become the prior odds for the next decision. And this is sometimes called Bayesian updating. But, you can just look at it as a way of using things that you have previously learned to inform your future decisions.

And this actually is pretty bad if you're one of these claimants. In Chip & PIN for example, one of the arguments is, maybe their cryptography went wrong, maybe someone factored some of these big numbers (computer systems like Horizon also have some cryptography to protect the integrity of their information).

But these are all fairly unlikely scenarios, and the likelihood ratio over here is actually an integral over all of these possibilities. And as the probability for one of these scenarios is small, then it just disappears from the equation, so it has no effect. What actually does have effect is things that we know are quite likely. So, claimants – or sub-postmasters – probably do commit fraud. They certainly do make mistakes. We also know that computer systems have bugs, and the Post Office is not disputing Horizon does have some bugs.

So when you put that into this sort of equation, the evidence is going to be pretty consistent with both scenarios. If the sub-postmaster is liable for something then you will see the evidence that looks like they're liable, and if they're not liable then you'll see evidence that is consistent with them being not liable, such as if their computer system went wrong.

And effectively what happens is that this bit of the equation just becomes 1.0 and because of the way multiplication works, disappears. Roughly speaking, the decision that's going to be made is based on the judge's prior belief: whether they think this person is honest versus that person is honest, and the evidence mostly disappears.

So that's kind of bad. But then, this is not the first case that's happened, there's been decades of litigation, in the case of Chip & PIN it's exactly the same, and we do the updating trick, and so the posterior odds get set to be the prior odds and this makes it even more likely that the claimant will be held liable. And because the decision of the previous case wasn't, "it was a 70% probability that this person was guilty". It was "the most likely explanation is that the person's guilty", then that amplifies this effect. So as more cases progress in a serial way then you end up with it being more likely to be considered that a person has acted fraudulently and less likely to be considered not to be liable as a result of some sort of computer problem.

Mybe we need some more formal evidence, we need some proofs, we like proofs. So all these sorts of things do is that they reduce the likelihood and hence the likelihood ratio of scenarios that were already pretty unlikely before. We know that people regularly make mistakes, but we don't regularly see computer bugs causing money to disappear, at least not in fairly well-written systems like Horizon.

And so these sorts of techniques don't actually improve the situation. Getting greater confidence in something that we're already quite confident about might feel nice from the perspective of the people designing the system, but it doesn't actually help resolve disputes.

There's a interesting quote that I found from a statistician, which is that, "It is far better to have an approximate answer to the right question, which is often vague, then an exact answer to the wrong question, which can always be made more precise". What I thought of when I saw this quote is that this is about having the contrast between having very strong arguments to irrelevant issues, like, "has this protocol been formally proved?" versus having more fuzzy answers to questions like, "did this particular bug cause this particular bit of money to disappear?"

So from this sort of basis, what can you do? One interesting aspect is that this court case is called a group litigation order. This is a particular UK thing. It's kind of like a class-action but lawyers will shout and scream at me if I suggest that, because it's got lots of differences. But one of the similarities is that rather than one person being involved as this claimant and then decisions being made serially, with that sort of Bayesian update thing going on in the back of the head of the judge – the decisions all get made together.

And now, the prior odds of liable versus not liable are not based on, "did this one person make a bad decision?" or, "did this one person screw up?" it's, "did all of these people screw up?" And when you multiply probabilities, assuming independence, you get an exponentially smaller probability.

And then it starts to be a lot more likely that maybe it was a computer problem that actually caused it. So not only is it interesting that this case going ahead at all is because of the large number of people and so the large sums that are useful for hedge funds to invest in. But also it's useful from the perspective of this sort of probability.

And another thing you can do is try to introduce some more transparency to the system. Horizon is horribly complicated and as a consequence its logging system is horribly complicated, and there's lots of disputes about the extent to which it represents reality. If there were a much simpler logging system of which you had much greater confidence that it was going to be independent of the existing computer system and also more likely to be correct, then you could have greater confidence in whether computer error had happened or had not.

And there was an intriguing part of the trial where it actually looked like they might have had this, where they talked about a Credence sub-system. What Credence was initially claimed to do was to be a log of keystrokes so if you could see an inconsistency between the keystrokes and the transactions then you had good evidence that something had actually gone wrong. It turned out it wasn't useful, it was a reconstruction of keystrokes based on the log, and so it isn't actually independent in a useful way, but that was interesting.

Another bit of information came out, was on old Horizon – Legacy Horizon. There's two versions. Today it's called Horizon Online, the old version was designed for situations where there's limited communication and actually sounds rather clever. So you have in a particular post office multiple computers, you have periodic synchronisation with the central Post Office computer, and they run some sort of algorithm, maybe it's a consensus algorithm, to make sure that they all have a consistent log of what actually happened at the end of it. But one of the intermediate steps of this is maintaining a local log. So if you can see discrepancies between a local log and an agreed log then that's also going to be quite interesting. Now actually, those logs, maybe they never existed, if they did exist, they're gone, and in any case new Horizon only has one log because it's permanently online. But these sorts of distributed systems might actually, by accident, have some interesting aspects from the perspective of transparency.

And another thing came up in the trial is the reluctance of the parties, particularly the Post Office, to actually disclose information because they said it was personally identifiable, it was commercially sensitive – in some cases they might be right. But it would also be quite useful for resolving disputes. And one of the aspects of the VAMS system, which Alex and my colleagues have worked on, is that we combine logs of what have happened with privacy enhancing techniques so that only certain information is disclosed. So maybe those sorts of privacy enhancing techniques could not only be used to protect against allegations of violating personal confidentiality, but also commercial sensitivity, and so allow more information to be disclosed in these sorts of trials without spending about 10 million pounds to argue what's going to be accepted and what's going to be not.

So I think one of the things is that we can do a bit better.

Simon Foley: So it's intriguing. I want to understand this. How it's taking a very sort of legalistic view to how judges make decisions, how decisions are made, but oftentimes they can put aside the law.

I'm thinking of an example at the University of Toronto, there was this famous case where there was a swimming competition and the rules of the competition said that the first person to put both hands on the end of the pool is the person who was deemed to have won the competition.

And so they announced the winner of the competition, and there's a court case subsequently because the second person said, "well I was the first person who put both my hands on the end of the swimming pool". And it turned out that the person who was judged to have won first by the organisers had just one hand. So when it went to court the judge threw it out and said, "this is not fair, it's unreasonable".

So in a framework of thinking like this, do you have any idea how you might be able to include some notion of fairness in this log of the...

Reply: So that particular point has come up, and the discussion is interesting. I'll skip to the last bullet point, which is that courts are limited by the law. So courts are not allowed to ignore the law, and this was explicitly stated in the Horizon trial when one of the barristers for the Post Office said to the effect of,

"You might think this is common sense but you must be careful not to follow common sense, you must follow the law. And if there's a deviation between law and common sense, judges must follow the law, even if it's stupid".

Simon Foley: I'm sorry if I wasn't quite clear. Because in the case of the swimming competition, the judge said the person who came in first is the person who came in first, even though the rules didn't apply to that person.

Reply: So there are laws about fairness which can overrule other types of laws. And that has happened in this case. So the first trial that has come to the end was about the contract and the conclusion of that trial is that some aspects of that contract were unfair and therefore should be removed. But that is because there is a law that says fairness in contract is more important than following the letter of the contract.

But in other aspects it's not okay to apply common sense. So this is one of the big differences between criminal and civil cases. A jury can make a decision on whatever basis that they want. They can think that, "This law is bad, and we'll find this person innocent because they did the thing but we think this law is bad". Judges are not allowed to do that.

Simon Foley: And equally in civil cases it's the balance of probabilities but in criminal cases...

Reply: So that's different, but that is also a different difference. So one of the reasons that sometimes bad criminal laws disappear, is because juries just refuse to convict. They think this is a stupid law, we're not going to send this person to jail even though they did the thing. Judges in civil cases when the judges are making decisions, they are beholden to follow the stupid law because it's the politician's responsibility to fix the stupid law.

And that's why, what my final bullet point is hinting at, that it might be the case that the judge will find that the Post Office had acted entirely unfairly, and the Post Office should not have deployed this computer system because the computer system was incapable of providing adequate evidence.

In one of the early cases on bank fraud pre-Chip & PIN the lawyers for the claimant argued that by presenting this computer system as evidence the bank was putting an unmeetable burden of proof on the person who was trying to get their money back. If that's the argument, these claimants could lose, and maybe there needs to be a law that says, "If a computer system is incapable of clearing someone who is innocent, then that computer system should not be permitted to be used in evidence". But there's no law, as far as I know, that says that, and so there could be a very inadequate result of this case, but that's the fault of the law, rather than the fault of this particular judge.

Ilia Shumailov: So to me it sounds like, when you talk about visuals, and when you talk about humans making mistakes and probabilities ... in practice, we definitely know that humans make a lot of mistakes, through negligence or corruption. And often enough those are not independent probabilities. And then the rules of stacking the probabilities suddenly change. I always, when I see somebody stealing, I also steal because I know then the problem is that I'm not going to quit. And as a matter of fact, I'm going to be stealing more the more we all steal.

In this framework of thinking, do you think that Bayes' rule is a good way to actually model this sort of misfit? Especially when the human's non-deterministic nature is considered?

Reply: There's a couple of parts to that. So one is like, is Bayes' rule the right thing to use? The book by ET Jaynes I think makes a convincing argument that there is no other sensible alternative. So there is only one set of laws of probability that makes sense, and that's that one, and all the other things that come from it.

Whether you should assume independence of stuff when it involves humans is a very different question. And I think for any individual, say any individual post office, then indeed, there is going to be some dependence between different incidents. But I think when you got two different sub-postmasters at different ends of the country that never talk to each other, then there's more argument that there's not going to be the same level of dependence.

Ilia Shumailov: Do they have unions or channels between them? And also when you consider their chance of their communicating versus we have now the data science – fairly reliable statistics – saying, how often we expect to see bugs in 1,000 lines of code. Have those probabilities been compared?

Reply: So there is a union but the union is very dysfunctional because they are 100% funded by the Post Office. And that's another thing that came up in the trial that just finished. There was a contract which was between the union and the Post Office which said that the union was not allowed to act in any way that would be detrimental to the interests of the Post Office. So, "union" in inverted commas.

Yes, sub-postmasters can communicate, but I'm not saying that the likelihood of one person committing fraud is entirely independent from another person committing fraud. I think it's safe to say that if you multiply these probabilities then you will get something that's smaller. Although it's not necessarily going to be that to the power of the number of people.

Ross Anderson: These types of arguments are very reminiscent of what we saw in the case against thirteen banks back in '92-'93. One of the arguments for the banks was that the likelihood of an accounting error was less than one in 30,000 so the lawyers on our side said well fine we've got 2,000 claimants so that's exactly the number you'd expect from a population of 60 million people.

The lawyers in that case succeeded in breaking up the class action into 2,000 individual cases in the small claims court. And the great majority of the claimants never got their money back. This is the case referred to in my paper "Why Cryptosystems Fail".

It turned out approximately two years later that a certain Andrew Stone was sent to jail for six and a half years for committing the offences. The banks were wrong and perhaps even disingenuous in arguing that the cases were not linked together; it turned out that they were. So you may get an outcome where you get a wrong result and the true cause is found only later or not at all.

Reply: So the particular fight as to whether these cases should be split up has been already had, and the Post Office lost. So it's going ahead with these 550 people. The Post Office certainly tried the same approach that you described the banks trying, and that didn't work out.

Frank Stajano: Who stopped them from doing that?

Reply: The person funding the group action. That's called the Justice For Sub-postmasters Alliance. But actually they are bankrolled by this big investment fund – they were the ones that got the lawyers to come together and then make this case that it should be a group litigation rather than an individual litigation. Otherwise it would be unsustainable for this sort of investment fund to deal with.

But I think another good point that Ross mentioned was these numbers. And the Post Office are certainly trying to use these sort of probability arguments against the claimants, and I think, another point related to – is probability useful? The right way to deal with this? I think yes.

Is assigning numbers the right way to deal with these sorts of cases? I'm much less convinced because the indication of certainty around the number means that you can overrule the more intuitive but equally valid views about, say, people's honesty. So this again becomes a victim of focusing on an accurate answer to the wrong question rather than an approximate answer to the right question.

Audio CAPTCHA with a Few Cocktails:
It's so Noisy I Can't Hear You

Benjamin Maximilian Reinheimer[1(✉)], Fairooz Islam[2], and Ilia Shumailov[2]

[1] Karlsruhe Institute of Technology, Karlsruhe, Germany
benjamin.reinheimer@kit.edu
[2] University of Cambridge, Cambridge, UK
{fairooz.islam,ilia.shumailov}@cl.cam.ac.uk

Abstract. With crime migrating to the web, the detection of abusive robotic behaviour is becoming more important. In this paper, we propose a new audio CAPTCHA construction that builds upon the Cocktail Party problem (CPP) to detect robotic behaviour. We evaluate our proposed solution in terms of both performance and usability. Finally, we explain how to deploy such an acoustic CAPTCHA in the wild with strong security guarantees.

Keywords: Acoustic CAPTCHA · Cocktail Party Problem · Natural language processing · Language comprehension

1 Introduction

ARPANET, a precursor to the modern Internet, was first presented to the public in 1972 at International Computer Communication Conference [37]. A revolutionary application appeared the same year – the email software. It was the first application for people-to-people communication on scale and remained the largest network application for over a decade. A lot has changed since then – a large proportion of the world is now connected and more and more devices are produced with built-in networking capability.

By 1998 it became apparent that criminals have found a way to use connectivity to their advantage [16] and since then the war with spam has begun [25]. Computer abuse, ranging from spam and identity theft to cyberbullying, is a common occurrence in the modern world – by now it inhabits all modern platforms and is largely commoditised [6,30,38,45]. It also scales, as abusers have figured out ways to automate their enterprises.

Completely Automated Public Turing Test To Tell Computers and Humans Apart (CAPTCHA) was created to stop automatic computer service abuse. All CAPTCHAs operate on a simple principle – they use problems that humans are good at and computers struggle to solve. Modern CAPTCHAs are ubiquitous and come in all forms and shapes. Most of them exploit the human ability to recognise objects even when only partial information is available.

© Springer Nature Switzerland AG 2020
J. Anderson et al. (Eds.): Security Protocols 2019, LNCS 12287, pp. 20–40, 2020.
https://doi.org/10.1007/978-3-030-57043-9_3

When first introduced, CAPTCHAs were simple and imposed low usability costs. So long as image-recognition technology was primitive and Internet crime was still in its infancy, distorted images were sufficient to stop most robots. But as more commerce moved online and CAPTCHA solving was suddenly worth money, solving services started appearing – e.g. *anticaptcha* [44]. In fact, anti-captcha was so popular and so widely used in Russian underground forums, that at one point people started to use its credit as a currency.

Today machine learning software is getting good at image recognition and systems are forced to use many additional markers to identify human behaviour. For example, Google, amongst other things, monitors cursor movement extensively to find automatic behaviour. However, such techniques impose a usability cost: instead of having to solve one simple task as in the early days, today people may be asked to solve a whole series of problems and are not usually given any feedback on why the system doubts their humanity.

Moreover, behavioural factors like cursor tracking are not themselves sufficient to limit automatic computer service abuse; CAPTCHA itself has to evolve too. Abusers collect data over time, allowing them to simulate human-like behaviour and find heuristics to solve tasks that were once hard for them. That, in turn, means that for CAPTCHA to be effective it has to evolve at least as fast as the attacker.

In this paper, we propose a new way to detect robots based on our human ability to separate overlapping human voices – referred to by psychologists as the Cocktail Party Problem. We evaluate our CPP CAPTCHA's performance against the best speech transcribers available currently and run several user studies to explore its usability costs. We discuss it's implications and investigate the naive attack performance. Finally, we describe how to run a cocktail-party CAPTCHA in the real world, and explore security guarantees.

We need new types of defences, and this paper presents one possibility. The remainder of this paper is structured as follows. Section 2 tells the story of CAPTCHAs and describes how our proposal relates to previous work in the field. Section 3 describes the necessary background information and describes conducted experiments. Section 4 evaluates the performance of our audio CAPTCHA mechanism in terms of both usability and protection. Finally, Sect. 5 explains how one can use it in practice.

2   Related Work

CAPTCHA was invented by von Ahn and Blum, and started being used at scale by websites which were happy for anyone to open an account (e.g. for webmail service) but did not want to let scripts open thousands of accounts [58]. The earliest CAPTCHAs involved reading text from distorted images, but a short time later, the first non-visual CAPTCHAs were introduced [34,58].

There is a substantial literature on visual CAPTCHAs and automated algorithms used to break them, with an arms race proceeding through the 2000s [7,13]. Audio CAPTCHAs were much less used in those early days (e.g.

for visually impaired users) and were initially evaluated only for their usability [36,54]; later they too became the target of attacks [56].

There have been attempts to combine visual and audio CAPTCHAs [29], where either the visual stimuli (images of an animal) or the auditory stimuli (animal sounds) can be recognised; other studies used bird noises and claimed promising results [48]. Another thread of research in the field of psychology exploited the mechanism of background speech, impairing short-term memory performance [20]. CAPTCHA designers have also attempted introducing cognitive complexity. Tam et al. proposed paraphrasing the question or answer to make life more difficult for machines, while still allowing humans to use contextual insight to solve the problem [56].

3   Methodology and Background

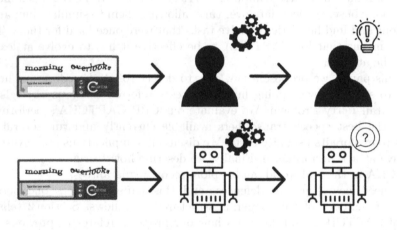

Fig. 1. reCAPTCHA process

3.1   What Is a Modern CAPTCHA?

Modern CAPTCHAs are trying to balance out four main objectives. First, a CAPTCHA must be solvable for humans; second, a CAPTCHA must be hard for robots to solve; third, it should be hard for the robots to collect system feedback; and fourth, a CAPTCHA should be able to evolve with little change to the overall experience. These objectives are further discussed below.

Human Usability with Images and Audio. Human handling of different types of noise is a well-understood problem, especially in the image classification domain [5,23,47]. For example, Geirhos et al. investigated human performance for an object detection task and compared it to the state of the art Deep Neural Networks (DNNs) [23]. Authors find that additional noise degraded performance for both humans and DNNs, but human performance degraded at a lower rate. It should be noted that DNNs were not exposed to the transformations considered by the authors in the training phase. Similarly, human comprehension of speech is well researched [27,46]. Humans non-linearly weight frequencies of acoustic signals and are better at distinguishing lower frequencies [42]. In practice, that means that humans can comprehend speech quite well, especially if the signal-to-noise (SNR) ratio in lower parts of the spectrum is large enough. It was also found that phase plays an equally important role in human understanding, particularly in low SNR settings [32,51]. Usability impacts of different CAPTCHA designs have been thoroughly evaluated both in terms of human solution accuracy and response time [12,48,59,60]. Additionally, anecdotal evidence was presented that even simple CAPTCHAs can drive legitimate users away [21].

Robot Usability. It is not clear what makes a problem hard. von Ahn and Blum, original creators of CAPTCHA, have defined an AI problem to be hard 'if the people working on it agree that it's hard' [2]. They argue that this definition captures the reality, and compare it to canonical cryptographic definitions, where cipher constructions are based on problems that are known to be hard.

Robot Data Collection. As more data gets harvested it becomes easier to use machine learning tools to automatically find solutions for CAPTCHAs. There are multiple ways to make learning harder for the attacker. First, the amount of unique data exposed to the attacker can be reduced. That can be done by supplying the same sample to the attacker, but with varying transformation on top of it. With features of just one sample present, it would learn to recognise that sample, rather than to generalise to a task. Second, noise can be added to the interaction with the CAPTCHA. This additional randomness could affect the convergence of the attacker. Randomness could come in different forms: supplying a sample from a completely different task and observing performance; or randomly passing or failing him. This randomness could also be controlled for a more complex interaction. By adding a skip button, one directly reduces the chances of getting a correct answer and allows for asking of an incorrect question. What is more, there is no simple way to go around it. An attacker needs to add a classifier to the overall system and learn it separately. That is because the skip button cannot be proxied using classification confidence, which was previously shown to be an ineffective metric across tasks [19,28]. Furthermore, by also asking two CAPTCHAs at the same time an attacker would struggle with attributing errors to made predictions. Finally, data could be supplied to the attacker with pre-defined bias, such that the attack would learn a backdoor [3,39]. Ultimately, the interaction with an attacker should not be thought of as many individual interactions, but rather it should be viewed as a sequence of decisions.

CAPTCHA Evolution. It is always a matter of time until CAPTCHA becomes solvable. In practice, that means that CAPTCHA systems should be built in such a way that it can be changed with relative ease, whilst preserving human usability levels. For example, Geirhos et al. noted that DNNs were struggling with unknown types of noise applied to objects for the object recognition task [23]. Evolution against a DNN attacker can then be build on top of that principle – over time applied noise should be changing both in terms of noise distribution and noise magnitude.

CAPTCHA Solution Costs. CAPTCHA solution services are a long established business that had been thoroughly studied both in technological [12] and business aspects [17,44]. Multiple online services offer services for solving popular CAPTCHAs. As of early June 2020, solving CAPTCHAs does not cost much. Depending on the platform it costs from 0.6$ to 2.5$ for 1000 CAPTCHAs. These services provide almost unlimited bandwidth for solving purely image-based CAPTCHA and from 5 to 7 per minute for more complex behaviour-based ones. Back in 2010, it was reported that those businesses use a hybrid solution approach, i.e. they solve it automatically if CAPTCHA is vulnerable, otherwise, humans from low-cost labour markets are hired [44].

CAPTCHA Example. Figure 1 shows an example of a CAPTCHA asked by reCAPTCHA, one of the most popular CAPTCHA providers. Here, the user is asked to transcribe two words: 'morning' and 'overlooks'. The CAPTCHA is easy for humans to solve: there are only two main transformations applied to the images and text occlusion is minimal. According to the principals described in Sect. 3.1, it is easy to evolve such a CAPTCHA in response to improving attacker performance: other transformations could be applied, and the dictionary could be expanded to include more special characters. Finally, the data collection principle

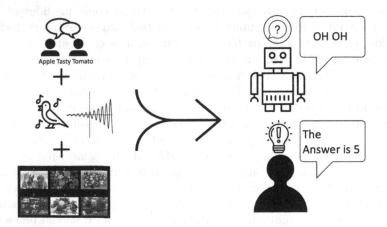

Fig. 2. CPP CAPTCHA process

described in Sect. 3.1 is also followed. The robot is not provided feedback on the performed transcriptions and, if a mistake is made, it would not know which of two words it was mistaken about[1].

3.2   What Is a Cocktail Party Problem and Why Does It Work?

Humans are much better than machines at disambiguating a single speaker from a group of people speaking at once [26]. That phenomenon is commonly referred to as a Cocktail Party Problem. In essence, it refers to cases where one or more voices are talking concurrently with the speech of interest. Background noise, consistent of natural human speech, serves as a form of semantic noise which should hinder human understanding less than it hinders machines. The Cocktail Party effect has already been investigated from numerous angles: from the general phenomenon [14], the cues that impact effectiveness [33,43], over the influence of working memory capacity [15] to the intentional control of auditory selective attention [24,50]. In this paper, we propose an acoustic CAPTCHA construction based on the Cocktail Party Problem phenomenon.

3.3   CPP CAPTCHA

We propose to use the Cocktail Party Problem to build a robust acoustic CAPT–CHA system as is depicted in Fig. 2. The problem itself can be formulated as follows. A user is provided a challenge speech sample M and a question q, such that $M = S_{orig} + \sum_{i=0..n} S_i + \sum_{j=0..m} N_j$, where S_{orig} is the speech of interest, $S_0..S_n$ are background speech samples and $N_0..N_m$ are non-speech noise samples. Question q is formulated in such a way that humans will be able to semantically extract S_{orig} from M, whereas computers will struggle to do so. Do note here, that question q can make semantic references to both speech background samples and noise. For example, the user may be asked "How many times did a bird sing after word'cat' was said by a female voice?". The user is asked to solve a tuple (M, q) and respond to the CAPTCHA system.

The construction described above is generic and encompasses a lot of different possibilities. In this paper, we describe and evaluate three different CPP CAPTCHA construction possibilities. We use speech signals comprised of either numbers, digits or individual words as both signals of interest and background speech. We assume that there is only a single speaker in the background S_0 and background noise is either no noise, bird singing, elephant sounds or white noise. Before starting the CAPTCHA the user gets question q explaining which voice he has to focus on: in this paper, we used the speaker's gender as the semantic information. Figures 3 to 5 display the introduction examples of our study, where participants could repeat the CAPTCHA and see the actual solution.

---

[1] reCAPTCHA uses two words, out of which the correct solution is known for one [44]. The correctness is assessed based on the editing distance of the provided solution and the control word.

First we start with the digit CAPTCHA, where two sets of 6 to 9 digits were read out by a female or male voice. The introduction screen is presented in Fig. 3. While listening to the CAPTCHA the user had to focus on the specified voice and enter the corresponding digits.

DIGIT CAPTCHAS: transcribe all digits said by the relevant voice

Example: Type in the digits said by the female voice.

Answer = 922016

Fig. 3. Example interface for digit CAPTCHAs

The second type is the character CAPTCHA, where two sets of 6 to 9 characters were read out by a female or male voice. Similarly to digits, participants were presented with an introduction screen as depicted in Fig. 4. While listening to the CAPTCHA the user had to focus on the specified voice and enter the corresponding characters.

CHARACTER CAPTCHAS: transcribe all characters said by the relevant voice

Example: Type in the characters said by the male voice.

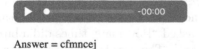

Answer = cfmncej

Fig. 4. Example interface for character CAPTCHAs

Finally we used a word CAPTCHA, where two sets of 3 to 6 English words were read out by a female or male voice. The introduction screen is presented in Fig. 5. The words in each set are related to one of a given set of images. After listening to the CAPTCHA, the user had to select the relevant image for the specified voice. For example, the participant would be told 'apple tasty tomato broccoli carrot cucumber' with a male voice, and a female voice would be saying 'rose nature tulip daisy buttercup'. The user would then be expected to pick the picture with vegetables (5) for male voice and picture with flowers (2) for female voice in Fig. 5.

WORD CAPTCHAS: pick the one image most related to the words said by the relevant voice

Example: Select the image related to the words said by the male voice.

Answer = 4

Fig. 5. Example interface for word CAPTCHAs

3.4 Ethics

The overall study is separated into two parts. First, we ran a preliminary study of the audio CAPTCHA mechanism. The participants were informed of their rights and both verbal and written consent was collected. As the study included extensive user interaction, we followed university guidelines and acquired ethics approval from the University of Cambridge Computer Laboratory Ethics Board. We made sure that the participants were not harmed in any way and no sensitive information was collected.

For the second usability evaluation, we followed the ethic guidelines of the Karlsruhe Institute for Technology. We made sure that all collected data followed university guidelines on ethical data handling and the most recent GDPR policies. As a study platform, we used SoSci Survey[2], that is compliant with the European Data Protection Regulations. As a recruitment platform, we used Clickworker[3]. Participants were clearly explained what the study was about and it's purpose. Expectations were set out and no deception was used. Participants were told that they could terminate their participation at any point without providing reasons and without any negative consequences. Their participation was 100% voluntary and payment of €3 per participant for 50 participants was provided.

---

[2] SoSci is a platform designed for running experiments https://www.soscisurvey.de.
[3] Clickworker is a platform similar to MTurk for finding participants in Europe https://www.clickworker.de.

3.5   Experiments

The aim of the experiments is two-fold. First, we aim to assess the user-friendliness of different CAPTCHA schemes to allow comparison. Second, based on the results acquired, we identify what features make audio CAPTCHAs user-friendly. For this, we use conventional usability evaluation following the ISO 9241-11 [1] definition of usability. The ISO standard has three main components:

– **Effectiveness:** the audio CAPTCHA is unambiguous and therefore easy to use;
– **Efficiency:** the audio CAPTCHA is solved a high percentage of the time and in as short a time as possible;
– **Satisfaction:** the audio CAPTCHA triggers a high level of satisfaction among the users, i.e. they should be satisfied and motivated to continue using it in the future.

Most people today are familiar with visual CAPTCHAs, as they are ubiquitous and are used to deter robot activity practically everywhere online. Although the users can occasionally be annoyed at CAPTCHAs, they are largely accepted. We aim to develop an audio CAPTCHA scheme that is at least as good in terms of usability. It should be noted, however, that people have been exposed to visual CAPTCHAs for the past 20 years and it is hard to reproduce the same learning artefacts. Measurements are collected in the following three forms:

– **Effectiveness:** Number of failed attempts at the audio CAPTCHA;
– **Efficiency:** Repetitions and duration until successful completion;
– **Satisfaction:** SUS Questionnaire [4,10,11,49].

3.6   Experimental Process

The study evaluates three forms of CAPTCHAs. The whole process is depicted in Fig. 6. Each type represents a different aspect of perception: numbers, letters, and entire words. First, the participants receive Informed Consent to read and accept. We then explain the procedure of the study. The participants are informed that participation can be terminated at any time without any consequences. After that, the participants are shown an example for each of the three CAPTCHA types. We explain how to deal with every type of CAPTCHA and

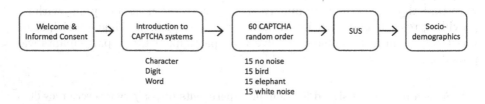

Fig. 6. Usability experiment pipeline

what the right solution is. The participants can listen to the CAPTCHA as often as they want until they feel confident in using it. Each CAPTCHA, regardless of type, consists of two voices – one female and one male. It is accompanied by a description such as:

- **Description 1:** "Transcribe all digits said by the relevant voice - example: type in the digits said by the female voice";
- **Description 2:** "Transcribe all characters said by the relevant voice - example: type in the characters said by the female voice";
- **Description 3:** "Word CAPTCHAs: pick the one image most related to the words said by the relevant voice - select the image related to the words said by the male voice".

Then the entire sequence of the 60 CAPTCHAs is presented randomly. To avoid framing and cognitive load effects, the sequence of CAPTCHAs gets reshuffled for every subject. Those CAPTCHAs are categorised based on their type: number, character, and word. Once participants finish solving CAPTCHAs, they get to the usability questionnaire. The questionnaire follows the standard usability guidelines of System Usability Score. To avoid framing and order effects, the order of questions is randomised. Finally, the study concludes with sociodemographic questions on gender, age, and highest educational achievement.

4   Evaluation

4.1   Usability

For the analysis of usability, we consider four different factors. First, we look at the primary total **number of correctly solved** CAPTCHAs. In each case, we distinguish the **noise type**. Then, to assess **order effects**, we split the CAPTCHAs into three groups depending on the period in which they have been solved. The participants have seen a total of 60 CAPTCHAs, we split the three groups into equal-sized bins: 1st – 20th, 21st – 40th, and 41st – 60th. By evaluating the recognition rate in such a way we can assess the learning effect. Finally, we consider the **number of errors**. Consequently, we distinguish how the rate of CAPTCHA recognition changes if one or two errors are allowed. Finally, the System Usability Scale values (SUS) are analyzed to assess the subjective perception of the CAPTCHAs.

First, we turn to the number of correctly recognized CAPTCHAs. It can be seen in Table 1 that the character-based CAPTCHAs have a significantly worse recognition rate (mean = 26.60%) when compared to both word (mean = 69.90%) and digit-based (mean = 71.80%) CAPTCHAs. The overall best performance was observed for digit-based CAPTCHAs without noise with 85.71% recognition rate, and the worst recognition was observed for character-based CAPTCHAs with bird noise with 18.78% recognition rate. Interestingly, we observe that in some cases participants recognise characters and words better in the presence of noise, than without it. We have two hypotheses regarding why

Table 1. Percentage of correct answers for CAPTCHA and noise types

Noise type	Digits ± std		Characters ± std		Word ± std	
None	**85.71%**	15.94	26.53%	18.43	68.57%	17.32
Bird	75.51%	20.11	18.78%	14.95	79.59%	18.93
Elephant	73.47%	23.23	**39.59%**	23.63	**81.22%**	19.75
White	57.55%	25.37	20.82%	17.78	48.98%	24.17
Overall	71.80%	21.17	26.60%	18.7	69.90%	20.04

this happens. First, it might be the case that participants focus more in the presence of noise. Given CPP CAPTCHA is a low to medium complexity task, a possible explanation could be found with the Yerkes-Dodson Law. It was previously found that a certain level of arousal is beneficial for task performance, and additional noise could just trigger that response [9,18,22,57]. Second, it might be the consequence of a shuffling procedure – some letters are harder to recognise when they overlap. The sequences were randomised for every participant and type of CAPTCHA. We have not controlled in the experiments that the overlaps are consistent across participants, and that could have affected the results. In the subsequent studies, both of those factors should be controlled for.

Table 2. Correct answers per position asked during the study

Type	1 to 20	21 to 40	41 to 60
Digits	4.13	**5.07**	**5.41**
Characters	1.67	1.88	2.04
Word	**4.33**	4.98	4.61
Overall	3.37	3.97	4.02

Next, we turn to the order effects. Table 2 shows how recognition rate changes over time. Here, it is noticeable that for all three types there is an increase in the number of correct answers over time. For all of the considered cases, except for word-based, the increase is observed through all of the time-periods. For word-based CAPTCHAs, improvement is only observed after the first period. Finally, we note that only in the digit-based CAPTCHAs, there is a significant increase for both transitions with p = .036, T = 2.162 and p = .007, T = 2.835.

In the third step, we consider how solvable the CAPTCHAs are when a participant is allowed to make a certain number of mistakes when making their transcription. Table 3 shows the results of the experiment. Note that we only consider the character- and digit-based CAPTCHA types here as word constitutes a binary choice. We find that participants were solving 71% of digit-based CAPTCHAs correctly without any errors, 91% with 1 error allowed and 96% with 2 errors allowed. Here, a significant performance increase of 20% is

Table 3. Correct answers per error tolerance

Type	0 Error	1 Error	2 Errors
Digits	**71%**	**91%**	**96%**
Characters	26%	65%	86%
Overall	48%	78%	91%

observed with just a single misclassification. An even more significant improvement is observed for character-based CAPTCHAs. Only 26% of CAPTCHAS are solved without any errors, but a single misclassification improved performance by almost 40% to 65%. With 2 errors allowed, we observe that performance improved by a further 20% up to 86%. Note here how close the human performance is for digit and character-based CAPTCHAs in the presence of just two errors. The complexity of digit and character tasks are extremely different – random guess probability of $\frac{1}{10^n}$ for n digits and $\frac{1}{26^n}$ for n characters.

Table 4. SUS Score for CAPTCHA types

Type	Mean	SD	Min	Max
Digits	**46.17**	**9.07**	27.5	**70.0**
Characters	44.54	8.25	27.5	67.5
Word	45.56	7.82	**32.5**	**70.0**
Overall	45.42	8.38	29.17	69.17
TapCHA [31]	85.0	–	–	–
Web tnterfaces [4]	68.2	–	–	–
Cell phones interface [4]	65.9	–	–	–
ReCAPTCHA v2 [31]	65.0	–	–	–

Finally, Table 4 presents the SUS values for different types of CAPTCHAs. It appears that for different CAPTCHA types there is no significant difference in terms of usability. For all three types, the mean values are in the range of about 45, with a minimum of around 30 and a maximum of 70. We find that acoustic CPP CAPTCHA performs consistently worse in terms of usability compared to the visual-based ones. Yet, the difference to the closest contender – reCaptcha v2 – is not too large. reCAPTCHA is a very widely used system, meaning it is really hard to control for learning effects. Moreover, Jiang et al. specifically recruited active web users [31]. Given that participants of our study encountered CPP CAPTCHA for the first time, we believe that with more careful design and control for learning effects the usability could be further improved.

4.2   Naive Transcription Performance

Now we turn to the adversarial evaluation. In this paper, we assume a naive attacker that is ignorant of the existence of the background noise in the sample. Although naive, that scenario represents a realistic case of a scalable attack in the real-world. For example, it was previously shown that acoustic reCAPTCHA can be easily solved using Google Cloud Speech out of the box with little to no modifications [8]. For the study, we chose Sphinx and Google Cloud Speech as benchmarks. To make it easier for the transcribers, unless stated otherwise, we used no additional noise and clean generated speech. We have attempted using recorded speech and got similar performance as is shown in Fig. 7. We decided to use generated speech as it presents an idealistic clean scenario. We turn to the case of a more skilful attacker in Sect. 5.

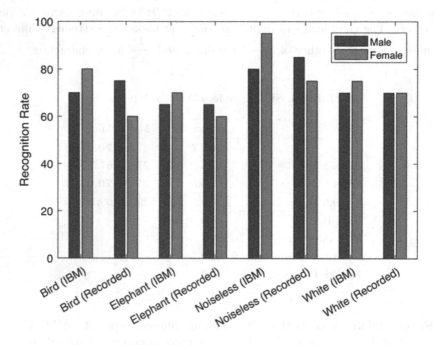

Fig. 7. Per-digit recognition rates for source-separated IBM and recorded digit CAPTCHAs, using a digit dictionary for Sphinx

Figures 8, 9 and 10 show the recognition rate for text generated with MaryTTs, IBM Text-to-Speech, and Google Text-to-Speech. As text transcription tools we chose Google Cloud Speech and Spinx. Overall, we observe that simply using transcribers does not work any more – the recognition rate for digits and characters is consistently low, even when reduced dictionaries are used.

First, we turn to per-character recognition rates which are shown in Fig. 8. Similarly, the character CAPTCHA recognition rates are low. Here, we further

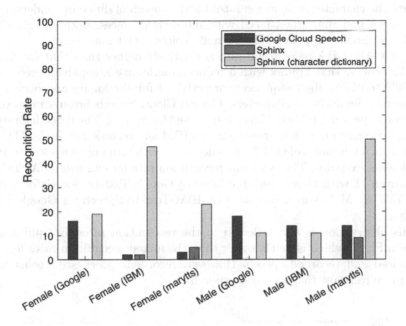

Fig. 8. Per-character recognition rate for character CAPTCHAs

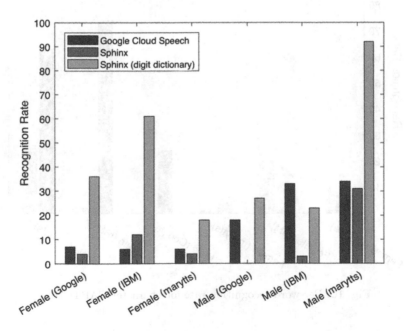

Fig. 9. Per-digit recognition rate for digit CAPTCHAs

evaluate the character recognition rates for the speech of different genders. Interestingly, we find that when faced with interleaved voices, both Google Cloud Speech and Sphinx appear to choose male voices over female voices.

Digit CAPTCHA recognition rate is relatively higher than that for characters. We observe that Sphinx with a reduced dictionary is capable of recovering from 60% to 95% of digit sequences correctly, yet full dictionary approaches perform worse. Similarly to characters, Google Cloud Speech favours male voices over female, yet conflicting evidence is observed for Sphinx. The detection rate for per-digit recognition with source-separated IBM and recorded digit CAPTCHAs ranges from a minimum of 60% for female voices with bird noises to close to 100% for noiseless scenarios. The per-word recognition rate for character CAPTCHAs ranges from 0% with Male speech produced by Google Text-to-Speech for Sphinx, up to 75% for Male voices produced by IBM Text-to-Speech for Google Cloud Speech.

This observation is also reflected in the recognition rates for Sphinx as is shown in Fig. 7, which is much higher than the mixed recognition rates for both synthesised and recorded speech. However, recorded speech still seems to be much more resistant than synthetic speech.

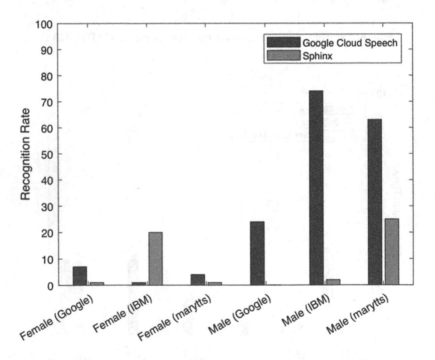

Fig. 10. Per-word recognition rate for character CAPTCHAs

To conclude, per-character, per-digit and per-word recognition rates are relatively poor. That is not surprising – the transcribers were not designed to solve multi-speaker situations. We do observe that digits are handled relatively better, which is consistent with the observation that it is the easiest of three tasks to solve complexity-wise.

Interestingly, we observe inconsistencies in the way that multi-speaker speech is handled. We see that different transcribers, when faced with a choice, consistently pick male voices over female. That finding suggests that similarly to other natural language models, transcribers used in this paper overfit to the dataset gender biases [41,55].

5   Conclusion and Discussion

In this paper, we have presented Cocktail Party Problem-based CAPTCHA construction. We have evaluated its performance in terms of usability and robustness against modern transcribers. We have observed that the Cocktail Party Problem does have an effect on the way transcription works, practically making it impossible for transcribers to be used out of the box. Interestingly, we observed that when faced with overlapping voices, transcribers have a gender bias, consistently picking male voices over female. Finally, we ran a user study to evaluate proposed CAPTCHA usability. We observe that participants could successfully solve it without prior experience and were getting better over time. We find that the usability scores were lower than the ones for the textual CAPTCHAs. Interestingly we observe that the closest contender is reCaptcha v2 – one of most commonly used visual-based CAPTCHAs – with a SUS difference between the two of 20. That, in turn, suggests that with more careful design and control for learning effects the usability of audio CAPTCHA based on the Cocktail Party Problem can be further improved.

CPP CAPTCHA in the Real World. CAPTCHA systems are not impenetrable. In the past, they have set off an arms race with new attacks and schemes being proposed several times a year. The same is to be expected for any new CAPTCHA that finds its way into use.

Same holds for the CAPTCHA construction described in this paper. Recently, a machine learning-based solution to the Cocktail Party Problem was proposed. In particular, Simpson described how one might go about generating a neural network that separates the speakers in a given audio file, with a network trained on the dataset of separated audio files [53]. The mechanism is based on the idea of binary mask generation and the network itself learns the relationship between the different frequencies of a human speaker.

We re-implemented Simpson's paper and evaluated the performance of our CAP-TCHA on a synthesised speaker against his CPP solver and standard text-to-speech transcribers. Using the method, we successfully managed to separate the speakers in the audio files and the speech to text system, and have been able to get the original text with 95% accuracy against almost 0% with CPP. Although a voice synthesiser represents an idealistic scenario (very idealistic scenario with perfect information and practically no task associated) of the attack with a very well-defined speaker, it is still representative of the machine learning ability to solve the problem.

Despite the success of the attack described above, we believe that the proposed solution is still deployable in the wild. We have seen successful attacks on image-based CAPTCHAs that ask a human to solve classification tasks, that we know computers solve much better [35]. There are several reasons why these solutions remain relevant. First and foremost, despite machine learning being able to perform a task very well, it can do so only for a local problem. Cloudflare simply changes the classification task every now and then, forcing the adversaries to either collect a new dataset or learn the task in an online manner. Both of those problems are already extremely hard but are made even harder with the help of a few heuristics. For example, if you suspect that the attacker is trying to do online learning you start to misguide that learning by saying that correct guesses are wrong and the wrong ones are correct. This will also allow the defender to embed trojans into the dataset [40]. Or one can simply ask the robot to solve multiple CAPTCHAs and not report to it if it solved any of them. Second, in practice, there is a lot more then just a single CAPTCHA, behavioural profiles are being built of an individual interacting with a system, which can also be used to detect fraudulent behaviour. For example, with audio one knows the minimum amount of time it should take for a user to solve a task. Similarly, one can also construct samples that she expects machine learning to solve slowly and measure how long it took the model to answer [52].

Visual and Language-Based CAPTCHAs. When compared to traditional visual CAPTCHA systems, language-based acoustic CAPTCHA represents a much richer interaction environment. Even if an attacker manages to learn to solve a local Cocktail Party Problem, it would still not destroy the CPP construction. First, the decision space for the attacker is still a lot larger than in the case of object detection. Language is a lot more discrete and interactions are a lot more subtle. Especially with audio in the analogue form – numerous distinct transformations can be used to diffuse human speech. There is little to no physical limitation on the way language is comprehended by humans, whereas there are large physical limitations to picture representations. Second, both natural language and acoustic natural language tasks are not yet solved by the state of the art machine learning. Although there have been models built which perform consistently well on a number of benchmarks, there is still no model available that is capable of solving all of the natural language comprehension tasks and quickly change between them. Third, most modern language models largely limit the language space with which they work. That is either done through reducing dictionary sizes or controlling the embedding space size. Performance is the issue here: if models are too complex or large they either do not fit in memory, take too long to train or have very large latency. In practice, that reduction is affordable for natural language tasks because models still extract information from unknown words by approximating them with known words. Same does not hold true for language-based CAPTCHAs, as the precision of the answer here is paramount. Finally, language and speech are really easy to change and numerous questions can be asked about the exchange of multiple speakers in an audio sample, with each one of those questions being of a different size. That makes the evolutionary principle of CAPTCHA construction particularly strong.

Future Research Directions. For future research, several approaches are worth pursuing. For example, in the field of word CAPTCHA, there is the possibility to use it entirely as an audio CAPTCHA and to design the response via audio playback. Furthermore, similar to visual CAPTCHAs, users could be allowed to select more than one image. Different languages could be used together for CPP construction to target multi-language or non-native speakers. Motoyama et al. previously categorised the manual labour pool of CAPTCHA solving services using CAPTCHAs in different languages [44]. The authors find significant differences in CAPTCHA service performance, suggesting that language mixture might be a potential way to control CAPTCHA complexity and protect against those services. reCAPTCHA already used a Navajo language speech as background noise, here we propose to extend it to many more languages [60]. Furthermore, the current study could be repeated with non-synthetic voices to evaluate the influence of human speech on performance and usability. The voices could also be modified in different facets, e.g. prosodic elements such as pitch and rate of speech. In the field of study design, users could be given the possibility to play CAPTCHA as often as possible. It would be interesting to see how the performance of robots changes compared to that of humans as they learn. Furthermore, the type of questions could be varied by linking them to the background noise, for example, "how often could you hear a bird in the background?". Finally, some CAPTCHAs showed apparent learning effects for the participants. Therefore, it would be interesting to conduct a longitudinal study to check if the familiarity with a CAPTCHA affects usability.

Acknowledgements. We thank Darija Halatova, Dmitry Kazhdan and Ross Anderson (all affiliated with Cambridge University) for valuable discussions and suggestions. Conducted research was partially supported with funds from Bosch-Forschungsstiftung im Stifterverband.

References

1. ISO 9241–11:2018(en) (2018). Accessed 18 Dec 2018
2. von Ahn, L., Blum, M., Hopper, N.J., Langford, J.: CAPTCHA: using hard AI problems for security. In: Biham, E. (ed.) EUROCRYPT 2003. LNCS, vol. 2656, pp. 294–311. Springer, Heidelberg (2003). https://doi.org/10.1007/3-540-39200-9_18
3. Bagdasaryan, E., Veit, A., Hua, Y., Estrin, D., Shmatikov, V.: How to backdoor federated learning. arXiv preprint arXiv:1807.00459 (2018)
4. Bangor, A., Kortum, P., Miller, J.: Determining what individual SUS scores mean: adding an adjective rating scale. J. Usability Stud. 4(3), 114–123 (2009)

5. Banko, E., Kortvelyes, J., Weiss, B., Vidnyanszky, Z.: How the visual cortex handles stimulus noise: insights from amblyopia. PLoS ONE **8**, e66583 (2013)
6. Bhalerao, R., Aliapoulios, M., Shumailov, I., Afroz, S., McCoy, D.: Mapping the underground: supervised discovery of cybercrime supply chains. In: 2019 APWG Symposium on Electronic Crime Research (eCrime) (2019)
7. Bigham, J.P., Cavender, A.C.: Evaluating existing audio CAPTCHAs and an inter-face optimized for non-visual use. In: Proceedings of the SIGCHI Conference on Human Factors in Computing Systems. ACM (2009)
8. Bock, K., Patel, D., Hughey, G., Levin, D.: unCaptcha: a low-resource defeat of recaptcha's audio challenge. In: 11th {USENIX} Workshop on Offensive Technologies ({WOOT} 17) (2017)
9. Broadhurst, P.: The Interaction of Task Difficulty and Motivation: The Yerkes Dodson Law Revived. Acta Psychologica, Amsterdam (1959)
10. Brooke, J.: SUS: a retrospective. J. Usability Stud. **8**, 29–40 (2013)
11. Brooke, J., et al.: SUS – a quick and dirty usability scale. Usability evaluation in industry (1996)
12. Bursztein, E., Bethard, S., Fabry, C., Mitchell, J.C., Jurafsky, D.: How good are humans at solving CAPTCHAs? A large scale evaluation. In: 2010 IEEE Symposium on Security and Privacy (2010)
13. Chellapilla, K., Larson, K., Simard, P., Czerwinski, M.: Designing human friendly human interaction proofs (HIPs). In: Proceedings of the SIGCHI Conference on Human Factors in Computing Systems. ACM (2005)
14. Cherry, E.C.: Some experiments on the recognition of speech, with one and with two ears. J. Acoust. Soc. Am. **25**, 975–979 (1953)
15. Conway, A.R., Cowan, N., Bunting, M.F.: The cocktail party phenomenon revis-ited: the importance of working memory capacity. Psychon. Bull. Rev. **8**, 331–335 (2001). https://doi.org/10.3758/BF03196169
16. Cranor, L.F., LaMacchia, B.A.: Spam!. Commun. ACM **41**, 74–83 (1998)
17. Danchev, D.: Inside India's CAPTCHA solving economy (2020). https://www.zdnet.com/article/inside-indias-captcha-solving-economy/
18. Denenberg, V.H., Karas, G.G.: Supplementary report: the Yerkes-Dodson law and shift in task difficulty. J. Exp. Psychol. **59**, 429 (1960)
19. DeVries, T., Taylor, G.W.: Learning confidence for out-of-distribution detection in neural networks. arXiv preprint arXiv:1802.04865 (2018)
20. Ellermeier, W., Kattner, F., Ueda, K., Doumoto, K., Nakajima, Y.: Memory disrup-tion by irrelevant noise-vocoded speech: effects of native language and the number of frequency bands. J. Acoust. Soc. Am. **138**, 1561–1569 (2015)
21. Elson, J., Douceur, J.R., Howell, J., Saul, J.: Asirra: a CAPTCHA that exploits interest-aligned manual image categorization (2007)
22. Gawron, V.J.: Performance effects of noise intensity, psychological set, and task type and complexity. Hum. Factors **24**, 225–243 (1982)
23. Geirhos, R., Janssen, D.H.J., Schütt, H.H., Rauber, J., Bethge, M., Wichmann, F.A.: Comparing deep neural networks against humans: object recognition when the signal gets weaker. arXiv preprint arXiv:1706.06969 (2017)
24. Getzmann, S., Jasny, J., Falkenstein, M.: Switching of auditory attention in "cocktail-party" listening: ERP evidence of cueing effects in younger and older adults. Brain Cogn. **111**, 1–12 (2017)
25. Goodman, J., Cormack, G.V., Heckerman, D.: Spam and the ongoing battle for the inbox. Commun. ACM **50**, 24–33 (2007)
26. Handel, S.: Listening: An Introduction to the Perception of Auditory Events. MIT Press, Cambridge (1993)

27. Heiko, P., Meine, N., Edler, B.: Sinusoidal coding using loudness-based component selection. In: IEEE International Conference on Acoustics, Speech, and Signal Processing (2002)
28. Hendrycks, D., Gimpel, K.: A baseline for detecting misclassified and out-of-distribution examples in neural networks. arXiv preprint arXiv:1610.02136 (2016)
29. Holman, J., Lazar, J., Feng, J.H., D'Arcy, J.: Developing usable CAPTCHAs for blind users. In: Proceedings of the 9th International ACM SIGACCESS Conference on Computers and Accessibility. ACM (2007)
30. Holt, T.J., Smirnova, O., Chua, Y.-T.: The marketing and sales of stolen data. In: Holt, T.J., Smirnova, O., Chua, Y.-T. (eds.) Data Thieves in Action. PSCYBER, pp. 19–43. Palgrave Macmillan, New York (2016). https://doi.org/10.1057/978-1-137-58904-0_2
31. Jiang, N., Dogan, H., Tian, F.: Designing mobile friendly CAPTCHAs: an exploratory study. In: Proceedings of the 31st British Computer Society Human Computer Interaction Conference (2017)
32. Kim, D.S.: Perceptual phase quantization of speech. IEEE Trans. Speech Audio Process. **11**, 355–364 (2003)
33. Koch, I., Lawo, V., Fels, J., Vorländer, M.: Switching in the cocktail party: exploring intentional control of auditory selective attention. J. Exp. Psychol. Hum. Percept. Perform. **37**, 1140 (2011)
34. Kochanski, G., Lopresti, D., Shih, C.: A reverse turing test using speech. In: Seventh International Conference on Spoken Language Processing (2002)
35. Krizhevsky, A., Sutskever, I., Hinton, G.E.: ImageNet classification with deep convolutional neural networks. In: Advances in Neural Information Processing Systems (2012)
36. Lazar, J., et al.: The SoundsRight CAPTCHA: an improved approach to audio human interaction proofs for blind users. In: Proceedings of the SIGCHI Conference on Human Factors in Computing Systems. ACM (2012)
37. Leiner, B.M., et al.: A brief history of the internet. ACM SIGCOMM Comput. Commun. Rev. **39**, 22–31 (2009)
38. Levchenko, K., et al.: Click trajectories: end-to-end analysis of the spam value chain. In: 2011 IEEE Symposium on Security and Privacy (2011)
39. Liao, C., Zhong, H., Squicciarini, A., Zhu, S., Miller, D.: Backdoor embedding in convolutional neural network models via invisible perturbation. arXiv preprint arXiv:1808.10307 (2018)
40. Liu, Y., et al.: Trojaning attack on neural networks (2017)
41. Lu, K., Mardziel, P., Wu, F., Amancharla, P., Datta, A.: Gender bias in neural natural language processing. arXiv preprint arXiv:1807.11714 (2018)
42. Mermelstein, P.: Distance measures for speech recognition, psychological and instrumental. Pattern Recognit. Artif. Intell. **116**, 374–388 (1976)
43. Moray, N.: Attention in dichotic listening: affective cues and the influence of instructions. Q. J. Exp. Psychol. **11**, 56–60 (1959)
44. Motoyama, M., Levchenko, K., Kanich, C., McCoy, D., Voelker, G.M., Savage, S.: Re: CAPTCHAs-understanding captcha-solving services in an economic context
45. Motoyama, M., McCoy, D., Levchenko, K., Savage, S., Voelker, G.M.: An analysis of underground forums. In: Proceedings of the 2011 ACM SIGCOMM Conference on Internet Measurement Conference (2011)
46. Paliwal, K.K., Alsteris, L.: Usefulness of phase spectrum in human speech perception. In: Proceedings of the Eurospeech (2003)

47. Rajashekar, U., Bovik, A.C., Cormack, L.K.: Visual search in noise: revealing the influence of structural cues by gaze-contingent classification image analysis. J. Vis. **6**, 379–386 (2006)

48. Sauer, G., Hochheiser, H., Feng, J., Lazar, J.: Towards a universally usable CAPTCHA. In: Proceedings of the 4th Symposium on Usable Privacy and Security (2008)

49. Sauro, J.: Measuring usability with the system usability scale (SUS) (2011)

50. Scharf, B.: On hearing what you listen for: the effects of attention and expectancy. Can. Psychol. (1990)

51. Shi, G., Shanechi, M.M., Aarabi, P.: On the importance of phase in human speech recognition. IEEE Trans. Audio Speech, Lang. Process. **14**, 1867–1874 (2006)

52. Shumailov, I., Zhao, Y., Bates, D., Papernot, N., Mullins, R., Anderson, R.: Sponge examples: energy-latency attacks on neural networks (2020)

53. Simpson, A.J.: Probabilistic binary-mask cocktail-party source separation in a convolutional deep neural network. arXiv preprint arXiv:1503.06962 (2015)

54. Soupionis, Y., Gritzalis, D.: Audio CAPTCHA: existing solutions assessment and a new implementation for VoIP telephony. Comput. Secur. **29**, 603–618 (2010)

55. Sun, T., et al.: Mitigating gender bias in natural language processing: Literature review. arXiv preprint arXiv:1906.08976 (2019)

56. Tam, J., Simsa, J., Huggins-Daines, D., Von Ahn, L., Blum, M.: Improving audio captchas. In: Symposium on Usable Privacy and Security (SOUPS) (2008)

57. Teigen, K.H.: Yerkes-Dodson: a law for all seasons. Theory Psychol. **4**, 525–547 (1994)

58. Von Ahn, L., Blum, M., Langford, J.: Telling humans and computers apart automatically. Commun. ACM **47**, 56–60 (2004)

59. Wang, S.Y., Bentley, J.L.: CAPTCHA challenge tradeoffs: Familiarity of strings versus degradation of images. In: 18th International Conference on Pattern Recognition (ICPR 2006). IEEE (2006)

60. Yan, J., El Ahmad, A.S.: Usability of CAPTCHAs or usability issues in CAPTCHA design. In: Proceedings of the 4th Symposium on Usable Privacy and Security (2008)

Audio CAPTCHA with a Few Cocktails: It's So Noisy I Can't Hear You (Transcript of Discussion)

Benjamin Maximilian Reinheimer[1(✉)], Fairooz Islam[2], and Ilia Shumailov[2]

[1] Karlsruhe Institute of Technology, Karlsruhe, Germany
benjaminmaximilian.reinheimer@kit.edu
[2] University of Cambridge, Cambridge, UK
{fairooz.islam,ilia.shumailov}@cl.cam.ac.uk

Everyone, my name is Benjamin, and from being a Postmaster, which, probably, most of you aren't, at the moment, to a topic that, I guess, most of you dealed in the past, CAPTCHAs, and our topic is, audio CAPTCHAs, with a few cocktails, it's so noisy I can't hear you.

First of all, you see a visual CAPTCHA and you think like adding some cocktails is pretty nice. So what's the general idea behind the system? Give me a second. Something is not working.

So that's an audio CAPTCHA which is currently used and I guess most of you could solve, it?

Frank Stajano: No.

Reply: Yeah. So first of all, what's a CAPTCHA? CAPTCHA is Completely Automated Public Turing Test to Tell Computers and Humans Apart, and as you realise this one might be solved by a computer but probably not by anyone in this room, so it's not by definition a problem that humans are good at and computers aren't.

So there's this Google reCAPTCHA problem, so the one you heard is an artefact from speech to text solvable CAPTCHAs of audio files in the past. In the past, audio CAPTCHAs were pretty easy to be solved by the reCAPTCHA. You just put in their audio transformation system and it could like solve every audio CAPTCHA, so they had to improve the audio CAPTCHA and you heard the improved version. Now the computer can't solve the problem but the human can't solve it either, because once they used concept noises like simple noises like white noise, in the background, first of all, or they used other regular noises like some sound just had changed but are on the same level. In the past, it was pretty easy, then they improved it and put more and more of this in the audio CAPTCHA and now it's not as easy as this question to answer like, Littlefoot's mother in the original Land Before Time, "Did you feel sad? Yes or no?"

That would be a question we would expect for a CAPTCHA because it's easy for us to solve.

© Springer Nature Switzerland AG 2020
J. Anderson et al. (Eds.): Security Protocols 2019, LNCS 12287, pp. 41–47, 2020.
https://doi.org/10.1007/978-3-030-57043-9_4

So our motivation is the following-

Frank Stajano: On that intangible CAPTCHA... if I had understood anything, what would have been my input to prove that I was human? What should I have done?

Reply: On the first one?

Frank Stajano: Yes.

Reply: You were supposed to input numbers, like digits. There was some digit audio tone in the background you could hear.

Frank Stajano: Oh okay, so I should have said some digits I had heard?

Reply: Yeah, you should have heard some digits like 7-3-1-something.

Frank Stajano: I really had no idea what the challenge was in that. Thank you.

Reply: I listened to it several times and I was no chance to even ... even with the answers you're supposed to give, there's no chance to find it, so yeah I think most people think CAPTCHA is a solved problem in the past, but wat about acoustic domain, so there's several ideas why acoustic CAPTCHAs are a thing of the future. One thing is that people have disabilities, so some people have not a proficiency in language to understand CAPTCHAs or can read, others have visual disabilities so for them audio CAPTCHAs is one thing.

Another thing is duplex-like systems, I don't know if you know Google Duplex, it's released I think last year and it can make phone calls as if it was a human and for the other side it's really difficult to tell if it's a human or not, and if you use systems like this you can attack your competitor if you're like a restaurant and you have other restaurant on the other side of the street and you want to make them lose money, you just use Google Duplex-like systems and attack them and make fake reservations and it's pretty easy, it's pretty cheap with systems like this.

So there's probably going to be some sort of CAPTCHA in the future or some sort of mechanism to make sure that these systems don't get misused and our idea is to use the cocktail party problem to produce audio CAPTCHAs and it's for two reasons; one, make usable and easy to solve CAPTCHAs, not as the one you heard before, and make it even difficult for the machine to break it, and definitely use more than one voice because there's some psychological effects that people at the cocktail party can really good selective hear one voice and differentiate from another and we want to build our system on this one.

So to have some effective form of thematic noise in the background, which the machine is difficult to break but is less intrusive for the human to understand and to comprehend, and you listen to a digit CAPTCHA, there are also character CAPTCHAs where you have to input characters and we have another preferred design we tested in our study which is about word base, because words are pretty easy for humans to understand and to relate words to different stuff, so we propose a scheme with only words.

One thing is the security is better because it has large data fields or it's more difficult for the machine to just randomly guess the correct answer, and in usability our idea was that humans are more likely to understand meaningful words and therefore are more effective in solving these CAPTCHAs, and we want to vary the number of words or randomly guessing words is also difficult for the machine, so we did two things; one was the usability part so we started people having some informed consent, some ethics then some study explanations, what is going to be expect for them in the next couple of minutes, then some examples, so they got all three example CAPTCHA types from our study and just can had the chance to familiarise with themselves using the CAPTCHA system so they have an idea how it sounds and how they expect to answer, and then they got audio CAPTCHAs, 60 in total, in a randomised order.

After this used this SUS that's the System Usability Scale, it's a pretty standard scale for asking questions about usability and them some social demographic questions for them. For the first study explanations are a bit more about methodology. We had two sets of digits, six to nine digits CAPTCHAs, one female and one male voice that would look like this. So that's for the digits part, the same for characters or six to nine characters, male and female voice. The same explanation, just this time with characters and I guess most of you find it more easy to understand than the one in the beginning of the talk, and then we have some CAPTCHA for words, like three to six English words, again with female and male voice, and they all relate to one image so they all have in common something and the user has to select one image out of a choice of images, it looks like this. So everyone has an idea which image is the correct one?

Frank Stajano: Four?

Reply: Yeah, four. So these words are not always in the picture like I think it said 'vehicle' which is more abstract but still only this one word would for a human be pretty easy to understand which picture is mentioned. So first of all we did some machine learning, we used state-of-the-art Google Cloud speech things and things only focused on characters, that's the character recognition, so as you can see things focus and characters is okay to about 50% recognition for IBM and MaryTTS voice but for the other voices it's pretty bad.

For digits, all of them are improving a bit. The male MaryTTS is okay with a recognition of over 90% and the female for IBM is okay with over 60% but all the others are really bad. Now surely you can say it's solvable with machine learning, just put in enough data and then we can solve it. For words we use these and as you can see for male it works.

From our research we found that the female voice is pretty bad with the current mechanism to solve, yeah?

Michael Millian: How did you, when you're measuring these male versus female voices, presumably a female voice is paired with a male voice, did you do any consideration of maybe this female voice is more recognisable with this male voice rather than that one?

Reply: So these, it only three voices for female and male and maybe Ilya can say a bit more because I'm more the usability guy for this study.

Ilia Shumailov: Yeah, so, long story short, it seems that there is an inherent bias every time you hear a female voice and a male voice together, even at the same gain level, the speech effects recognised that you go for the male voice irregardless, so it seems like there is a bias generally... maybe I'm not claiming it is there for sure because nobody knows.

Reply: I guess that was the question.

Martin Ukrop: Was there any bias like in the human participant as well because hearing the sample I also found the male voice is easier to understand and hear in examples, even though I was sometimes to supposed to hear for the female voice?

Ilia Shumailov: So I made the study we were asking to-

Reply: We were only asking about the female voice because previous studies with some slightly different people gave the feedback that they preferred the female voice to listen to, but yeah, I think that's individual and you can change it around.

Ilia Shumailov: Yeah but certainly, overall the goal of this study was to show that actually there is a much easier way to build systems which are tricking the [inaudible] that's available out there, by not putting some journalistic voices that we heard in the beginning from reCAPTCHA but just by using special psychological effects.

Reply: So let's move on to the usability study for the humans, so that's for the-

Frank Stajano: So because the two voices that are mixed and need to be distinguished are male and female and because the female is usually higher frequency, would it be possible for an attacker to use some kind of spectral analysis and say the female's going to be higher and then isolate that based on that?

Ilia Shumailov: We actually took state-of-the-art machine learning and we were capable of suppressing both female and male voices, however this does not mean that you can't rig the system because the fact that we've managed to separate and just transcribe the speech does not mean you can actually make intelligible. As we can see, the percentages are okay, this is the attack on the CAPTCHA that I put on the speakers.

What happens in practice if you involve such a system because the most expensive part is in the character adaptation. What did I say, how many times did the cat say 'meow', and all those problems are actually not solvable. Locating how many speakers in the room, separation of those individual speakers is the sort of problem, however humans are capable of it. This is why images must be used in the mind to distract away from the actual objects within the image and make decision.

Jim Blythe: So this is interesting, but this sort of raises, to this high level the question where you try to stay one step or two steps ahead of the automated systems. . . how long did it take you to find something that's simple to create, that humans can do right now that the machines can't, because to use a system like this you're going to have to be continually doing this, as the automated recognition systems catch up to you.

Ilia Shumailov: Right now [inaudible] underground for once, people felt [inaudible] as a means of currency, so long story short people adapt systems when they try to solve those problems; the more complex the problem is, the more [inaudible] you are required to actually solve it. I think I saw a paper which is basically the journalistic voice you heard from the audio and then for images your classic line of traffic lights, car crossings and other things.

Reply: Maybe you should switch to the usability. So for now we looked at accuracy, so first we looked at the digits and we had four different background noises, like there was no background noise, there was some birds chirping at the background, there was some elephant in the background and there was some static white noise in the background. For digits you can clearly see white noise was okay but not a good result.

Without none 85% had everything correct, so it's not per digit, it's having all the digits in one CAPTCHA correct in one try. All the participants only had one try, trying the CAPTCHA to solve it then they went onto the next CAPTCHA. For characters, as you can see people were not as good as for digits, and the ranking changes a lot. Now elephant is the best, If you could say, from really bad results so here only on average like 26% of the CAPTCHAs could completely be solved in one try, and for words, words are equally to overall to the digits but again this time elephant and bird are the best with none being a bit below, which is quite surprising so, from our results, it seems people can solve them better with some noise in the background, as you were talking about disrupting the people.

For this word CAPTCHA even have a positive influence, after this we asked the participants to rate this system, System Usability Scale, it's like 10 items about "I would use the system in the future", "I think the system is complex", "I I think I would need help for this". Sadly, overall, all three CAPTCHA types are like 45 around, which is not a good value, so normally above 68 is good score, everything below is okay-ish, everything below 35 is really bad so we have to look into why people, being for some of the CAPTCHAs pretty good in solving them, rated them pretty bad in usability.

Maybe it's because they didn't get feedback but right now we don't know, but there's a question. Give a second.

Martin Ukrop: Thanks. How many participants did you have?

Reply: It's 50 participants. 50 participants, who all had to solve 60 CAPTCHAS.

Lydia Kraus: I was wondering, whether you compare to your results from the audio CAPTCHA like the System Usability Scale results, with our studies that also used the same scale in the context of the visual CAPTCHAs.

Reply: Yeah, we found a few studies who used the same scale, most of them used different scales. Some of the visual CAPTCHAs in the past, not the current ones, like one generation before were around 70%, so still not really good, but better than ours.

Lydia Kraus: Okay, follow-up question: do you think ... does it make sense to substitute the visual CAPTCHAs with the audio CAPTCHAs? Like if people seem to like the visual CAPTCHAs more?

Reply: As it's not the same study, I would not say people like visual CAPTCHAs more from my own personal experience lately, I had a lot of problems solving the visual CAPTCHAs because I often tend to click too many of the fields if you have some visual to click, because I apparently act as a machine. If there's some small part in line one corner, I click it and the machine would click it but most people don't, do that marks me as a machine so I have to redo them like 10 times, so having not the same participants in the same study with the same generation, I would not say they liked visual CAPTCHA more.

Currently I would like to investigate why it's so bad, so we didn't give them feedback if they were correct or not, so maybe people thought they were like really bad even though they weren't as bad as they did, so that's something for the future I think we have to investigate.

Fabio Massacci: One question sorry. You've rendered things in English, right?

Reply: Yeah. In English in the UK with English native speaker.

Fabio Massacci: Okay. With this then you may try a different nationality, may have different-

Reply: Sure.

Ilia Shumailov: So, coming back to these usability score, the reason why they decided to put both overall and [inaudible] here, is from, first of all, comparing images to audio is not the same. We are, by now, already used to images. It would be quite hard to find people that haven't seen CAPTCHAs. So, when you ask people to rate CAPTCHAs, as a design user study, unless you explicitly deceive them into thinking that this is not a part of the study, it's very hard to get proper comparison. Right? That's the first thing. The second thing is, the best response, the maximum response for each of these categories was around 70. Okay? So the reason why we normalise this is because if you try to compare with images, some people are so used to sorting images, now that they give you, what was it? 85 or 90 in the study or so, the maximum they were reporting for images.

Reply: Yeah.

Ilia Shumailov: So comparing them is a little bit hard. Okay? So this is why normalised values showing that this okay, is some waterproof way to compare doing them again. One is not a substitute for the other. Audio CAPTCHAs are also necessary because. Imagine you're a restaurant. You want to increase your sales, right? There are two restaurants on your street. What you do is, you get a [inaudible] calls the time the other restaurant and says, "Okay, can I please make a reservation" using multiple different voices. If you put the incentive aside, and to say, okay, there are means of solving this by asking for credit card numbers as you're making reservation. It is extremely hard to protect the voices.

Frank Stajano: Thanks, Diana, with all due respect, if I were the owner of a restaurant, and I have to put this in front of potentially paying customers, I rather just have disruption than risk people not booking at my restaurant because they have to book through this. This seems very [inaudible] for people to go through before booking, whereas they would just book to a restaurant that doesn't have a CAPTCHA.

Reply: Okay. Just one more point. As we only allowed one try, on the last slide I only showed 100% completion. We looked at how many mistakes do the people do for both characters and digits, and for characters it's more interesting because you can clearly see that people seem to do one mistake and then you'll jump from 26 to already 65% of correct characters hey found and allowing two mistakes is already 86.

One thing we found is, it seems to be there are characters that people are really bad to understand like B and P and stuff like this, so one idea for the future would be, you could use this to invert this stuff, so if someone can correctly guess this character at this one specific position, it might be a machine because humans can't do it. So that's an idea in like combine things that humans are possible to solve and things that are just, humans are really bad in solving, to combine in one CAPTCHA and have this as [inaudible] ... and I think then that's it. Thank you.

Understanding Humans

Shaping Our Mental Model of Security

Saša Radomirović[✉]

School of Mathematical and Computer Sciences, Heriot–Watt University,
Edinburgh, UK
sasa.radomirovic@hw.ac.uk

Abstract. The IT industry's need to distinguish new products with new looks, new experiences, and new user interface designs is bad for cybersecurity. It robs users of the chance to transfer previously acquired security-relevant knowledge to new products and leaves them with a poor mental model of security.

Starting from a comparison with physical safety, we explore and sketch a method to help users develop a useful mental model of security in cybersystems. A beneficial side-effect of our methodology is that it makes precise what security requirements the user expects the system to fulfill. This can be used to formally verify the system's compliance with the user's expectation.

1 Introduction

The safety of consumer products has tremendously improved over the course of the last century. In some industries, notoriously the automotive industry, safety improvements have been achieved in spite of a significant push-back by the industry and only after many hard-fought legal battles [6,8]. Unfortunately, now that consumer products are increasingly being connected to the Internet we may be about to regress on safety. We have never really been secure in cyberspace, but we were physically safe from cyber attackers until the IT industry began to connect everything and the kitchen sink to the Internet.

In the IT industry security issues are still largely the customer's problem. Only the largest vendors provide automatic security patches for their products and only for a limited time. When the vendor ceases to provide security updates, the customer must buy new products or risk security breaches due to unpatched vulnerabilities. New products and services attempt to distinguish themselves with new looks, new user interface designs, and new functions. This leaves some users disoriented and thus vulnerable to attacks.

Even though user interface design is a well-researched area and user experience is directly related to a product's success, some people still struggle to comprehend computing technology, and fail to interact correctly with it, simply because there is always a learning curve to a new technology. Some of those that do comprehend technology now will eventually lose touch with its latest trends. When a new technology goes on to marginalise and eliminate previously established technologies, those unfamiliar with it will be forced to learn to use

© Springer Nature Switzerland AG 2020
J. Anderson et al. (Eds.): Security Protocols 2019, LNCS 12287, pp. 51–59, 2020.
https://doi.org/10.1007/978-3-030-57043-9_5

it. This problem is aggravated by the fact that different mobile apps, web apps, applications, and all the Internet of Things devices making their way into people's homes use different design patterns, different terminology, and different interfaces. It further steepens the learning curve and increases user errors due to confusion and misunderstanding, which may be exploited by an attacker.

Therefore, in order to design systems that are better at keeping users and the Internet at large secure, we must ensure that independently designed systems represent security-critical interfaces in a unified manner. In this paper we explore the use of security signs to communicate security-relevant information and instructions. The purpose of this paper is not to discuss what the best graphical or auditory representation for security signs and signals is, but to discuss what types of instruction or information must be conveyed. We shall therefore refrain from suggesting any shape, color, symbol, or sound for any sign or signal.

2 Users' Mental Model of Security

A mental model is a cognitive representation of external reality. It is a functional, simplified representation of reality, a working model [7]. We form our mental models through trial and error. To improve our mental model we need interactive feedback. Wash and Rader [9] observe that information security provides very little direct feedback to users. This makes mental models for information security difficult as the positive or negative consequences of security-critical decisions may not manifest themselves in time to be associated with the decisions made. It follows that (design) changes are bad for people's mental model of security.

As long as our rapidly evolving hardware and software systems keep on changing the location, terminology or graphical representation of security-critical settings and notifications, we can expect that users' mental models of security-critical functionalities will be poor. To guide users through security-critical processes and decisions we must therefore either always make the costly assumption that the user's working model of the system is very poor, or support users in creating better mental models by keeping the presentation and functionality of security-critical elements of systems the same. Clearly, the second option is preferable, but it requires standardisation.

Standardised signs and signals are a crucial tool to reduce the risk of accidents in safety-critical systems. For example, we all rely on "green for go" and "red for stop" on the road. The standardisation of this choice of colors keeps those of us who can distinguish these colors safe even in places we haven't been to before. "Green for go" is not innate to us, but we are able to transfer this knowledge to new, previously unseen environments.

We can therefore expect that user security would benefit greatly if there was agreement on standard signs and signals for security and privacy options and notifications across applications and platforms. If future versions of applications and new technologies keep to such a standard, it would allow users familiar with previous technologies to transfer their accumulated knowledge to the new technology.

At present, we are in the unfortunate situation that the location and representation of security settings and notifications not only change between vendors, but even on a yearly basis from one major version of a software to the next. To give just one example, in an update of the iOS mobile phone operating system, the behaviour of the Bluetooth and Wi-Fi buttons in "Control Center" changed while their appearance (shape, color, and symbol) remained the same. In iOS 10 these buttons turn the respective services on and off. In iOS 11 these buttons temporarily disconnect some devices, but the respective service remains on[1] and the system continues to provide access to the service [2,3]. The result of such an interface tweak is that the users' mental models further diverge from reality.

3   Shaping Our Mental Model of Security

Our position is that human-computer interfaces should provide security-relevant information with standardised security signs. Ideally, the security signs alone should provide enough information for the user to understand the security implications of an action (or inaction) to the user's assets.

In the following we explore how signs and signals could be designed to support a user's security-critical decisions. We start with safety signs that are commonly found at workplaces and public areas in the European Union and are standardised by ISO 7010.

3.1   From Safety Signs to Security Signs

Safety signs help people to safely navigate a physical space. There are essentially four types of safety signs distinguished by shape and color in ISO 7010. A red circle indicates a prohibition, a blue disk indicates an obligation (a mandatory action), a yellow triangle indicates a warning, and a green rectangle indicates a safe way (a safe condition)[2]. These shapes and colors are combined with pictograms to convey what the safety instruction or information relates to. For example, a cigarette in a red circle indicates that smoking is prohibited, a helmet on a blue disk indicates that head protection must be worn, a lightning bolt in a yellow triangle is a high voltage warning, and a phone in a green rectangle indicates the location of an emergency phone.

The obligation and prohibition signs give instructions about what to do or not to do in an environment. The warning and safe way signs provide information about dangers and safety features in the environment. If we are lost in a hospital, a "no unauthorised persons" and a radiation warning sign on a door should prevent us from trying to find our way out through that door. The prohibition sign instructs us not to enter, the warning sign informs us of the danger.

---

[1] A new symbol is introduced in iOS 11 for the state in which the Bluetooth or Wi-Fi service is off. Unless the respective service is off to begin with, this state cannot be reached from within Control Center in iOS 11.

[2] Signs indicating the location of fire equipment are depicted on red rectangles.

Our familiarity with safety signs could perhaps be leveraged to communicate security requirements and warnings with such signs to users. However, our focus in the following is on the instructions and information that can be conveyed with the four types of signs. Indeed, the four types of safety signs discussed are not sufficient to signal all security conditions. Safety signs are intended to minimise risk to a subject's safety in an environment that the subject has no or only limited authority over. For example, they must be set up by employers in workplaces as part of their duty of care to their employees. The safety signs are a communication from the employer to the employees.

In contrast, the responsibility to keep a user's assets secure in cybersystems is shared between the user and their system and it requires a two-way communication between the user and the system. The user inputs data into the system and has some control over the system. The system is supposed to store, processes, and protect the user's data as directed. Both user and system may signal an obligation or prohibition to each other. To avoid confusion, we must therefore distinguish between signs that represent an obligation/prohibition imposed on the user and signs that represent an obligation/prohibition imposed on the system. For example, if a system uses safety signs to communicate instructions to users, it would use a blue disk and red circle respectively to signal an obligation and prohibition imposed on the user. Consequently, obligations and prohibitions that the user wishes to impose on the system would have to be represented by shapes and colors that are clearly distinct from those used for safety signs.

Moreover, since the user has a choice whether to impose a restriction on the system, there must also be related signs for its opposite, i.e., for the "release from obligation" and the "permission" types of instructions. From a security requirements perspective, these instructions could be represented by a single type, i.e. a "no restriction" type, as they do not impose a restriction on the system. In practice, however, it might be clearer from a user's perspective to have distinct signs for the two types. We will refer to the no restriction type in the rest of the paper.

We argue below that these new types of instructions suffice to represent security requirements for standard data security properties. To this end, we must first define what security means.

3.2 Security Requirements

A security requirement is a set of acceptable system behaviours. If the system's behaviour is in the acceptable set, the system satisfies the security requirement. We say that the system is secure if it satisfies all of the user's security requirements. Otherwise the system is not secure.

Standard data security requirement types concern the control of read and write permissions to data and resources and impose availability and functionality requirements on services and resources. It is well-known that the former requirements are prohibition type requirements and the latter obligation type requirements.

With the security signs discussed in the preceding section, the user can define security requirements by setting obligations and prohibitions to be imposed on the system. It follows that the security signs can represent standard types of security requirements.

Once the obligations and prohibitions imposed on the system are set, the user *expects* the system to be secure, i.e., meet all imposed obligations and prohibitions. However, the system will frequently be unable to meet all user-imposed requirements, for example due to external factors, such as power loss, or conflicting requirements imposed by the user. The notion of system security defined above is impractical as it prevents the analysis of how the system and user can resolve some benign violations of security requirements. We therefore relax the conditions and define *user security* as the absence of bad surprises for the user. More precisely, we allow the system to break a user-defined security requirement if it previously informs the user about the need to change a requirement and offers options to do so. Thus the user's expectation of which security requirements hold is defined by the choices the user makes in the system's interactive dialogs and the information that the system communicates to the user. User security is satisfied if the system satisfies the user's expected security requirements.

For user security to be satisfiable in a non-trivial system, the security signs must be expressive enough for the system to communicate violations of security requirements to the user and provide options to resolve them. We discuss this next.

3.3   Communicating with Security Signs

Users may have control over a wide range of services, from an alarm clock to voice command recognition. A typical service runs in the background without a prominently audible or visible user interface. Enabling a service creates an obligation for the system to eventually or continuously perform a task. Similarly, a user can launch applications obliging the system to perform an immediate task. The user can define permissions and prohibitions by granting or revoking the permission for a service or application to access data or a device. For example a voice command recognition service may be prohibited to access information about the user's contacts while a messaging application may be permitted to access the microphone. The system communicates the obligations and prohibitions that the user can control and these are all represented as obligations and prohibitions imposed on the system.

Compliance and Violation. A user's security requirements (i.e., obligations and prohibitions for the system) may be impossible for the system to satisfy. In this case the system must alert the user with a warning sign and provide information about the violated requirement. To avoid confusion, a sign representing a violation of an obligation or prohibition, which is of an information type, must be distinguishable from the obligation and prohibition signs which denote an instruction. We therefore need a violation type whose signs are related to but clearly distinct from obligation, prohibition, and no restriction signs.

In order for the system to inform the user about the reason for a violation, the sytem may also need to refer to security requirements that are satisfied. We thus also need signs of a compliance type that indicate satisfied security requirements. Note that compliance and violation signs may refer to restrictions imposed on the system or the user.

The information alerting a user to a potential security violation is therefore composed from several signs: First, a warning sign to indicate that the user's security has been or is at risk of being violated. Second, the violation sign for the one or more security requirements that cannot be fulfilled. Third, the reason (if known) for the violation of the aforementioned security properties which are compliance or violation type signs.

If there are one or more options for the user to resolve the situation, the user must be presented with these options. This can be achieved with a safe way type sign followed by the available options which we will discuss in the next section.

We briefly give examples for various types of obligation violations that could occur.

1. Obligation violated due to a prohibition imposed on the system.
   The system may be unable to run a voice messaging application because it does not have permission to access the microphone.
   To alert the user, the system would signal a warning sign, a violation sign for the obligation imposed on the system to run the voice messaging application, and a compliance sign for the prohibition to access the microphone.
2. Obligation violated due to an obligation violation by the user.
   The system may be unable to run a voice messaging application because it does not have a microphone or may be unable to install security updates because it is operating on low battery power.
   In both cases there is a lack of an external resource which is impossible for the system to control. It is the user's obligation to provide the resource, i.e., ensure that there is a microphone, a sufficiently charged battery, or a power supply.
   To alert the user, the system would signal a warning sign, a violation sign for the obligation imposed on the system and a violation sign for the obligation imposed on the user to provide the missing resource.
3. Obligation violated due to an obligation imposed on the user.
   Similarly to the previous example, a portable loudspeaker may be unable to play music while it is being recharged. As recharging the device is an obligation imposed on the user, the system would signal a warning sign, a violation sign for the obligation imposed on the system and a compliance sign for the obligation imposed on the user to provide the missing resource.
4. Obligation violated due to another obligation imposed on the system.
   The system may be unable to perform a backup operation of a storage device while it is repairing the files system of the same storage device.

5. Obligation violated due to a prohibition imposed on the user.
   The system may be unable to open a file because the user is not authorised to access the file.

We have thus seen that the introduction of violation and compliance signs enables the system to communicate its state to the user. It remains to discuss the communication of options provided to a user to define security requirements or resolve a violation or conflicting set of requirements.

Options. To maintain or return to a secure state, i.e., satisfy the user's expected security properties, the system must allow the user to choose from all available options.

The security sign types defined thus far allow us to represent options for security requirements by signalling the present state with a compliance type sign and signalling the available options with obligation, prohibition, and no restriction signs. The user's choice can then be represented by changing the compliance type sign to the new state or by signalling a warning, as discussed above, if the user's choice leads to a security violation.

In some cases, the system must signal an option involving an obligation or prohibition to be imposed on the user. Such options are only available when the user is not fulfilling the necessary obligation or prohibition. Thus, such options are signalled with a violation type of the obligation or prohibition imposed on the user and the corresponding obligation or prohibition type. For example, if one of the options is for the user to plug in a currently unplugged device into an electricity supply, then the system would display a violation of the obligation imposed on the user to plug in the device and the obligation for the user to plug in the device.

4 Discussion

We have merely explored the feasibility of security signs with respect to the types of information that must be communicated between a user and a system. We have seen that a communication system could be based on 9 different types of signs: Warning signs and safe way signs to alert the user and provide information on how to resolve a problem. Obligation and prohibition signs imposed on the system and respectively on the user to communicate instructions and a type for no restriction imposed on the system. Finally, compliance and violation signs to indicate a state. Four of these types are analogous to standard types of safety signs which provide warnings, information, and instructions to people. The new types extend these to communicate instructions from a user to the system and for the system to communicate its current state to the user.

We have not discussed the number of symbols that this approach would require. There is clearly a trade-off between the memorability of a number of signs and symbols for users and the expressivity of the resulting language, and it is not certain that there is a good solution.

A non-negligible benefit for a system that implements standardised signs as sketched in this paper is that it makes precise what security requirements the system must satisfy. This makes it easier to formally test the system's conformance to the promised behaviour as signalled to the user, the user security property defined above, as well as other security and usability properties, such as robustness to human error. Moreover, the type and number of signs appearing in user interface dialogues can be used to estimate the complexity of the information the system communicates to its user.

We have tacitly assumed that the system is trustworthy. This assumption is too strong and real-world systems will be using accidentally or adversarially misleading security signs. For example, phishing and overlay attacks [1,10] are conceivable, but their impact on systems with security signs and their mitigation should be the same as for a system without security signs. A potentially interesting, more specific attack vector could be dark design patterns that are well-known in the advertising industry. These are user interface designs that guide the user towards an unfavourable outcome for the user. A simple dark pattern would be to use the tyranny of the default: Many users are weary of changing default settings or simply do not take the time to explore preference settings. A system could set unfavorable default security settings for the user and make them hard to find. Thus the deployment of security signs in itself would certainly neither guarantee that users' security nor their mental model of security improves.

5   Related Work

Mental models in cybersecurity have been investigated from a few different angles. We mention two that use a formal methods approach.

Combéfis and Pecheur [4] use labeled transition systems to describe the behaviour of a system and the user's mental model of it. They present an algorithm that computes from a system model the minimal mental model that a user must have in order to properly use the system. The minimal mental model is equivalent to the system model modulo a variant of weak bisimulation.

In his PhD dissertation, Houser [5] developed a formal model of user mental models and applied it to discover dangerous user-system interactions within the context of a cloud data storage system and analyse the threats faced by recipients of phishing emails.

6   Conclusion

We have sketched a method to help users develop a useful mental model of security in cybersystems. The basic idea is to always expose users to the same standard signs in the same security context. The security signs may be meaningless to a novice in the beginning, but their repeated use and the user's observation of the effects that follow gradually shape and improve the user's mental model. A wide-spread adoption and consistency across different platforms and software versions would ensure that users' mental models remain accurate across different systems and help reduce security risks due to confusion and misunderstanding.

References

1. Aonzo, S., Merlo, A., Tavella, G., Fratantonio, Y.: Phishing attacks on modern android. In: Proceedings of the 2018 ACM SIGSAC Conference on Computer and Communications Security, CCS 2018, Toronto, ON, Canada, 15–19 October 2018, pp. 1788–1801. ACM (2018)
2. Apple Inc. iPhone User Guide, 2017. https://help.apple.com/iphone/10. Accessed 30 Dec 2019
3. Apple Inc. iPhone User Guide 2018. https://help.apple.com/iphone/11. Accessed 30 Dec 2019
4. Combéfis, S., Pecheur, C.: A bisimulation-based approach to the analysis of human-computer interaction. In: ACM SIGCHI Symposium on Engineering Interactive Computing Systems, pp. 101–110 (2009)
5. Houser, A.M.: Mental models for cybersecurity: a formal methods approach. PhD thesis, Department of Industrial and Systems Engineering, University at Buffalo, State University of New York (2018)
6. Jensen, C.: 50 Years ago, 'Unsafe at Any Speed' shook the auto world. The New York Times, 27 November 2015. Section B, p. 3. https://www.nytimes.com/2015/11/27/automobiles/50-years-ago-unsafe-at-any-speed-shook-the-auto-world.html. Accessed 30 Dec 2019
7. Jones, N.A., Ross, H., Lynam, T., Perez, P., Leitch, A.: Mental models: an interdisciplinary synthesis of theory and methods. Ecol. Soc. 16(1), 46 (2011)
8. Mashaw, J.L., Harfst, D.L.: The Struggle for Auto Safety. Harvard University Press (1990)
9. Wash, R., Rader, E.J.: Influencing mental models of security: a research agenda. In: 2011 New Security Paradigms Workshop, NSPW 2011, Marin County, CA, USA, 12–15 September 2011, pp. 57–66 (2011)
10. Yan, Y., et al.: Understanding and detecting overlay-based android malware at market scales. In: Proceedings of the 17th Annual International Conference on Mobile Systems, Applications, and Services, MobiSys 2019, Seoul, Republic of Korea, 17–21 June 2019, pp. 168–179. ACM (2019)

Shaping Our Mental Model of Security
(Transcript of Discussion)

Saša Radomirović[(✉)]

School of Mathematical and Computer Sciences, Heriot-Watt University,
Edinburgh, UK
sasa.radomirovic@hw.ac.uk

This talk is not on a completed piece of research, it is a work in progress. One of our biggest challenges at the moment is how to improve cyber security and people are at the heart of it. A lot has been written about safety and human error. There's also been, for a long time, this thought that humans are the weakest link in security. If we could just take the human out of the loop, we would have safer systems, or more secure systems. Whether we are better off with or without the human in the loop, we cannot avoid people being part of security. And one way to keep people secure is to teach them something, and this is where the mental model comes in.

As humans, we are primed to read each other's faces. For instance, I taught this information security class—it must have been mig-in-the-middle attacks that I was talking about—and I had one student who enjoyed himself a lot in that class: he was smiling all the time. And, as I was talking, I thought, "Ah, this is great. Somebody's actually enjoying this presentation." But then, as I walked around, I saw that actually he had a cell phone in front of him and he was enjoying some YouTube video. So I went from reading a face, making an inference about that person's mental state and trying to figure out what it is that he perhaps is enjoying, to realising that my mental model of what he was doing was completely off.

A mental model is a cognitive representation of external reality. It is just a model, it is something that is in our head, it can be completely wrong; but the point is, it is all we have to help us explain what might be happening in the world around us. And these mental models allow us to understand causal relations, in order to solve a problem. A typical problem we might want to solve is turning on a TV. It's a completely abstract thing. There's a remote, it is not connected to a TV; yet, if we push a certain button, the TV goes on. We don't need to understand how infrared LEDs work, we don't need to understand how electricity works. If we have a sufficiently good model of remotes and TVs, it will allow us to turn on the TV. If it doesn't turn on, we will perhaps have a more refined model to look for missing batteries in the remote, to check the plugs, and so forth.

So a mental model is a simplification of reality, and it is very much a working model. Before babies take their first steps, they already experiment with the world around them. They learn about gravity by dropping things all the time. Anybody who's had kids has been driven insane by them dropping food all the

© Springer Nature Switzerland AG 2020
J. Anderson et al. (Eds.): Security Protocols 2019, LNCS 12287, pp. 60–68, 2020.
https://doi.org/10.1007/978-3-030-57043-9_6

time or any other object that they can get hold of, while they're forming a mental model of gravity.

We don't have to just experiment all the time, we can also be taught a mental model of something and this typically happens, say, with traffic lights. We don't have to be run over by a car to understand that red means stop and green means go. This can also be communicated to us.

So communication, experimentation, and observation are very important ingredients for us to form a mental model. If we then look at cyber space, what we realise as we go from a physical world to a virtual one is that it is much more difficult to form a good mental model. For instance, if I have some data that I want to get rid of, say on a piece of paper, then in the physical world, I can burn it or I can shred it and the destruction is immediate. I can tell the paper is gone, I can tell the data is gone. But if I try to achieve the same thing on a computer, by deleting a file, I will perhaps hear a sound that a trash can makes as it is being emptied, and what I see is that the representation of the file has vanished. But I do not have the same assurance that I have in the physical world that its data has been destroyed, and maybe it hasn't.

I want to make another couple of comparisons between the physical and the abstract world. If we look at representations of objects on a computer, they typically make reference to physical objects that we know, for which we already have a mental model. Take physical switches. You will find better or worse designed ones. You will find those that are very clear in what position they're in, that is, on or off. You will find those that are very unclear in what positions they might be. But in the physical world what you also get is additional feedback that says whether it's on or off. If I want to turn on a lawn mower, it doesn't matter whether I can tell what the on or off position of the switch is. If it is on, it will make a noise; and I will get some feedback about what's happening and I will start learning which position means "on".

As we move again to cyber space, we have better and worse representations for these switches, but the fact that frequently the feedback is not immediate makes it harder to learn what the switch does. If I turn a preference setting on or off, I will not necessarily get immediate feedback that something has happened or will happen. Here I'm taking the example of privacy settings. Frequently these privacy settings are not something you will immediately experience: they are something that will have an influence on things you will do later. If I perhaps don't want to be tracked, I would turn all location services off, but this type of setting is something that will only over time have any ramifications. I will not get immediate feedback. So it will be much harder for me to form a good mental model of what it means that the button representing this setting is on or off.

The next thing about mental models is that change is very bad. It takes time for us to form a mental model. As I said, it takes experimentation, it takes feedback to understand how something works, to have an anticipation of what a controlled mechanism does. If systems start changing we have to adapt our mental model and that comes at the cost of errors and again a learning-from-feedback loop. What I'm showing on this slide is how an operating system has changed the delete confirmation dialog over several releases. It changed from preventing an accidental delete action to reconfirming an intended delete action: At first, the highlighted button on the right in the confirmation dialog was to not actually do what you intended to do. In a later release the button on the right would still not do what you intended to do, but the dialog highlighted the intended action's button. In the present release the delete button is both emphasised and on the right.

These changes are subtle and perhaps very few people have accidentally deleted a file due to them. But think of more complex systems, of being under time pressure, and of controlling processes where the consequences won't be immediate. Unlike the deletion of the file, which I will likely notice quickly, if I'm controlling something in a complex system that will have an effect only down the line, in a few days, then these types of changes will lead to errors.

This is essentially what my talk is about. How do we shape people's mental models to prevent errors due to change and lack of understanding? How do we shape people's mental models in order to keep them secure in cyber space? As I said, change is bad for your mental model. If I look at a future based on what the hot topics are these days, well then we will have lots of Internet of Things gadgets. For each one of them, we will have to form a new mental model of what it does. For each one of them, there may be this delay between performing an action and receiving feedback that allows us to learn how it functions. Whatever it is that will come up in the future, there will be lots of change.

Now people in this room will probably deal reasonably well with this change. We love technology and we will try to study it, but most people will not do any of this. Most people will depend on the gadget they're buying to give them clear feedback so that they can control it in a secure fashion, whatever *secure* means in that context. And, even for us, I would say that technological change will become a burden over time. Over time, as you age, you start losing interest in some of the latest things. And, as you lose interest, you also lose touch: your mental model of how things work starts degrading. So, while the younger crowd evolves and knows what a "thumb up" means, it doesn't mean anything to you. You do not have a mental model for what it means to click on a thumb up on a web page. And this slowly has ramifications into other parts of life that then start using, say, a thumb up as a sign, as a mental model aid for a certain action.

In that sense, change is bad; and, as we cannot avoid change, we somehow need to make sure that we keep people safe. As we cannot rely on experimentation and discovery alone to shape people's mental models, the best way to keep people safe is to communicate potential dangers to them, say using signs and symbols. If you think of the early days of the Internet when we stopped communicating face to face and started communicating by email and still being under time pressure and having to communicate quickly, it frequently happened that you would have a conversation where the other side completely misunderstood what you wrote. They didn't see your face while you were writing your message, they read it out of context, or didn't realise it was tongue-in-cheek. There was miscommunication because there was lack of feedback in the text that was there.

So you would think perhaps that now the emojis that are raining down on us could help. However, a study showed that the same emoji conveys different meaning and emotion to people, depending on the platform they're seeing it on. So a symbol such as the "grinning face with smiling eyes" that is actually meant to convey an emotion fails at doing this because of the vendors' freedom to create their own version of it. And this means that we need standardised signs if we want to help people with their mental model.

I've already used the example of traffic lights as something that we can teach to each other. Because they're universal, anywhere on Earth that I know of, if you're trying to cross the street, green will mean go, red will mean stop. And people typically get this part right, as opposed to what side of the road vehicles are driving on and which way you're supposed to look when you're trying to cross the street. The fact that this is not standardised leads to mistakes when people used to continental Europe's traffic visit the British Isles. Standardisation helps prevent these types of mistakes.

Safety signs have colour coding and shapes that indicate safe conditions, warnings, obligations, and prohibitions. If you compare this with security, you will not find many symbols that are universal and that will communicate a security purpose to you. The things that come to mind are locks used for public key crypto, shields that indicate some sort of protection and we also see keys and fingerprints.

Michael Millian: One thing I've noticed on this topic is when I have been working with older people and finding a website where they can download a file. Sometimes there'll be a download button and then there'll be five ads on the website, also with download buttons. Somehow I have this mental model of which one's the right one just by looking at it, but I have no way to explain to anybody else how I constructed this mental model or how they can construct it.

Reply: Exactly. This is something that we would want to be able to communicate with some sign. I have only one suggestion for how we could do it. I'll come back to it in a minute.

Jonathan Anderson: I guess a related point is when you see all of the download buttons you also see people putting padlocks in various places, in places where they don't mean what you think they mean. It means what they want you to think it means, in a way that would be harder to do in the physical world. If I walked around Trinity putting up signs saying "you must do this, you must do that", the porters would come and say, "pardon me, sir". That would stop. But in a context where generally (for graphic design reasons or whatever) we want to be able to put arbitrary experiences in front of users, is there any hope?

Reply: Yes. Why does it not work in the physical world? Because there are people or institutions who have the authority over a certain space. You wouldn't be able to put up a misleading sign here on the grounds because somebody will pass by and then take it off. In cyber space anybody can post anything anywhere, but removing misleading content is difficult. So, since we are on this topic, let me skip to it in my presentation.

There's this one manufacturer of laptops that had the idea to put a touch bar on their keyboards. One thought that I had when I first saw it is that this could be great for security. The manufacturer now has a small display that they can control, that *only they* have the authority over. But they didn't go for that. They opened it up for everybody, unfortunately. But if we were to post any kind of security signs, if we were to have any signifiers for "confidential", "integrity-protected", and so on, these signs would have to be communicated in a space where we have learned that the sign is trustworthy, as long as it is in that reserved space and we trust the manufacturer of this device.

Frank Stajano: In the very pertinent example that was just made of the download buttons, it should be remarked that the owner of that page is explicitly saying, "I will rent out those few square pixels to someone else just because I'm going to get some millicent when someone clicks on it, and I don't give a damn what they do with it." And that the people who put the ad up do something very misleading by putting the download button that pretends to be part of the rest of the page. But there could be conceivably someone who says, "I'm willing to make a slight profit by renting out some of my page real estate, but I want to retain some control over what they do." And they could conceivably pre-screen the ads and say, "you are not allowed to insert anything that looks like a download button". They don't do that, but they could.

Reply: I guess they could; but, when we look at the economic incentives of ads, it seems to me that we have lost this war big time. No technological solution will make this better. Unless we find other financial incentives that make it better, I don't think that we will get very far with this. These ads are well known to steal everyone's bandwidth, they're expensive for me as a cell phone user if they're being downloaded, they have security vulnerabilities. But as long as somebody is paying the sites, why would they fix it?

Frank Stajano: Yes. What I mean is that, if the entity providing the page (which is the reason why the user goes there) cared about the safety of the user, it would be a different situation than if the person putting up the page cared just about making maximum profits, regardless of what happens to the user. I think it's only in that second case that they just let ads on regardless of their content. And in fact sometimes they will even attract people just for the purpose of making money through the ads they're keeping there.

Reply: Yes, but I don't think it is economically viable, even for the page owners who care, to do the right thing. In essence, the market seems to be such that they are renting out space, as you said. Right behind that space, it's a bidding war of different advertisers trying to understand who's actually on that page and whether they want them to look at their ad. Somehow the economic reality is such that even if the page owner wanted to, he would not be able to only allow a trustworthy advertiser.

Frank Stajano: And that's not how the market works at the moment, but it is not inconceivable that in another universe the market will say, "I will only make ads that are proper, and that don't have kiddie porn, for example, they don't have fake download buttons, etc."

Bruce Christianson: One of the problems at the moment is there's no standard interface. So, even for people who are minded to be well-behaved, the model for what we have to do is incompatible between different parts of the same page. So what you're arguing is that standard interfaces will help people evolve towards similar mental models, is that correct?

Reply: Yes, and part of my argument is indeed standard interfaces, standard signs—I'm hoping we can find other aides for mental models—would be a step towards getting everybody to understand what it is. But then the second part is indeed how do you prevent this from being hijacked, for example by overlay attacks.

Bruce Christianson: Yeah. My question is: how wide does the interface have to be? How much space does it have to contain and how explicit does that space have to be, in terms of being represented, for your approach to work, where there are lots of other people with, perhaps, other ideas?

Lydia Kraus: I find the problem that you raise (with the consistency across interfaces) interesting, but I would like to raise another issue: maybe we need to change our mental model of security first. Maybe not change, but think about what we want to communicate to the users. Basically, I don't think that this very simple model of "this is secure and this is not secure" is a good solution. Because there are so many properties that we would need to cover and somehow you would need to have users understand that there are different properties, not just secure or not secure. And, on the other hand, maybe we need to help users to evolve their mental model, because security is a process and what is secure today doesn't have to be secure tomorrow. And how would we explain that to people?

Reply: Yes, I agree with much of what you say. One issue that you raised is that there are sometimes trade-offs to be made in security. One example is, if you were to install Dropbox fresh today, then, the next time you connect a camera, a screen pops up asking you, "Do you want to automatically back up all the pictures on your camera to Dropbox?" And this raises, as you just mentioned, a trade-off; in this case between "Do I want to protect the integrity of my pictures? I don't want to lose my pictures" versus "Do I also want to protect my privacy?" But if we can somehow standardise a signage for people to understand what integrity is, what privacy is, and if we can associate this meaning with symbols, then we can indicate to the user what trade-offs the user is about to make.

There's of course the issue of trust. I need to trust the provider of an app to honestly display these signs. This is very similar to the situation where I need to give privileges to an app when I don't know whether the app is malicious or not. We are all familiar with the permissions system on mobile devices where an app must ask for permission to have access to your location, contacts or camera. And those permissions could be displayed as symbols that are standardised and in a secure manner, so that I know the app itself cannot control the symbols. It is the trusted manufacturer that controls the symbols.

Jim Blythe: I guess I apologise for going in a different direction, but I think that's what we're supposed to do here. Talking about width, but also looking at the depth of the mental model... All the examples have been visual symbols that tell the user what to do, which is great, but in many cases users can make their own choices about what they do in security. What we might want to move towards is a more persuasive view point. We want to tell people why they should be doing this and that's where mental models can be great because you might be able to tap into a user's mental model and come up with something that says, "Okay, if the firewall is a physical wall, then this is why it should be a bit higher right now. This is what's coming at you." Or other ways to exploit the way that they're currently thinking of it. So that means a slightly deeper mental model which tries to understand what symbols users are actually processing, what models they have, why are they doing the things they're doing and what are the trade-offs? And that leads to a second question: have you thought about how you get the mental models that people are currently using so that you could evolve those, perhaps, or work within that framework?

Reply: Studies have been conducted on what people are thinking when they're interacting with these systems, but they're always very particular to a small case. In the bigger picture, I don't see how it is being done. What schools currently do is to give guidance to their pupils about behavioural etiquette on the Internet. What keeps you safe, what are the dos and don'ts. This is, in some sense, a start towards providing a mental model of what is safe and what is not. If we can tap into this with some standardised signage that is then also being reinforced by software applications and not subject to the constant design changes "because this looks cooler than that", then we could have a more persistent way of communicating at a high level "the choice you're about to make has the following implications." The deeper level I think will then have to evolve over time because not everything can be communicated in these simple terms.

Jovan Powar: I want to say something, related to Frank's point, which I think is also instructive to understand the incentives that you have to play with when it comes to getting a software update as the website owner and is to comply with this kind of stuff. You said that it would be good to be able to basically say, "You can't have an ad that has something like a download button on it." Well, most major ad exchanges do actually check this and they have automated checks to say that you're not doing the download button. The problem is that the sites that these things show up on are the things where maybe they've been blacklisted by the major ad exchanges or something. You've essentially got a black market. If I'm a person who wants to start an advertising exchange, then I allow people to say download and then all the people put download things on me, and the people who can't get ads from the other people get it with that same download. Does that make sense?

So it's that classic problem whereby, if you want to really strengthen the ecology around something, the best thing to do is criminalise it. The problem here is that this is also the problem with incentives, in that you have to convince your software makers to comply with this and then you have to have some kind of consensus that it works with their incentives, as well as anything else. And the problem is that, in a lot of the cases, these website owners don't bear the cost of things going wrong. So you don't have to just make it understandable to the user, but you've also got to make it understandable to the software maker in a way that makes them have a stake in it.

Reply: Yes. I see this as a big problem as well. Perhaps on the web most of the problems we're having nowadays are most obvious, but it is not only about that aspect. There is a barrier between the web browser and my system where we could shield users, at operating system level, from some of the things that could happen. When downloading anything off the Internet, we're nowadays facing the "are you sure you want to execute something you downloaded?" dialog. This is where we could put up defences that relate to the mental model. What Frank mentioned and what you're referring to, these are much more hairy issues. I agree with your remarks.

Martin Ukrop: I generally like the idea of standardising the security signage, though I see a different problem. Has anyone looked into the mental model of a privileged space? With the example of the download thing, the real download button is in the space that is privileged to the website owner, while for the other ones it's in a space that usually is unprivileged because it's an advertising box. A similar example is the fav-icon in the browser that used to be next to the URL bar. If you put a padlock (meaning a secure site) in the fav icon, it doesn't actually mean secure because that's an unprivileged space. While, if it had been two pixels to the right in the privileged space, it would have had a different connotation.

Reply: Yes, and so this is why I don't think we can solve this within the context of a screen, of a browser, or of anything where it is very difficult for the user to tell contexts apart. This is exactly what gets me excited about the possibility of having a device-controlled or operating-system-controlled space that is going to support the mental model with trustworthy information, separate from everything else that's going on. It will still be a challenge of course to create a link between what the user is looking at, what the user's mental model of the page displayed to him is, and the signage on this protected space. There are still challenges there, but I think it's the only way we can make a step forward. With anything else, you're right, it's impossible to distinguish.

Michael Millian: I really like this idea of standardising the signage, but it has been very difficult for our whole field to do this. We frequently run into the problem. There's the comic about, "There are seven standards. Let's create one universe of standards where there are eight standards." Perhaps there are lessons throughout history to be learned about how we got the common signage that we have now because surely that didn't start out as universal signage. And it still isn't completely universal, but it's much more standardised. So maybe looking at the process of how those unified could teach us some lessons.

Reply: I agree. But I also don't think that we need to necessarily start right now with standardising the signage. We can start with the following perhaps. What you see here are Firefox settings for security and privacy—in Georgian. The only reason I can tell it's security and privacy is because I clicked there. If even the UI developer cannot tell what's going on here, then something's wrong. So, perhaps, in the first instance, we should support the user with simpler signage to help with this long text that for most people could just as well be written in a foreign language, to help with too many options where it is not immediately clear which one is the safe one or what the trade-offs are and what the consequences are. This alone would make things better. Over time we can see whether (as with safety) we start to converge towards the same signs or whether we need another competing standard, but hopefully not.

Social Constructionism in Security Protocols

A Position on Human Experience, Psychology and Security

Simon N. Foley[✉] and Vivien M. Rooney

Department of Information Security and Communication Technology,
Norwegian University of Science and Technology, 2815 Gjøvik, Norway

Abstract. Understanding the human in computer security through Qualitative Research aims at a conceptual repositioning. The aim is to leverage individual human experience to understand and improve the impact of humans in computer security. Embracing what is particular, complex and subtle in the human social experience means understanding precisely what is happening when people transgress protocols. Repositioning transgression as normal, by researching what people working in Computer Network Defense do, how they construct an understanding of what they do, and why they do it, facilitates addressing the human aspects of this work on its own terms. Leveraging the insights developed through Qualitative Research means that it is possible to envisage and develop appropriate remedies using Applied Psychology, and thereby improve computer security.

Keywords: Social aspects of security and privacy · Security requirements · Psychology · Qualitative Research methods · Computer Network Defence · Threat intelligence

1 Introduction

A variety of approaches have been considered when analysing how user behaviour can influence the objectives of a security protocol. For instance, at the most basic level, a separation of duty protocol can be verified as protecting a transaction should one of the subscribing parties misbehave [10]. Approaches, such as security ceremonies, are intended to model complex patterns of human-system interaction and how user-(mis)behaviour might impact the objective of the security protocol in which they play a part [2,8]. Such approaches have tended to focus on modeling the observable behavior of the users. More recently, it has been suggested that this analysis should be extended to incorporate the user as a human, and consider the human persona, societal norms, and so forth [5,13,14]. For example, does a separation of duty protocol achieve its objective if the users involved have a casual regard to rules which they may circumvent in order to

© Springer Nature Switzerland AG 2020
J. Anderson et al. (Eds.): Security Protocols 2019, LNCS 12287, pp. 69–81, 2020.
https://doi.org/10.1007/978-3-030-57043-9_7

help each other out? Notwithstanding the technical challenges of developing and reasoning about such models, there has been little consideration of what it means to use these models and how we come to understand and diagnose the human participation in security protocols.

Our position is that Social Constructionism provides a means to help understand and diagnose how humans experience security protocols. We argue that Qualitative Research methods can be used to systematically discover what it means to the participants to engage in a security protocol. This meaning can be in terms of their emotional, sensory, physical, volition and intellectual experiences. This presents the reality of how the participant experiences the security protocol. For example, how ambivalence or a stressful situation might lead to a perfunctory check of a separation of duty requirement. We are interested in using psychological theories to help diagnose and understand these experiences of participants in a security protocol and how these experiences may impact the protocol objectives; these insights may in turn help identify potential remedies. We are also interested in systematically developing rigorous models of this human experience that could be used as part of a formal analysis of the interoperation between human experience and protocol operation.

In this paper we explore this position through a use-case concerning a protocol for sharing threat information among computer network defenders.

2   Social Constructionism and the Human Experience of Technology

As social beings, humans make sense of the world around them in a social context, in interaction with others. In the process of describing and explaining a situation, or a series of events, the process of doing so is how we create that situation or those events. Our understanding of a situation or events is developed in the same way. This approach to understanding how people make sense of their world is a Social Constructionist one. Adopting this approach to understanding an experience with technology means that people construct that experience in dialogue. As people explain and describe their experience with technology, or with a particular aspect of technology, such as in their work environment, they are constructing its meaning. In the same way, if technology is part of a particular experience, or if it is the aspect of experience that we are particularly interested in, then the framework for researching and understanding that technology, or that aspect of technology, is a social framework.

Experience is something that continues to elude concise definition [17], however, for practical purposes, there are several interrelated components of which it is comprised:

- *Emotional* responses to, for example, people, spaces, events, outcomes, processes, memories.
- *Sensory* apprehension of the environment.
- *Physical* factors of the body and how they interrelate with the environment.

- *Volition* of individual desires and choices, taking account of, for instance, wishes, needs and values.
- *Intellectual* reasoning based on knowledge and beliefs.

These components of experience interrelate, for instance, take the example of a person making a difficult decision in a high stress environment. Their experience of making that decision can encompass all of the components, perhaps in conflict with each other, perhaps as inseparable from each other, as a decision is reached, and as the person makes sense of the process at the same time.

When we want to understand what is happening between people and technology, adopting a focus on human experience, rather than on what is observable, facilitates delving into the meaning that an artifact has for an individual. This approach allows us to uncover how the components of experience can interplay, for instance, how intellectual and volitional components can be in conflict with each other, and how such conflicts are given meaning as individuals reconcile them in dialogue. We can uncover that physical and intellectual components of the same experience are intertwined, and what this means for the individual. Thus, rather than being limited in our understanding to a cognitive approach of what is observable, or focusing on facilitating ease of interaction with technology, as a Human-Computer Interaction approach might, we can understand how and why a *human being* constructs meaning of their experience of technology.

3   Use Case: Cyber Threat Information Sharing

The exchange of threat information within sharing communities is a recommended practice for individuals working in Computer Network Defence, such as Security Operations Centres (SOCs) and Computer Security Incident Response Teams (CSIRTs). Studies report that effective information sharing and collective problem solving are required for a successful security incident response [1,18–20]. There are risks when sharing communities span multiple organizations and it is important that sensitive information about threats, their remediation and legal and organizational requirements are safeguarded. NIST special publication 800-150 [15] provides guidelines on sharing cyber threat information, with recommendations on how sharing relationships should be established and how individuals should participate in these sharing relationships. This collection of procedural and technical controls are regarded as a security protocol intended to mitigate the risks associated with the human-intensive information sharing activity.

For the purposes of exploring our position in this paper we describe a security protocol that provides a (very much simplified) interpretation of the spirit of NIST 800-150. Figure 1 defines this protocol as follows:

- The organization approves a Memorandum of Understanding (MoU) setting the constraints for exchanging threat information in a sharing community involving external parties who are considered trustworthy. The organization

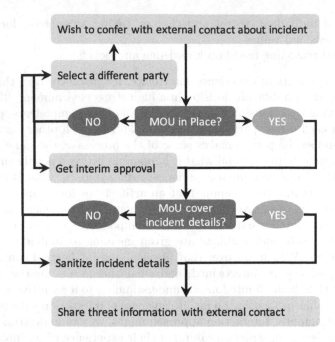

Fig. 1. Simplified threat information sharing protocol.

should proactively establish such sharing communities as part of its security processes and is discouraged from setting up new MoUs during security
incidents.
- In the course of an ongoing security incident, a computer network defender
  wishes to confer with an external contact who is believed to be defending a
  similar incident:
  - If an MoU exists for the external party, then information sharing may
    proceed subject to the constraints of the MoU.
  - If the MoU does not exist for the desired external party then the defender
    should seek a different party for which an MoU exists.
  - An exception to this procedure is possible. If the trusted sharing commu-
    nities cannot provide useful threat intelligence then the defender either
    requests an MoU to be established or else obtains interim approval from
    a line-manager to share limited information with the external party with
    careful recording of information disclosed.

4   Uncovering Human Security Experience

From the Social Constructionist perspective, research findings are regarded as a
situated interpretation, applicable to its particular context, and therefore open
to subsequent reinterpretation. This contrasts with the Positivist perspective,
where findings are regarded as a universal truth. The Social Constructionist

approach being advocated in this paper has been used to research experiences with technology. One example is a project concerning the experience of Computer Network Defenders. The constructionist approach to Grounded Theory [6] was adopted, as an inductive approach to methodology is appropriate [22]. The data gathering technique of semi-structured interviewing was used [16], also cohering with the Social Constructionist perspective [22]. In this research project on the experience of Computer Network Defense, semi-structured interviews were conducted with people working in Security Operations Centres and in Computer Security Incident Response Teams. The focus was on each individual's experience of work. The transcribed interviews were analysed using Grounded Theory techniques, such as line by line coding, the development of categories and themes, and memo writing. The theoretical analysis resulted in five themes [19], summarized in Table 1.

Table 1. Emergent themes and theories of Computer Network Defenders (from [19]).

Theme	Description	Amenable to change	Applicable theory
Intrinsic positive	Regarded as being inherently positive, not needing explanation, therefore less salient to creating identity	Don't want to change	Social identity
Created positive	Explained as positive, therefore highly salient to creating identity	Don't need to change	Social identity relational dialectics
Intrinsic negative	Inherent aspects of the work, negatively regarded, less salient for team identity	Can't change	Social identity cognitive dissonance
Created negative	Negative aspects of the work less relevant to creating team identity	Want to change	Social identity
Areas of tension	Aspects of work regarded with ambivalence, highly salient for team identity	Want to change	Social identity cognitive dissonance

In order to illustrate the outcome of the research, our focus in the current paper is on one particular phenomena that emerged during the Grounded Theory analysis of the transcribed interview data. This is the experience of information sharing in the context of the work of Computer Network Defenders. The Appendix gives examples of categories and line by line codes relevant to the context, action and meaning around the phenomena of sharing threat information by Computer Network Defenders in the course of their work. The following describes the experience of information sharing, and some of the components that interplay to create that experience. Line by line sample codes from the Appendix are included for convenience. In the following description of the phenomena surrounding threat information sharing, the relevant Grounded Theory codes are identified using a sans-serif font.

How the phenomena of information sharing is constructed by the Computer Network Defenders draws on multiple components of their experience. One component is procedures, and these are regarded variously as being: inflexible, something that slows you down during a crisis, yet as being important in an organisational context, and useful (proceduresSlowYouDown).

Another component of the experience of information sharing is the crisis itself, where speed in developing a workaround and a solution is critically important (workaroundNotInProcedures)(crisisSolvedSpeed). The importance of achieving this is bound up not alone in deploying one's skills and knowledge individually and as part of the team within the organisation (crisisWholeTeamWork), (crisisBeingAlone), it is also bound up in the social identity that is created by being part of the wider community of defenders (cyberDefendersCommunity). The span of this community of defenders extends beyond the organisational boundary (communicationWithNonTeam), and herein lies the tension of sharing information (cyberDefendersTension).

Being part of the community of Computer Network Defenders is regarded as akin to being a firefighter, and the fight is a global one against cyber attacks and cyber terrorism (cyberDefendersUnited), (cyberThreatsGlobal). Creating this identity is a very positive aspect of the experience of Computer Network Defense work. As such, being a member of this global community is important, and solving a problem during a crisis, an attack, means that people want to employ all of the resources at their disposal, including sharing and obtaining information outside of the organisation (externalLinksImportant), (linksWithOthersImportant). In this way, while procedures remain important, the membership of the global community can outweigh adherence to procedures. The ensuing dilemma around information sharing that is faced during a crisis (informationRequired), (informationSortingImportant), is rooted in these varied factors, and simultaneously in a context where other tensions are also at play. Examples are tensions between different organisational agendas, such as those tensions between legal (regulatorsLegalAgenda), marketing and financial (crisisAssigningResponsibility).

For Computer Network Defenders, the experience of information sharing is characterised by contradictions, conflicts and unresolved tensions. The experience that is constructed is particular, complex and subtle, embedded in multiple overlapping contexts.

5   Explaining Human Security Experience

We take two perspectives on the Grounded Theory analysis of the human experience of the security protocol. Firstly, we draw upon existing psychological theories related to the identified phenomena in order to better understand the human experience: this can help identify potential remedies for improving the protocol, helping the individual or simply accepting that something cannot be changed. Secondly, we consider how the Grounded Theory analysis might be used to develop rigorous models of aspects of the human experience for the purposes of understanding and diagnosing how an individual impacts the objectives of security protocol and vice-versa.

5.1 A Psychological Perspective

Understanding how Computer Network Defenders construct their experience of work provides insights into the process of how sense is made of the actions that people take in a particular situation. We can understand how a person perceived what they were doing, from their perspective, how this act made sense to them. We understand how, for instance, a protocol may be transgressed, and how sense was made of this act by the transgressor. This Social Constructionist approach facilitates the explanation and interpretation of experience in an abstract way, meaning that we can delve into the process of sense making, and develop a theoretical model that is valid in a particular situated context. This way of understanding the experience of Computer Network Defenders contrasts with Positivism, in that a predictive model is not possible. What is possible is the application of theory from Social Psychology to the emerging phenomena as a way of positioning the results of the study for practical purposes.

In [19] we proposed that Social Identity Theory [21], Relational Dialectics Theory [3,4] and Cognitive Dissonance [9] could be used in order to shed light on how people make sense of their experience of Computer Network Defense work. The potential of Social Identity Theory is to provide all stakeholders with the means of understanding, for instance, the components, significance and means of establishing Social Identity in the context of individuals and teams engaged in Computer Network Defense. Another phenomena that emerged from the research project concerned the manner of communication within the Security Operations Centre and Computer Security Incident Response Teams. We proposed [19] that this constructive and democratic way of communicating be incorporated into staff training, framing what is an emerging team activity by Relational Dialectics Theory [3]. Other aspects of experience that emerged in the research project centred around Areas of Tension, the fifth theme that was identified during data analysis. This concerns the phenomena of information sharing as discussed above, and among other areas of tension identified is the use of intuition. The generation of psychological stress for Computer Network Defenders is associated with such areas, and it was proposed that Cognitive Dissonance Theory would be a useful way of understanding and ameliorating these issues [19].

5.2 Towards a Socio-technical Perspective

Recognising that the codes uncovered during a Grounded Theory analysis of semi-structured interview data can be interpreted as probabilistic variables [11], a qualitative elicitation methodology has been developed [12] whereby a Bayesian Network can be systematically built from a Grounded Theory analysis of interview data. The resulting model represents a machine-interpretable encoding of the identified phenomena. It is used in [12] as a means to elicit Attribute Based Access Control policies where the codes/variables uncovered during analysis represent the policy attributes.

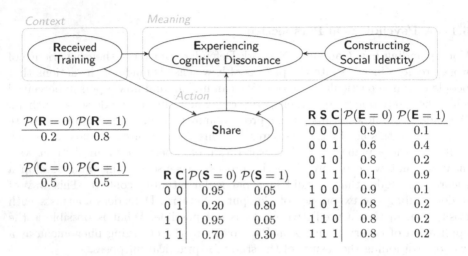

$$P(R = 0) \quad P(R = 1)$$

$P(R = 0)$	$P(R = 1)$
0.2	0.8

$P(C = 0)$	$P(C = 1)$
0.5	0.5

R C	$P(S = 0)$	$P(S = 1)$
0 0	0.95	0.05
0 1	0.20	0.80
1 0	0.95	0.05
1 1	0.70	0.30

R S C	$P(E = 0)$	$P(E = 1)$
0 0 0	0.9	0.1
0 0 1	0.6	0.4
0 1 0	0.8	0.2
0 1 1	0.1	0.9
1 0 0	0.9	0.1
1 0 1	0.8	0.2
1 1 0	0.8	0.2
1 1 1	0.8	0.2

Fig. 2. Simplified Bayesian Network of sharing experience

We are exploring how this approach might be adapted to develop machine-interpretable models that represent a part of the human experience of security protocols. Figure 2 depicts a Bayesian Network of aspects of the human experience concerning the sharing of cyber-threat information. For the purposes of this paper we present it as a thought-experiment whereby the model represents what might be constructed from a Grounded Theory analysis carried out in our study of computer network defenders [19]. The probabilistic variables correspond to some of the codes uncovered during the study and their relationship (dependencies and transitional probabilities) is intended to represent the human experience of the participant interacting with the security protocol. These include

- Constructing Social Identity: the defender is constructing their Social Identity, making sense of what they are doing by being part of a community defending against threat. The community may be a specialised technical community, known personally to the defender. The community may be a global community of defenders who fight against cyber terrorism. In this context they are especially likely to do this when there's a potential crisis unfolding, and they wish to confer with other community members, sharing, seeking and comparing information about the phenomena that are being observed.
- Experiencing Cognitive Dissonance: disquiet arising from the experience of the defender of multiple realities that conflict with each other. This generates psychological stress; an additional burden on people working in the already high pressure environments of SOCs and CSIRTs. Lessening Cognitive Dissonance

can help to improve functioning. For example, when conflicting realities have differing interpretations of procedures (in this case, whether or not an MoU is in place).

– Share: sharing threat information with colleagues outside the organization and contrary to procedure. More likely coincides with the defender enacting multiple realities and experiencing cognitive dissonance owing to procedure violation.

How the Bayesian Network can be systematically generated in practice using the approach in [12] is a topic of ongoing research. The semi-structured interview scripts, marked-up during Grounded Theory analysis, provide a meaning for the interviews, and machine learning is used on this marked-up data to build the Bayesian Network based policy that represents the relationships between the identified phenomena. In the generated model three kinds of variables are identified:

– *Context* variables that represent participant beliefs about the context of the actions in which they engage. For example, whether there is an MoU in Place with an external party or whether the defender has recently Received Training to help them recognise and address cognitive dissonance.
– *Action* variables that represent the decisions that can be made by a participant to engage in an action. For example, the decision to contact and Share threat information with an outside party.
– *Meaning* variables represent the meaning of the experience by the participant when engaging, or otherwise, in an action in some context. For example, the participant is Constructing Social Identity or Experiencing Cognitive Dissonance.

Based on the interviews, the Bayesian Network in Fig. 2 reflects that it is considered likely that defenders have Received training ($\mathcal{P}(\mathbf{R} = 1) = 0.8$) and that it is uncertain whether or not they are Constructing a social identity ($\mathcal{P}(\mathbf{C} = 1) = 0.5$), in the absence of any other information. The likelihood a defender is Experiencing cognitive dissonance depends on their training, whether they are constructing a social identity and whether they are Sharing threat information externally.

This Bayesian Network can be used as a tool to help explore and diagnose the human experience of interacting with the security protocol. We used the SamIam tool [7] to explore sharing based on the Bayesian Network defined in Fig. 2.

Computing directly from this network, and in the absence of any particular observations, the likelihood of external sharing is relatively low ($\mathcal{P}(\mathbf{S} = 1) = 0.22$) as is the likelihood of staff experiencing cognitive dissonance ($\mathcal{P}(\mathbf{E} = 1) = 0.21$). If specific phenomena (variables) have been observed then we can use the most probable explanation (MPE) for remaining unobserved variables by computing the maximum a-posteriori probability instantiation of all the variables given the evidence. For example, if we have evidence of external sharing ($\mathcal{P}(\mathbf{S} = 1) = 1$) then, in the absence of any other observations, the most probable explanation is that defender(s) are constructing their social identities

$(\mathcal{P}(\mathbf{C} = 1) = 0.89)$ and it is less likely that they are experiencing cognitive dissonance $(\mathcal{P}(\mathbf{E} = 1) = 0.45)$ since they are usually trained $(\mathcal{P}(\mathbf{R} = 1) = 0.8)$. However, if a compliance audit determines that they have not received training $(\mathcal{P}(\mathbf{R} = 1) = 0)$, then the most probable explanation is that they are experiencing cognitive dissonance $(\mathcal{P}(\mathbf{E} = 1) = 0.86)$ in the course of constructing their social identities $(\mathcal{P}(\mathbf{C} = 1) = 0.94)$.

In addition to helping to understand the human-experience of interacting with a security protocol, the Bayesian Network provides a machine-interpretable model that could play a role in the analysis of how human-experience can impact the objectives of the security protocol itself. For example, by providing a means to 'program' aspects for personas in Behavorial Computer Science [14] or for the human aspects of security ceremonies at Levels V (Communal) and IV (Personal) in the Bella-Coles-Kemp model [5]. These are future directions for the research.

6   Conclusion

In this paper we consider the elicitation and analysis of human experience in security protocols and the role that this plays in achieving the objective of the protocol. In the course of our research we observe that contemporary systems merit and require nuanced methodologies in order to better understand the user experience in what is a convoluted socio-technical context. Analysis of the phenomena using the psychological theories may help in remediation at a particular level, however they also point to the immutability of some practices and activities. This leads to the conclusion that notwithstanding the goals of user-centred security, sometimes human transgression might more usefully be re-conceptualized as a normal part of the status-quo.

Acknowledgement. This work was initiated at IMT Atlantique and completed at NTNU. It was supported, in part, the Norwegian National Security Authority and by the Cyber CNI Chair of Institute Mines-Télécom which is held by IMT Atlantique in Rennes, France.

A   Some Categories and Codes From the Use Case

The following provides examples of some of the uncovered categories and codes that are relevant to the phenomena of cyber-threat information sharing that emerged during Grounded Theory analysis, as part of a study on cyber network defenders.

A.1   Category: Procedures

Line by Line code (number of occurrences)
procedures/Absence/Creativity (2)
procedures/ImportanceOf (5)
proceduresSlowYouDown (1)

A.2   Category: Crisis Resolution and Team Work

Line by Line code (number of occurrences)
crisis/WholeTeamWork (3)
work/CrisisBeingAlone (3)
workaround/NotInProcedures (2)

A.3   Category: Inherent Goods/Those Gaining Approval

Line by Line code (number of occurrences)
crisis/Solved (5)
crisis/Solved/Speed (2)
intuition/roleInTheWork (2)
procedures/Absence/Creativity (2)

A.4   Category: Crises Described in Detail

Line by Line code (number of occurrences)
crisis/Solved/Relief (3)
crisis/Solving/TakesTime (1)
crisis/Solved/Speed (2)
crisis/TimeLine (3)
identifyingTheCrisis (2)
identifyingTheCrisisEnd (8)
work/CrisisBeingAlone (3)

A.5   Category: Tension Between Differing Agendas

Line by Line code (number of occurrences)
communicatingWithNonTeam (4)
regulatorsLegalAgenda (8)
tension/QualityServiceCommercialGoal (5)

A.6   Category: The Company Commercial Matters

Line by Line code (number of occurrences)
askingForHelpOutsideTeam (2)
crisis/AssigningResponsibility (3)

A.7   Category: Being Part of Community

Line by Line code (number of occurrences in the data)
cyberDefendersCommunity (3)
cyberDefendersTension (2)
cyberDefendersUnited (6)
cyberThreatsGlobal (16)

externalContextImportant (5)
externalLinksImportant (8)
firefighterMercenariesRole (13)
informationSharingImportant (13)
informationToConfirmIncident (4)
linksWithOther[deleted]sImportant (6)

A.8   Category: Information on Cyber Security and Defense

Line by Line code (number of occurrences in the data)
informationRequired [deleted] (11)
informationRequired[deleted]Burden (1)
informationSecurityImportant (8)
informationSharingManaged (11)
informationSortingImportant (13)

References

1. Albanese, M., et al.: Computer-aided human centric cyber situation awareness. In: Liu, P., Jajodia, S., Wang, C. (eds.) Theory and Models for Cyber Situation Awareness. LNCS, vol. 10030, pp. 3–25. Springer, Cham (2017). https://doi.org/10.1007/978-3-319-61152-5_1
2. Basin, D.A., Radomirovic, S., Schmid, L.: Modeling human errors in security protocols. In: IEEE 29th Computer Security Foundations Symposium, CSF 2016, Lisbon, Portugal, 27 June–1 July 2016, pp. 325–340 (2016). https://doi.org/10.1109/CSF.2016.30
3. Baxter, L.A.: Voicing Relationships. Sage Publications, London (2011)
4. Baxter, L.A., Braithwaite, D.O.: Relational dialectics theory. In: Baxter, L.A., Braithwaite, D.O. (eds.) Engaging Theories in Interpersonal Communication: Multiple Perspectives, pp. 349–361. Sage Publications, London (2008)
5. Bella, G., Coles-Kemp, L.: Layered analysis of security ceremonies. In: Gritzalis, D., Furnell, S., Theoharidou, M. (eds.) SEC 2012. IAICT, vol. 376, pp. 273–286. Springer, Heidelberg (2012). https://doi.org/10.1007/978-3-642-30436-1_23
6. Charmaz, K.: Constructing Grounded Theory. Sage Publications, London (2006)
7. Darwiche, A., et al.: Samiam: Sensitivity analysis, modeling, inference and more. UCLA Automated Reasoning Group. http://reasoning.cs.ucla.edu/samiam. Accessed on 05 Aug 2019
8. Ellison, C.M.: Ceremony design and analysis. IACR Cryptology ePrint Archive **2007**, 399 (2007). http://eprint.iacr.org/2007/399
9. Festinger, L.: A Theory of Cognitive Dissonance. Stanford University Press, Palo Alto (1957)
10. Foley, S.N.: A nonfunctional approach to system integrity. IEEE J. Sel. Areas Commun. **21**(1), 36–43 (2003). https://doi.org/10.1109/JSAC.2002.806124
11. Foley, S.N., Rooney, V.M.: Qualitative analysis for trust management. In: Christianson, B., Malcolm, J.A., Matyáš, V., Roe, M. (eds.) Security Protocols 2009. LNCS, vol. 7028, pp. 298–307. Springer, Heidelberg (2013). https://doi.org/10.1007/978-3-642-36213-2_33

12. Foley, S.N., Rooney, V.M.: A grounded theory approach to security policy elicitation. Inf. Comput. Secur. **26**(4), 454–471 (2018). https://doi.org/10.1108/ICS-12-2017-0086
13. Johansen, C., Jøsang, A.: Probabilistic modelling of humans in security ceremonies. In: Garcia-Alfaro, J., et al. (eds.) DPM/QASA/SETOP -2014. LNCS, vol. 8872, pp. 277–292. Springer, Cham (2015). https://doi.org/10.1007/978-3-319-17016-9_18
14. Johansen, C., Pedersen, T., Jøsang, A.: Towards behavioural computer science. In: Habib, S.M.M., Vassileva, J., Mauw, S., Mühlhäuser, M. (eds.) IFIPTM 2016. IAICT, vol. 473, pp. 154–163. Springer, Cham (2016). https://doi.org/10.1007/978-3-319-41354-9_12
15. Johnson, C., Badger, L., Waltermire, D., Snyder, J., Skorupka, C.: Guide to cyber threat information sharing. Technical report. NIST Special Publication 800–150. National Institute of Standards and Technology, MD, USA (2016). https://csrc.nist.gov/publications/detail/sp/800-150/final
16. Kvale, S.: InterViews. An Introduction to Qualitative Research Interviewing. Sage Publications, London (1996)
17. Lallemanda, C., Groniera, G., Koenig, V.: User experience: a concept without consensus? Exploring practitioners' perspectives through an international survey. Comput. Hum. Behav. **43**, 35–48 (2015). https://doi.org/10.1016/j.chb.2014.10.048
18. Paul, C.L., Whitley, K.: A taxonomy of cyber awareness questions for the user-centered design of cyber situation awareness. In: Marinos, L., Askoxylakis, I. (eds.) HAS 2013. LNCS, vol. 8030, pp. 145–154. Springer, Heidelberg (2013). https://doi.org/10.1007/978-3-642-39345-7_16
19. Rooney, V.M., Foley, S.N.: What you can change and what you can't: human experience in computer network defenses. In: Gruschka, N. (ed.) NordSec 2018. LNCS, vol. 11252, pp. 219–235. Springer, Cham (2018). https://doi.org/10.1007/978-3-030-03638-6_14
20. Sundaramurthy, S., McHugh, J., Ou, X., Wesch, M., Bardas, A., Rajagopalan, S.: Turning contradictions into innovations or: how we learned to stop whining and improve security operations. In: Symposium on Usable Privacy and Security (SOUPS). USENIX (2016)
21. Tajfel, H., Turner, J.: An integrative theory of intergroup conflict. In: Austin, W.G., Worchel, S. (eds.) The Social Psychology of Intergroup Relations, pp. 33–47. Brooks/Cole publishing, Monterey (1979)
22. Twining, P., Heller, R.S., Nussbaum, M., Tsai, C.C.: Some guidance on conducting and reporting qualitative studies. Comput. Educ. **106**, A1–A9 (2017). https://doi.org/10.1016/j.compedu.2016.12.002

Social Constructionism in Security Protocols (Transcript of Discussion)

Simon N. Foley$^{(\boxtimes)}$ and Vivien M. Rooney

Department of Information Security and Communication Technology, Norwegian University of Science and Technology, 2815 Gjøvik, Norway

This is joint work between myself and my co-author, Vivien Rooney. I'm a computer scientist, and Vivien's an applied psychologist. We're interested in understanding how humans experience working with security protocols. And, when I use the word "security protocol", I mean it in the most general sense: a set of rules that people and machines are supposed to follow.

As an overview of what we mean by social construction for security, let's start by looking at the Equifax data breach from 2016. The problem was that they had not updated their copy of the software package Struts, and as a consequence, a vulnerability in the software was exploited and there was a large data breach. When the breach was considered by the US House of Representatives committee on oversight and government reform, the Equifax CEO testified that "the human error was that the individual who's responsible for communicating in the organisation to apply the patch, did not." The individual involved testified that "To assert that a senior vice president in the organisation should be forwarding vulnerability alert information to developers three or four layers down in the organisation on every alert just doesn't hold water, doesn't make any sense. If that's the process that the company has to rely on, then that's a problem".

Here we have security controls in place and two different views. Whether it's their actual view or a contrived view, it suits my purposes as an example. One person's view was that it was human error and that it was this person's fault. The other view was that, "No, it's not my fault, it's stupid controls."

As technical people, we think, "I could observe this system. I could study the controls that are in place for software update. I could study what the humans are doing, and out of this, I would probably have found this vulnerability." But there's another dimension that goes beyond just looking at, or observing, what people are doing, and that is, how do we make sense of the humans themselves and how they're experiencing this technology. We might be tempted to look at these specific controls from the designer's point of view; their view of how the security works is a valid reality. And equally for the end-user, their view of what is happening is also a valid reality.

Let's look at an indepth example of this. Last year we conducted a study of people who worked as network defenders in Security Operations Centres (SOCs) and Security Incident Response Teams (CSIRTs). We wanted to understand how those individuals working as front line defenders were experiencing working within the system.

J. Anderson et al. (Eds.): Security Protocols 2019, LNCS 12287, pp. 82–88, 2020.
https://doi.org/10.1007/978-3-030-57043-9_8

Within these systems there are many rules and procedures that the defenders are expected to follow. Among other things, we wanted to understand whether they actually follow these procedures. Are they experiencing things that, as individuals, might cause problems following procedures? I'll talk a bit more about the details in the second half of the talk. To give you a you a sense, here's an extract from a semi-structured interview that Vivien carried out with one of the defenders in the study. The question was, what happens when you're in a crisis situation and you see there's a possible attack or threat, and you want to find out more information?

There's rules that one is supposed to follow. Are they followed all the time? You can see in the transcript of the discussion with the interviewer, that the participant in the interview is coming to understand their interpretation of what they actually do on the ground. The participant says: "Oh everyday we're really aware that, we know if there's an issue, the quickest way is to call the person who is doing it, who's working an issue." They're talking about the issue, but then, that's not the procedure. It emerges that "I think in the organisation, the procedure is one thing, but maybe we're doing something different."

From the interview, "Well, this is informal", "Yes, and they encourage it", "And is it acceptable?" And the answer is, "Well, most of the time, it's acceptable. There's a way to do it." And you can see they're sort of hedging it, so in a sense, they're coming to an understanding of what it is they're actually doing on the ground. I'll talk a little bit about the psychology behind this later and how that can affect those working in SOCs and CSIRTs, in our experience.

Through the interview the participant is constructing an understanding of their experience of working in the SOC or CSIRT. As they explain and describe their own experience with systems and technology, they're constructing its meaning to themselves. This does not come through checkboxes or prepared survey questionnaires, but through dialogue. In this way both the interviewer and the participant come to understand things that either might not have realised beforehand. It's jointly constructed understandings that form the basis of a shared reality of the participant. In this reality, most of the time they follow procedures, but sometimes they're not. And, of course, the meaning of their experience of working with this technology will change over time.

Frank Stajano: Would it be too cynical to say it's acceptable not to follow the strict procedure, so long as nothing bad happens? But, if something bad happens, then it's your fault. That seems to be the case of when people say, "well, following procedure will take forever", so everybody knows that we can take shortcuts, but we know that we are not supposed to". And in fact, that goes to the point that, when people want to go on strike without going on strike, they would say "I will not strictly follow the procedure" and they're screwed just as badly.

Reply: That is the point. We learned that individuals who work in these situations have different social identities. That they have the identity of a person who works in the organisation, someone who follows procedures, because that is good. There are good reasons why you need to follow procedures, even if it is just to cover yourself. But equally, they have an identity within their team and, what we saw in the interviews was that, within a team, people have a sense of camaraderie. There's a crisis. We need to defend against this crisis, and these procedures can become at a remove from the crisis: we know they're there, but we're not really following them right now. However, we then need to be mindful about how we report the crisis, because, if in my report I write "Frank didn't follow the procedure, and Frank contacted somebody outside the organisation" then that may get Frank into trouble, which might threaten the identity that I see myself having within this team.

There's another social identity which is that, as an individual defender, I have a network of contacts; I'm part of a global community of defenders and we have a common worthy goal; I identify myself with this community and this is important to me. What I'd like to be able to do is to phone one of my contacts in the community and say, "We're witnessing this traffic coming into our system. We think it's part of a threat. Are you seeing anything like this?".

There's definite procedures and guidelines in this case. For example, NIST Special Publication 800-150 recommends that there be a Memorandum of Understanding in place between the defender's organisation and that of their contact. Defenders are supposed to follow the MoU which precisely defines the kind of information that they are allowed share with their contact. But in a crisis, you're not going to be paying to much attention to that. Also, when you look at the defenders as individuals, they liken themselves to being firefighters defending, fighting the good fight as part of a global community. This is important to them and is part of this identity.

This is something that can influence whether they follow the rules. The defenders have different social identities "I'm a person who works for the organisation", "I'm a person who works within a team", "I'm a person who's part of a global community". And each identity may treat rules differently. Defenders construct and manage these different realities of themselves. This can result in cognitive dissonance and can produce psychological stress on the individual, which can then influence their performance within the group.

This was one result in our wider study and was one of the sources of tension that we found within SOCs and CSIRTs, this issue of having multiple social identities and the resulting cognitive dissonance. We could ask, on the one hand, "how can we help people who work in these situations deal with these issues". But then, on the other hand, sometimes you can't fix these issues. When we talk about security and when we talk about people following rules, the lawyers say, "You must follow these rules". But the reality of the situation is that as individuals, they have many more complicated things going on that they're having to deal with. So, maybe from the company's point of view, maybe they need to change what they mean by security.

Jovan Powar: I agree. I found some of the thrust of what you're saying is that, if we're going to reason about these systems that we need to understand the constructive meaning of them, the shared reality of the people who actually use them. But, there's an experimental problem there, isn't there, because when you're doing this interview, you are guiding things, and they're coming to you, like you said, they're coming to the realisation of how systems work, but that is a joint reconstruction driven by what you've imprinted to the systems. So, if we're really trying to understand it, how do you get that constructive understanding from the people on their own that is useful.

Reply: There's two points here to consider. One is that I don't do these semi-structured interviews because I'm pretty sure that I would lead the person into technical explanations of things. My co-author is an Applied Psychologist. She conducted the interviews and as a Qualitative Researcher she is careful how she prepares for, and conducts, the semi-structured interviews, so as to avoid leading the person in their answers. The second point is that as a research method, this is social constructionism. The interpretation that the defender is forming is an interpretation from their shared experience of working. But equally, it's an interpretation based on the dialogue that they have with the person who's doing the interview. So, it is possible that you could have another interviewer of this person and they could come up with a slightly different theory. And that's the nature of social construction.

Jovan Powar: When you're talking about their interaction with the security procedures, even asking them questions about it on its own might be a bias that you're introducing because if you're looking at. For example, a failure, and you're asking them about all the procedures. If they didn't have an understanding of the procedure then—if the reality was nil or very different—you're making them form an understanding of it at the point of interview, which is not the same as what they originally understood.

Reply: Let's go back to the transcript fragment from the interview. I can't recall the original question that lead to this discussion in the interview, but it would not have been an explicit "do you share information outside the organisation". It might be along the lines, "Okay, so you work in a SOC and your job is to deal with threats, what is that like?" and encourage them to expand on that. It is difficult to do this kind of interviewing without introducing bias, but it can be done. Nevertheless, you do make a good point.

That's the jointly constructed understanding and humans change their mind all the time. They reinterpret and come up with different explanations about what they're doing and what they think about them; they change their mind and what they do over time. Except of course for Vulcans who never change their mind. If security operations centre were run by Vulcans, then of course they'd follow procedures and fully understand their experience of it. What we want to do is to build understandings of the human understanding of our human experience of security systems

We use Qualitative Research methods to do this. In particular, Vivien likes to use the Grounded Theory. It's socially constructed grounded theory, used to help to uncover what's happening among people. In this study it was cybersecurity defenders. Having used the method to identify what's happening, she studies the psychology of the human in the phenomena. What are they feeling? What are they thinking? What are they experiencing? Qualitative techniques are good for discovering unknown knowns. Finding out about the things you didn't realise you knew. We can map this activity into the model that Giampaolo Bella and Lizzy Coles-Kemp proposed in 2012. Our work on the human experience would map into the communal and personal levels.

We're using qualitative research as a means to uncover the human experience. This is not human behaviour nor are we trying to model the behaviour of these individuals. We're looking at what people's emotional responses are. How are they feeling about things, sensory awareness, physical environments, and situations[1]. Is it hot. Is it cold? Are they upset? Are they tired? Are they really annoyed about something? How does that influence their experience. Their desires, their choices, they're very ambitious. They want to do things. They want to do good and use their intellectual reasoning.

This is that what is happening in the security protocol, the security system, along with its users, is a social construction. It is by engaging with the individuals involved that we can come to an understanding of what's happening.

Michael Millian: We have a very interesting anecdote from the hospital down the road that our department does some work with. For security of the computers that the doctors use, somebody put in some software that used the webcam on the computer to make sure there was a human in front of it. A human walks away and the screen locks after five seconds. But this interrupted the workflow of the doctors who would need to change their gloves every time they walked away from the computer. So, they discovered that if they put a large coffee cup over the webcam, the screen would just stay on. It's very interesting how often the people designing the security protocols don't interface with the users who are going to be using the security protocols. And then these two groups of people just end up being at odds with each other.

Reply: That's a good example of how people work around ill-considered design. There's lots of great examples of poor design in Don Normans book on the design of everyday things. While not specifically about design for computer security, it's about good user-centered design. User centered security promotes the idea that we should not blame the user; in a sense we should "blame" the designer because their design is ill-considered. Many times this is true. But I'm not so sure it should always apply. Read the transcript of the dialog with the defender. I know "blame" is not a good word to use, but in a sense you might like to blame the defender in this case (about threat information sharing). It's not the designer's fault. Equally, it's not the defender's fault.

Jim Blythe: I'd like to push back a bit on that. I don't think that security makes you always blame the designer and not the user. We should also be mindful of

---

[1] This is nicely depicted in Munch's, *The Dance of Life* (1900).

Angela Sasse's paper, the user is not the enemy. But what we have is a kind of mismatch between what the user expected and what the designer has got. And it might be one fault or another, the notion of fault here is a tricky one. That's why the notion of blame itself is tricky. And the other thing I'd like to point out about this example is that we're talking about defenders who are not your typical end-user. But I want to say that end users have entered into a social contract with the technology they're using, which is that, as we've said before, we shouldn't overburden them with what it's doing. These defenders are professionals who should have had some process which may not exist, which could be the organisation's fault.

Reply: My co-author would say, "You should not talk about blame." I'm trying to be contentious to push people to think about, the tension that goes on between these two views. And you're quite right that in this case, that defenders are not your conventional users, and we're not thinking about it in terms of typical end-user/consumer computer interaction.

Lydia Kraus: I'm thinking that maybe it's not about blaming one side or the other side, and maybe it's a communication problem in the end. Perhaps the challenge is to find a constructive way to satisfy both sides.

Reply: I agree. I'm trying to capture human transgression in the security protocol. We may usually think of human transgression as error. Perhaps, we should re-think it: transgression becomes a normal part of security. At the moment I don't have a concrete answer about how this might be adequately modelled in the protocol. At what point is a tolerated transgression no longer tolerated?

We want to build a model of human experience so that we can then study how it interacts with the conventional models that we would use for describing a security protocol. At the moment I'm using a Bayesian Network to represent the relationship between attributes representing human experience and the system state and actions carried out by those humans. The Bayesian Network is elicited as part of the Grounded Theory analysis. Analysis may then provide some insight about the security of the system. Perhaps an increase in cognitive dissonance has become evident in the system: defenders are enacting multiple identities arising from a recent increase in external sharing. A remediation might be to help the individuals by providing them with training, or perhaps by strengthening team identity.

Our focus to date has been on identifying the phenomena and providing a psychological understanding. We haven't considered remediation to a great extent. In our study of the SOCs and CSIRTs we identified positive things and negative things about the experience of defenders; things that one could change and things that could not be changed; things that should change, things that should not change. With limited resources, you'd spend them on the things that you should change. The example in the paper is about how threat information is shared amongst cyber defenders.

Jonathan Anderson: I think you see some cognitive dissonance in regulated professions. Engineers, doctors, lawyers, et cetera, where you've got these multiple identities that you're active in sometimes and make decisions. While analysts in a SOC might not exactly have the same kinds of credentials, I think that's true for the people who do critical things, like pilots and ship's captains. Is there anything that we can learn from those kind of environments that helps understand this better?

Reply: That's a good point. In some of the regulated professions, such as air-pilots, they tend not to have a culture of blame. When there is an incident, the culture is to be open and report and learn. They're not inclined to shoot the messenger. It would be interesting to explore what this culture is in the case of network defenders.

Jim Blythe: You mentioned there were three components and one was a socio-technical, and that was really good. I noticed that the notion of teamwork comes in a lot from the description that you gave. But your focus on socio-technical is for individuals. I know that a number of psychological groups look at defenders, explicitly studying the teams and their construction. What you think about that?

Reply: It's not something that we had analysed in depth. While there is some mention of teams in the data, our focus has been more on the individual, and for example how they think about themselves and their relation to the team and social identity.

Fabio Massacci: Do you consider how the strong time pressure affects these people working in the SOC? They get zillions of messages and some point they have to take a decision, they are expected to, they have to do something.

Reply: In our study there were five different themes and the most interesting one was the theme around tensions. One of the issues within this we identified was the use of intuition by defenders. Within the SOC, they're not supposed to use their intuition; they are expected to follow procedures. However, sometimes they avoided following procedures as they slowed things down; they use their intuition in order to get something done. Dealing with these multiple realities, the cognitive dissonance can result in stress.

Fresh Perspectives

Bounded Temporal Fairness for FIFO Financial Markets

Vasilios Mavroudis[✉]

University College London, London, UK
v.mavroudis@cs.ucl.ac.uk

Abstract. Financial exchange operators cater to the needs of their users while simultaneously ensuring compliance with the financial regulations. In this work, we focus on the operators' commitment for fair treatment of all competing participants. We first discuss unbounded temporal fairness and then investigate its implementation and infrastructure requirements for exchanges. We find that these requirements can be fully met only under ideal conditions and argue that unbounded fairness in FIFO markets is unrealistic. To further support this claim, we analyse several real-world incidents and show that subtle implementation inefficiencies and technical optimizations suffice to give unfair advantages to a minority of the participants. We finally introduce, ϵ-fairness, a bounded definition of temporal fairness and discuss how it can be combined with non-continuous market designs to provide equal participant treatment with minimum divergence from the existing market operation.

1 Introduction

First-in-first-out (FIFO) markets process incoming messages in the same temporal order they arrive to the matching engine. Thus, reaction time to market events is one the most important factors in the competition for scarce resources. Following the introduction of electronic trading, many firms sought to decrease their reaction time to market events by automating their strategies (i.e., algorithmic trading) and by improving their technology (e.g., optimize their trading models, establish faster network links, upgrade their software and hardware stacks). Over time, this evolved into a technological arms race between several firms competing for better placement at the order book[1]. The average reaction time has drastically reduced, initially from seconds to milliseconds, and soon after down to microseconds and nanoseconds.

For any FIFO market race to be fair, participants must be treated equally and compete only on the basis of their respective reaction times. In this work, we argue that unconditionally equal treatment of the participants in FIFO markets is becoming increasingly difficult to achieve. This is primarily due to FIFO's implementation and infrastructural requirements that are hard to consistently meet in practice. For example, exchanges (whose participants may have

---

[1] Orders who occupy the top of the order book have better access to liquidity [10].

© Springer Nature Switzerland AG 2020
J. Anderson et al. (Eds.): Security Protocols 2019, LNCS 12287, pp. 91–103, 2020.
https://doi.org/10.1007/978-3-030-57043-9_9

nanosecond-scale reaction times) must ensure that their infrastructure does not introduce any delays that could alter the relative arrival times of competing orders [25,28,31]. However, networking equipment (e.g., network switches) is rarely certified to guarantee equal latency on all ports at a nanosecond scale [25]. To better understand the deployment complexities of FIFO order-matching, we study several real-life incidents where exchanges failed to maintain a level playing field for all market participants. Most of these incidents were due to unintentional, subtle infrastructural inefficiencies but, in certain cases, participants intentionally further exacerbated the timing discrepancies through technical[2] optimizations. Based on the insights from our survey, we then argue that unbounded temporal fairness is an elusive goal and introduce a bounded extension. This more practical version of fairness could improve the microstructural transparency of financial exchanges as well as allow participants to determine if the degree of temporal fairness provided by an exchange is acceptable given their strategies.

Overall, this paper makes the following contributions:

- Defines the implementation and infrastructure requirements that must be fulfilled by every exchange using an unbounded FIFO order-matching policy.
- Surveys several "unfairness" incidents from financial exchanges and investigates their root causes.
- Introduces a bounded version of fairness that improves the market transparency towards participants and could serve as a reference point for regulators.

2 Preliminaries

In this section, we introduce some fundamental concepts of electronic markets and outline the operation of modern exchanges.

2.1 Market Structure

Figure 1 illustrates the different actors and components of an electronic market and their interactions. Market participants (P_i) submit their *orders* to the exchange either through brokers or directly to the exchange's gateways. Brokers are used by participants who trade low volumes, while those with higher volumes usually prefer to place their computers in the exchange's premises (i.e., colocation) and connect directly to the exchange (i.e., direct market access). In both cases, the exchange receives the incoming orders through its gateways which filter out invalid orders and forward the rest to be matched. To balance the load and reduce latency under heavy traffic conditions, exchanges tend to deploy several order gateways very close to the matching engine [30].

---

[2] In this work, we use the term "technical" to refer to knowledge, machines, or methods used in science and industry. This is not to be confused with "technical analysis" that refers to the analysis of statistical trends.

Once an order is received, it is placed in the *order book* where the matching algorithm ranks, pairs and fills it with those of other participants.[3] Once a match is found, the order is closed and removed from the book, if the entire open quantity of the order has been filled. Otherwise, the book's record is updated to include only the remaining (unfilled) quantity. Participants remain up to date on their pending orders and the state of the order book through the market's data feeds which are routed through the exchange's update servers. Depending on their feed subscription type, participants may receive only periodic snapshots of the order book or near-realtime updates on the trading activity.

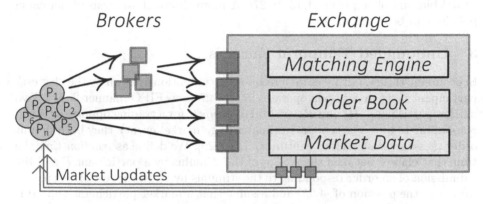

Fig. 1. Illustration of the components of an electronic financial exchange. Participants submit their orders through their brokers (orange rectangles) or directly to the exchange's gateways (blue rectangles). The gateways then forward all valid orders to the matching engine, which pairs bids and offers and updates the order book with the remaining quantities. Market participants remain up to date with the market by subscribing to one of the available market feeds. (Color figure online)

2.2 Order-Matching Policies

Order-matching policies specify the manner by which a financial exchange must process (e.g., rank, match, hide) the order messages it receives from market participants. Currently, one of the most commonly used policies is FIFO (also known as first-come-first-serve matching) [37]. Under this policy, the matching engine processes order messages in the same temporal order in which the messages were received. Consequently, in markets with scarce resources, participants who react fast to market events have higher allocation chances compared to participants with slower reaction times.

In modern exchanges, this speed-related competition has three different manifestations depending on the roles of the competing parties i.e., maker vs. maker,

---

[3] A more thorough treatment of the limit order book is provided by Gould et al. [16].

taker vs. taker and maker vs. taker[4]. In the first case, makers compete with other makers for the best position in the queue at each price level in the limit order book. An order that is earlier in the queue at a price level is much more likely to get filled than one positioned later in the queue [13,35]. Similarly, takers compete with other takers for favorably-priced bids and offers of scarce resources [13]. The first taker order to the market has access to the full offered volume, while subsequent ones have a lower chance of getting filled, as the volume decreases. A maker who is trying to cancel their "stale" bid or offer may also compete with taker(s) who are trying to lift that bid or offer. This practice is called "sniping" and involves fast takers buying assets from or selling assets to slower makers at 'stale' bid and offer prices [4,13,21,27]. A more thorough analysis of matching policies can be found in [20].

3   Unbounded Temporal Fairness

In economic theory, fair races for a resource in contention are won by the "fastest" participant if the order book operates in a *continuous* FIFO manner [4,17]. Two market participants P_A and P_B are said to *compete* for a trading opportunity *op* if responding to the same economic stimulus (e.g., market event), they both submit order messages that seek to capture *op* [1,27,29]. We define as *reaction time* the time that elapses between the receipt of the stimulus by a participant P and the submission of an order responding to the stimulus by P. In the rest of this paper, we adopt the position of [4,17] and assume that a market participant's speed is a function of their (direct or indirect) investment in technology i.e., the more a participant spends the faster they are expected to be. With this in mind, we can now provide a definition of temporal fairness in financial exchanges [27,29]:

Definition 1. *Temporally Fair Race: Given a market event occurring at time t_e, a race between two participants P_A and P_B with reaction times r_A and r_B is fair, if for the arrival times of their orders (t_A and t_B) it holds that: $t_A = t_e + r_A + l$ and $t_B = t_e + r_B + l$, where l is constant.*

The constant l represents the various transmission delays of the exchange's infrastructure (e.g., network link latency for market updates, order transmission latency, order processing latency). A more relaxed version of this definition that seeks to bring slower and faster participants onto "equal footing" has been discussed in [27,29,32,33]. We can now define when an exchange is temporally fair.

Definition 2. *Temporally Fair Exchange: A financial exchange is considered temporally fair, if all the races between all possible pairs of its participants are always temporally fair.*

---

[4] In finance literature, "market makers" provide liquidity to the market (i.e., post resting orders that populate the limit order book), while "takers" remove liquidity by placing orders that are 'marketable' (so immediately match with makers' orders causing those maker orders to be removed from the book). These roles are not fixed and participants transition from maker to taker depending on the side of the trade they take.

4 FIFO Requirements

Intuitively, FIFO matching appears to conform with the above definition of temporal fairness by-design (see Sect. 3) as orders are ranked and matched based on their relative arrival time at the exchange's engine. However, a FIFO market design can maintain its fairness properties only if orders always reach the matching engine in the same relative order they were sent. Similarly, market updates should reach all the colocated participants simultaneously so as to ensure that no one has more time to react. More formally, a FIFO deployment is temporally fair if it remains compliant with the following three requirements at all times:

Consistent & Simultaneous Market Updates
Given a market event e occurring at time t_e and two colocated participants who receive the corresponding market update at times t_A and t_B respectively, it must always hold that $t_A - t_e = t_B - t_e$, for every possible pair of participants.

Preserve Relative Submission Order
Given two colocated participants whose orders were sent at times t_A and t_B and arrived at the matching engine at times t'_A and t'_B, it must always hold that $t'_A - t_A = t'_B - t_B$.

Honor Price-Time Priority
Given an order o_A that arrives at the matching engine at time t_A and a competing order[5] o_B that arrives at t_B, if $t_A < t_B$, it must always hold that o_A will be executed before o_B (unless o_A is explicitly cancelled by the participant).

5 Practical Considerations

As outlined in Sects. 3 and 4, temporally fair markets require that participants compete solely on the basis of their reaction time while every other factor of the system remains constant for all of them. However, the practicality of these strict requirements is questionable. We now survey various incidents from the relevant literature as well as legal reports and show that in various cases participants experienced favourable or unfavourable order submission latency or market update delay due to technical inefficiencies.

Infrastructure Jitter. Electronic exchanges comprise a plurality of hardware and software components that exhibit small non-constant variations in their processing times. For example, modern computers are optimized for maximum performance (i.e., instruction throughput) and thus do not guarantee deterministic execution times. This is due to speculative execution, cache eviction in the presence of competing processes, charge-to-read and data prefetching that contribute to variances in the process execution runtimes in a range between a few nanoseconds to a few hundred microseconds [15,34]. Furthermore, distributed

---

[5] The term "competing orders" refers to lit orders for the same instrument that reside on the same order book side and price level.

network architectures (such as those used by major financial exchanges) also introduce discrepancies in the processing times and asymmetries in the data dissemination speed. This is attributed to the various performance differences between replicated components. For instance, an order gateway may be significantly less crowded compared to the rest of the gateways, thus providing favourable submission times to its users [39]. To address this, market operators strive to maintain their systems perfectly symmetrical and load balanced at all times with nanosecond [25] precision. While this can reduce the magnitude of the problem, differences cannot be fully eliminated even if the exchange uses and fine-tunes the exact same hardware and software in all of its replicated components.

Uneven Information Dissemination. Another potential point of failure with regards to temporal fairness are the market operations that involve information dissemination. Such operations, if not implemented carefully, have the potential to introduce discrepancies in the times that information is received by different participants. For example, Tick-by-Tick data feeds update participants after every change in the order book and must be received by all subscribed participants simultaneously. However, perfect synchronicity is technically challenging to achieve in practice. In a relevant incident, the data feed servers at the National Stock Exchange (NSE) of India were reportedly transmitting the updates in a sequential, non-randomized manner to the subscribed participants, while the order gateways differed in capabilities and loads [39]. In particular, market updates were transmitted in the same order participants logged in (on a per server basis), thus enabling participants with knowledge of this technicality to gain an advantage by logging in early. This resulted in unfair races as some participants were consistently receiving market updates before everyone else (Requirement 1 in Sect. 4). From a technical perspective, one-shot multicast could potentially decrease the latency discrepancies by transmitting all the updates *almost* simultaneously[6]. Unfortunately, even in this case, the inter-arrival discrepancies are reduced but not eliminated [22]. During the same incident, participants were also found to actively delay updates to others by unnecessarily occupying positions in the queue of update servers they were not using [39]. Similar practices have been reported in various other exchanges and markets [12,14,18].

Request Broadcasting. As discussed in Sect. 2.1, major exchanges have a modular (cf. monolithic) architecture with several replicated components to improve their responsiveness and minimize their downtime. However, component replication can have an impact on fairness as there may be fluctuations in the performance of the different components over time. Participants can take advantage of such discrepancies even if they have no information about the performance of the individual components (e.g., order gateways). In past incidents, participants were found to simultaneously broadcast copies of their orders to

---

[6] Multicast based on fanout-spitting or application-layer multicast overlay services suffer from delay problems similar to those of unicast [36].

all available gateways [6]. This practice improves the likelihood that their order will be routed through one of the faster (e.g., less loaded) gateways thus outracing competing participants who do not replicate their orders (Requirement 2 in Sect. 4). Various exchanges have taken measures to counter order replication, usually by limiting the number of simultaneous connections that are permitted per participant [8,9,12,14].

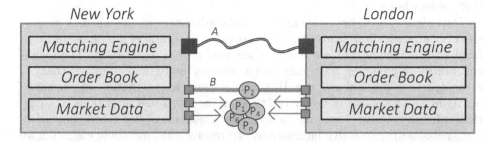

Fig. 2. Illustration of how out-of-band channels can impair fairness in exchanges with decentralized order books. In such exchanges, orders submitted at the local order book (e.g., New York) may be routed to one of the geographically distributed nodes (e.g., London) that offers the best price. The nodes route orders to each other through a direct high-bandwidth network link (A), while participants are updated through the market data feeds of each order book. However, this structure assumes that there is no link B that provides lower latency than A. If such a link becomes available, participants can use it to front-run orders as they are routed across the nodes.

Out-of-Band Channels. A common practice for market participants is to use private fast network links to aggregate market data from multiple venues so as to take better informed trading decisions. In centralized exchanges, this practice does not violate any of the fairness requirements as the order submission latency and the update-feed delays remain constant. However, fast external links may have an adverse effect on the fairness of exchanges with decentralized order books. Such exchanges maintain several geographically-distributed nodes (i.e., order books) that use a network link to route incoming orders to the node that currently offers the best price (Fig. 2). Thus, an incoming order that gets submitted in London may be routed to New York to be matched. However, this assumes that any participant who observes an incoming order in London will not be able to reach the New York book before the order is routed there. While in most cases this is a reasonable assumption (such very low-latency links across continents are limited), the ICAP EBS venue's [11,18] inter-region routing link was outperformed by the Hibernia Express link, thus advantaging participants who had subscribed to it. To address the problem, the operator introduced a speedbump (i.e., a short constant delay) that alleviated the latency advantage provided by the faster network link [11].

Communication Protocol Violations. In networks that use store-and-forward switching, each complete transmission unit (e.g., frame, packet) is copied to the switch's memory buffer and checked for potential errors (e.g., cyclic redundancy checks) before it gets forwarded to the next node. Therefore, the processing time of each message by the switch depends on its size as the whole unit must be received before any checks are performed. In 2015, a market participant was found to exploit this process by intentionally truncating data fields in their outgoing orders. This resulted in invalid data in some non-critical fields but gave them an advantage over other competing participants as switches would process their orders faster [6,7].

Participants have been also found to take advantage of the inherent properties of communication protocols. In networks, large messages are often split into fixed-size fragments that are sent to their destination sequentially. The recipient stores the incoming fragments into a memory buffer and combines them to reconstruct the original message. However, message fragmentation may result in ambiguity with regards to the arrival times of incoming messages. This is of particular importance in electronic exchanges as fragments of two competing orders (i.e., messages) may arrive interweaved. To resolve this, matching engines have introduced tie-breaking policies that allow them to determine the relative order of incoming orders in a consistent manner. One such policy timestamps incoming orders based on the arrival time of their first fragment (e.g., IP packet). This timestamp is then used to determine their relative precedence in the order book. Unfortunately, this policy is prone to *optimistic messaging*, a form of technical gaming. Optimistic messaging relies on the fact that orders are timestamped with the arrival time of the first fragment but cannot be reconstructed until all fragments have arrived [19,23,25]. A strategic participant can exploit this to establish precedence in the book for orders they may intend to submit in the future. For example, given an economic event that is to occur at a specific time t_e, a participant preemptively sends a fragment of an order shortly before t_e (a few milliseconds early) to establish precedence in the order book. Then, depending on the outcome of the event, the participant can decide to trade on the news and transmit the rest of the order's fragments, or drop the incomplete order (e.g., by invalidating the network/application-layer checksum in the remaining fragments). Depending on the variant used by the participant, the pre-event fragments may contain the fields of the order that are not trade-specific (e.g., participant ID) or may contain event-depend data if the event has only a few potential outcomes.

Unintended Order Interactions. Electronic markets paved the way for sophisticated order types that realize conditional interactions with the order book. However, the additional complexity introduced by those orders, made it more difficult for operators to account for all possible interaction scenarios. For example, certain order types (e.g., intermarket sweep orders, hide and light orders) could under specific conditions overtake other orders who preceded them in the execution queue (Requirement 3 in Sect. 4) [3,26]. While these order types were available to everyone, their existence and operation was poorly communicated thus resulting in an unfair asymmetry between the participants who were aware of their operation and those who did not [2,3,5,40]. In another occasion, the interaction between two order-types on New York Stock Exchange enabled participants to use pegging orders to detect the presence (but not the volume) of hidden orders [38]. As a result, participants who exploited this design flaw could retrieve additional information on the current state of the order book compared to those that relied only on the market feeds. While this order interaction was a bug, it highlights how unintended corner-cases may occur in exchanges with complex microstructure.

6   Bounded Temporal Fairness

As discussed in Sect. 4, an exchange that guarantees fairness unconditionally must ensure that all updates arrive simultaneously to all its colocated participants. However, unlike *price, time* is continuous and thus simultaneity is unrealistic, especially considering the various hardware and software imperfections. We thus argue that *unbounded* fairness is an elusive goal. Instead, fairness should be considered with regards to a clearly defined *reference frame*. We now introduce bounded versions of the definitions given in Sect. 3 that provide such a reference frame.

Definition 3. ϵ-*Bounded Temporally Fair Race: Given a market event occurring at time t_e, a race between two participants P_A and P_B with reaction times r_A and r_B is ϵ-fair, if for the arrival times of their orders (t_A and t_B) it holds that: $t_A = t_e + r_A + l \pm \epsilon/2$ and $t_B = t_e + r_B + l \pm \epsilon/2$, where l is constant.*

As before, the constant l represents the various transmission delays of the exchange's infrastructure, while ϵ quantifies the time scale at which the current infrastructure of the exchange can provide fair treatment between the participants. For example, a switch that consistently offsets one of its ports by 1 ms can provide ϵ-fairness for $\epsilon = 1$ ms, as the faster participant in races where $\|r_A - r_B\| > 1$ ms will still win the race (assuming the rest of the infrastructure exhibits no jitter). For brevity, we refer to ϵ-bounded temporally fair races as ϵ-fair.

Definition 4. (ϵ, δ)-*Bounded Temporally Fair Exchange: A financial exchange is considered temporally fair with respect to bounds ϵ and δ, if the races between all possible pairs of its participants are ϵ-fair with probability greater than or equal to δ.*

In the above definition, δ represents the probability that a race between two orders will be ϵ-fair. We introduced δ, as past works have shown that the probability distributions of the latency in distributed systems (both in financial exchanges and in other applications) exhibit long tails [24,25]. In a practical setting, the operator can derive ϵ and δ by monitoring the discrepancies occurring in their system. Some techniques and measurement tools for this purpose have been discussed in [25].

Overall, the above definitions provide a more practical notion of temporal fairness as they relax the requirements for strict simultaneity in market updates and complete precedence-preservation in orders. *Bounded* fairness can improve the transparency of financial exchanges and allow participants to determine if the degree of temporal fairness provided by an exchange is acceptable given their strategies. Moreover, ϵ and δ could serve as a well-defined reference point for regulators and could drive a positive competition between exchanges.

Note, however, that these definitions do not make a statement about the races that take place beneath the ϵ boundary. This leaves a blind spot, where all the races with reaction-time differences less than ϵ could be consistently won by the slowest competing participant. Operators can try to decrease ϵ (and increase δ) by upgrading their infrastructure but similarly participants are also getting consistently faster and more sensitive to subtle differences. We argue that non-continuous market designs at ϵ timescales could solve this problem by uniformly distributing the victories between participants for races beneath ϵ [27,29,32,33]. In these market designs, the majority of the participants will experience a FIFO market, while the small minority of ultra-fast traders will be still guaranteed at least equal treatment at all scales.

7   Conclusions and Future Directions

This work discusses the gap between economic theory and the unavoidable complexities that emerge when theoretically "fair" market models are implemented. We focus on FIFO order-matching and its infrastructural and implementation requirements that "fair" deployments must fulfill. Our survey of the literature and relevant sources suggests that technical challenges make full compliance with these strict requirements unrealistic. Instead, we propose a bounded version of fairness that takes into account the unpredictability of hardware and software systems. The bounds clearly define the degree of fairness that participants can expect from an exchange and can be tightened further as the operators refine their infrastructure. For cases that fall outside these bounds (i.e., very low latency competition), discrete-time policies can be applied to guarantee at least equal participant treatment.

Acknowledgments. We thank the attendees of the workshop for the insightful discussion and the valuable feedback. Moreover, we would like to thank David Kohan Marzagão for his input with regards to our definitions of fairness. Vasilios Mavroudis was partially supported by University College London and BinanceX through the Tradescope project.

References

1. Angel, J.J., McCabe, D.: Fairness in financial markets: the case of high frequency trading. J. Bus. Ethics **112**(4), 585–595 (2013)
2. Australian Securities and Investments Commission: Report 331: Dark liquidity and high-frequency trading (2013). https://download.asic.gov.au/media/1338878/info178-published-15-January-2014.pdf
3. Bodek, H.: The Problem of HFT: Collected Writings on High Frequency Trading & Stock Market Structure Reform. Decimus Capital Markets LLC, Norwalk (2013)
4. Budish, E., Cramton, P., Shim, J.: The high-frequency trading arms race: frequent batch auctions as a market design response. Q. J. Econ. **130**(4), 1547–1621 (2015)
5. Buti, S., Consonni, F., Rindi, B., Wen, Y., Werner, I.M.: Sub-penny and queue-jumping. Charles A. Dice Center Working Paper (2013–18) (2015)
6. CME Group: Slides from new iLink architecture webinar (part I) (2014). http://web.archive.org/web/20141005062026/www.cmegroup.com/education/new-ilink-architecture-webinar.html
7. CME Group: Notice of Summary Access Denial - NYMEX-16-0600 (2017). https://www.cmegroup.com/notices/disciplinary/2016/11/NOTICE-OF-EMERGENCY-ACTION/NYMEX-16-0600-ELDORADO-TRADING-GROUP-LLC.html#pageNumber=1
8. CME Group: CME Group Customer Forum (2018). https://www.cmegroup.com/globex/resources/files/customer-forum-q4-2018.pdf
9. CME Group: Introducing CME Group (2019). http://web.stanford.edu/class/cs349f/slides/CME%20Group%20Overview%20Stanford
10. Cont, R., Kukanov, A., Stoikov, S.: The price impact of order book events. J. Financ. Econom. **12**(1), 47–88 (2014)
11. Detrixhe, J., Mamudi, S.: A New Fast Lane for Traders Spurs Plan to Thwart Exploiters, 2 August 2015. https://www.bloomberg.com/news/articles/2015-08-13/a-new-fast-lane-for-traders-spurs-plan-to-thwart-exploiters
12. EBS Service Company Limited: EBS Dealing Rules - High Level Summary (2012). http://image.exct.net/lib/fef6127172670c/d/1/EBS%20Dealing%20Rules%20High%20Level%20Summary%20July%202012%20_4_.pdf
13. Farmer, D., Skouras, S.: Review of the benefits of a continuous market vs. randomised stop auctions and of alternative priority rules (policy options 7 and 12). In: Manuscript, Foresight. Government Office for Science (2012)
14. Garnham, P.: Foreign exchange: EBS vows to remove unfair advantages (2012). https://www.euromoney.com/article/b12kjjrny27stq/foreign-exchange-ebs-vows-to-remove-unfair-advantages
15. Godbolt, M.: Memory and caches: how they work, and how they affect performance (2018). https://www.youtube.com/watch?v=vDns3Um39l0
16. Gould, M.D., Porter, M.A., Williams, S., McDonald, M., Fenn, D.J., Howison, S.D.: Limit order books. Quant. Financ. **13**(11), 1709–1742 (2013)
17. Harris, L.: What to do about high-frequency trading. Financ. Anal. J. **69**(2), 6–9 (2013)
18. Howorka, E., Horsfall, P., Iaccheo, S., Merold, M., Steyn, S.: Distribution of Data to Multiple Recipients. US Patent 2007/0124419 (2007)
19. Hurd, M.: The Accidental HFT Firm (Forthcoming, Negative Latency Chapter) (2019). https://meanderful.blogspot.com/2018/06/negative-latency.html. Accessed 28 Mar 2019

20. Janecek, K., Kabrhel, M.: Matching algorithms of international exchanges. Technical report, Citeseer (2007)
21. Kirilenko, A., Kyle, A.S., Samadi, M., Tuzun, T.: The flash crash: high-frequency trading in an electronic market. J. Financ. **72**, 967–998 (2017)
22. Klöcking, J.-U., Maihöfer, C., Rothermel, K.: Reducing multicast inter-receiver delay jitter - a server based approach. In: Lorenz, P. (ed.) ICN 2001. LNCS, vol. 2093, pp. 498–507. Springer, Heidelberg (2001). https://doi.org/10.1007/3-540-47728-4_49
23. Lariviere, D.A., Hosman, B.P., Peck-Walden, P.I., Studnitzer, A.L., Bonig, Z., Nagarajan, M.: Message processing protocol which mitigates optimistic messaging behavior. US Patent App. 15/851,067, 28 June 2018
24. Li, J., Sharma, N.K., Ports, D.R., Gribble, S.D.: Tales of the tail: hardware, os, and application-level sources of tail latency. In: Proceedings of the ACM Symposium on Cloud Computing, pp. 1–14. ACM (2014)
25. Lohr, A.: Open Day 2019: T7 infrastructure and latency (2019). https://www.deutsche-boerse.com/resource/blob/1637232/da0ae611905acda0d7502260903a0835/data/Open-Day-2019_T7-Latency-Roadmap_Andreas-Lohr_final.pdf
26. Mavroudis, V.: Market manipulation as a security problem: attacks and defenses. In: Proceedings of the 12th European Workshop on Systems Security, p. 1. ACM (2019)
27. Mavroudis, V., Melton, H.: Libra: fair order-matching for electronic financial exchanges. In: Proceedings of the 1st ACM Conference on Advances in Financial Technologies, pp. 156–168. ACM (2019)
28. Melton, H.: Ideal latency floor. US Patent App. 14/533,543, 5 November 2014
29. Melton, H.: A fairness-oriented performance metric for use on electronic trading venues. In: 2017 International Conference on Computational Science and Computational Intelligence (CSCI), pp. 1027–1030. IEEE (2017)
30. Melton, H.: Understanding and improving temporal fairness on an electronic trading venue. In: 2017 IEEE 37th International Conference on Distributed Computing Systems Workshops (ICDCSW), pp. 1–6. IEEE (2017)
31. Melton, H.: On fairness in continuous electronic markets. In: Proceedings of the International Workshop on Software Fairness, FairWare@ICSE 2018, Gothenburg, Sweden, 29 May 2018. pp. 29–31 (2018)
32. Melton, H.: On fairness in continuous electronic markets. In: 2018 IEEE/ACM International Workshop on Software Fairness (FairWare), pp. 29–31. IEEE (2018)
33. Melton, H.: The paradoxical effects of jitter on fairness in financial exchanges: engineering implications. Working paper (2019)
34. Metamako: MetaApp 32: An adaptable platform that enables intelligence at the network edge leveraging FPGA, x86_64 server and 5ns layer 1 switching technology (2017). https://www.xenon.com.au/wp-content/uploads/2017/06/MetaApp32_data_sheet.pdf
35. Moallemi, C., Yuan, K.: The value of queue position in a limit order book. Confronting Many Viewpoints, Market Microstructure (2014)
36. Prabhakar, B., McKeown, N., Ahuja, R.: Multicast scheduling for input-queued switches. IEEE J. Sel. Areas Commun. **15**(5), 855–866 (1997)
37. Preis, T.: Price-time priority and pro rata matching in an order book model of financial markets. In: Abergel, F., Chakrabarti, B.K., Chakraborti, A., Mitra, M. (eds.) Econophysics of Order-driven Markets, pp. 65–72. Springer, Milano (2011). https://doi.org/10.1007/978-88-470-1766-5_5
38. Securities and Exchange Commission: Securities Act of 1933 Release No. 10463, March 2018. https://www.sec.gov/litigation/admin/2018/33-10463.pdf

39. Securities and Exchanges Board of India: Order in the matter of NSE Colocation (2019). https://www.sebi.gov.in/enforcement/orders/apr-2019/order-in-the-
matter-of-nse-colocation_42880.html
40. United States of America before the Securities and Exchange Commission: In the
Matter of UBS Securities LLC, Exchange Act Release No. 74060 (2015). https://
www.sec.gov/litigation/admin/2015/33-9697.pdf

Bounded Temporal Fairness for FIFO
Financial Markets
(Transcript of Discussion)

Vasilios Mavroudis[✉]

University College London, London, UK
v.mavroudis@cs.ucl.ac.uk

I'll take advantage of the five-minute grace period to make my main points early on. Then, I'll move on and introduce some fundamental concepts as I understand that not everyone is necessarily familiar with all the details of modern exchanges.

So, why do I think that security can help with market manipulation? The answer is that besides "classic" manipulation where traders try to mislead the market and give the false sense that 'there is lots of activity around a particular stock', there are other manipulation techniques that are based solely on technical factors. In particular, these techniques exploit inefficiencies in the exchanges's infrastructure and the way the exchange operates.

While we'll talk primarily about stock exchanges, most of these considerations apply also to cryptocurrency or other types of exchanges. Even if in practise their order-matching processes and infrastructure are still not very advanced. In stock exchanges, particularly in the US, there is an ongoing debate on how legal or ethical are certain trading strategies. The outcome of this debate will likely prompt significant changes in the market regulations. However, there are valid arguments from both sides and it will take rather long until a consensus is reached.

Luckily, when modelling security threats, we have a bit more freedom to make our own assumptions about acceptable and unwanted behaviours.

One can consider a particular behaviour unwanted and say, "Well, I don't want this to happen in my system" and thus I'll adjust their threat model accordingly.

We've seen this happening and I'll later give some examples of market operators who did that. So, even if something is not illegal or if it is borderline ethical, we can say, "In my experience this harms the market and thus we will prevent it in our exchange" and take appropriate measures. In a nutshell, you can design the whole system to work the way you want it to.

However, one may expect that attempting such changes is utopian, as regulators and market participants are not willing to accept substantial changes to the market structure.

It turns out that the financial sector is quite flexible. There are various new and older exchanges that do things in a bit of an unorthodox way to address manipulation problems.

J. Anderson et al. (Eds.): Security Protocols 2019, LNCS 12287, pp. 104–112, 2020.
https://doi.org/10.1007/978-3-030-57043-9_10

Moreover, I'd like to emphasize that technical problems often have technical solutions. I'll present some of them later on, but I'm sure there are many solutions to be proposed.

To better understand how markets work we can consider open outcry markets and try to recreate one in this room. For example, if we all had a commodity that we would like to trade, we could start advertising to each other how much of that commodity we each have, how much we're selling, or how much we're buying.

If we do this long enough, we will even come up with a complete signalling code. This is only part of it. It was actually very complex. It's hard actually to memorise it but I guess you learn it after a few years in the market. This is how things worked, back in the day, but then computers came and this changed drastically.

By 2008, people had started using computers on the trading floor and moved away from hand signaling. Soon they even moved off the exchange's premises. This picture is from 2016 when the same trading floor is completely empty. That's UBS, Stamford, in the US.

This is how exchanges look now. There is actually nothing to see apart from their computers. This is the architecture of a modern electronic exchange. The "market participants" here are traders and investors who want to buy or sell. We also have brokers who route orders to the exchanges on behalf of smaller participants. However, large trading firms won't route their orders through a broker as this means additional delay and fees. This already raises some questions about certain things that may be "unfair".

Then, you have the exchanges and the regulators. The regulators make sure that everything is transparent and fair, to the degree that's possible. Modern electronic exchanges comprise three components. The limit order book, which lists all the open buy and sell orders. The matching engine which matches open orders together, and the data feeds, which report back to the traders the state of the order book and successful matches.

This is a screenshot of an order book. Orders are ranked in descending price, and thus the order at the highest price-level appears at the top. Similarly, sell orders are ranked in ascending price and the order selling at the lowest price is ranked first.

The difference between the highest buying order and the lowest selling one is the "spread" of the market. But what is an order? There are actually several order types. Sometimes even hundreds of them if we consider their variants. The simplest type is "market order" where you express you interest to buy or sell a quantity of an instrument without specifying a price. Then, the market sells to you or buys from you at whichever the best price is at the moment. That's a bit risky but it is useful if you want to quickly unload or quickly buy something.

What most traders use is limit orders where you also specify the maximum price you are willing to pay if buying or the minimum price you are willing to accept if selling. Besides these, there are several other conditional order types. For instance, iceberg orders are interesting. If a trader doesn't want to influence the price of a particular stock, but wants to buy a large quantity they can use an iceberg order that exposes only parts of their total quantity at a time.

If a trader uses an iceberg order to buy 100 pieces of a stock, the order may display a demand for 10 shares at a time. When the first 10 shares are bought, it will ask for another 10. There are lots of variants but the general idea is that you don't want to reveal your quantity all at once.

There are also "anonymous" orders which work similarly to "normal" order types but also conceal the identity of the trader that submitted them. For example, an influential investor selling a particular stock may influence its market price, and thus they may prefer to use anonymous orders to avoid leaking their position. It should be noted that the market regulators and operators have full access to the identity of the market participants regardless of the order type used.

There are also "hidden" orders that provide only pre-trade transparency. Which means that everyone is going to see the order details once it gets filled. But the order will not appear in the order book before that. Moving on to the actual security part; we should define what a "fair" market is. The US and EU regulations are good starting points. They are not identical but they treat various aspects of the market in the same manner.

Overall, a fair market should fulfill seven properties. Only one of them, the "trading integrity", concerns the behaviour of investors and traders while the rest concern the exchange operators. Trading integrity entails, and this is part of the regulation, that market participants should not submit orders unless they intend to trade.

This is clearly to prevent manipulation. For example, a participant cannot repeatedly submit an order for a million shares of one particular stock and cancel them a millisecond later, as this will influence the price. However, "trading intent" is very hard to prove or disprove, so there is an enforcement problem there.

Besides this particular problem, there are also several other smaller or larger ones that we will discuss. Actually, for each one of these seven properties, there has been at least one case where an exchange failed to maintain it and the regulators got involved. For example, the "operational transparency" property entails that the structure and the operation of the exchange should be known to everyone. Moreover, if you're trading on a particular exchange, everyone should have access to the same order types as well as all the details of their operation.

"Fair market access" means that no market participant should have unfair advantages over other participants when submitting or altering orders. For example, it is not fair if someone's orders appear in the order book several minutes after they were submitted, while other traders experience a much lower latency.

"Symmetric access to information" refers to the data feed latency and how it may vary between participants, thus giving unfair headstarts to some of them. "Order queue integrity" refers primarily to the order book shown earlier. What happens if there are two buy or sell orders at the same price level? Which of them gets filled first? The obvious thing to do is to rank them based on their arrival time. However, in practice things get more complicated as different order types interact in various ways with the order book. For instance, exchanges often prioritise "public" orders over "anonymous" or "hidden" ones. Because of these and other operational details, order ranking is often quite complex. In some cases, this complexity enabled participants to exploit little-known implementation details to have their orders ranked higher than those of their competition, even if their orders arrived later.

"Participant anonymity" refers to "anonymous" and "hidden" order types and their ability to protect the trader's identity or order details. We have introduced some of the basic order types and exchange properties, and we will now move on to the actual market abuse/manipulation part.

Market abuse refers to two types of behaviour: "Insider trading" and "Market Manipulation". In this work, we are not concerned with insider trading and instead focus on certain types of market manipulation. Manipulative behaviour takes three forms in modern exchanges: Misleading information, where a market participant knowingly publishes misleading information to influence the price of an asset; False trading signals where participants trade with an intend to mislead others; and Technical manipulation.

To better understand technical manipulation, we can assume an adversary Adv, similar to those considered in computer security. In this case, Adv is a sophisticated market participant who has invested in technology, in particular, high computational power, direct access to the exchange and very-low latency links. In practice, such participants maintain their own inter-exchange communication links. Initially, they had their own fibre optic cables between their premises and the exchanges. These allowed for a much lower roundtrip latency, a few milliseconds compared to the Internet or even leased lines, and was enough to outrace most of the market participants at the time. Simultaneously, exchanges started offering "colocation" options so that firms could house their computers inside the exchange's premises. This shrunk the transmission times even further. An interesting detail about colocation is that all co-located firms get the same cable length, ±1 m. This ensures that a firm housed on the ground floor next to the matching engine has the same transmission latency as a firm housed on the third floor.

Jeff Yan: What you're describing actually is allowed by the SEC... what you're talking about really is the asymmetry between institutional investors versus other investors?

Reply: Yes. Is the question about colocation specifically? Or in general about these practises?

Jeff Yan: Yes, for example, their fast cable, the fast wi-fi connections between the big investors and the institutional investors and the stock exchanges in the US. But those are all approved by the FCC.

Reply: Yes, they are.

With regards to colocation, it's definitely legal but there are opposing views about its fairness. One side is concerned by the fact that colocated firms have an advantage over everyone else who is not colocated. However, the other side counterargues that colocation ensures that all colocated firms are on equal footing and experience almost the same latency. Overall it's a long discussion about what's ethical and what's not.

Besides fiber optic cables, participants nowadays use also microwave, short-wave and even laser links. For example, this was a proposal for a tower in Dover that aimed to connect the UK with Europe. Of course, to take advantage of their fast links, participants also need to have high processing capacity. Given the magnitude of the roundtrip improvements provided by these links, a slower computer is enough to offset any transmission advantages. Adv has also in-depth knowledge of the market structure and very good understanding of the exchange's processes.

Frank Stajano: I'm not sure if I understand fully the incentives of all the parties participating. Under the possibly wrong assumption that the exchange wants to maintain fairness for all: If we are talking about milliseconds making a difference, would it not be easy for the exchange to say, "I am going to work, not in a continuous-time basis, but on a clock basis." And say, "I'm going to do trades every hundred milliseconds and whoever gets into that batch, gets done.

Reply: Absolutely. This is actually a design that has been proposed in some prior works. It works but the batch length needs to be much larger than the "uneven delays" it tries to "equalize".

Alastair Beresford: An additional tack is to say what actual real value comes out of doing this high-frequency trading at all, and why not just impose a small tax on any transaction that's being utilised on the parties. And maybe get rid of all this entirely. Is it really actually providing us any social utility?

Reply: Both very good points.

Yes, batch auctions have been proposed but I'm not aware of any exchanges using it. Having said that, exchanges are surprisingly progressive, so they've deployed some other countermeasures. But to answer your question, I agree a few milliseconds don't add any social value. It's not that our economy is changing at a microsecond or even millisecond rate.

Alastair Beresford: So has the batching been done?

Reply: Not this particular design of batch auctions. It has been proposed in some papers though. Other, simpler countermeasures have been deployed. Most of them work by introducing some delay to incoming orders. However, there are various criticisms about added delays as people argue that market participants have an outdated view of the market and the orders that appear open may no longer be. They sometimes refer to this phenomenon as "house of mirrors".

It an intense debate as it's hard to define what's fair and what's not.

Frank Stajano: You had something you said was a matching engine that matches deals and the first thing I thought when I saw that part of your slide was okay, either they do it in a randomise fashion or there's going to be a deterministic order in which Apple gets traded before Yen.

Is that going to be an unfairness that is taken into account? If everybody knows? If everybody tries to get the name of their share at the beginning of the day, or things like that?

Reply: Different stocks are matched independently. You can think of it as simultaneous auctions. There are several order books, each one for a particular stock.

Frank Stajano: You could have the same argument for buyers. If I had several traders and I have to match all these things, which one went first?

Reply: There are lots of discussions and various problems with that. Each instrument has its own order book and in theory price-time priority is enough to rank orders. However, reality is more complex as different order types interact differently with the book. For example, in the past, there were some order types that would, under certain conditions, be placed ahead of other orders that arrived earlier at the same price-level. Some participants took advantage of this to outrace their competition, but not everyone was aware of that feature. In fact, many participants were not even aware of the existence of those orders. I attribute these kind of problems, in part, to the complexity of the regulatory directives. Regulators add clauses trying to prevent unfairness and unwanted phenomena, but the more complex you make a system, the more prone it is to errors. In that particular case, those complex order types were introduced as a response to an update in the matching regulations. This problem has now been fixed but if we look into these phenomena from the operators' side, it is obvious that there are conflicting interests. Operators want to maintain their markets healthy and fair but they also want to keep their biggest customers happy and accommodate their needs. As mentioned previously, changes have to be approved by the SEC but it is not always easy to predict or comprehend all the potential implications of a seemingly simple change or order type.

Besides these, there are several other technical manipulation techniques. Some of these techniques provide clear monetary gains, while others make sense only as part of a larger trading strategy. However, all of them directly breach one of the properties mentioned previously. To name a few, traders may employ pinging techniques, stuff the market with orders, snipe on stale orders, jump ahead on the price-time queue, or use optimistic messaging. I will elaborate on a few of them.

The first manipulation technique, latency fingerprinting, breaches the anonymity property of "anonymous" orders, which conceal the trader's identifier by replacing it with a generic identifier. In electronic markets, the participants and the exchanges use the FIX protocol to craft and parse messages; for example to submit new orders or alter open ones. Each FIX packet has a timestamp field which is filled by the trader when the message is sent. Once the message arrives at the exchange and is placed in the order book, the participants receive an update. Thus, a participant who has access to a fast data feed, can use these two timestamps to estimate the transmission delay of the message. The transmission delay is relatively stable for each participant as it is due to the latency of their network link. Given a table that maps the network link latencies to individual participants, one can infer with reasonable accuracy the identity of a firm submitting an anonymous order. To build such a table, one can measure the latency of non-anonymous orders submitted by the same participants.

"Sniping" is one of the oldest tricks in the book. It's possible just because not everyone is equally fast in their reactions to market events, and because the delays in order transmission may differ substantially, and unfairly, between participants. For example, let's say you own a car and you have assigned to a car-dealer to sell it for 500 GBP. However, a particular event, for example a movie, causes this particular car model to became highly sought-after and thus its market value increases. Sellers of this particular model will now call their car dealers and ask them to increase the price accordingly. Sniping occurs when a buyer attempts to hit the market before this price update occurs so as to buy the traded asset at the previous, now "stale" price. This allows them to immediately sell the asset back at the actual, higher market price. In exchanges, faster participants take advantage of slower ones by trying to match their "stale" orders, before the later update their order prices.

Sasa Radomirovic: I remember discussing this with some people from a business school, but this is a feature, not a bug. That's why they want a faster connection than some. Because in theory there is no difference between this and some other signal like the Brexit declaration of May or whatever. So this is not considered something you can have countermeasures for, because that's part of the game. You can exploit whatever information is out there to beat the market.

So I wouldn't include this into the measures for which you want to have a technical countermeasure. You may want to have a business countermeasure, as Frank said, do things in bulk, but otherwise, it wouldn't be something that you can do anything about.

Reply: Yes this is indeed how the markets currently work. It is unclear, however, how good or bad this is for the markets in general. For instance, there are some exchanges, such as the IEX, that use a "speedbump" to prevent some of these practices. IEX adds a 350 μs fixed delay on every order. While fast traders still have an advantage over slower ones, the "speedbump" allows the exchange to reprice orders pegged to the National Best Bid and Offer. Other exchanges use variable delays to all or certain order types.

But I agree being faster than other participants is not necessarily a problem per se. It depends how one gains one's speed advantage. There are cases where the exchange's infrastructure imposes uneven delays to the different participants. For example, the participants assigned to an order gateway A may be disadvantaged over those that use a gateway B, as A is less capable or more congested. In practice, those delay discrepancies are very hard to completely "equalize" due to the distributed and complex infrastructure of modern exchanges.

Beside technical countermeasures, there are also other regulatory counter-measures. For example, the SEC runs a whistleblower program where researchers submit their manipulation evidence and receive large monetary awards in cases of successful convictions.

One can also redesign the market to be more resilient to manipulation. This is what Frank Stajano suggested in his question above and can be found in the literature as "frequent batch auctions". I think it's a very good idea. Probably the way we should move forward. Additionally, some of the problems mentioned earlier can be addressed individually with specific patches. For instance, latency fingerprinting can be easily addressed by the participants themselves by adding noise to their timestamps.

Finally, I'd like to touch a bit on a recent patent from 2018. It is concerned with "optimistic messaging" and proposes ways to address it. To better explain optimistic messaging, let's assume a trader T who is competing with other market participants around a specific economic event happening at a particular time. Depending on the outcome of that event, T and their competition decide to place a bid at the market or not. T is equally fast with everyone else but can employ optimistic messaging tricks to outrace them. T knows in advance the bid that is to be placed if the event has a positive outcome, thus they can prepare the order beforehand. This enables them to split the FIX order-message into its TCP segments and transmit all but one of them before the event actually occurs. Once the event occurs, if T decides to bid, they send the remaining packet. Otherwise, they simply drop it. Alternatively, T can send invalid checksums or use other order invalidation tricks. In some cases, traders have been found to transmit their TCP packets out of order. They first submitted the event-agnostic packets (with fields such as the "participant identifier") and once the event occurred the remaining ones with the actual buying/selling price. Overall, optimistic messaging provides a headstart to traders as it allows them to initiate their order transmission earlier than everyone else.

Sasa Radomirovic: So what you showed us were defences against what's perceived unethical or unlawful behaviour, but at the very beginning you showed us properties we would like to have. The defences seem reactive and then they just lead to, as you said, more complexity. It defends one thing, but then opens up another. Has anybody looked at starting from the properties we want to have, leading us to impossibility results. I'm thinking of things like Arrow's theorem for voting where you can have preferences expressed for a stock that you want to buy, offering more or less money and if you get to record this in the right way, it seems to be the moving part too, we see that we cannot achieve all the nice properties we want to now.

Reply: None that I'm aware of actually. You mean in using formal methods to try to perhaps exhaustively or in a smarter way?

Sasa Radomirovic: Right, yes, formal methods. If you were to strip a lot of interesting stuff away, to do it.

Reply: Yes, we could take such an approach and I am not aware of any prior works doing that already. Currently, the markets are optimised for quick price discovery, while manipulation and other practical problems seem to be an afterthought.

Mismorphism: The Heart of the Weird Machine

Prashant Anantharaman[1]([✉]), Vijay Kothari[1], J. Peter Brady[1],
Ira Ray Jenkins[1], Sameed Ali[1], Michael C. Millian[1], Ross Koppel[3],
Jim Blythe[2], Sergey Bratus[1], and Sean W. Smith[1]

[1] Dartmouth College, Hanover, NH, USA
pa@cs.dartmouth.edu
[2] Information Sciences Institute, University of Southern California,
Los Angeles, CA, USA
[3] Sociology Department, University of Pennsylvania, Philadelphia, PA, USA

Abstract. Mismorphisms—instances where predicates take on different truth values across different interpretations of reality (notably, different actors' perceptions of reality and the actual reality)—are the source of weird instructions. These weird instructions are tiny code snippets or gadgets that present the exploit programmer with unintended computational capabilities. Collectively, they constitute the weird machine upon which the exploit program runs. That is, a protocol or parser vulnerability is evidence of a weird machine, which, in turn, is evidence of an underlying mismorphism. This paper seeks to address vulnerabilities at the mismorphism layer.

The work presented here connects to our prior work in language-theoretic security (LangSec). LangSec provides a methodology for eliminating weird machines: By limiting the expressiveness of the input language, separating and constraining the parser code from the execution code, and ensuring only valid input makes its way to the execution code, entire classes of vulnerabilities can be avoided. Here, we go a layer deeper with our investigation of the mismorphisms responsible for weird machines.

In this paper, we re-introduce LangSec and mismorphisms, and we develop a logical representation of mismorphisms that complements our previous semiotic-triad-based representation. Additionally, we develop a preliminary set of classes for expressing LangSec mismorphisms, and we use this mismorphism-based scheme to classify a corpus of LangSec vulnerabilities.

1 Introduction

Mismatches between the perceptions of the designer, the implementor, and the user often result in protocol vulnerabilities. The designer has a high-level vision for how they believe the protocol should function, and this vision guides the creation of the specification. In practice, the specification may diverge from the

© Springer Nature Switzerland AG 2020
J. Anderson et al. (Eds.): Security Protocols 2019, LNCS 12287, pp. 113–124, 2020.
https://doi.org/10.1007/978-3-030-57043-9_11

initial vision due to real-world constraints, e.g., hardware or real-time requirements. The implementor then produces code to meet the specification based
on their perceptions of how the protocol should function and, in some cases,
how the user will interact with it. However, incorrect assumptions may produce
vulnerabilities in the form of bugs or unintended operation. A user—informed
by their own assumptions and perceptions—may then interact with a system
or service that relies upon the protocol. A misunderstanding of the protocol
and its operation can drive the user toward a decision that produces an unintended outcome. Ultimately, the security of the protocol rests on the consistency
between the various actors' mental models of the protocol, the protocol specification, and the protocol implementation. A *mismorphism* refers to a mapping
between different representations of reality (e.g., the distinct mental model of
the protocol designer, the protocol implementor, and the end user) for which
properties that ought to be preserved are not. In the past, we have used this
concept and an accompanying semiotic-triad-based model to succinctly express
the root causes of usable security failures [25]. We now apply this model to protocol design, development, and use. As mentioned earlier, many vulnerabilities
stem from a mismatch between different actors' representations of protocols and
the protocol operation in practice, e.g., the HeartBleed [11] vulnerability embod-
ies a mismatch between the protocol specification, which involved validating a
length field, and the implementation, which failed to do so. Therefore, it is natural to adopt the mismorphism model to examine the root causes of protocol
vulnerabilities. That is precisely what we do in this paper.

In this paper, we examine protocol vulnerabilities and the mismorphisms
upon which they are rooted. We develop a logic to express these mismorphisms,
which enables us to capture the human mismatches that produce in vulnerabilities in code. Finally, we use this logical formalism to catalog the underlying
mismorphisms that produce real-world vulnerabilities.

2   Related Work

The notion of mismorphism closely parallels the views expressed by Bratus
et al. [8] in their discussion of exploit programming:

> "Successful exploitation is always evidence of someone's incorrect assump-
> tions about the computational nature of the system—in hindsight, which
> is 20-20."

The mindset embodied in this quote forms the foundation for the field of
language-theoretic security (LangSec).[1] Exploitation is unintended computation

---

[1] We only give a brief primer of LangSec in this paper. For those who are interested in
learning more we recommend consulting the LangSec website [7].

performed on a *weird machine* [24] that the target program harbors. [2] Weird machines comprise the gadgets within a program that offer the adversary unintended computational capabilities to carry out an attack, e.g., NOP sleds, buffer overflows. Weird machines were never intended by protocol designers or implementors but organically arose within the protocol design and development phases. For instance, consider a designer who intends to design a web server program. The implementor of the software attempts to sanitize the input, but unwittingly lets malicious input through. This enables the adversary to supply unexpected input, resulting in unexpected behavior. The adversary repeatedly observes instances of unspecified program behaviour and uses these observations to craft an exploit program that they run on the exposed weird machine; this weird machine may serve as a Turing machine or otherwise expressive machine for the supplied input, the exploit program. To the designer, it was just a web server program; to the exploit programmer it provides an avenue of attack.

LangSec advocates taking a principled approach—one that is informed by language theory, automata theory, and computability theory—to parser design and development to eliminate the weird machine. LangSec facilitates the construction of safer protocols that behave closer to the way that designers and implementors envision by identifying best practices for protocol construction, such as parsing the input in full before program execution and ensuring the parser obeys known computability boundaries for safer computation. It also delivers tools such as Hammer and McHammer to achieve these goals [15,20].

Momot et al. [18] created a taxonomy of LangSec anti-patterns and used it to suggest ways to improve the Common Weakness Enumeration (CWE) database. Erik Poll [22] takes a different approach, classifying input vulnerabilities into two broad categories—flaws in processing input and flaws in forwarding input—and discusses examples from both categories in detail.

Pieczul and Foley studied Apache Struts code over a period of 12 years and systematically analyzed code changes and the nature of the security vulnerabilities reported [21]. They observed interesting phenomena pertaining to vulnerabilities and code security—and they developed a phenomena lifecycle that captures how these phenomena appear alongside developer awareness about the security problem.

We build upon this prior research, viewing mismorphisms as precursors to the weird machine. Our work is motivated by the belief that identifying and categorizing the mismorphisms that produce weird machines is a valuable step in systematically unpacking the causes of vulnerabilities and ultimately addressing them.

---

[2] For the reader interested in learning more about weird machines: Dullien [10] provides a formal definition for understanding weird machines and shows that it is feasible to build software that is resilient to memory corruption. Bratus and Shubina [9] also present exploit programming as a problem of code reuse, discuss how the adversary uses code presented by the weird machine to carry out the exploit, and describe colliding actors' abstractions of how the code works.

3   A Logic for Mismorphisms

Here, we provide a very brief primer on mismorphisms and present a logical model for capturing them. Our work here builds upon our earlier efforts to build a semiotic-triad-based mismorphism model [25], which was, in turn, inspired by early semiotics work by pioneers Ogden and Richards [19]. The logical representation presented here blends temporal logic with the idea of multiple interpreters. Following this section, we demonstrate how this logical model can be used to classify underlying causes of LangSec vulnerabilities by providing a preliminary classification using real-world examples.

In the context of this paper, a mismorphism refers to a difference in interpretations between two or more interpreters. That is, we can think of different interpreters (e.g., people) interpreting propositions or predicates about the world. In general, it is good when the interpretations agree and are in accordance with reality. However, when a predicate takes on a truth value under one interpretation but not another interpretation, we have a mismorphism, which may be a cause for concern. In our earlier applications, we found these mismorphisms were useful in understanding and classifying usable security failures and user circumvention. Here, we apply them to protocol and parser security. As mismorphisms deal with interpretations of predicates and how interpretations differ between interpreters, it's easy to see why formal logic provides a natural foundation to represent them.

We use the words *predicate* and *interpretation* in similar—albeit, not identical—manners to the common formal-logic meanings, e.g., as presented by Aho and Ullman [6]. However, instead of a binary logic, we use a ternary logic similar to Kleene's ternary logic [13, 16].[3] We refer to a predicate as a function of zero or more variables whose codomain is $\{T, F, U\}$ where T is true, F is false, and U is uncertain/unknown. We refer to an *interpretation* of a predicate as an assignment of values (which may include U) to variables, which results in the predicate being interpreted as T, F, or U. A predicate is interpreted as T if after substituting all variables for their truth values, the predicate is determined to be T; it is interpreted as F if after substituting all variables for their truth values, the predicate is determined to be F; if we are unable to determine whether the predicate is T or F, the predicate is interpreted as U.

The interpretation must be done by someone (or perhaps something) and that someone is the *interpreter*. In this paper, common *interpreters* include the oracle O who interprets the predicate as it is in reality, the designer D, the implementor I, and the user Y. We note that some interpreters may not have adequate information to assign precise values to the variables that ensure the predicate is interpreted as T or F. It is in these instances that the predicate may be interpreted as U. In this paper, we use $P|_A$ to denote the interpretation of predicate P by interpreter A.

To represent mismorphisms we need a way to express the relationship between interpretations of a predicate. Thus, we have the following:

---

[3] We do not specify a specific ternary logic system for evaluating predicates in this paper.

[Predicate] [Interpretation Relation] [List of interpreters]

The interpretation relations over the set of all predicate-interpreter pairs are k-ary relations where $k >= 2$ is the number of interpreters there are in the interpretation relation—and each k-ary relation is over the interpretations of the predicate by the k interpreters. The three interpretation relations we are concerned with in this paper are: the interpretation-equivalence relation ($\underset{\text{interp.}}{=}$), the interpretation-uncertainty relation ($\underset{\text{interp.}}{\overset{?}{=}}$), and the interpretation-inequivalence relation ($\underset{\text{interp.}}{\neq}$).[4] These relations are defined as follows, where each P represents a predicate and each A_i represents an interpreter:

- $P \underset{\text{interp.}}{=} A_1, A_2, \dots A_k$ if and only if P, as interpreted by each A_i, has a truth value that's either T or F (never U)—and all interpretations yield the same truth value.
- $P \underset{\text{interp.}}{\overset{?}{=}} A_1, A_2, \dots A_k$ if and only if P takes on the value U when interpreted by at least one A_i.
- $P \underset{\text{interp.}}{\neq} A_1, A_2, \dots A_k$ if and only if P interpreted by A_i is T and P interpreted by A_j is F for some $i \neq j$.

There are a few important observations to note here. One is that the oracle O always holds the correct truth value for the predicate by definition. Another is that if we only know the $\underset{\text{interp.}}{\overset{?}{=}}$ relation applies, we won't know which interpreter is uncertain about the predicate or even how many interpreters are uncertain unless $k = 2$ and one interpreter is the oracle. Similarly, if we only know that the $\underset{\text{interp.}}{\neq}$ relation applies, we do not know where the mismatch exists unless $k = 2$. That said, knowledge that the oracle O always holds the correct interpretation combined with other facts can help specify where the uncertainty or inequivalence stems from. Last, the $\underset{\text{interp.}}{=}$ relation will not be applicable if either the $\underset{\text{interp.}}{\overset{?}{=}}$ or the $\underset{\text{interp.}}{\neq}$ interpretations are applicable; however, $P \underset{\text{interp.}}{\overset{?}{=}} A_1, \dots A_k$ and $P \underset{\text{interp.}}{\neq} A_1, \dots A_k$ can both be applicable simultaneously.

The purpose of creating this model was to allow us to capture mismorphisms. Mismorphisms correspond to instances where either the interpretation-uncertainty relation or interpretation-inequivalence relation apply.

It may be valuable to consider some natural extensions to this logical formalism. In select cases, we may consider multiple interpreters of the same role. In these instances, we assign subscripts to distinguish roles, e.g., D, I_1, I_2, O. Also,

---

[4] Note that for $k = 2$, if we confine ourselves to predicates that take on only T or F values, the relation $\underset{\text{interp.}}{=}$ is an equivalence relation in the mathematical sense, as one might expect, i.e., it obeys reflexivity, commutativity, and transitivity.

there are temporal aspects that may be relevant. Predicates can be functions of time and so can the interpretations. While we use the common $v(t)$-style notation to represent a variable as a function of time within a predicate, in select cases we consider the interpreter as a function of time, e.g., $I_4^{t_3}$ means the interpretation is done by implementor I_4 at time $t = t_3$.

4   Preliminary Classification

Here, we describe various classes of mismorphisms using the mathematical notation we just developed. All the vulnerabilities we catalog fall into one of the categories of mismorphisms we describe below.

4.1   Failed Assumption of Language Decidability

Any input language format needs to be decidable for the implementor to be able to parse and make sure that there are no corner cases when the program can enter unexpected states or fail to terminate. When the designer assumes a language L is decidable (in the absence of proof, that it is), the program may harbor the potential for unexpected computation.

For one example, the Ethereum platform uses a Turing-complete input language to enable its smart contracts. It is demonstrably more difficult to build a parser for such an input language. Such added complexity led to the Ethereum DAO disaster [27], in which all ethers were stolen, forcing the developers to perform a highly controversial hard fork. As a result, some developers built a decidable version of Solidity called vyper [12].

We define such a language mismorphism by the form:

$$L \text{ is decidable} \underset{\text{interp.}}{\overset{?}{=}} O, D \tag{1}$$

A diagrammatic representation of the above formalism can be found in Fig. 1.

4.2   Shotgun Parsers

Shotgun parsers perform input data checking and handling interspersed with processing logic. Shotgun parsers do not perform full recognition before the data is processed. Hence, implementors may assume that a field x has the same value at time t and time $t + \delta$, but the processing logic may change the value of the field x in an input buffer B.

This mismorphism relation is seen below:

$$B(t) = B(t + \delta) \underset{\text{interp.}}{\neq} O, I \tag{2}$$

Implementors may expect the buffer to be intact across time, but that is not observed to be the case. Shotgun parsing can cause mismorphisms in two distinct ways. First, a partially validated input may be wrongly treated as though

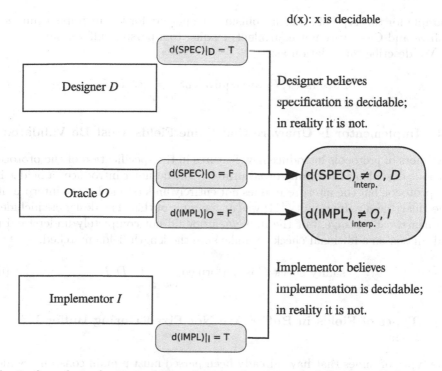

Fig. 1. One class of mismorphism where implementors and designers both disagree with the reality that the language is actually undecidable.

it is fully validated. Suppose Implementor 1 performs the shotgun parsing and knoww the input to be only partially validated. Then, Implementor 2 works on execution and assumes the input is fully validated by the time the code segment is executed. This type of a shotgun parser mismorphism can be represented as follows:

$$B \text{ is accepted} \underset{\text{interp.}}{\neq} I_1, I_2 \tag{3}$$

Second, the same implementor may perform shotgun parsing and be responsible for working on the execution code. But they may interpret the same protocol differently during those different times. This type of a mismorphism can be represented as follows:

$$B \text{ is accepted} \underset{\text{interp.}}{\neq} I^{t_1}, I^{t_2} \tag{4}$$

4.3   Parser Inequivalence for the Same Protocol

Designers of protocols intend for two endpoints to have the exact same functionality, and build identical parse trees. The Android Master Key bug [14] is an apt example for this type of a mismorphism. The parsers for the unzipping function in Java and C++ were not equivalent, leading to a parsing differential.

We describe this relation as:

$$\text{Parsers } P_1, P_2 \text{ are equivalent } \underset{interp.}{\neq} \quad O, D, I \tag{5}$$

4.4 Implementor Is Unaware that Some Fields Must Be Validated

Designers of protocols introduce new features in the specification of the protocol without describing them fully or accurately. The designer introduces a field x in the protocol, but the interpreter does not entirely understand how to interpret it. The Heartbleed vulnerability [11] was an example of this. The designers included the heartbeat message, but the implementors did not completely understand it and missed an additional check to make sure the length fields matched.

$$\text{sanity check } C \text{ is performed } \underset{interp.}{\neq} \quad O, D, I \tag{6}$$

4.5 Types of Fields in Buffer Are Not Fixed During Buffer Life Cyle

The types of values that have already been parsed must remain constant. Sometimes, implementors assume field x is treated as type $t(x)$ throughout execution. In reality, the field may be treated as a different type at certain points during execution.

$$type(x) \text{ is fixed } \underset{interp.}{\neq} \quad O, D, I \tag{7}$$

5 A Catalog of Vulnerabilities and Their Mismorphisms

Below, we provide a small catalog of some vulnerabilities and the mismorphisms that we believe produced them.

Shellshock: Bash unintentionally executes commands that are concatenated to function definitions that are inside environment variables [17].

$$\text{sanity check } C \text{ is performed } \underset{interp.}{\neq} \quad O, D, I$$

The sanity check C here makes sure that once functions are terminated, the variable shouldn't be reading commands that follow it.

Rosetta Flash: SWF files that are requested using JSONP are incorrectly parsed once they are compressed using *zlib*. Compressed SWF files can contain only alphanumeric characters [26].

$$\text{sanity check } C \text{ is performed} \underset{\text{interp.}}{\neq} O, D, I$$

The specification of the SWF file format is not exhaustively validated using a grammar. The fix uses conditions such as checking for the first and last bytes for special, non-alphanumeric characters.

Heartbleed: The protocol involves two length fields, one that specifies the total length of the heartbeat message; the other specifies the size of the payload of the heartbeat message [11].

$$\text{sanity check } C \text{ is performed} \underset{\text{interp.}}{\neq} O, D, I$$

Sanity check C involves verifying the length fields l_1 and l_2 match.

Android Master Key: The Java and C++ implementations of the cryptographic library performing unzipping were not equivalent [14].

$$\text{Parsers } P_1, P_2 \text{ are equivalent} \underset{\text{interp.}}{\neq} O, D, I$$

Ruby on Rails - Omakase. The Rails YAML loader doesn't validate the input string and check that it is valid JSON. And it doesn't load the entire JSON; instead, it just starts replacing characters to convert JSON to YAML [23].

$$\text{sanity check } C \text{ is performed} \underset{\text{interp.}}{\neq} O, D, I$$

Sanity check C should first recognize and make sure the JSON is well-formed, before replacing the characters in YAML.

Nginx HTTP Chunked Encoding: Large chunk size for the Transfer-Encoding chunk size trigger integer signedness error and a stack-based buffer overflow [2].

$$B \text{ is accepted} \underset{\text{interp.}}{\neq} I_1, I_2$$

The shotgun parser works on execution without validating the value of the length field, which could be much larger than allowed, thereby causing buffer overflows. All implementors must work with the same knowledge, and the input must first be recognized fully.

Elasticsearch Crafted Script Bug: Elasticsearch runs Groovy scripts directly in a sandbox. Attackers were able to craft a script that would bypass the sandbox check and execute shell commands [4].

$$L \text{ is decidable} \underset{\text{interp.}}{\overset{?}{=}} O, D$$

Developers of Elasticsearch had to explore the option of abandoning Groovy in favor of a safe and less dynamic alternative.

Mozilla NSS Null Character Bug: When domain names included a null character, there was a discrepancy between the way certificate authorities issued certificates and the way SSL clients handled them. Certificate authorities issued certificates for the domain after the null character, whereas the SSL clients used the domain name ahead of the null character [1].

$$\text{Parsers } P_1, P_2 \text{ are equivalent} \underset{\text{interp.}}{\neq} O, D, I$$

Although having a null character in a certificate is not accepted behavior, certificate authorities and clients do not want to ignore requests that contain them. So they follow their own interpretations, resulting in a parser differential.

Adobe Reader CVE-2013-2729: In running length encoded bitmaps, Adobe Reader wrote pixel values to arbitrary memory locations since there was a bounds check that was skipped [3].

$$B \text{ is accepted} \underset{\text{interp.}}{\neq} I_1, I_2$$

The code used a shotgun parser where the implementor of the processing logic assumed all fields were validated. The bounds check was never performed.

OpenBSD - Fragmented ICMPv6 Packet Remote Execution: Fragmented ICMP6 packets cause an overflow in the mbuf data structure in the kernel may cause a kernel panic or remote code execution depending on packet contents [5].

$$\text{sanity check } C \text{ is performed} \underset{\text{interp.}}{\neq} O, D, I$$

Implementors of the ICMP6 packet structures in OpenBSD did not understand how to map it to the existing `mbuf` structure, and then validate it.

6 Conclusion

In this paper, we proposed a novel approach to categorizing the root causes of protocol vulnerabilities. We created a new logical model to express mismorphisms, grounded in the semiotic-triad based representation of mismorphisms explored in our earlier work. We then used this logical model to develop a preliminary set of mismorphism classes for capturing LangSec vulnerabilities. Finally, we created a small catalog of vulnerabilities and demonstrated how our classification scheme could be used to classify the mismorphisms those vulnerabilities embody.

Acknowledgement. This material is based upon work supported by the United States Air Force and DARPA under Contract No. FA8750-16-C-0179 and Department of Energy under Award Number DE-OE0000780.

Any opinions, findings and conclusions or recommendations expressed in this material are those of the author(s) and do not necessarily reflect the views of the United States Air Force, DARPA, United States Government or any agency thereof.

References

1. CVE-2009-3555 The Mozilla Network Security Services (NSS) fails to properly validate the domain name in a signed CA certificate, allowing attackers to substitute malicious SSL certificates for trusted ones. Available from Vulners. https://vulners.com/exploitdb/EDB-ID:26703
2. CVE-2013-2028 Nginx HTTP Server 1.3.9-1.4.0 Chunked Encoding Stack Buffer Overflow. Available from Rapid 7. https://www.rapid7.com/db/modules/exploit/linux/http/nginx_chunked_size
3. CVE-2013-2729 Adobe Reader X 10.1.4.38 - BMP/RLE heap corruption. Available from Vulners. https://vulners.com/exploitdb/EDB-ID:26703
4. CVE-2015-1427 The Groovy scripting engine in Elasticsearch before 1.3.8 and 1.4.x before 1.4.3 allows remote attackers to bypass the sandbox protection mechanism and execute arbitrary shell commands via a crafted script. Available from Vulners. https://vulners.com/cve/CVE-2015-1427
5. OpenBSD's IPv6 mbufs remote kernel buffer overflow. Available from Vulners. https://vulners.com/cert/VU:986425
6. Aho, A., Ullman, J.: Foundations of Computer Science: C Edition, Chapter 14, July 1994. http://infolab.stanford.edu/~ullman/focs.html
7. Bratus, S.: LANGSEC: Language-theoretic Security: "The View from the Tower of Babel". http://langsec.org
8. Bratus, S., Locasto, M., Patterson, M., Sassaman, L., Shubina, A.: Exploit programming: from buffer overflows to "Weird Machines" and theory of computation. Login USENIX Mag. **36**(6), 13–21 (2011)
9. Bratus, S., Shubina, A.: Exploitation as code reuse: on the need of formalization. IT-Inf. Technol. **59**(2), 93–100 (2017). https://doi.org/10.1515/itit-2016-0038
10. Dullien, T.F.: Weird machines, exploitability, and provable unexploitability. IEEE Trans. Emerg. Top. Comput. (2017). https://doi.org/10.1109/TETC.2017.2785299
11. Durumeric, Z., et al.: The Matter of Heartbleed. In: Proceedings of the 2014 Conference on Internet Measurement Conference, pp. 475–488. ACM (2014). https://doi.org/10.1145/2663716.2663755

12. Ethereum: Pythonic Smart Contract Language for the EVM. https://github.com/ethereum/vyper
13. Fitting, M.: Kleene's three valued logics and their children. Fundam. Inf. **20**(1–3), 113–131 (1994). http://dl.acm.org/citation.cfm?id=183529.183533
14. Freeman, J.: Exploit (& Fix) Android "Master Key". http://www.saurik.com/id/17
15. Hermerschmidt, L.: McHammerCoder: a binary capable parser and unparser generator, https://github.com/McHammerCoder/McHammerCoder
16. Kleene, S.C.: Introduction to metamathematics (1954)
17. Mary, C.: Shellshock attack on linux systems-bash. Int. Res. J. Eng. Technol. **2**(8), 1322–1325 (2015)
18. Momot, F., Bratus, S., Hallberg, S.M., Patterson, M.L.: The seven turrets of babel: a taxonomy of LangSec errors and how to expunge them. In: 2016 IEEE Cybersecurity Development (SecDev), pp. 45–52, November 2016. https://doi.org/10.1109/SecDev.2016.019
19. Ogden, C.K., Richards, I.A.: The Meaning of Meaning: A Study of the Influence of Language upon Thought and of the Science of Symbolism. Harcourt Brace and Company, San Diego (1927)
20. Patterson, M.: Parser combinators for binary formats, in C. https://github.com/UpstandingHackers/hammer
21. Pieczul, O., Foley, S.N.: The evolution of a security control. In: Anderson, J., Matyáš, V., Christianson, B., Stajano, F. (eds.) Security Protocols 2016. LNCS, vol. 10368, pp. 67–84. Springer, Cham (2017). https://doi.org/10.1007/978-3-319-62033-6_9
22. Poll, E.: LangSec revisited: input security flaws of the second kind. In: 2018 IEEE Security and Privacy Workshops (SPW), pp. 329–334. IEEE (2018). https://doi.org/10.1109/SPW.2018.00051
23. Rezvina, S.: Rails' Remote Code Execution Vulnerability Explained. https://codeclimate.com/blog/rails-remote-code-execution-vulnerability-explained
24. Shapiro, R., Bratus, S., Smith, S.W.: "Weird Machines" in ELF: a spotlight on the underappreciated metadata. In: Proceedings of the 7th USENIX Conference on Offensive Technologies. WOOT 2013, USENIX Association, Berkeley, CA, USA (2013). http://dl.acm.org/citation.cfm?id=2534748.2534763
25. Smith, S.W., Koppel, R., Blythe, J., Kothari, V.: Mismorphism: a semiotic model of computer security circumvention. In: Proceedings of the 2015 Symposium and Bootcamp on the Science of Security, p. 25. ACM (2015)
26. Spagnuolo, M.: Abusing JSONP with rosetta flash. https://miki.it/blog/2014/7/8/abusing-jsonp-with-rosetta-flash/
27. Torpey, K.: The DAO disaster illustrates differing philosophies in bitcoin and ethereum. https://www.coingecko.com/buzz/dao-disaster-differing-philosophies-bitcoin-ethereum

Mismorphism: The Heart of the Weird Machine (Transcript of Discussion)

Prashant Anantharaman[✉]

Dartmouth College, Hanover, NH, USA
pa@cs.dartmouth.edu

As Jon mentioned, this is one of our two talks at this workshop. My colleagues Vijay and Michael, over here, will be presenting later in the morning. In this talk, I'll introduce what mismorphisms are, and some of the things that we work on, which are LangSec and weird machines. And I'll talk a bit more about some of the work we did in this paper. We want some insight from all of you about what we can do to improve our work. And we have some holes that we've identified that we want your help fixing.

What really are mismorphisms? Mismorphisms are, in essence, mismatches between how humans think about the same thing differently. A really nice example is the open source null character bug that was discovered by Dan Kandinsky and team. An attacker could use a domain name: the attacker owns the domain name, which is badguy.com, and the attacker crafts this certificate request and sends it to the certificate authority. The certificate authority reads this as, "Okay it's .Badguy.com"—it essentially means that it's a subdomain owned by the attacker. And then the certificate authority grants the certificate. So there's a null character over here. And a null character in a domain is not supposed to be allowed.

How the certificate authority handles this null character, and how the browser handles this null character, is different. And the exciting thing about this bug was that you could actually have something like a wild card in the beginning, which would mean that this domain gets cut. For example, the browser was actually reading this as the thing that is before the null character. This would necessarily mean that the attacker has a certificate that says that it's paypal.com, but it's actually not that. If it had a wildcard certificate, it would match any domain. The certificate is for any domain because the browser thinks the thing before the *null* character is what the certificate is for. Whereas the certificate authority thought the thing after the *null* character is what it was for.

This is a typical example of what a disconnect could be. How do we really go about cataloging these disconnects? What are mismorphisms? Mismorphism is a disconnect between what the reality is, what the person actually imagines it to be, and the symbol that is used to signify the reality. You can see that the three are distinctly different. The same can actually be applied to a security setting where there is a reality, and there is what we think (the mental model) and then how it's actually represented in the wild. And there is a disconnect between these three, and this is what we are actually getting to in this paper.

© Springer Nature Switzerland AG 2020
J. Anderson et al. (Eds.): Security Protocols 2019, LNCS 12287, pp. 125–131, 2020.
https://doi.org/10.1007/978-3-030-57043-9_12

This paper also deals with LangSec. Language-Theoretic Security (LangSec) says that the parser, which is the first part of the code that actually processes any input, is literally a decider for the input. The parser decides if the input is something that is a part of the language or not, and only if it is a part of the language it accepts the input. If it is not a part of the language, then you let it out.

Parsers actually are an essential part of weird machines. A weird machine is something that processes some input, and it runs some unintended computation. The computation that a weird machine runs is not intended, but it's accidentally present by design. It could be through poor design, or it could be through the lack of knowledge that this language is actually not decidable sometimes. Weird machines could stem from a bunch of these reasons. Our insight over here is this that mismorphisms lie at the heart of these weird machines.

What we are doing over here is that we are describing how different programmers might have thought differently, leading to various bugs. We are cataloguing some past bugs that we encountered and, in this paper, we are trying to come up with a formal notation for how we think these mismorphisms could have occurred.

We use three standard notations in this paper. The first one is the interpretation equivalence, the second one is interpretation uncertainty, and the third one is interpretation inequivalence. Basically, the intuition over here is that there is a predicate P and then there are interpreters A_1 through A_k. If it's an interpretation equivalence, then the interpreters A_1 through A_k all think the same about the predicate. So they arrive at the equal truth value for the predicate. In case of the interpretation uncertainty there is at least one interpreter A_1 through A_k who thinks that the value is uncertain and we are not really sure if it's going to be true or false for that predicate. And I think the inequivalence is intuitive over here. It is the case that there is at least one A_1 through A_k whose value doesn't match the other ones.

These are just three examples of mismorphisms that we came up with. There are many more in our paper. One specific thing is the Ethereum DAO disaster where the language was actually not decidable, the O and the D over here are the oracle and the designer. The designer assumes that the language is decidable, but then, in reality, the language is not decidable. We've categorized it as an interpretation uncertainty there. Shotgun parsers are one of the root causes for LangSec or input handling bugs. What we mean is that there's a buffer B that the implementer assumes doesn't change over time, whereas in reality the buffer actually changes over time because it's a shotgun parser. A shotgun parser is basically a parser where you perform input handling and processing interspersed, so the LangSec principle is this that you perform all input handling distinctly, separate from the rest of your code. You validate all your input and then only start processing, whereas in a shotgun parser you do input handling and processing interspersed in your code. A shotgun parser would be categorized in this way.

Let us see a couple of examples of how we arrived at these mismorphisms. One example is the Heartbleed bug. In a standard request, you say that "If you're alive then just reply back with this particular string in it." And there are two length fields involved over here. There is a length field included within the heartbeat request, and there is a length field for the overall packet. And obviously, both need to match in some way. And over here you could say, "Send me this forty thousand letter word called blah" when in reality the word 'blah' is just four characters. There is a mismatch over here, and the two length fields should have been validated. You could basically say that there is a sanity check where the oracle, the designer, and the implementer's interpretations don't really match over here, and the length field should have been validated.

Another example is what I mentioned earlier: the null character bug. There are two parsers, P_1 and P_2. These two parsers are meant to be equivalent since they are endpoints of the same protocol. In reality, they represent the view of the oracle, the designer, and the implementer. Hence, it's inequivalence between their interpretations.

That brings me to the discussion questions. We were wondering what sort of user interface could we actually build to help protocol developers or protocol implementers to actually catalog these vulnerabilities or submit these vulnerabilities to some central entity that we could build. And, we were wondering how we could actually go about making such a thing useful. I'll leave the floor to a discussion.

Jonathan Anderson: It seems like one of the interfaces that's most relevant to things like the Heartbleed attack, even leaving aside for a moment the interface for submitting examples—it's just the complexity of APIs, in the sense that Heartbleed didn't happen because people didn't have APIs for validating fields, it was because it was too annoying to use them so they hand-rolled something that sucked. I guess if you're studying language security, are you also coming up with ideas that are relevant for designing interfaces in ways that developers will align reality with the expression of what their code is trying to do?

Reply: Yep, that's totally relevant. Because one important thing that we're looking at through this work is to actually understand how these mistakes actually occur. And then, how you can actually build language principles to avoid them from occurring and how you can actually build tools that would help a developer not make the same mistakes again and again.

Frank Stajano: This classification of things depending on how the interpreters differ in their interpretation of the predicate seems to me to be very sensitive to the set of interpreters that you have. So, if you have a bland or a stupid interpreter, then we all agree that something may in fact be wrong. We have to have ingenious or devious or creatively written interpreters to actually uncover the discrepancies that your method would then classify as a mismorphism.

So, where do these interpreters come from? What's the general method for, given a new vulnerability, saying, "well, let me now feed it to a sensibly diverse group of interpreters to see if there is a mismorphism."

Reply: The way we actually went about it was to understand how protocols are implemented. For example, in Heartbleed, there are a group of protocol designers, and there are a group of people who actually implement these protocols. You have a group of people who design it and a group of people who actually implement it, and then there's the reality. We were actually looking at these three groups, we were not looking at any random interpreter. We were just looking at people who actually have something to do with these protocols and their implementations.

Frank Stajano: Thank you.

Alastair Beresford: So are humans an interpreter as well? For example, if you ask for a certificate for a domain such as paypal.com or badguy.com, that's a valid sub-domain but people misinterpret part of that as paypal.com in some cases. Is that part of your model or not? Is that a helpful viewpoint?

Reply: I don't really know. Vijay?

Vijay Kothari: We were thinking about that. We didn't really discuss that specific example in the current iteration of the paper, but yes, it's very interesting, thank you.

Fabio Massacci: I want to keep going on Frank's point. It's actually an interesting idea. From the software engineering perspective, you say, "Well, let's ignore all the complexity of the internal structure, just look at the parser." If the two parsers of the CA and the parser of Firefox interpret the string in the same way, then there will be fewer errors later on. You think that this would be a feasible approach?

Reply: What you just said is what the whole field that we are working on, LangSec, is about. We are trying to say, "How do you build parsers based on the formal specification of a protocol?" To be able to say to each other, these two protocols are equivalent.

Fabio Massacci: What I meant is you want to test the interoperability of the parser only, rather than proving that the parser is correct. Parsers are very difficult beasts to formalise correctly.

Reply: The thing is that it also depends on the language of the protocol. It needs to be within the equivalence boundary of the Chomsky hierarchy. It cannot be beyond the equivalence boundary to be able even to say that these two are interoperable. It's not something that you can just have a robust set of test cases or fuzzing cases for it. To be able to prove that two parsers are equivalent, it has to be within a specific boundary on the Chomsky hierarchy.

Michael Millian: Prashant touched on this briefly, but we do use fuzzing to some degree to get at this. But he is absolutely right that to prove it in a formal sense, for all inputs, that they're going to handle it the same way, it takes a little bit more than just fuzzing, but it takes exactly the formal proof.

Jovan Powar: Further to that point, the software design aspect of it is essentially like unit testing in API, right? You throw a lot of stuff at it and make sure, not that they're correct but that they do the same thing. And that's attacking the problem from the downstream end of it, where you've got the design system and you're checking that it behaves correctly. And obviously that is much harder to do because of the problems faced get much bigger.

What do you think of the idea of attacking from the language point of view and trying declarative languages, where you have to compare the declaration of the API correctly and lots of different things, and then leave it up to the implementation of the language to do it, which reaches a much smaller problem space to prove the correctness of the language?

Reply: I think, right now one of the more significant problems is that specifications themselves are inadequate or unclear, which is why the implementers end up implementing them differently or end up missing sanity checks, for example.

One of the overall goals of the entire field of security should be to come up with a better way of describing specifications of protocols so that at least such vulnerabilities would be fewer.

I do agree with what you said.

Michael Millian: To partially answer that question and to be more specific about some of the flaws in specifications themselves, something that we see more frequently than we would like, is a specification for a protocol that has a state machine or some kind of formal description of what a packet should look like and what fields should look like. But then, in prose, the specification offers more description on that or puts extra constraints. So, if you don't read all of the prose carefully, you're going to end up with different implementations based on how closely you read the document.

Reply: There has been work, quite recently, on studying these state machines of various OpenSSL implementations in operating systems, and they did end up quite different from each other. In practice we have seen that, although there is a specification, the specification is written in a way that the implementations end up being significantly different from each other.

Lydia Kraus: Thanks, this is an interesting topic and I'm wondering when I see your questions on the discussion slide, what is your conceptual idea of the whole thing? Is it something like a translator that translates the designer's mental model to the programmer's mental model?

Reply: That's an excellent question. One of our more important motivations in the field of LangSec is to have formal specifications written in a way that it can translate to code in a one-to-one mapping way. So, yes. The answer is yes. To have a way that you can have a one-to-one mapping from what the designers mental model is to what the reality of the code is.

Sasa Radomirovic: I've collected a few follow-ups. I'll start with Alastair. This was the "Is a human a weird machine," question. I think phishing attacks would be a case where the human has one idea of what's going on, whereas the attacker is creating a different mental model to match. Then, a more recent discussion on specifications and then annotating it with text. I think a couple or more years ago at this workshop there was a suggestion that we specify protocols in a way that, if you deviate from the specification, when implemented your implementation just wouldn't be correct any more, it wouldn't interact with our clients. But it seems to be a very expensive way of making interactions work. If you haven't specified thing carefully, many cases do not work, because you deviate from the specification. But then on the other side, if you wanted to do this formally, that seems very expensive too. And in the end it seems to be only with one code base that is being shared among everybody in order to ensure that everything is being implemented the same.

I feel like I would use it now too. I'm wondering: can you do more than this?

Reply: I agree with what you said. There's not much we can do, which is why we want to discuss this.

Michael Millian: I, for one, and my lab more broadly, are strongly for the position, closely related to what you said, which is reducing to a single code base. The way I like to think of this is moving towards a world where parser writers don't really roll their own parser, the same way that crypto-library writers don't really roll their own crypto. You really need to know what you're doing to get this right, and so for all the protocols we should have a couple standard libraries that have been proven correct, and that everybody can just call. We don't have that yet. We're working on that. But I think that's the ideal world we should be moving towards.

Simon Foley: I guess for me, this is really my interpretation which is different from formal verification of the codebase. A remark: a couple of years ago, we looked at struts, which is an MVC implemented in Java and widely used. We looked at the security controls in that, and I'm thinking that what we saw in the mistakes, and the way they were implemented in the security control were very likely mismorphisms. What we'd done is over a 12 year period, we've looked at how vulnerabilities have been set out against that particular security control, and then the developers were in turn, fixing those vulnerabilities. And they made the same mistakes over and over again along with a bunch of other issues; we gave a presentation a couple of years ago here. I was thinking, what we saw were people misinterpreting a graph so the implementors of struts was misinterpreting this particular security control over and over again, and I'm trying to think, "Well, I wonder would it be useful, or how you might capture these things as mismorphisms."

It could also be useful for you if you wanted to do a study, to go back and look at something like struts that has a large number of vulnerabilities posted against it. A lot of them are the same kind of vulnerability as the one I spoke about yesterday about EquiFax is exactly the kind of vulnerability we'd been seeing five or ten years ago. And it might help you to identify patterns and mismorphisms that could be usable in a more general way.

Reply: What you describe is something that we can capture in our particular categorization. What you described is essentially a mismatch between what the designer intended with the API and what the implementer actually grasped from the API. It's something that we have looked at in specific instances, but we have not looked at one giant code base over a long period.

Simon Foley: Yeah, and in this case the designer was the implementer.

Reply: Oh, okay.

Simon Foley: A quick example would be as follows: the security control was doing whitelist checking against OGNL code that was being sent to the NBC in order to set internal settings and the designer would see a vulnerability posted and say, "oh, I must fix this", and as a sort of knee-jerk reaction would have said "oh, add some more checks," but they didn't think the problem through, and so they really only half-fixed it. You see this happening over and over again.

Now, describing each one, I think it could be described as a mismorphism. The bigger challenge is the fact that the designer, who designed it, didn't quite capture what they really intended. So, it's going back to the sort of social constructivism that they didn't engage in what was it that they were trying to describe and, just kind of getting into this half-baked fix.

Reply: Yeah, that's really interesting because, while we were looking through this, we were also looking at how a bug like Heartbleed originated, and how it was patched later on. So, the way the patch was implemented again was something we call a shotgun parser. It was patched in line and not in a separate place where you perform all the input validation first, and then go on to processing. I think it would be interesting to look at how bugs were patched later on and how the same mistakes were repeated.

Human Limitations in Security

Human Limitations in Security

Affordable Security or Big Guy vs Small Guy

Does the Depth of Your Pockets Impact Your Protocols?

Daniele Friolo[1], Fabio Massacci[2], Chan Nam Ngo[2(✉)], and Daniele Venturi[1]

[1] Sapienza University of Rome, Rome, Italy
{friolo,venturi}@di.uniroma1.it
[2] University of Trento, Trento, Italy
{fabio.massacci,channam.ngo}@unitn.it

Abstract. When we design a security protocol we assume that the humans (or organizations) playing Alice and Bob do not make a difference. In particular, their financial capacity seems to be irrelevant.

In the latest trend to guarantee that secure multi-party computation protocols are fair and not vulnerable to malicious aborts, a slate of protocols has been proposed based on penalty mechanisms. We look at two well-known penalty mechanisms, and show that the so-called see-saw mechanism (Kumaresan *et al.*, CCS 15), is only fit for people with deep pockets, well beyond the stake in the multi-party computation itself.

Depending on the scheme, *fairness is not affordable by everyone* which has several policy implications on protocol design. To explicitly capture the above issues, we introduce a new property called *financial fairness*.

1 Introduction

Multi-party computation (MPC) allows a set of mutually distrustful parties to compute a function of their secret inputs, in a distributed manner. MPC is an abstraction of several important cryptographic tasks, including, e.g. electronic auctions, voting, online gambling and lotteries, valuation of assets, and privacy-preserving data mining [30]. While its foundations have been laid in the 1980's by showing that every (polynomial-time) function can be computed securely via an MPC protocol [13,22,35], only recently MPC has become of practical interest.

The objective of this paper is to review, jointly, the economic fairness of MPC in conjunction with the shadow of the future.

Penalties as the Crypto-solution to MPC Unfairness. The security guarantees of MPC in the ideal world implies *privacy* (i.e., nothing but the output is revealed), *correctness* (i.e., the output is correctly computed), *independence of inputs* (i.e., a corrupted party cannot make its input dependent on the honest parties' inputs), *guaranteed output delivery* (i.e., corrupted parties are not able to prevent honest parties from receiving their output), and *fairness* (i.e., corrupted parties receive the output if and only if the honest parties do as well). Unfortunately, a seminal

J. Anderson et al. (Eds.): Security Protocols 2019, LNCS 12287, pp. 135–147, 2020.
https://doi.org/10.1007/978-3-030-57043-9_13

result of Cleve [15] shows that there are cryptographic tasks, such as coin tossing, for which fairness is unattainable when a majority of the parties are dishonest.

The introduction of decentralized payment systems, such as Bitcoin [33], gave rise to a new approach in how to obtain fairness even in applications without honest majority, in the form of *penalty mechanisms*. Each party publishes a transaction containing a time-locked deposit with amount, say, q, which can be redeemed by honest players after a certain amount of time, in case of malicious aborts during the protocol execution. If no malicious abort happens, the deposit can be withdrawn by the owner by redeeming the transaction upon completion of the protocol. This yields some fairness by a financial compensation [2,7].

Penalties and Financial (Un)fairness. While the above approach is certainly sound from the cryptographic perspective, and in fact it has been applied successfully from online poker [27] to fair exchange [17], to the best of our knowledge its soundness from the economics perspective is much less understood, and this is a potential issue as it is particularly important to consider security and economics objectives as one in Fintech applications [32].

In particular, the key assumption in all penalty-based-MPC protocols is that eventually honest parties would be made whole, and therefore it does not matter how much money they should put into escrow during the execution of the protocol. While this is true when q is a LaTeX symbol in a crypto paper, it is far from true when q is actual money in one's wallet or bank account: for most have-nots delayed payments look bad [10], and for the wealthy there is always the opportunity cost of not investing the money in better endeavours [29]. For example, in a classical experimental study [8], individuals asked to chose between immediate delivery of money and a deferred payment for amounts ranging from \$40 to \$5000 exhibited a discount rate very close to the official borrowing rate. These results are consistent across countries (e.g., [8] in the US and [1] in Germany). Individuals and companies exhibited varying degree of risk aversion [10,29] but they all agree that money paid or received "now" has a greater value than the same amount of money received or paid "later" [3].

In this paper we look at two penalty mechanisms and show that one of them is only fit for the "big guy" with even bigger pockets, well beyond the money at stake in the MPC itself. "Small guys" have no options but either rushing to be first, or participating to the protocol would simply be out of their pocket. In summary, *cryptographic fairness and financial fairness are not the same*, which has several policy implications on protocol design.

2   MPC and Fairness

Table 1 lists some attacks to fairness in real-world scenarios for MPC. For instance, in poker (Texas hold'em), a player might abort the protocol, to avoid any monetary loss, after he learns that his own cards are not good enough to win the current hand. Similar issues apply to all card games involving online

Table 1. Real-world examples where an attacker might take advantage by aborting the protocol before the honest parties learn the output

Application	Attack
Poker	The adversary in the last round, upon seeing all cards (including his own secret faced down card), learns that he will lose and aborts
Lottery	The adversary in the last round, sees the final number, learns that he is not the winner and aborts
Digital exchange	The seller receives the payment and decides to abort without sending the digital good to the buyer

gambling. Fairness is also a big issue in *digital auctions*[1] and *digital exchanges* (e.g. [31]), where any of the sellers could defraud an hypothetical buyer by aborting the protocol right after receiving the payment.

Given Cleve's impossibility result, several works attempted to find mitigation to the fairness problem. Examples include achieving fairness for specific functionalities [4,23,24], relaxing the security definition in several ways [11,19,20], and using a public bulletin board [14]. For instance, Cachin and Camenish [11] consider a model where a partially trusted third party is used in the real world to restore fairness (without taking part to the actual protocol), whereas Pinkas [34] achieves fairness by using a variant of timed-commitments and blind signatures.

As mentioned in the introduction, a recent major trend is to guarantee some form of fairness via penalty mechanisms, and those systems go greatly with decentralized coins, as we illustrate in the next section.

3   Penalty Mechanisms as the Universal Cure

The idea of achieving fairness via financial compensation through penalty mechanisms originates in the work by Andrychowicz *et al.* [2]. In particular, their penalty mechanism is based on Bitcoin. The idea here is that a malicious player is discouraged to abort the protocol prematurely, as the latter would cause a financial loss, used as a compensation for the honest players, that is larger than what the player would actually lose if he remained in the protocol.

At the beginning of the protocol, in order to engage in the penalty mechanism, the players need to deposit some amount of coins, in a so-called *escrow account*. In practice, however, one cannot initialize a penalty mechanism with a self-claimed account, since the cash that gets deposited into the escrow account

---

[1] The most cited example is the Danish sugar beet auction, where 1200 farmers auctioned their production [9]. However, an actual reading of the paper reveals that only three servers performed MPC over the secret shares generated by the bidders. One server was run by researchers, whereas the other two servers were run by industry associations. In such a set-up, fairness was not an issue because individual bidders did not actually run the MPC protocol, and thus could not abort it.

must originate from a system where each transaction is acknowledged by every party, as in, e.g., Zerocash [6]. This allows everybody to publicly verify validity of the transactions resulting from the protocol's operations, and thus to credit each account with the due amount, thus making the employment of penalty mechanisms in tandem with digital currencies a natural design choice.

A penalty mechanism is implemented as a sequence of *claim-or-refund transactions* (CRT). Intuitively, a CRT allows a payer to *conditionally send* some money to a payee. The payee will receive the money if s/he presents a satisfying assignment (or witness) to a predicate specified by the payer in the condition, e.g. s/he has sent the output to all parties in the computation phase. Typically, the CRT can be redeemed only after a certain time, which allows honest players to redeem the transaction first in case they did terminate the protocol.

Subsequent work refined the idea of using penalty mechanisms and financial compensation to better fit real-world settings of interest, as we summarize in Table 2. We describe two popular penalty mechanisms in the next section. For further discussions related to incentives, see [5].

Table 2. Penalty protocols

Paper	Type of penalty system
Secure MPC with penalties	
KB16 [26]	CRTs, secure function evaluation with ordered output delivery, and the see-saw mechanism [27]
ADMM14 [2]	"Timed commitments" [34] on Bitcoin
KMSWP16 [25]	Secure function evaluation with penalties, realized via Ethereum smart contracts
Poker	
KMB15 [27]	CRTs and the see-saw mechanism
DDL17 [16]	Stateful contracts, and publicly verifiable checkpoints on the blockchain
Lottery	
ADMM14 [2]	General-purpose MPC with penalties with Bitcoin scripts
Digital exchange	
GBGN17 [21]	Escrow protocols and fair exchange (special case of fair comp.)

4   The See-Saw and Hawk Penalty Mechanisms

The See-Saw Mechanism. Kumaresan *et al.* [27,28] design MPC protocols for a special functionality called *secure cash distribution with penalties* (SCD). SCD includes an initial deposit phase where all parties must freeze some money. Afterwards, during the computation phase, the players provide inputs and obtain the outputs. In the distribution phase, the deposited money is redistributed among the parties (possibly according to the output of the computation phase). SCD is *drop-out tolerant*: any party aborting during the computation phase will have to pay penalties to all parties using their deposit. The protocol can be made reactive by allowing multiple stages during the computation phase.

The crucial contribution of [27] and [28] is the *see-saw mechanism*, which provides a way to keep the cash deposited in *escrow*. As such it forces the parties to reveal their next message during the computation phase in a round-robin fashion. The witness required by the CRTs to release the funds refer to a subset of parties that learned the output (up to the current step of the reveal phase), and if the payee releases his transcript to the next player, then receives the money. In practice, a CRT can be realized using either Bitcoin scripting language (albeit not widely supported), or a Turing-complete language, as e.g. in Ethereum [18]. The sequence of deposits is claimed in the *reverse* order.

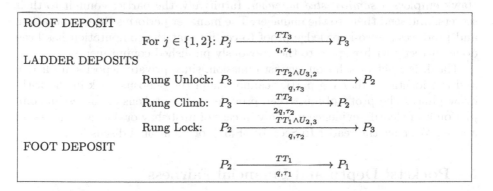

Fig. 1. Locked Ladder mechanism of [27], in the case of 3 parties. We write $P_i \xrightarrow[kq,\tau_{2i-1}]{TT_j} P_j$ as a shorthand for "P_i deposits kq coins in the escrow, that can be redeemed by P_j if and only if he exhibits a valid transcript TT_j before the timeout τ_{2i-1} in the reveal phase". The value $U_{i,j}$ is the dummy token that *locks* the CRT in order to avoid coalition attacks.

The see-saw mechanism leverages two sub-mechanisms: the locking and the ladder mechanisms (Fig. 1). Using the locking mechanism, a CRT is "locked" until all the transactions before it have been claimed. A party P_i that has to move after a party P_j will need to obtain a dummy token $U_{i,j}$ from P_j as a part of the condition of the CRT from P_j to P_i, while party P_j can only claim one's own CRTs (in the rounds before P_i) if s/he presents $U_{i,j}$ for P_i in the next round.

As for the locked ladder mechanism, the protocol proceeds in three subphases: roof, ladder, and foot deposit. In the roof deposit phase each party P_j

$(1 \leq j \leq n-1)$ sends a CRT to P_n. After that, it starts the ladder deposits sequence where (a) in the Rung Unlock step, each party P_i $(2 \leq i \leq n-1)$ receives a locked deposit from each party P_j $(1 \leq j \leq i+1)$; (b) in the Rung Climb step, a party P_i receives a CRT from P_{i+1}; and (c) in the Rung Lock step, a party P_j $(1 \leq j \leq i+1)$ receives a locked deposit from P_i. Finally, after the foot deposit phase, the deposits are claimed in reverse order.

The parties must stake an *increasing deposit in a fixed order*, since order of revelation is important for the see-saw mechanism to work [27, p. 7]. This might interfere with security goals if who started the process ought to be confidential.

The Hawk Mechanism. Another penalty mechanism is the one introduced in Hawk [25, Appendix G, §B]. Here, all parties first run an off-chain secret sharing based MPC protocol where each party receives its own share of the output. Then in an on-chain protocol, all parties start by depositing some money that can only be claimed after sending the corresponding share of the output. An aborting party's deposit is redistributed among the honest parties.

To handle the secure computation and enforcing a correct cash distribution, Hawk employs a *semi-trusted manager*. Intuitively, the parties commit to their secrets, and send them to the manager. The manager performs the computation, and produces a zero-knowledge proof to certify that the computation has been done correctly with respect to the previously published commitments.

Hawk is a better solution against omission, since private deposits are frozen and the identified aborting parties cannot claim the deposits back in the withdraw phase. The protocol must then provide security tokens of successful completion and identify evidence not only in case of misbehavior, but also in case of aborts. We refer the reader to Sect. 10 of [31] for additional discussion.

5   Pockets' Depth and Financial Fairness

The experimental evidence about inter-temporal economic choices is that money paid or received "now" has a greater value than the same amount of money received or paid "later". As a result, the present valuation of a quantity of money received later is discounted by what is called a *discount rate*. Such discount rate may depend on the level of risk aversions [29], or on the confidence in the certainty of future payments and on life expectancy [10]. The discount function may also have different functional forms (e.g. exponential, hyperbolic, etc.) and may have different values for borrowing or receiving money, as well as depend on the amount that is actually at stake [3].

The basic model is sufficient for our purposes[2]: a quantity of money q received after a time t is exponentially discounted at a constant discount rate Δ, i.e.

$$q_{now} = \begin{cases} qe^{-\delta t} & \text{(continuous case)} \\ q\frac{1}{(1+\Delta)^t} & \text{(discrete case)} \end{cases} \tag{1}$$

---

[2] More sophisticated models actually exacerbates our findings.

To provide a basic reference value for Δ, the rates for several central banks as measured on December, 30 2018 are reported in Table 3. They are the rate at which commercial banks can borrow money from the central bank to adjust their capital requirements. The value of the continuous rate or discrete rate from Eq. (1) can be easily inverted from one another by equating the compounding period: a yearly rate of 0.25% corresponds to a continuous rate of 0.223%.

Table 3. Sample of Central Banks Rates

Institution	Instrument	Overnight	Hourly
Bank of England[7]	Bank Rate	0.75%	0.062%
Central European Bank[8]	Marginal Lending Facility	0.25%	0.021%

At this point we want to analyze how the different penalty mechanisms behave in terms of their inter-temporal choices, as we have described in Sect 4.

Hawk by Kosba et al. [25] is rather straightforward in this respect. Everybody has to deposit the same amount at the same time and can withdraw it as soon as the semi-trusted manager has done its job.

See-Saw by Kumaresan et al. [27] requires a more careful analysis, as the inter-temporal payment schedule by the parties is clearly different even in the three-party case of Fig. 1: P_1 only makes a roof deposit, whereas P_2 makes both a foot deposit and a rung lock deposit, and P_3 must make two ladder deposits, one of them for twice the amount of coins.

To provide a visual feeling of how a protocol treats its parties, Fig. 2 illustrates the amount of coins deposited during the first phase (in red), and the coins withdrew in the last 5 steps (in blue). During the reveal phase, we represent the withdrawals as a deposit decrease for each of the three player (P_1, P_2 and P_3).

Figure 3 shows what happens with four parties. The protocol is twice longer, and the highest deposit is also larger, being proportional to the number of parties. Essentially, the first party P_1 must only deposit q into the escrow and immediately after the half of the protocol steps (at $t = 11$) is made whole again. For the protocol security design this is necessary, as P_1 is the party who makes available the result first to the other parties in the MPC.

The second party P_2 must have bigger pockets than P_1: before the protocol gets to the release phase, it had to deposit four times the amount of P_1. Yet, its treatment is slightly more favorable than P_3 and P_4 who have to lock into the escrow during the deposit phase (red) almost five times more coins than P_1 (and 20% more than P_2) for almost 50% longer time before they can withdraw them during the release phase (blue). If q is actual dollars instead of q, they are not going to be happy.

It is true that P_1's deposit is earlier in the protocol, so it is more valuable than the later deposits of P_3, and the even those of P_4. However, the distance is

142   D. Friolo et al.

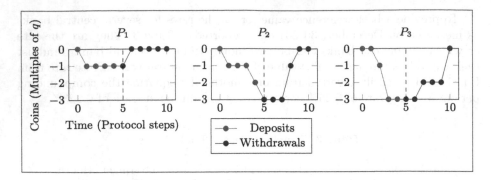

Fig. 2. Deposits and withdrawals in Kumaresan's See-Saw mechanism [27], in the case of 3 parties. Party P_1 has to keep into the escrow a much smaller amount of coins q during the deposit phase (red), and can withdraw them earlier in the reveal phase (blue) than P_2 and P_3, who gets the worst of it. (Color figure online)

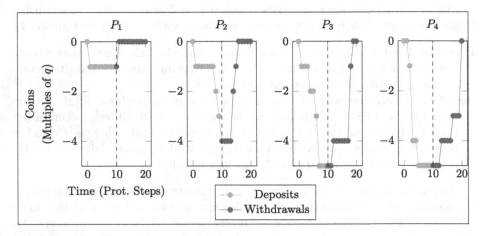

Fig. 3. Deposits and withdrawals in Kumaresan's See-Saw mechanism [27], in the case of 4 parties. (Color figure online)

not so large to justify such a five-fold increase. Not even hyper-inflation would make up for the difference in the deposit.

To provide a quantitative valuation of the qualitative analysis above, we consider the *poker* case [27], where every party assumes to obtain the same reward at the end (scoop the plate). We introduce a definition of what makes a protocol financially fair.

Definition 1. *Let i be a party of a protocol with a final identical reward, $c_i(t, \pi)$ be the down payments that party i is asked to commit at step $t \geq 0$ of the execution path π, and let Δ_i be the discount rate of party i. A cryptographic protocol with a common reward is financially fair iff for every pair of parties i and j, and every execution path $\pi_{i,j}$ involving parties i and j,*

$$\sum_t c_i(t, \pi_{i,j}) \frac{1}{(1 + \Delta_i)^t} = \sum_t c_j(t, \pi_{i,j}) \frac{1}{(1 + \Delta_j)^t}. \tag{2}$$

We can now calculate the results of the outcome for each player for the plain execution in the case where everything goes smoothly. For simplicity we assume that all actors have the same discount rate, and calculate the *net present value* (NPV) of Kumaresan's See-Saw mechanism for each party.

$$NPV(P_1, \Delta, q) = -\frac{q}{1 + \Delta} + \frac{q}{(1 + \Delta)^6} \tag{3}$$

$$NPV(P_2, \Delta, q) = -\frac{q}{(1 + \Delta)} - \frac{q}{(1 + \Delta)^4} - \frac{q}{(1 + \Delta)^5}$$
$$+ \frac{2q}{(1 + \Delta)^8} + \frac{q}{(1 + \Delta)^9} \tag{4}$$

$$NPV(P_3, \Delta, q) = -\frac{q}{(1 + \Delta)^2} - \frac{2q}{(1 + \Delta)^3} + \frac{q}{(1 + \Delta)^7} + \frac{2q}{(1 + \Delta)^{10}} \tag{5}$$

A similar analysis can be done for four parties, and we have written a small Java program that, for a given Δ, computes the net present value, and hence the financial fairness, for all parties. Table 4 reports the corresponding value for a range of discount rate, including those of the Central Banks listed in Table 3.

Table 4. Net present value of Kumaresan's See-Saw [27] for $q = 100\$$ and three parties

	NPV by Discount Rate		
Party	0%	0.021%	0.062%
P_1	0$	−0.08$	−0.25$
P_2	0$	−0.25$	−0.74$
P_3	0$	−0.27$	−0.80$

Even under the simplified assumption that the discount rate does not depend on the amount of deposit locked into an escrow and with constant exponential discount, Kumaresan's See-Saw protocol is only financially fair for a discount rate of 0%, when money cost nothing. A moderate discount rate of 0.75%, well below the US Federal Rate, would make the protocol significantly unfair for P_2 and P_3 wrt P_1.

Proposition 1. *Kumaresan's See-Saw mechanism is financially unfair for a uniform deposit quota $q_1 = q_2 = q_3 = q$, and a discount rate $\Delta > 0$ that is constant across the parties.*

Notice that for P_2 and P_3 the net present value is close, so that the protocol could be adjusted by asking P_3 to deposit a smaller value than P_2 an so on. Put differently, *it is possible to achieve financial fairness if we ask parties to pay a different amount.* Once the distribution of inter-temporal deposits and withdrawals is known, a protocol can be made financially fair by setting different deposit quotas, i.e. equating $NPV(P_1, \Delta, q_1) = NPV(P_2, \Delta, q_2) = NPV(P_3, \Delta, q_3)$, and solving for q_1, q_2 and q_3. Notice that such solutions depend on the discount rate Δ, and thus different discount rates might imply different values of q_i.

Proposition 2. *For the continuous discount rate of 0.223% and a stake of $q = 100\$$, Kumaresan's See-Saw mechanism would be financially fair up to 1¢ for three parties by setting $q_1 = q = 100\$$, $q_2 = 33\$$, $q_3 = 31\$$.*

Table 5 shows the deposit and withdrawal schedule that each party should make to make the protocol fair. Different levels of risk aversions or risk seeking (after all we are talking about poker) might be applicable. In particular the large difference between q_1 and q_2, q_3 may generate different behaviors. The acceptability of this theoretical scheme may be the subject of an experimental paper.

Table 5. Deposit/Withdrawal adjustments to make Kumaresan's See-Saw mechanism financially fair for a stake $q = 100\$$ and a continuous discount rate $\Delta = 0.062\%$.

P	1	2	3	4	5 ·	Maximum · Deposit ·	6	7	8	9	10
	...... Deposit Phase							.... Reveal Phase			
						Original See-Saw Protocol					
P_1	-100\$				·	**-100\$**	· +100\$				
P_2	-100\$		-100\$	-100\$ ·		**-300\$**	·		+100\$	+100\$	
P_3		-100\$	-200\$		·	**-300\$**	·	+100\$			+200\$
						Adjusted Protocol for financial fairness at discount rate $\Delta = 0.062\%$					
P_1	-100\$				·	**-100\$**	· +100\$				
P_2	-33\$		-33\$	-33\$ ·		**-99\$**	·		+66\$	+33\$	
P_3		-31\$	-62\$		·	**-93\$**	·	+31\$			+62\$

Even if money costs nothing, a gap in the financial capacity makes a huge difference when large amounts at stake, as apparent from Figs. 2–3, and Table 5.

Consider, for instance, a real futures market, as described in [31]: the single smallest contract has a value of 1 million (real) dollars.

In the worst case with N traders, the required deposit to some traders is $(2N-3)q$. In a low-frequency market (Lean-Hog futures, Lean Hog LHZ7) there are only few tens of traders (Table 3 from [31] reports 15–33 traders), but still the last trader would have to deposit assets 67x times the stake of the trader completing last, and in large markets (Eurodollar GEH0 from Table 3 in [31] reports between 14–520 traders, with an average of 200 traders) more than 1037x times larger.

While these deposits would be returned at the end of the protocol, during the protocol's execution some traders would have to deposit around one billion dollars in an escrow account to make an order worth one million!

6 Design Implications and Conclusions

Financial fairness implies novel failure modes and novel design challenges for protocol designers: *If the inter-temporal distribution of money is important for the end users, then understanding how a penalty mechanism locks and releases escrow deposits to the players is critical for its success.*

Indeed, if the humans (or organizations) embodying Alice and Bob are unhappy of the way actual money is distributed, then they are not going to use the protocol, no matter how secure and cryptographically fair it claims to be. Put simply, Kumaresan's See-Saw mechanism [27] is not affordable by everyone.

Our work highlights several important research questions. For instance: Can we enrich the standard security definition of some MPC tasks of interest, such as decentralized poker or multi-party lotteries, so that it directly accounts for financial fairness? Can we design penalty mechanisms that provably achieve financial fairness in those applications? Answering the above questions in the affirmative would have important consequences on secure protocol design, as it would allow, e.g., to prove a composition theorem, in the style of [12], enabling to use sub-protocols as parts of more complex protocols in a modular way, while automatically keeping financial and cryptographic fairness. We leave exploring these directions as future research.

Acknowledgment. This work is part of CyberSec4Europe (cybersec4europe.eu), a project that has received funding from the European Union's Horizon 2020 research and innovation programme H2020-SU-ICT-03-2018 under grant agreement No. 830929.

References

1. Ahlbrecht, M., Weber, M.: An empirical study on intertemporal decision making under risk. Manage. Sci. **43**(6), 813–826 (1997)
2. Andrychowicz, M., Dziembowski, S., Malinowski, D., Mazurek, L.: Secure multi-party computations on bitcoin. In: Proceedings of IEEE SSP, pp. 443–458 (2014). https://doi.org/10.1109/SP.2014.35
3. Angeletos, G.M., Laibson, D., Repetto, A., Tobacman, J., Weinberg, S.: The hyperbolic consumption model: calibration, simulation, and empirical evaluation. J. Econ. Persp. **15**(3), 47–68 (2001)
4. Asharov, G., Beimel, A., Makriyannis, N., Omri, E.: Complete characterization of fairness in secure two-party computation of boolean functions. In: Dodis, Y., Nielsen, J.B. (eds.) TCC 2015. LNCS, vol. 9014, pp. 199–228. Springer, Heidelberg (2015). https://doi.org/10.1007/978-3-662-46494-6_10
5. Azouvi, S., Hicks, A., Murdoch, S.J.: Incentives in security protocols. In: Matyáš, V., Švenda, P., Stajano, F., Christianson, B., Anderson, J. (eds.) Security Protocols 2018. LNCS, vol. 11286, pp. 132–141. Springer, Cham (2018). https://doi.org/10.1007/978-3-030-03251-7_15
6. Ben-Sasson, E., Chiesa, A., Garman, C., Green, M., Miers, I., Tromer, E., Virza, M.: Zerocash: decentralized anonymous payments from bitcoin. In: Proceedings of IEEE SSP, pp. 459–474 (2014)
7. Bentov, I., Kumaresan, R.: How to use bitcoin to design fair protocols. In: Garay, J.A., Gennaro, R. (eds.) CRYPTO 2014. LNCS, vol. 8617, pp. 421–439. Springer, Heidelberg (2014). https://doi.org/10.1007/978-3-662-44381-1_24
8. Benzion, U., Rapoport, A., Yagil, J.: Discount rates inferred from decisions: an experimental study. Manage. Sci. **35**(3), 270–284 (1989)

9. Bogetoft, P., et al.: Secure multiparty computation goes live. In: Dingledine, R., Golle, P. (eds.) FC 2009. LNCS, vol. 5628, pp. 325–343. Springer, Heidelberg (2009). https://doi.org/10.1007/978-3-642-03549-4_20

10. Brown, J.R., Ivković, Z., Weisbenner, S.: Empirical determinants of intertemporal choice. J. Financ. Econ. **116**(3), 473–486 (2015)

11. Cachin, C., Camenisch, J.: Optimistic fair secure computation. In: Bellare, M. (ed.) CRYPTO 2000. LNCS, vol. 1880, pp. 93–111. Springer, Heidelberg (2000). https://doi.org/10.1007/3-540-44598-6_6

12. Canetti, R.: Universally composable security: a new paradigm for cryptographic protocols. In: Proceedings of IEEE FOCS, pp. 136–145 (2001)

13. Chaum, D., Crépeau, C., Damgård, I.: Multiparty unconditionally secure protocols (extended abstract). In: Proceedings of ACM STOC, pp. 11–19 (1988)

14. Choudhuri, A.R., Green, M., Jain, A., Kaptchuk, G., Miers, I.: Fairness in an unfair world: fair multiparty computation from public bulletin boards. In: Proceedings of ACM CCS, pp. 719–728 (2017)

15. Cleve, R.: Limits on the security of coin flips when half the processors are faulty (extended abstract). In: Proceedings of ACM STOC. pp. 364–369 (1986)

16. David, B., Dowsley, R., Larangeira, M.: Kaleidoscope: an efficient poker protocol with payment distribution and penalty enforcement. In: Meiklejohn, S., Sako, K. (eds.) FC 2018. LNCS, vol. 10957, pp. 500–519. Springer, Heidelberg (2018). https://doi.org/10.1007/978-3-662-58387-6_27

17. Dziembowski, S., Eckey, L., Faust, S.: Fairswap: How to fairly exchange digital goods. In: Proceedings of ACM CCS. pp. 967–984 (2018)

18. Ethereum: a next-generation smart contract and decentralized application platform (2015)

19. Even, S., Goldreich, O., Lempel, A.: A randomized protocol for signing contracts. Commun. ACM **28**(6), 637–647 (1985)

20. Garay, J.A., MacKenzie, P.D., Prabhakaran, M., Yang, K.: Resource fairness and composability of cryptographic protocols. J. Cryptol. **24**(4), 615–658 (2011). https://doi.org/10.1007/11681878_21

21. Goldfeder, S., Bonneau, J., Gennaro, R., Narayanan, A.: Escrow protocols for cryptocurrencies: how to buy physical goods using bitcoin. In: Kiayias, A. (ed.) FC 2017. LNCS, vol. 10322, pp. 321–339. Springer, Cham (2017). https://doi.org/10.1007/978-3-319-70972-7_18

22. Goldreich, O., Micali, S., Wigderson, A.: How to play any mental game or a completeness theorem for protocols with honest majority. In: Proceedings of ACM STOC, pp. 218–229 (1987)

23. Gordon, S.D., Hazay, C., Katz, J., Lindell, Y.: Complete fairness in secure two-party computation. J. ACM **58**(6), 24:1–24:37 (2011)

24. Gordon, S.D., Katz, J.: Complete fairness in multi-party computation without an honest majority. In: Reingold, O. (ed.) TCC 2009. LNCS, vol. 5444, pp. 19–35. Springer, Heidelberg (2009). https://doi.org/10.1007/978-3-642-00457-5_2

25. Kosba, A., Miller, A., Shi, E., Wen, Z., Papamanthou, C.: Hawk: the blockchain model of cryptography and privacy-preserving smart contracts. In: Proceedings of IEEE SSP, pp. 839–858 (2016)

26. Kumaresan, R., Bentov, I.: Amortizing secure computation with penalties. In: Proceedings of ACM CCS, pp. 418–429 (2016). https://doi.org/10.1145/2976749.2978424

27. Kumaresan, R., Moran, T., Bentov, I.: How to use bitcoin to play decentralized poker. In: Proceedings of ACM CCS, pp. 195–206 (2015)

28. Kumaresan, R., Vaikuntanathan, V., Vasudevan, P.N.: Improvements to secure computation with penalties. In: Proceedings of ACM CCS, pp. 406–417 (2016)
29. Lee, B., Veld-Merkoulova, Y.: Myopic loss aversion and stock investments: an empirical study of private investors. J. Bank. Fin. **70**, 235–246 (2016)
30. Lindell, Y., Pinkas, B.: Secure multiparty computation for privacy-preserving data mining. IACR Crypto. ePrint Ar. 2008 (2008)
31. Massacci, F., Ngo, C.N., Nie, J., Venturi, D., Williams, J.: FuturesMEX: secure, distributed futures market exchange. In: Proceedings of IEEE SSP, pp. 453–471 (2018). https://doi.org/10.1109/SP.2018.00028
32. Massacci, F., Ngo, C.N., Nie, J., Venturi, D., Williams, J.: The seconomics (security-economics) vulnerabilities of decentralized autonomous organizations. In: Stajano, F., Anderson, J., Christianson, B., Matyáš, V. (eds.) Security Protocols 2017. LNCS, vol. 10476, pp. 171–179. Springer, Cham (2017). https://doi.org/10.1007/978-3-319-71075-4_19
33. Nakamoto, S.: Bitcoin: a peer-to-peer electronic cash system (2008)
34. Pinkas, B.: Fair secure two-party computation. In: Biham, E. (ed.) EUROCRYPT 2003. LNCS, vol. 2656, pp. 87–105. Springer, Heidelberg (2003). https://doi.org/10.1007/3-540-39200-9_6
35. Yao, A.C.: How to generate and exchange secrets (extended abstract). In: Proc. of IEEE FOCS. pp. 162–167 (1986), https://doi.org/10.1109/SFCS.1986.25

Affordable Security or Big Guy vs Small Guy (Transcript of Discussion)

Chan Nam Ngo(✉)

University of Trento, IT, Trento, Italy
channam.ngo@unitn.it

Our talk today is about "Affordable Security" and we dub it "Big Guy versus Small Guy" in the sense that Big Guys are the one who have a lot of money and Small Guys are the poor guys.

Here we are referring to the MPC Fairness problem. Just in case you don't know what is MPC: it is the short form of Secure Multiparty Computation which allows some mutual distrusting parties to jointly compute a global function without revealing their secret inputs to each other. MPC guarantees many security properties but among them this one (MPC Fairness) is the most interesting one to us: it guarantees that the corrupted parties only obtain the outputs if the honest parties do.

This property has an interesting impact in real life applications. For example, in poker MPC, when you are the one who move last and you have already seen all the cards so you know that you are not winning, without Fairness you can just take back your stake and leave ... Obviously this is not what we want. The same happens to lottery: when you see the final number, you know that you are not going to win, without Fairness, again, you can just take back your stake and leave ...

MPC Fairness can be guaranteed if there is honest majority among parties (e.g. if we implement the MPC using secret sharing techniques, more than half of the parties is needed to reconstruct the final outcome [1]). Without honest majority there is no "real solution" to this MPC Fairness problem. There are however some workarounds, e.g. penalizing the corrupted parties and compensating the honest parties in MPC does provide some form of MPC Fairness.

Several solutions exist in the market, e.g. Secure Computation with Coins, brought to you by the bright minds of MIT. In particular, there were several algorithms that have been published in Crypto '14 [2], CCS '15 [3] and CCS '16 [4]. Among them, let us take a look at the See-Saw mechanism (CCS '15). In our talk today let us actually run this protocol for real. Note that the protocol is secure but not ours, so if during the run there is something happens to your pocket: all disclaimers apply!

In fact there is also another mechanism that provides "penalty as a solution to MPC Fairness" which is called the Hawk mechanism (S&P '16, [5]) but in our talk today we will mostly focus in See-Saw. The idea of "penalty as a solution to MPC Fairness" is pretty simple: 1) you ask everybody to deposit in escrow before starting the MPC; and then 2) you run the MPC; 3) after the MPC each party can withdraw the deposit only if it can present a proof of participation

J. Anderson et al. (Eds.): Security Protocols 2019, LNCS 12287, pp. 148–156, 2020.
https://doi.org/10.1007/978-3-030-57043-9_14

(obtained in the second step of this protocol). Obviously the aborting parties cannot show the proof of participation because they didn't participate! So they cannot withdraw. And we can use that deposit of the aborting parties as a compensation to the parties that actually did the MPC. That is why this is only a workaround, not a real solution, because the honest parties still don't obtain the output (but they are compensated).

So, everybody happy? No, unfortunately not ... Because for penalty to make sense the money have to be real, which means that all the deposits and the withdrawals are actual fund transfers: 1) What if a party must deposit more than another one? We will see this when we run the protocol; and 2) what if a party must deposit more than what it is worth comparing to the outcome of the MPC? and 3) certainly a party will want to deposit as late as possible and withdraw as early as possible because they don't want to keep their money locked in escrow for too long time, especially when they need to borrow the money to run the MPC, e.g. the poor guys don't have enough money to put in escrow so they have to borrow it from a bank and interest rates certainly apply here ...

So, old problem solved, which we call the Crypto Fairness, but unfortunately new problem introduced, which we call Financial Fairness. We are going to have five participants (Bruce, Martin U, Alastair, Martin K, Vashek) to join our little experiment: it will be moderated by Fabio Massacci and we ask the base chip to be only one.

Fabio Massacci: It's 1 GBP for winning (putting down 1 GBP on the table), if you would win.

Reply: Yes, 1 GBP for the winner. The base chip is only 1: EUR, GBP, USD are all welcomed. We are going to proceed in rounds. In each round we will ask you to give us some money (deposit step), or we will give you back some money (withdrawal step).

To simplify the MPC, we have asked each participant to write down a secret random number in a piece of paper which we will simply: open, compute the sum, divide it by 5 and plus 1. The participant of the corresponding index will be the winner.

This is the See-Saw algorithm for the case of three parties (show the slide with the algorithm in Fig. 1 of the main paper): 1) it starts with the roof deposit phase in which everybody gives money to the last guy; then 2) it proceeds to the ladder deposit phase which consists of three different steps of rung unlock, rung climb, and rung lock, in which the parties give money to each other in escrow; and finally 3) the floor deposit phase in which the second party gives the money to the first party in escrow.

Fabio Massacci: So I will start collecting. I think first I need the roof deposit. So, 1 GBP each please. Thank you ... (collecting the money) I will collect whoever is ready first. Thank you ...

So, the roof deposit is done. Okay, so now we have rung unlock. Okay, very good. Rung unlock: Vashek, 5 GBP ... You cannot complain unless you want to abort in which case you lose already your 1 GBP. I need 1 GBP from Martin K. So, I need 1 GBP from you (Martin K), Thank you! Oh, sorry, yes. Vashek, 1 GBP. Okay, so now we are done.

We move to the next step. Rung climb: Vashek, one more GBP. Okay, now Martin K, we need 4 GBP.

Martin Kleppmann: What?

Fabio Massacci: It's free, it's the protocol, I mean ...

Martin Kleppmann: I'm not sure I understand this protocol. I'm out of GBP coins.

Fabio Massacci: So, you are the poor people. You've lost already your two GBP coins.

Reply: You cannot afford the security, we are very sorry.

Fabio Massacci: So Alastair, we need two GBP from you. Now, I think we are done with the rung climb. Except, unfortunately, Martin K has aborted.

Now, we go to rung lock. Martin K, you owe one more GBP but you are gone. So, now, Alastair, one more GBP. And now we are finally at rung climb: Alastair, 1 GBP. Now we are in rung lock, so the last step. Good. Alastair, two more GBP.

Martin Ukrop: In case you didn't notice there are two more things in the protocol.

Fabio Massacci: No, your time is coming, don't worry.

Martin Ukrop: That's exactly why I'm worried.

Fabio Massacci: So, now, you (Martin U) only have to give 4 GBP. Okay, we're done. Thank you for your custom. So, I think we can go over to the next.

Reply: Okay, so unfortunately Martin K cannot proceed. But if everything went well, in the end, Bruce only need to deposit 1 GBP. Martin U has to deposit 5 GBP. Alastair has to deposit 6 GBP. Martin K has to deposit 7 GBP, but he cannot afford it. And Vashek needs to deposit 7 GBP.

So, the problem is clear, right? Martin K has to *deposit 7 GBP*, just to *win 1 GBP*. This is just to visualise what is the problem (show the slide with Fig. 2 in the main paper). Some parties only need to deposit a few coins, but the other parties, especially the one who move last, have to deposit much, much more. This is the case of four parties (show the slide with Fig. 3 in the main paper), so, the first one only need to deposit 1 GBP, but the last one has to deposit 5 GBP.

Let's consider a real life example: if you are building an MPC for futures trading which actually has from 10 to 500 parties. This is what we are going to see (Table 1). In a low trading day, with only 15 traders, in the worst case you have to deposit 27 times the amount that you need to deposit as a base unit q. And in the high day, you need 67q.

Table 1. Penalty as a solution to fairness [3] in futures trading

Market	Lean hog		EURdollar	
Days	#Parties	Deposit	#Parties	Deposit
Low	15	27q	14	25q
Normal	17	33q	199	395q
High	33	67q	520	1037q

Martin Ukrop: We are supposed to deposit extra GBP from the starting 1 GBP, deterministic? If we were to run this again with the same examples, it would be exactly this way?

Fabio Massacci: Yes.

Martin Ukrop: Okay, thanks.

Reply: Yes, it is deterministic, and everybody has to move in fixed order. What if you are talking about EURdollar futures? So, for a EURdollar contract, which is 1 million USD per contract, and we are only talking about one contract here, and in one round. If you have more than 500 traders, you need to *deposit 1 billion USD, just to trade 1 million USD*. This is just one round. If you have more rounds, this will be worse, certainly.

So, this is the first problem that we want to discuss about this See-Saw protocol. The second problem is that money "now" always has more value than money "later". Of course, money deposited later and withdrawn earlier (the party that move first) is more valuable comparing to other parties' money. Certainly you don't want to lock up your money as you can also use it elsewhere: you have better usage for it instead of putting in someone's safe, especially if you need to borrow money from the bank to actually afford the security that you want.

To quantify this phenomenon we use what we call the Net Present Value (NPV) as a metric. For this we only have a really simple model which is just the simple bank interest rates to start with. This is the formula which can use to compute the NPV of each party in the case of three parties. So, it is pretty simple here (Eq. 1 in the main paper). You deposit in the 1st round and you only withdraw in the 6th round. So, you have already lost some money, because you lock it up. You lock up q in 5 rounds, right? And it is worse for the case of the third party. So, you lock up your money in the 2nd round, in the 3rd round, and only in the 7th and the 10th round you can get your money back.

If it is only 100 USD at stake, just by participating in this protocol, you lose around 8 cents as the first party. This is already the least damage to the luckiest person participating in the MPC. For the unlucky one, the last one, he will lose 27 cents, and that is only for 100 USD. If we are trading 1 million USD, with 1 billion USD in deposit, that is even more severe.

So, now, do we really think that there are possible trivial solutions? We so far only mention the amount that you have to deposit, and you can withdraw. So, it is not really related to any security protocol or any cryptographic primitive so far. So can we simply move from this really unfair deposit and withdraw sequence to a sequence in which we just modify the amount deposit, to make it fair? This is clearly one possible solution, right? But, unfortunately, based on the security protocol, if, for example, here, if we accept this sequence of deposit (Table 5 in the main paper). If P_2 aborts, P_1 only gets 33 USD as penalty comparing to 100 USD that he should receive (as in the original protocol).

Can we conclude that solutions not be so trivial when you are balancing the deposit? In which you want to make sure that everybody deposit, more or less, the same, but in the actual protocol, you can see here (Fig. 1 in the main paper), you are not just locking up your money somewhere, but you are actually giving it to another party to lock it in escrow. So, it is not so trial to modify the sequence that you can maintain the Fairness in Crypto and the Fairness in Finance at the same time. Of course, if the receivers are not well-balanced, for example P_2 learns the final outcome but he doesn't want to proceed, instead of losing 100 USD, he can just lose 33 USD.

The takeaway in this talk: the inter-temporal distribution of money is important. So, if we are going to design a penalty protoco, especially for financial services, then we need to understand how the lock and release of the escrow works, because it is gong to be critical for the success of the penalty solution. As we can see here, the bright minds from MIT cannot give a workable solution for futures trading. Nobody is going to *deposit 1 billion USD just to trade 1 million USD* and that is just the problem on the surface, right? As we look into the NPV there is also this unfairness of P_1's very late deposits but very early withdrawal. This deeper problem prevents a penalty solution to be applicable in practice.

Sasa Radomirovic: So, your party that's holding the money in escrow needs to be trusted.

Reply: Not exactly, in these works, they consider the model of claim or refund transactions and it can be implemented with a trusted bank, or it can also be implemented using Bitcoin and some cryptocurrency, like Ethereum. Basically the claim or refund transaction works in this way: you send a time lock transaction in Bitcoin, after the time lock period the money will be refunded to the sender. But before the time lock if the receiver of the money can present some proof of participation then he can claim the money. So, money goes two ways, depending on the receiver aborts or continues. So, it doesn't need to be trusted.

Sasa Radomirovic: Right, but you then need to monitor the Bitcoin network, so you're pulling out on time that you don't miss any deadlines.

Reply: Yes, but it is not so difficult: a Bitcoin transaction needs one hour to be consolidated.

Sasa Radomirovic: Right, it seems to me a very expensive solution, considering that if you were to upset the trusted third party you could get away for free, in terms of dollar amount. With a trusted third party we can solve the fairness problem. Without the trusted third party it seems to be very difficult.

Reply: But sometimes there might not be a trusted third party, otherwise, why do we need security research anymore?

Frank Stajano: In 2008, so more than 10 years ago, at this workshop, I presented with Richard Clayton, a protocol called CyberDice [6], predated the Bitcoin paper, and it was a way of running a lottery for mutually distrustful participants without a trusted third party and without a way of putting money on the table, because there was no table and because they were all distributed across the internet.

In the absence of Bitcoin, which hadn't been introduced yet, we had something that relied on, essentially, an unforgeable ledger for recording transactions. And we relied on distinguishing between the people who are running the game, for they might be crooked, and the people who were transforming bitstreams into currency, and vice versa. The people who were doing this transducing mechanism, had no interest in the game. They were just checking that these things had several properties, and if they didn't, they wouldn't do the conversion into money.

You would first have to deposit something to get bitstream out of that, which you could then use to play on the internet. And when you got a, say, winning bitstream, they would check that the rules had been followed before paying out. Because everybody had to buy their own bitstream to convert their money to bitstream at certain time I don't think that this would encourage the problems of some people having to keep the money locked longer than others.

Reply: In my perspective, the bitstream is actually the Bitcoin network. Because the miners who run in the bitstream ledger don't have interest in this game, in this MPC, that they're running. And the parties that run the game, are actually just running an MPC. But probably the rules are pretty flexible for the bitstream, right? So, you can check arbitrary conditions.

The reason why this claim or refund transaction model is interesting is because we only need to rely on a simple primitive, which is the Bitcoin network, which is already deployed in practice. If we, for example, are using Ethereum, which has a virtual machine that allows more flexible rules to be checked rather than just "you claim when you present the proof of participation, or the transaction will be refunded to the original sender". Then it will be much more similar. So, I think that your CyberDice is a sort of Ethereum but not the simple Bitcoin with the claim or refund transaction model?

Frank Stajano: I don't see why there should be a very long delay, a significant difference in the time that the money is locked into the system for different players. If we are talking about the game which has a number of rounds, and then finishes. Why shouldn't it be all over in a short period of time?

Reply: So, you are talking about the second problem that we are presenting here: that money now has more value than money later. The reason why it has a problem, because if, for example, we are using Bitcoin as the ledger for the claim or refund transaction, one transaction actually needs one hour to be consolidated. And in the case of three parties for just one round, it takes 10 h, because, as you can see, there are 10 rounds. So, if we are talking about the really small amount of money, 100 USD, then you only lose from 8 to 27 cents. But if you are talking about a much higher bet, for example in the case that we are running the futures trading, then you have to put a stake 1 billion in which means you are going to lose, I think, 10 million times higher of just 8 cents if you are borrowing 1 billion from the bank and you have to pay the hourly rate interest.

Frank Stajano: It's going to be over in 10 h, unless you're in Brazil with higher inflation, it's not going to make a difference if you use just the interest of penalties, is it? At this rate, the other guy, maybe not 10 h, but I don't know nine hours.

Fabio Massacci: So, 10 h is not very much, if you're talking about 100 USD, but if you're talking about a couple hundred millions, it's a lot of money. This amount of money, and I'm not talking about Brazil, this is the Bank of England, if you borrow money from the Bank of England for one day, then it will charge you a lot of money if you borrow it at once. So, in this case, it would be something like 10 million times more that you have to pay interest. Which is a lot. But answering your question it depends on how the game finishes, if it is really an MPC there is a bit of asynchrony. So you can assume that some parties will give money at certain rounds, and then you have to wait for the second party to give his answer to the MPC and then you have to wait for third party . . . So, people will actually delay so that they are the last one going forward. That's why we need to maybe sit down and look into exactly how this protocol works, to see whether this can be fitting to this problem, or not.

Jonathan Anderson: Could you go back to the slide where you have your various motivations, like lottery and trading and things for multiparty computation?[1]

---

[1] This slide shows Table 1 in the main paper.

So, it seems to me that these use cases are quite different, both in terms of the scale, but also the existence of trusted third parties. Because, on the one hand, if you're talking about people playing online poker, and you don't trust poker.com, or what have you, that's one thing. If you're talking about borrowing hundreds of millions of GBP from the Bank of England on an overnight lending rate, well, then there's clearly a trusted third party, if you're trading millions of GBP for EUR, or something. So, it seems like some of the claims that you're making are making assumptions from one domain and applying them to the other, where maybe they're inappropriate.

Reply: Well, fair enough. But I think that borrowing money from the Bank of England, has nothing to do with this protocol, because you're just borrowing the money, and maybe you convert it into Bitcoin, so you can actually use it in the penalty protocol if you really want to use it, so I don't see how they connect here. I mean, the Bank of England is not a trusted party to the protocol at all.

Jonathan Anderson: Okay, so that's true, but I guess I'm slightly sceptical that someone is going to exchange 200 million GBP for EUR using a mechanism that doesn't have a legal recourse of transaction receipts, and lawyers, and judges, and higher judges, and higher courts, etc.

Bruce Christianson: You just tie your money up for years, going through all that.

Jonathan Anderson: Well, that may be true, but I think that's probably still better than tying your money up for an indeterminate amount of time and hoping that no one comes along with a longer chain, or else having to depend on secretive cabal developers who produce a code that says which locks in the blockchain all chains have to flow through, and things like that. I mean, you're exchanging one kind of trust for another, and the people who spend hundred of millions of pounds on currency exchanges are probably the kind of people who trust large institutions more than they trust private code.

Reply: Well, fair enough. Thank you!

References

1. Goldreich, O., Micali, S., Wigderson, A.: How to play any mental game or a completeness theorem for protocols with honest majority. In: Proceedings of ACM STOC, pp. 218–229 (1987)
2. Bentov, I., Kumaresan, R.: How to use bitcoin to design fair protocols. In: Garay, J.A., Gennaro, R. (eds.) CRYPTO 2014. LNCS, vol. 8617, pp. 421–439. Springer, Heidelberg (2014). https://doi.org/10.1007/978-3-662-44381-1_24
3. Kumaresan, R., Moran, T., Bentov, I.: How to use bitcoin to play decentralized poker. In: Proceedings of ACM CCS, pp. 195–206 (2015)

4. Kumaresan, R., Vaikuntanathan, V., Vasudevan, P.N.: Improvements to secure computation with penalties. In: Proceedings of ACM CCS, pp. 406–417 (2016)
5. Kosba, A., Miller, A., Shi, E., Wen, Z., Papamanthou, C.: Hawk: the blockchain model of cryptography and privacy-preserving smart contracts. In: Proceedings of IEEE SSP, pp. 839–858 (2016)
6. Stajano, F., Clayton, R.: Cyberdice: peer-to-peer gambling in the presence of cheaters. In: Christianson, B., Malcolm, J.A., Matyas, V., Roe, M. (eds.) Security Protocols 2008. LNCS, vol. 6615, pp. 54–70. Springer, Heidelberg (2011). https://doi.org/10.1007/978-3-642-22137-8_9

Human-Computability Boundaries

Vijay Kothari[1]([✉]), Prashant Anantharaman[1], Ira Ray Jenkins[1],
Michael C. Millian[1], J. Peter Brady[1], Sameed Ali[1], Sergey Bratus[1],
Jim Blythe[2], Ross Koppel[3], and Sean W. Smith[1]

[1] Dartmouth College, Hanover, NH, USA
vijayk@cs.dartmouth.edu
[2] Information Sciences Institute, University of Southern California,
Los Angeles, CA, USA
[3] Sociology Department, University of Pennsylvania, Philadelphia, PA, USA

Abstract. Human understanding of protocols is central to protocol
security. The security of a protocol rests on its designers, its implementors, and, in some cases, its users correctly conceptualizing how it
should work, understanding how it actually works, and predicting how
others will think it works. Ensuring these conceptualizations are correct
is difficult. A complementary field, however, provides some inspiration
on how to proceed: the field of language-theoretic security (LangSec)
promotes the adoption of a secure design-and-development methodology that emphasizes the existence of certain computability boundaries
that must never be crossed during parser and protocol construction to
ensure correctness of design and implementation. We propose supplementing this work on classical computability boundaries with exploration
of human-computability boundaries. Classic computability research has
focused on understanding what problems can be solved by machines or
idealized human computers—that is, computational models that behave
like humans carrying out rote computational tasks in principle but that
are not subject to the natural limitations that humans face in practice. Humans are often subject to a variety of deficiencies, e.g., constrained working memories, short attention spans, misperceptions, and
cognitive biases. We argue that such realities must be taken into consideration if we are to be serious about securing protocols. A corol-
lary is that while the traditional computational models and hierarchies
built using them (e.g., the Chomsky hierarchy) are useful for securing
protocols and parsers, they alone are *inadequate* as they neglect the
human-computability boundaries that define what humans can do in
practice. In this position paper, we advocate for the discovery of human-
computability boundaries, present challenges with precisely and accurately finding those boundaries, and outline future paths of inquiry.

1 Introduction

Humans are integral to the conception and operation of protocols. They lay out
the initial vision, create the specification, implement the protocol, and wittingly

© Springer Nature Switzerland AG 2020
J. Anderson et al. (Eds.): Security Protocols 2019, LNCS 12287, pp. 157–166, 2020.
https://doi.org/10.1007/978-3-030-57043-9_15

or unwittingly make use of it. Due to humans' close and varied interactions with protocols during their design, development, and operation, we must - if we want to secure protocols - account for humans' intrinsic limitations in understanding protocols.[1]

The genesis of a protocol vulnerability often lies in some human failure or deficiency, e.g., the copy-and-paste blunder that produced the Apple *goto fail* vulnerability [16]. The designer may introduce mistakes or create the specification under incorrect assumptions. Or the implementor may fail to correctly conceptualize the specification, e.g., due to cognitive constraints. Or perhaps the user may misunderstand the protocol, driving them toward behaviors that jeopardize security. (While some may not consider the previous example to be a protocol vulnerability, it has the same form as one; it is a predictable failure of the protocol design-and-development process, which can be used as a reliable conduit for attack.)

Our thesis is that a whole class of vulnerabilities could be averted if we better understood human limits to computability and took a principled approach to protocol design and development grounded in such an understanding.

In the remaining sections of this paper, we: discuss Turing's notion of computability; provide a brief primer on the field of language-theoretic security (LangSec), which informs our work; present the idea of complementing LangSec with the incorporation of human-computability boundaries; discuss challenges in defining human-computability boundaries and follow-on work; discuss related work; and conclude.

2   The Human Computer

Today, Turing machines are often thought of as computational models for modern-day electronic computers; however, Turing very much had humans in mind during his conception of the Turing machine. As Jack B. Copeland points out in his discussion on the Church-Turing thesis:

> "Turing introduced his machines with the intention of providing an idealized description of a certain human activity, the tedious one of *numerical computation*. Until the advent of automatic computing machines, this was the occupation of many thousands of people in business, government, and research establishments. These human rote-workers were in fact called *computers*. Human computers used effective methods to carry out some aspects of the work nowadays done by electronic computers. The Church-Turing thesis is about computation *as this term was used in 1936*, viz. human computation[.]" [7].

---

[1] While the discussion in this paper focuses on protocols, the notion of human-computability boundaries is certainly applicable more broadly.

In Turing's seminal paper [22], in which he proved the Entscheidungsproblem is not, in general, solvable, he also introduced the Turing machine, along with the notion of computability. Turing wrote, in the paper, that: "Computing is normally done by writing certain symbols on paper. We may suppose this paper is divided into squares like a child's arithmetic book." In the same paper, Turing uses "the fact that the human memory is necessarily limited" as justification for the finite state property of Turing machines.[2]

Despite Turing's inspirations to model human computation, Turing machines are not adequate in fully capturing all aspects of human computation in protocol and program design, development, and use. It was never meant to do this. The Turing machine was a computational model that dealt with an ideal - a human in principle, not in practice. More importantly, human computation at the time was envisioned narrowly as rote processes carried out by humans. It was never intended to capture how humans design, develop, conceptualize, and use computer programs and protocols, in the fashion they do today. While we still have human computation in the present day, the role of humans and the tasks they perform are fundamentally different—and any computational models we use to capture human computation must reflect this reality.

3   LangSec and Computational Models

Language-theoretic security (LangSec) [5] incorporates the theoretical insights offered by language theory, automata theory, and computability theory into a design-and-development methodology that averts common pitfalls responsible for producing numerous protocol and parser vulnerabilities. It advocates separating the parser from the execution environment, modeling the parser as a formal grammar, ensuring the grammar does not exceed certain computability boundaries on an extended version of the Chomsky hierarchy, and ensuring that the parser is a *recognizer* or more precisely a *decider*, i.e., it rejects all bad inputs and accepts all good inputs. In essence, LangSec tells us how to design protocols and parsers based on our understanding of the limitations of machines. That is not to say that LangSec does not acknowledge or address human causes of protocol and parser vulnerabilities. On the contrary, Bratus et al. in their discussion of exploit programming [6], note that many exploits are manifestations of incorrect computability assumptions. LangSec aims to rectify these assumptions within the design-and-development process. Furthermore, successful application of LangSec principles *requires* reducing human error. For example, the parser combinator toolkit Hammer [17] helps eliminate user error by assisting the implementor in creating a parser that matches the specification grammar. We contend that, while LangSec is vital and has made great strides toward securing protocols, it alone is insufficient. Specifically, there is a limit to what can be achieved by considering traditional computability boundaries alone. (Of course, one might argue this would not be a problem if we could eliminate the human

---

[2] We note that not everyone held this view. For example, Shagrir provides discussion on Gödel's rejection of this assumption [19].

from all parts of the protocol life cycle—including design, development, and use; as far as we can tell, we're not quite there yet.)

We propose supplementing the field of LangSec with work that explores human-computability boundaries. Classical computational models, such as the Turing machine are excellent for capturing what machines can do; however, they are generally not well-suited for capturing what actual humans can do with and especially without aids. In practice, humans have finite memories—and often inadequate knowledge to understand protocol workings in comparison to machines. They have short attention spans. They are subject to cognitive biases and often make mistakes in reasoning in predictable ways. These deficiencies manifest in bugs during protocol and parser conceptualization, coding bugs, and user error, all of which endanger security.

We argue that we must acknowledge these human deficiencies, understand why and how they occur, develop solutions to begin addressing them, and finally we must update our protocol and parser design-and-development processes in accordance with such findings. We hope this initial position paper will lay some groundwork for further inquiry that helps in securing protocols and parsers.

4   Human-Computability Boundaries

Using an extended version of the Chomsky Hierarchy that differentiates between non-deterministic and deterministic pushdown automata, LangSec recommends staying within either the boundary of Turing-decidability (linear-bounded automata) or the stricter boundary of parser-equivalence decidability (deterministic pushdown automata), depending on the problem at hand. The *exact* class boundaries for these decision problems are not part of the five-class extended Chomsky hierarchy, e.g., the Turing-decidability boundary lies at recursive languages. The extended Chomsky hierarchy, however, is natural for humans to interpret and allows sufficient expressiveness to still be useful in the design and development of parsers and protocols.

Human-computability boundaries—the boundaries that specify what *actual humans* can do with the capabilities they possess and the deficiencies they are subject to—are a different beast altogether. Fitting human-computability boundaries to an extended Chomsky hierarchy is futile as there exist grammars within the class of regular grammars—i.e., grammars that can be expressed with finite state automata—that humans, in general, fail to conceptualize correctly. We do not know exactly where these human-computability boundaries lie, but the discovery of them may be instrumental in securing protocols and parsers. This observation is captured in Fig. 1. The ovals correspond to classes of grammars (or languages or automata) in the five-class extended Chomsky hierarchy. LangSec boundaries are drawn at linear-bounded automata and deterministic pushdown automata, whereas the oddly-shaped blob corresponds to a single idealized human-computability boundary. *If this boundary were representative of reality, we would want to constrain ourselves to the intersection of the blob and the appropriate LangSec computability boundaries during protocol and parser construction.*

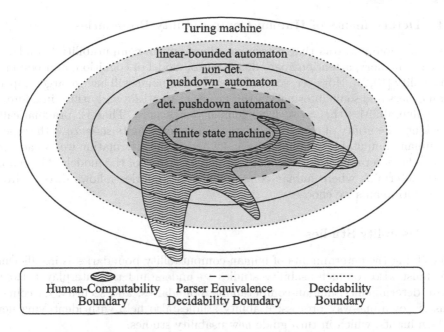

Fig. 1. Human-Computatability and LangSec Boundaries.

In practice, however, things are more complex. We can imagine different human-computability boundaries corresponding to different human roles and protocol interactions. We can also imagine fuzzy boundaries where the uncertainty comes from the variance of human attributes over a sub-population. We might consider human deficiencies of a probabilistic nature and aim to ensure most users are unsusceptible to a given flavor of attack based on protocol misconceptions; then, we may design and develop the protocol around this aim. If we know *a priori* what tools the various actors have at their disposal, the model we choose and boundaries we choose should take this into account. In short, the model used to express human-computability boundaries should be rooted in the protocol at hand, as well as the relevant sub-populations and their capabilities.

5   Challenges and Future Work

In the previous section, we introduced the notion of human-computability boundaries and motivated the need for their discovery. However, there are a wide variety of challenges associated with accurately and precisely defining where these boundaries lie, developing models to capture them, and utilizing them in practice. In this section, we briefly touch on these threads and suggest directions for future research.

5.1   Determinants of Human-Computability Boundaries

There are many factors that determine where human-computability boundaries lie, e.g., memory, attention span, dual-process model of cognition, and bounded rationality [10,21]. However, some of these determinants will have a larger impact than others and some information will be easier to attain and utilize in addressing vulnerabilities that arise from human deficiencies. That is, pragmatically speaking, the utility of exploring a determinant rests on its *salience* with respect to human-computability boundaries and whether the information we can acquire about the determinant is *actionable*. The effectiveness of the models that enable us to determine where human-computability boundaries follows directly from the determinants we choose.

5.2   Usability Studies

Identifying the determinants of human-computability boundaries is insufficient. We must also conduct usability studies to understand the interplay between these determinants, human-computability boundaries, and security. Of course, this is not a one-way process; usability studies also help with identifying new determinants, which in turn guide new usability studies.

   One example of a genre of usability studies we are interested in involves collecting concrete metrics for code complexity. Two classes of metrics are based on: (a) what the programmer can readily observe in the code and (b) what is represented in the abstract syntax tree (AST) for the program inputs in computer memory. As we mentioned earlier, program inputs are handled by code called parsers. Examples of metrics of the first type include lines of parser code and complexity per line of parser code, e.g., how many atomic structures such as combinators are used or represented in each line of code (on average or in the worst line). Examples of metrics of the second type include AST depth, number of branches, and tree balance.

5.3   Understanding Roles

Drawing useful human-computability boundaries requires understanding which roles are pertinent, the goals associated with the roles, the tools afforded by each role, and the interplay between each role and the protocol. Such understanding must be reflective of the protocol at hand and the application domain. The protocol and application domain may warrant consideration of additional roles or sub-roles that we have not discussed.

5.4   Developing Models

We've discussed the importance of defining where and how the protocol is used, determining the roles of the various human actors, identifying the determinants of human-computability boundaries, and gathering the requisite data grounded in usability studies to draw human-computability boundaries.

The next step is then to incorporate these findings into a model that captures human-computability boundaries in a way that enables us to reason about the security of the protocol. It may be infeasible to draw perfect or even close-to-perfect boundaries for human computability. Understanding *some* limitations, however, can go a long way in addressing vulnerabilities.

The power of the model used to capture human-computability boundaries lies its utility in the design and development of safe protocols. While it may be infeasible to draw perfect or even close-to-perfect boundaries for human computability, all is not lost. Indeed, it may be better to capture a few limitations in a manner that enables us to design and develop safe protocols than many in a way that does not. As we discussed earlier, one inspiration for this paper was in developing human-computability boundaries that complement LangSec boundaries. In pursuit of this objective, we may wish to develop models similar to those of the classical automata, such as Turing machines, to capture these boundaries. While even these models will not neatly fit within the extended Chomsky containment hierarchy used in LangSec, they would still be rooted in automata theory, which is certainly convenient. After all, understanding the commonality of two models of one type is generally easier than understanding the commonality of two models of different types.

We note that there has been some interesting, recent work on developing models for end users (e.g., [1,4,11]) that can assist in safe protocol and program construction. Another approach might be to extend the compliance budget work of Beautement et al. [2] to a cognitive budget for human agents.

6   Related Work

Jeanette M. Wing expounded on computational thinking as an essential mindset that everyone would benefit from, thereby providing a strong pedagogical basis for incorporating computational thinking into college and pre-college curricula [24]. She writes:

> "Stating the difficulty of a problem accounts for the underlying power of the machine—the computing device that will run the solution. We must consider the machine's instruction set, its resource constraints, and its operating environment." [24]

This mindset is crucial in efficiently solving problems on machines. In this paper, we argue for a parallel notion: Just as we must understand the computational capabilities of the machines that humans use, we must understand computational capabilities of humans as they interact protocols and programs, e.g., as they conceptualize and reason about code during development.

For completeness, we note that in recent years, human computation has developed into a field in its own right, e.g., [14,18,23]. The work in this field, however, is largely tangential to our work in this paper. Our interests are in developing an understanding of human-computability boundaries as they pertain to secure program and protocol design, development, and use. That said, in the past two decades, there has been some exciting research efforts to capture humans in protocol and parser design. Below, we touch on a few particularly relevant ones.

In 2007, Carl Ellison [8] presented the notion of ceremony [3] as a natural extension to the network protocol. A ceremony incorporates everything conventionally thought to be out-of-band to the protocol, e.g., UI interactions, human-human interactions, provisioning tasks. This holistic view of the protocol as a ceremony enables the security practitioner to better conceptualize and analyze protocol security. Since then, researchers have expanded on the idea of ceremonies. Notably, Bella and Coles-Kemp [3] pursued a formal model of security ceremonies with multiple layers: information, operating system, human-computer interaction, personal, and communal.

Johansen et al. [11] argued for the development of a new discipline, Behavioral Computer Science, lying at the intersection of behavioral sciences, ubiquitous computing and Internet of Things (IoT), and artificial intelligence. This discipline blends the study of HCI, modeling, and the notion of computational trust. The authors argue we must rethink the rational agent models often used for human behavior by acknowledging that: differences exist between humans' experienced utility, predicted utility, and remembered utility [13]; humans employ the dual-process model of cognition wherein they may invoke either a fast, knee-jerk, intuitive, and automated response or a slower, deliberate, rational response [12,20]; and humans are subject to all sorts of heuristics that affect their judgements [9]. The authors then discuss approaches to building models that capture this complexity, grounded in the Bella-Coles-Kemp model discussed earlier [3].

Basin et al. [1] studied the security of protocols in the presence of human error. They developed a formal model that includes human agents whose behavior may deviate from the behavior assumed by the protocol specification. They captured human error using two approaches: (1) a skilled human approach that begins with an infallible human agent who knows the protocol specification and modifies it to allow for a small number of mistakes; (2) a rule-based approach that begins with an untrained human that does not know the protocol specification and imposes a set of rules upon human agent behavior that dictate permissible behaviors. They then demonstrate how these two approaches can be used to formally model fallible humans with the Tamarin verification tool [15]. They also do a case study to show how this modeling approach can be used to discover human-based vulnerabilities in a protocol, and they use the model to compare different authentication protocols.

The most relevant work we've seen to our paper is by Blum and Vempala [4]. They proposed a model of human computation for end users in studying the security of protocols. They argued that traditional notions of computability cannot blindly be applied to humans and that, instead, human computational models must take into account the reality that human processing power is inferior to that of computers. They argued that human computation occurs in two dis-

---

[3] As noted by Carl Ellison: "The term 'ceremony' was coined for this purpose by Jesse Walker of Intel Corporation." [8].

tinct phases: a pre-processing phase and a processing phase. Accordingly, they developed a model for human computation—a variant of the Turing machine—and introduced the notion of a schema to be the human analog to a computer algorithm. Finally, they applied this model to different problems. Our paper certainly has some overlap with this work. However, we explore notions of human-computability boundaries more generally. We are also not solely concerned with users; we also focus on human designers and implementors. Last, we are interested in combining models of human computability with traditional computability models.

7 Conclusion

We argued that security rests, in large part, on acknowledging and accounting for human deficiencies in the design and development of network protocols. Existing LangSec work highlights theoretical computability boundaries along the extended Chomsky hierarchy for which the decidability and parser equivalence decidability problems are solvable. Accordingly, recommendations to stay within these computability boundaries along with tools and other LangSec developments are valuable in guiding secure protocol and parser construction. However, as we argue in this paper, they alone are insufficient. We discussed the notion of human-computability boundaries, highlighted the difficulty in understanding and defining them, and discussed open challenges for future work.

Acknowledgement. This material is based upon work supported by the United States Air Force and DARPA under Contract No. FA8750-16-C-0179 and Department of Energy under Award Number DE-OE0000780.

Any opinions, findings and conclusions or recommendations expressed in this material are those of the author(s) and do not necessarily reflect the views of the United States Air Force, DARPA, United States Government or any agency thereof.

References

1. Basin, D., Radomirovic, S., Schmid, L.: Modeling human errors in security protocols. In: 2016 IEEE 29th Computer Security Foundations Symposium (CSF), pp. 325–340. IEEE (2016)
2. Beautement, A., Sasse, M.A., Wonham, M.: The compliance budget: managing security behaviour in organisations. In: Proceedings of the 2008 New Security Paradigms Workshop, pp. 47–58. ACM (2009)
3. Bella, G., Coles-Kemp, L.: Layered analysis of security ceremonies. In: Gritzalis, D., Furnell, S., Theoharidou, M. (eds.) SEC 2012. IAICT, vol. 376, pp. 273–286. Springer, Heidelberg (2012). https://doi.org/10.1007/978-3-642-30436-1_23
4. Blum, M., Vempala, S.: The complexity of human computation: a concrete model with an application to passwords. arXiv preprint arXiv:1707.01204 (2017)
5. Bratus, S.: LANGSEC: Language-theoretic security: "The View from the Tower of Babel". http://langsec.org. Accessed 2 Jan 2019

6. Bratus, S., Locasto, M., Patterson, M., Sassaman, L., Shubina, A.: Exploit programming: from buffer overflows to "weird machines" and theory of computation. Login USENIX Mag. **36**(6), 13–21 (2011)
7. Copeland, B.J.: The Church-Turing Thesis. In: Zalta, E.N. (ed.) The Stanford Encyclopedia of Philosophy. Metaphysics Research Lab, Stanford University, Spring 2019 edn. (2019)
8. Ellison, C.: Ceremony design and analysis. Cryptology ePrint Archive, Report 2007/399 (2007). https://eprint.iacr.org/2007/399
9. Gilovich, T., Griffin, D., Kahneman, D.: Heuristics and Biases: The Psychology of Intuitive Judgment. Cambridge University Press, Cambridge (2002)
10. Herley, C.: So long, and no thanks for the externalities: the rational rejection of security advice by users. In: Proceedings of the 2009 workshop on New Security Paradigms Workshop, pp. 133–144. ACM (2009)
11. Johansen, C., Pedersen, T., Jøsang, A.: Towards behavioural computer science. In: Habib, S.M.M., Vassileva, J., Mauw, S., Mühlhäuser, M. (eds.) IFIPTM 2016. IAICT, vol. 473, pp. 154–163. Springer, Cham (2016). https://doi.org/10.1007/978-3-319-41354-9_12
12. Kahneman, D.: A perspective on judgment and choice: mapping bounded rationality. Am. Psycholog. **58**(9), 697 (2003)
13. Kahneman, D., Thaler, R.H.: Anomalies: utility maximization and experienced utility. J. Econ. Perspect. **20**(1), 221–234 (2006). https://doi.org/10.1257/089533006776526076
14. Law, E., Ahn, L.V.: Defining (Human) computation. Synth. Lect. Artif. Intell. Mach. Learn. **5**(3), 1–121 (2011)
15. Meier, S., Schmidt, B., Cremers, C., Basin, D.: The TAMARIN prover for the symbolic analysis of security protocols. In: Sharygina, N., Veith, H. (eds.) CAV 2013. LNCS, vol. 8044, pp. 696–701. Springer, Heidelberg (2013). https://doi.org/10.1007/978-3-642-39799-8_48
16. Naked Security, Sophos: Anatomy of a "goto fail" - Apple's SSL bug explained, plus an unofficial patch for OS X!, February 2014. https://nakedsecurity.sophos.com/2014/02/24/anatomy-of-a-goto-fail-apples-ssl-bug-explained-plus-an-unofficial-patch/. Accessed 3 Jan 2019
17. Patterson, M.: Parser combinators for binary formats, in C. https://github.com/UpstandingHackers/hammer. Accessed 4 Jan 2019
18. Quinn, A.J., Bederson, B.B.: Human computation: a survey and taxonomy of a growing field. In: Proceedings of the SIGCHI Conference on Human Factors in Computing Systems, pp. 1403–1412. ACM (2011)
19. Shagrir, O.: Gödel on turing on computability. In: Olszewski, A., Wole'nski, J., Janusz, R. (eds.) Church's Thesis After Seventy Years, pp. 393–419. Ontos Verlag (2006)
20. Sloman, S.A.: Two systems of reasoning. In: Gilovich, T., Griffin, D., Kahneman, D. (eds.) Heuristics and Biases: The Psychology of Intuitive Judgment. Cambridge University Press, Cambridge (2002)
21. Smith, S.W.: Security and cognitive bias: exploring the role of the mind. IEEE Secur. Privacy **10**(5), 75–78 (2012)
22. Turing, A.M.: On computable numbers, with an application to the entscheidungsproblem. Proc. London Math. Soc. **2**(1), 230–265 (1937)
23. Von Ahn, L.: Human computation. In: Proceedings of the 2008 IEEE 24th International Conference on Data Engineering, pp. 1–2. IEEE Computer Society (2008)
24. Wing, J.M.: Computational thinking. Commun. ACM **49**(3), 33–35 (2006)

Human-Computability Boundaries
(Transcript of Discussion)

Vijay Kothari(✉) and Michael C. Millian

Dartmouth College, Hanover, NH, USA
vijayk@cs.dartmouth.edu

Vijay: The origin of many protocol vulnerabilities is the human. Humans fail predictably, and they fail often. This paper is mostly dealing with how do we acknowledge these failures. Moreover, how do we start designing protocols in such ways that humans are less likely to fail and cause these vulnerabilities down the road?

Two examples that are particularly relevant deal with Heartbleed and URLs. Prashant spoke about Heartbleed before[1], and there's a mismatch between the length field and the actual payload. Another example is URLs. The end user could be looking at a URL, and there's all this weird structure that most users probably do not understand. You can do something like username at password, colon, and then display the rest of the URL. You can use special characters that people don't understand. So, if we were to redesign the underlying protocols in such a way, that we want to minimize the usability failures, how would we go about actually doing that?

This example [on the slides] is for Microsoft SafeLinks. Somebody sends you a URL, and SafeLinks will take that URL and do this vetting process. So this particular URL has two redirects, and the protocol allows for that. SafeLinks fails on this, so we'd classify this as a correct URL. How do we start going about addressing those sorts of problems?

Humans are a source of vulnerabilities. We can think of economic theory—and humans don't behave exactly like the models from economic theory might suggest. Cognitive biases constrain them. They have limited memory, short attention spans, misperceptions. How do we acknowledge all of these problems and design around them? Our focus in this paper is primarily on automata theory.

Prashant spoke earlier about LangSec. A significant component of LangSec involves constraining the grammar that the parser runs on to be very, very small. So you use a more constrained language or grammar rather than a more expressive one. So can we design automata around humans? That's one of the core foci in this paper, and Michael will speak a little bit more on that.

Michael Millian: For automata and comparing machine automata to some model of human automata, we're going to use the Chomsky Hierarchy from language theory as a jumping off point. For people who aren't as familiar with this, or

---

[1] "Mismorphism: The Heart of the Weird Machine", these proceedings.

© Springer Nature Switzerland AG 2020
J. Anderson et al. (Eds.): Security Protocols 2019, LNCS 12287, pp. 167–174, 2020.
https://doi.org/10.1007/978-3-030-57043-9_16

it's been a while, there are these different states in the hierarchy describing how complex your machine is, from regular expressions, which can be characterized as finite state machines, all the way up to Turing machines, that can do anything computable.

In the field of LangSec, we define a couple more boundaries. So we've got this decidability boundary. This follows from language theory. Once you move beyond linear bounded automata, you run into the decidability problem and the halting problem. We have the other boundary, the parser equivalence boundary. This also follows from standard language theory.

If you've got two separate parsers, two different implementations of the same grammar, can you tell if they're equivalent? Also, the limit there is non-deterministic, push-down automata, or deterministic-context-free. Those are equivalent. If you get more complex than that, you are not able to prove that two separate implementations of your parser are correct, and you might get parser differentials. Moreover, that's something we'd like to avoid.

That's all on the machine side. When we start trying to put humans into this, it's not entirely clear what kind of parsers humans implement in their heads. There are regular expressions that humans can understand quite easily, but others that they can't. Anybody who's looked at an extended regular expression would be familiar with the sensation of, "I have no idea what this is trying to express." At the same time, machine-like i^n, j^n, k^n, for the n value is not regular, but humans have no problem matching that. Also, there are other Turing-complete languages that humans have no problem reasoning about but require more complex machinery.

So the problem is how do we model what humans are capable of doing, so that we can design protocols and languages that humans are capable of building—and, in the cases where it's too complex, make tools to supplement human deficiencies. So some of the open questions that we have that we'd love to put up for discussion are, can we use automata theory to model humans? Alternatively, can we modify it in some way, to model humans? Is there any way that we can start getting at defining human computational boundaries? If not something that looks like the Chomsky model, some other model? Can we acknowledge and design around some deficiencies in a formal way? Moreover, maybe approximate or more probabilistic approaches would be a good jumping off point. We'd love to hear from people any thoughts or input that you have.

Lydia Kraus: Thanks. It's an interesting topic, and could you go back to the second slide? Humans systematically fail. Well I think that maybe in the best case we could learn from failures. I'm wondering whether you have thought about that in your context? And maybe like the goal of somehow trying to omit the systematic failures is aiming a bit high? How about having something like a secure default instead of just aiming so high to avoid all mistakes because some of them might actually be something positive? And you learn from it?

Michael Millian: My first instinct to that is even if you're making a model that allows you to learn from mistakes. The ultimate goal is still not to make a mistake, right? So, it sounds like you are also trying to build a model that acknowledges human faults and tries to work around them. But by systematizing what it looks like to make a mistake and then fix it?

Lydia Kraus: Yes, I'm just wondering, I feel it is hard to avoid any mistakes because that's the way people function. So, you don't need to answer now.

Vijay: Yes, that'd be great to discuss. I guess one thing that comes to mind is that—Yes, you're right—we're probably not going to be able to get everything. So, could we maybe find, say, 90% of the common mistakes? Perhaps we could get rid of or deal with those early in the design phase, when I think that the costs are generally pretty low if you deal with it early, rather than later on. I guess what I'm thinking is if we were at a point where we were deciding how URLs are to be structured, or URIs are to be structured, what could we have done to get rid of the problems that attackers use to conduct phishing attacks?

Michael Millian: Much in the same way as the Chomsky Hierarchy, you get to Turing complete languages, and you run into the halting problem. You can't design something that will solve every problem. Humans run into the same kind of situation. However, can we define constraints or subclasses where we could say, if you put these constraints on the problem, humans can deal with it, and do it safely, as long as they follow the constraints?

Fabio Massacci: So, compared to the Turing hierarchy level, there has been some work as I mentioned, in the software engineering community, in particular by Andreas Zeller, that actually show that with very little effort just staying down on the context-free languages, you can actually generate an automatic parser, that'd sort of be an envelope of the things that shouldn't happen.

So this does not create a precise boundary of the things that cannot happen or should not happen. But for example, he was able to show that just with this very simple envelope, that limits what should not happen, you can catch most of the mistakes, like Heartbleed or others. This was very simple. So you may have something that you can say, okay, let's have an approximation of the possible human behaviours and after this one with the context free, you could actually be the security monitor. Let's call it this way. You could actually check this shouldn't happen. And if this is so, then you have lots of things. And this will be an army that we can actually manage.

Michael Millian: Yes. We've been looking at the same stuff in our lab. I'm not sure we've encountered that research. So we will look into it. However, we are also dealing with ways to automatically generate parsers so that you can avoid some of these vulnerabilities.

One of the tools we use is called Hammer. To use the IPV4 header as an example of a protocol you might want to build a very naïve way would say, "Oh you know, it's just some number of bits, all concatenated with each other." What our tool looks like is on the left there. We can see the sequence focus variables, like the version, the IHL, and then we define what each of those is.

So for version, you might have a choice between four and six, if you want to accept IPV4 and IPV6. This is very summarised. However, we also have some notion of checking the length fields at the time of parsing so you don't have to do that computation later because it should be encapsulated. Also, the point of discussing this is that maybe we can use as a model the abstract syntax tree that you build when you are parsing your message and reason for a particular protocol. If there is a depth or a branch factor on the tree at a certain point, it becomes more difficult for humans to reason about the tree when it gets to a certain size, as just maybe one example for ways we can get at this human decidability problem.

Fabio Massacci: What is the human? Is the human a developer of the protocol parser or the human is user of...

Michael Millian: The developer of the protocol.

Vijay: We were also thinking more broadly. I believe that for Hammer, it's the developer as Michael was saying. But it could be developers/implementers, the designer or the user.

Simon Foley: Fabio had mentioned Zeller. My understanding of that work was that he was looking at the past behaviour of the API, and mining from that normal interaction of the API? So, it wasn't captured in human behaviours, it was captured with what the normal interaction with the API is.

Ross Anderson: There are many other problem domains where the interface between humans and computation is the root task and the one that springs immediately to mind is probability theory, where humans are much better at a frequentist approach to probability. Alternatively, to dealing with probability problems when these are made socially salient. And both of those make me slightly skeptical about the idea that we will get a useful definition of a boundary between human and machine computation, which can be expressed in terms of the mechanics of machine computation. Because mechanics of the brain are somewhat different. And therefore the definition of the boundary is perhaps more readily made, in terms of human capabilities rather than automata capabilities.

Vijay: Yes, I think you are correct. However, I think even if we get marginal improvements, it would be useful. For example, you can think that perhaps we could restrain the number of states to twenty in a protocol, and that might be infeasible for most protocols. In select cases, I think we can probably compare specifications based on what humans can do using automata theory and still have gains.

So, the reason why we are looking at automata theory is to blend LangSec with the capabilities of humans because we have something like Hammer that we are developing. And so we can even get marginal improvements on top of that?

Michael Millian: I don't think I mentioned what Hammer is. But Hammer is just a parser combinator tool. In formal language theory, the parser is just a combination of operators like concatenation and Kleene star. And Hammer is just an implementation of those combinators that you can compose together to write your protocol in a way that it looks like a grammar.

Sasa Radomirovic: I think humans' capabilities vary widely. So we cannot ask what humans' capabilities—humans, as all of us—are. I think even an individual's capabilities will vary widely over a day or a period of time. So it seems to me that the stratify approach is the only way to model humans. To make any model of humans would be to say for some or many perimeters within this range we will have 50% of the humans—or on a good day, most people can do it and on a bad day, some can't. So, I don't think we can achieve that by defining just one model of human.

Michael Millian: Yes, that's a very good point. And I'm not sure that's what we are trying to do but we are trying to understand exactly what the constraints on humans are. Like what kind of problems are completely unsolvable by humans by which maybe we mean, nobody is going to get it correct. Maybe we mean 99% of people, are going to make a mistake on this. And then what kinds of problems are easily solvable, where most people are going to get it right most of the time. There's obviously going to be variance. But we want to try to capture what that looks like and draw boundaries around it, so that we can design tools and design workflows that work with humans to maximize their potential for success.

Vijay: I think we can think about things probabilistically, as well. And another thing is, yes, there's a ton of variance in humans. But we can still think about if we're worried about developers in one part of the protocol and users in another. Maybe there's certain types of features that are common to developers and common to users. So there might be a little bit of stratification we can still do. We are still thinking about this.

Fabio Massacci: So again, sorry. I want to keep insisting human versus different types of humans. Because even from the questions that you get from the audience, clearly everyone here has a different understanding of what's human. So probably human computability is the wrong title.

If you have developers in mind, it's one thing. If you have a normal user, like people who are victims of typo-squatting, that is a different type of user. So you should probably decide what you are doing. Are you helping the developers to understand exactly how they can get correct parsing tree and so on, or are you understanding that humans like myself or my mother when we're browsing on the internet seeing "paypaI", but the i instead of the l is the wrong thing. These are different things. So you should definitely decide which is your human. Is the human a developer or is the human a user? Because it's a very different class.

Vijay: I agree, but I think there are different approaches, depending on what class you are dealing with. I don't believe that we need to necessarily restrict it, only to developers or only to users, but we use different approaches. For example, we were doing a usability study right now, where we're looking at how people parse URLs.

Fabio Massacci: Who is "people"?

Vijay: General users—to better understand why users are susceptible to attacks. So, URL attacks go back twenty years. There are research papers that study this. In some of the modern browsers, we change the way that URLs look, so it's tailored to human deficiencies, as we call them in the paper. So in this study, we ask users to classify URLs and how safe they are, and we track their eye gaze. So, Michael spoke about Hammer. In this study, if we follow users' eye gaze and we can find what types of problems users run into and what kind of attacks they're probably most susceptible to, just by the way that they're parsing the actual URLs. So that might be useful in trying to find user boundaries.

Michael Millian: The distinction that you've drawn is a good one and we're interested in such distinctions in this paper.

Benjamin Ylvisaker: Another variable that seems really important to me is length of study. If looking at a regular expression or a grammar or something like that, if I just glance at it, it might like look line numbers. But for someone who spent an hour or a day or year studying it might think "This is a perfect obviously and I understand all the ins and outs of this." So if you're studying with real people that's...

Michael Millian: Yes that's a really good factor to make sure we look at.

Jonathan Anderson: I think another distinction you might want to tease apart is not just different categories of level of training or level of expertise but also, for the different categories of computation that you're talking about, we have computers that are doing similar kinds of things or doing something that's a subset of other things that the computer might do. Whereas I think, when you look at people who are, for example, engaged in their primary task with lots of attention and focus, versus people who are cruising through something that's just on their way to something that they want to do—I mean I'm not a psychologist, but I gather that it's completely different processes in ways of sense-making that are employed. So that might be an important distinction to get into as well. Because you may have very different ways of even describing the way that people are trying to walk through this sense making process when they're engaged in it for different reasons.

Vijay: Yes that's a really good suggestion.

Michael Millian: That's something that we're sort of doing with the URL study. It's not specifically tied to automata theory but we were thinking about that.

Jonathan Anderson: But in that case, if you're asking people, "Is this URL safe?" that means you're asking them to turn on the part of the brain that thinks about safety, when they're looking at the URL. That's maybe not the natural condition for looking at a URL or for clicking on something.

Vijay: The way that we are planning to do the study, subject to having enough participants of course to do the study in full, is that we were thinking about priming them beforehand. So there are various ways you can do it, you can watch a video or something else. We're not sure that it would be precisely like the encounter they would have in real life. We'll try to explore that.

Jim Blythe: We are also exploring models of human behavior that do take that exact difference into account, or at least we try to model the different processes and the fact that somebody will give one answer under one set of priming circumstances and another under a different set.

As you saw in this paper, we're just looking at the way that this lays out over the computability hierarchy. We drew the straight, broad preliminary piece, where we don't look at all these aspects. Thank you, that's certainly one that we would want to include, as we refine the human boundaries.

Jeff Yan: There is growing literature of computational thinking. Have you looked into that?

Jeannette Wing wrote an article on computational thinking, which started a large literature. I'm not sure actually how to answer the grand question you ask in the paper. I'm curious whether Jeannette's work could inform your study.

Vijay: We'll certainly take a look.

Jim Blythe: I know a little about that. Yes, I think it's a very interesting point. I mean it's a way to help people shape their thinking about these processes...

Jeff Yan: Yes. Exactly.

Jim Blythe: ...and it might bring them closer toward this. So it would be very interesting to see how that ...

Jeff Yan: Thinking in a computational way.

Jim Blythe: Yes. And using this framework might be a way of figuring out if that is actually helpful in terms of reducing vulnerabilities, for example, or other benefits.

Daniel Thomas: I think this might come back to the audio CAPTCHA talk yesterday[2]. Because there's the consideration of doing the task the first time. And maybe you don't understand it. Maybe you have the expertise to have another go and try again and revisit something. That can be very different kind of problem than the, "You must get it right the first time as you hear it, in a very time-constrained context" thing.' Whereas you can make your guess and listen again and check whether you are right.

Michael Millian: Yes. Repetition is an interesting factor that's related to time spent on the problem but distinct.

Ilia Shumailov: Yes we evaluated this effect and we actually found that there is some statistical significance in the training. So for the audio CAPTCHA there is an actual training process in there which we can measure and the differences are significant

Simon Foley: Have you considered when you ask this question, how it fits into the framework that Bella proposed where they looked at the number of levels going from the lowest level of the operating system and protocols up to the human interface and the human persona and then the social view of the human. So they talk about what is your model. Actually for the human-computer interface part, they looked at a limited model of personas, the different personas that people have when interact with the system. . . they have an Isabelle model of the human, in this case. And then from the probabilistic point of view, there's some work that Audun Josang from the University of Oslo did to capture human behaviour. So it might give you some hints about where you position what you mean by the human behaviour. Is it the human behaviour at the interface? Is it the human behaviour from the persona point of view? Or is it something other than that?

Vijay: I've heard of the personas work, but I don't know it very well. Yes, we will look at it. Thank you.

---

[2] "Audio CAPTCHA with a few cocktails", these proceedings.

Secure Sharing and Collaboration

Challenges in Designing a Distributed Cryptographic File System

Arastoo Bozorgi[1]([✉]), Mahya Soleimani Jadidi[2], and Jonathan Anderson[2]

[1] Department of Computer Science, Memorial University,
St. John's, NL A1B 3X9, Canada
`ab1502@mun.ca`
[2] Department of Electrical and Computer Engineering, Memorial University,
St. John's, Canada
`{msoleimanija,jonathan.anderson}@mun.ca`

Abstract. Online social networks, censorship resistance systems, document redaction systems and health care information systems have disparate requirements for confidentiality, integrity and availability. It is possible to address all of these, however, by combining elements of research in both filesystems and security protocols. We propose a set of techniques and combinations that can be employed to move beyond the current centralized/decentralized dichotomy and build a privacy-preserving optionally-distributed cryptographic filesystem. Such a filesystem, prototyped as *UPSS: the user-centred private sharing system*, can be used to build applications that enable rich, collaborative sharing in environments that have traditionally either avoided such interaction or else suffered the costs of out-of-control sharing on untrustworthy systems. We believe that our combination of filesystems and security protocols research demonstrates that sharing and security can go hand in hand.

Keywords: Privacy by design · Online social networks · Cryptographic file systems · Distributed file systems

1 Introduction

Private information about individuals is, today, stored in centralized repositories that must be trusted fully to perform access control faithfully. Alternative approaches have been proposed that distribute data in peer-to-peer networks, but they lack the availability required by real-world systems that process personal information. Online social networks, censorship resistance systems, document redaction systems and health care information systems have apparently-disparate requirements for confidentiality, integrity and availability. However, we believe that these problems are tractable if re-cast as filesystems problems, with a research goal of developing filesystems that incorporate both centralized and distributed components without sacrificing user privacy.

© Springer Nature Switzerland AG 2020
J. Anderson et al. (Eds.): Security Protocols 2019, LNCS 12287, pp. 177–192, 2020.
https://doi.org/10.1007/978-3-030-57043-9_17

The four use cases we have identified have differing, even contradictory, requirements (Sect. 2). For example, the requirement for centralized auditing of access to health care data is in direct opposition to the needs of a censorship-resistant online social network. However, we believe that there is a set of filesystems and cryptographic techniques that can be employed together, in various combinations, to meet each use case's requirements individually.

Techniques from modern copy-on-write filesystems can be combined with cryptographic capabilities, convergent encryption and distributed systems concepts in order to implement filesystem primitives with untrusted storage at global scale (Sect. 3). Untrusted block stores may be centralized for high performance or distributed for availability in the face of a censor, with local storage acting as either a cache or a seed as appropriate. Subsets of both files and directory trees can be selectively shared among users and applications, with mutability controlled by application-specific policy enforced only on user- or organization-controlled systems. Separating the control plane of policy enforcement from the data plane of bulk storage yields a hybrid filesystem that can be applied to centralized or distributed use cases.

We have begun to build a prototype of such a hybrid filesystem: *UPSS: the user-centred private sharing system*. This filesystem can be accessed as a traditional Unix filesystem or—perhaps more compellingly—incorporated directly into applications as a library. The UPSS API allows applications to interact with the system without knowledge of underlying structures such as the storage medium, and to provide more sophisticated sharing protocols than can be supported by the traditional POSIX filesystem API. Combining the research in both filesystems and security protocols, the UPSS project strives to enable systems with rich collaboration *and* strong user control in contexts as disparate as health care and censorship-resistant social networks.

2   Motivation: Use Cases

The requirements for our privacy-preserving distributed filesystem stem from four use cases that are not well-served by the state of the art:

- online social networking with untrusted service providers,
- censorship-resistant social networking with network partitioning,
- corporate file sharing with redaction integrity and
- health care data sharing with privacy and audit requirements.

A summary of the four use cases' requirements can be found in Table 1.

Table 1. Requirements derived from OSN (S), censorship-resistant network (C), redaction integrity (R) and health care (H) use cases

Requirement	S	C	R	H
High availability (connected network)	✓		✓	✓
Availability in network partition		✓		
Untrusted storage	✓	✓		✓
Partial/subset sharing	✓	✓	✓	✓
Scalable to large user base	✓		✓	✓
Sharing reciprocity ("merge requests")	✓	✓	✓	✓
Peer-to-peer storage and caching		✓		
Access auditing				✓

2.1 Online Social Network

General-purpose online social networks require high availability, frictionless content sharing and high overall standards for ease of use. Users—and the applications they employ—interact with shared content; any social application platform must be able to provide this access while still allowing for user control over that sharing. In addition to the above, however, it is desirable for any design incorporating centralized elements to *not trust the provider*. That is, although a central store of data may be required for availability and performance reasons, that provider need not have access to the plaintext of users' data.

As we describe in Sect. 3.1, it is possible to share immutable directory trees among users of a centralized data store while maintaining strong confidentiality, integrity and availability properties. This can be accomplished with well-understood cryptographic and filesystem techniques. The challenge of building a practical OSN from these raw materials is in the handling of shared *mutable* content. It must be possible to describe mutation in terms of operations that can be checked for consistency when performed by multiple authorized users. For example, updating a tree of shared content can be expressed as a "merge request" that replaces one immutable tree with another one, as long as the new tree references the original as its predecessor.

Thus, we make the following observations about the requirements for a privacy-preserving distributed filesystem being used as the basis for an OSN:

1. The requirement for high availability rules out techniques that base their security and functionality guarantees on the use of peer-to-peer networks—some centralized storage will be required.
2. Centralized providers must only have access to encrypted data, ideally without information about metadata such as file sizes.
3. Users should be able to easily delegate access to shared content, both to applications and to other users.

4. The requirement for massively scalable performance rules out techniques that impose heavy computational or network burdens on servers, such as secure multi-party computation or private information retrieval.
5. It should be possible to manage mutable directory trees with operations that can be checked for consistency, e.g., "merge requests".

2.2   Censorship-Resistant Social Networking

Reliable and widely adopted information systems need to be resilient against any censorships by authorities such as governments. Decentralization of server modules could be an effective approach for this issue, as any central point is a kind of weakness for the system. Inevitably, most of systems contain centralized management and decision making modules, for example, user authorization on the cloud storage should be done centrally. Peer-to-peer connections are a solution to reduce the risk of being blocked. Along with this idea, caching techniques are another effective ways to improve system's high availability. Thus, to provide a reliable and safe censorship-resistant information system, we can accommodate following fundamentals about the system's underlying filesystem to support stated requirements:

1. The requirement for decentralization leads to different sharing protocol on the filesystem that lets users to have peer-to-peer data sharing. Necessarily, we need a backup storage for those cases in which one of principles is offline. The sharing approach should handle backups as well. The connection protocol should work for different users behind NATs. Similar inspiring protocols have been introduced before, such as Session Traversal Utilities for NAT (STUN) [23], for finding users' public IP addresses and ports. Figure 1 shows this situation.

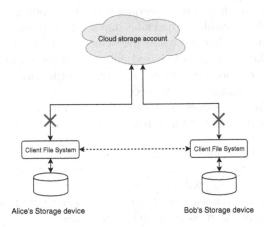

Fig. 1. Applied censorship to the central point of the system

2. Along with peer-to-peer connections, the requirement for system's high availability results in different caching techniques which support various periods of time for cached data. The filesystem can handle data caching based on users' share requests. In this way, having permanent cached data is also possible. Expired cached data could be removed in different ways such as having a garbage collector that runs periodically.

2.3   Redaction with Integrity

A common requirement for large organizations—both commercial and governmental—is the ability to release documents and information selectively in response to information requests and legal discovery. Current approaches to such information sharing involve the redaction of documents and a one-way release of information. Linking redacted documents to their original versions is a manual process that provides little technical assurance of integrity. A chain of custody for such information may be asserted by the releasing organization but may not, using current techniques, be verified by the receiving party.

It is desirable to be able to release portions of documents in a manner that provides strong integrity verification and linking to the original document. Sharing part of a file or a directory hierarchy should be efficient and should allow linking to commitments for unredacted versions without revealing any redacted information. In addition, it may be desirable to provide a mechanism for changes to released content to be shared back to the original, unredacted document, enabling new communication patterns and—potentially—better strategies for internal information compartmentalization. We can thus observe that:

1. Directory hierarchies and even files should be sharable *in part*, as subsets of their unredacted originals.
2. Shared subsets should be linkable to original, unredacted documents with strong integrity.
3. Changes to redacted documents should be re-sharable back to redacting parties in a way that permits two-way collaboration over partial views.

2.4   Health Care Data Sharing

Health care information systems have several requirements in common with OSNs such as high availability and data sharing within the network. One additional requirements, however, is the need for auditing of accesses to patient data. This acts as a disincentive for health care workers to access the private information of patients they are not caring for. However, in the context of a privacy-preserving system, the requirement for audit records should not cause arbitrary patient data to be exposed to the network security team.

One barrier to innovation in the health care context is the dichotomy between "trusted" and "untrusted" systems and the enormous effort required to certify a system as "trusted". A filesystem that afforded the ability to securely share strict subsets of patient data could enable new innovations. Applications running on such a platform could be executed with lower stakes, as the impact of an application accidentally leaking data without context, e.g., image data with no patient identifiers attached, would be less than if the application implicitly had access to complete patient records. This is anologous on the partial data sharing requirement described in Sect. 2.3, but in a very different environment.

We thus make the following observations about the challenges of building health information systems atop a privacy-preserving distributed filesystem:

1. Confidentiality must be maintained from both system administrators and health care workers who do not require patients' information in the course of providing care.
2. Access to patient data should be auditable without revealing patient information to auditors.
3. It should be possible to provide new applications with access to data subsets without implying access to complete patient records.

3   UPSS: The User-Centred Private Sharing System

To design a system which can provide a fundamental basis for the majority of the requirements discussed in Sect. 2, we use some key ideas of existing systems, mainly discussed in Sect. 4, to design our system as a new filesystem associated with efficient sharing mechanism. By introducing UPSS, we try to meet confidentiality, high availability, data integrity, and an efficient sharing mechanism, all integrated into a system to serve a wide range of other applications.

To support confidentiality, we use cryptographic techniques to provide an end-to-end sharing system, which stores user data in a secure way on the storage, with user-controlled privacy. To provide a high level of availability, users' storages or cloud storage accounts can be used as temporary or even permanent caches to maintain other users' data online. Consequently, this data replication leads to data inconsistency problem which is reduced to version control problem by storing user data in immutable objects in our system. UPSS suggests a content-addressing mechanism for data blocks on storage through cryptographic hashes obtained from blocks' content and their physical locations on storage.

Our system is constructed out of four main layers, which are depicted in Fig. 2. In this section, we discuss UPSS, a User-centered Private Sharing System in more details and explain how UPSS can meet the discussed requirements.

3.1   Immutable DAGs

Data is stored in UPSS as a set of fixed-size immutable encrypted blocks. These blocks, which are encrypted and named according to a hash of their ciphertext, are linked together in a Merkle DAG (Directed Acyclic Graph). Merkle DAGs are used to describe files, directories and versions of both. Immutable blocks are encrypted using symmetric keys derived from cryptographic hashes of their content, a technique known as *convergent encryption* [9], and named using the

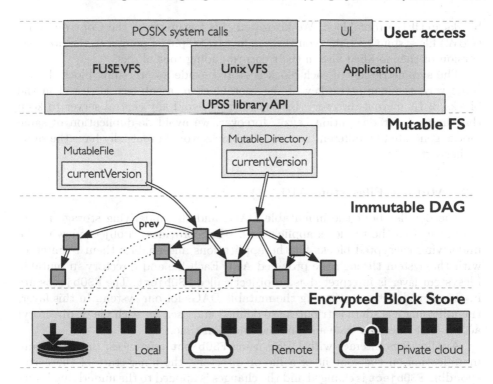

Fig. 2. Layers in the UPSS prototype. Encrypted block store stores ciphertext blocks, which are generated from plaintext blocks in immutable Merkle DAGs (thick arrows represent block pointers). A mutable filesystem is exposed as a library API, which can be consumed directly by applications or adapted to a conventional filesystem API.

cryptographic hash of their ciphertext, a technique known as *content-addressable storage*. The name of a block and the key that can be used to access it are referred to as a *block pointer* $BP_B = (n_B, k_B)$, given by:

$$k_B = h(B)$$
$$n_B = h\left(E_{k_B}\{B\}\right)$$

where n_B is the name of a block and k_B is the key used to decrypt it. A block pointer can thus be seen as a cryptographic *capability* [8] to read a block, though not necessarily to modify it (see Sect. 3.3). The block pointer to the root node of a file or directory implies the ability to access arbitrary quantities of content, up to an entire filesystem.

By defining blocks to be immutable, we reduce the data inconsistency problem to a version control problem. A file modification causes a new version of the file to be created and this modification affects the whole path up to the parent blocks until the root block. We borrowed this feature from the Copy-on-Write (CoW) file systems. Version controls are met by keeping a pointer to the previous version of the modified files in their corresponding root blocks.

The symmetric key of each block is stored inside its preceding block. In the same way, the symmetric key of the root block in a sub-tree is stored in the blocks of the parent directory. In this way, we avoid any central server to keep the chain of our decryption keys. Moreover, we avoid de-duplication of same blocks generated by different users as the blocks would eventually have the same ciphertext.

3.2   Mutable Filesystem API

All the details about the immutable DAGs and the underlying storage model is hidden from the top level applications. UPSS provides an object view of the underlying encrypted blocks for the applications and enables them to interact with the system through the provided API. Each file and directory in mutable filesystem layer is interpreted as an object called FSObject. The FSObjects are in-memory objects constituting the mutable DAGs for our system. In this layer, the following metadata attributes are defined and used for each file or directory: access time, creation time and the modification time.

Applications interact with UPSS using FSObject references. In case of any modification on the content of a file or directory, the inner state of the corresponding FSObject is changed and the changes is applied to the underlying layers to reflect the file/directory's modification. However, the object reference remains the same. This process is done in background and is transparent from the top level applications. The results can be returned by callback functions provided by the API's methods. This approach can also make a non-blocking modification process from the applications' viewpoint running on the upper level.

The FSObjects enables us to have structured files, which can support some functionalities not supported by the classical Unix filesystems that interpret the files as unstructured byte arrays. One of the functionalities supported by UPSS is guaranteeing the data consistency of the shared files between users. To do so, the system should define a consistency model, suitable for distributed systems. One applicable solution is to define the file structures as a Conflict-free Replicated Data Type (CRDT) [12,25,26] to guarantee that shared files on different replicas converge, by defining a Strong Eventual Consistency (SEC) model, which leverages mathematical properties such as monotonicity in a semilattice and/or commutativity, which ensure the absence of conflict. An add-only DAG is an example of a CRDT data type [25] suitable for a distributed filesystem with file sharing and redacting integrity.

3.3   Share Control Module

Providing a mechanism to share data, either on a multiuser system or over the network in distributed systems, is a crucial feature for various information systems. According to the requirements described in Sect. 2, a sharing module on top of our filesystem is responsible to support different scenarios for both central-ized and peer-to-peer data sharing. To have a very flexible, and also extensible design for the future, we considered the sharing module as another application above the UPSS API library, shown in Fig. 3, along with other applications such as Unix VFS or FUSE VFS, etc. Thus, the subsequent integrated system potentially supports a wide range of required use cases for information systems.

As a primary prototype, this module is divided into two principal sub-modules that handle share requests and data transmissions separately. The share control module is an application, mainly responsible to manage share requests, in terms of the sharing protocol, version control, users' privileges and access controls. This module receives or sends share requests. Once the request is pro-cessed and the user and privileges are authorized, the share control module makes related modification on shared data through the UPSS API.

On the other side, data transmission accomplishes using the sharing block store which communicates with the local block store or the local caches of the system and other remote block stores. Figure 3 represents this module. These features distinguish UPSS from the other systems described in Sect. 4.

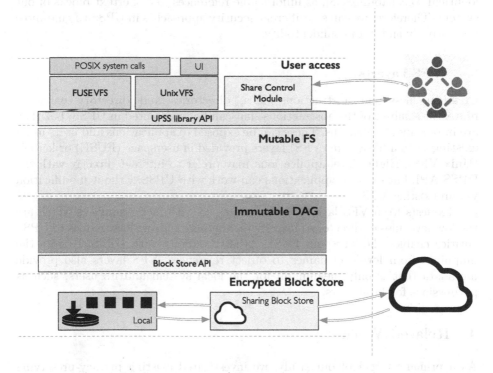

Fig. 3. Sharing module includes two sub-modules, share control module and sharing remote block store, to manage share procedure and data transmission control

As another important issue that rises about data sharing, this module handles users' access controls. When we talk about data sharing between users and their privacy, accessibility appears as the other important issue. In UPSS, the concepts of permissions and privileges are raised in different layers and vary based on the scope in which the user is defined. For example, for local users in a multiuser system, a file can be shared with traditional POSIX permissions such as "read", "write" and "execute". However, for non-local users in the network involved with share and merge requests, we need to define additional policies and definitions to provide a user-centered privacy scheme through access controls. For example, any user can share data with others, but nobody obtains or modifies data without the right privileges. Data modification would be done after user authorization, which can be achieved using cryptographic techniques such as public keys and certificates. For remote users, modifying data could be followed with merge or pull requests. The sharing protocol considers users' access rights before the main procedure of the request accomplishes. The rest of the procedure would be done in the mutable layer, as it is implicitly shown in Sect. 3.2. The corresponding mutable block would be added to the mutable Merkle DAG associated with the block pointer to its ciphertext block. Here, the application of block pointers is identical to capabilities [8], as unforgeable references to ciphertext blocks of our system. Therefore, we can see different security approaches in UPSS to guarantee user privacy and data confidentiality.

3.4 VFS Layer(s)

Classical filesystem abstractions—files, directories and directory entries—represent a subset of the abstractions that can be represented in UPSS, but they are important abstractions. These can be exposed to applications and users using existing virtual filesystem (VFS) layers provided in userspace (FUSE) or kernels (Unix VFS). Higher-level applications may prefer to interact directly with the UPSS API, but existing applications can work with UPSS without modification via an existing VFS.

Requests from VFS layers can be addressed with inode numbers which are the low-level files or directories identifiers. Mapping the low-level names to UPSS entities enables the VFS and FUSE APIs to interact with UPSS. Besides the mappings from low-level names to object references, VFS layers also provide metadata that is only meaningful for the local system and its users, such as permissions for local users.

4   Related Work

As a primary target of our study, we investigated existing privacy-preserving approaches mainly in online social networks. First, we started with studying different systems and modules regardless of their type, scope and the system level in which they are integrated and employed, to find their key ideas, cons, and pros. The only common feature between all of them is their effort to place additional user privacy, especially against OSN server providers. As we expanded our target to have a secure and privacy-preserving filesystem, we continued with an investigation on several filesystems, focusing on their provided security features. We summarize these studies starting from OSN tools to filesystems.

4.1 Online Social Network Systems and Tool

Privacy on social networks can be discussed in different ways. The old well-known and well-supported issue is users privacy against each other. But, the matter remained hidden behind the first issue was users privacy against OSN servers and providers. Efforts to support the first feature, caused the community to forget about the providers until recent years. Eventually, attempts to improve privacy in centralized OSN systems appeared. Because of the centralized architecture of most adopted OSNs, such as Facebook and Google Drive, primary proposed approaches tended to be centralized in design. Lockr [29], FlyByNight [14], NOYB [10], Scramble [1] and CP2 [22], all can be counted as important and effective tools in this category. In addition to centralization, we can categorize privacy countermeasures and approaches in other ways. Using cryptographic techniques or providing user-controlled privacy are other effective features.

Lockr [29] and Scramble [1] are browser plug-ins which restricts accesses through user-defined access control lists. Although this feature makes a flexible privacy scheme, it still suffers from storing plaintext data on OSN servers, including user data and users relationships. FlybyNight [14] and CP2 (short for "Cryptographic privacy protection") [22] protect user data by some encryption mechanism with this difference that CP2 can also protect the relationships between users by determining the users with some unique pseudonyms. In NOYB [10], users' profiles are partitioned into smaller clusters called *atoms*, and the atoms of one user are substituted with atoms of another user in the same cluster pseudo-randomly, and then the encrypted index of each atom is stored in a dictionary. The authors of FaceCloak [15], introduced a mechanism in which the users' private data is stored encrypted in a user-trusted third-party server, while some other fake data related to encrypted data are stored in OSN servers in plain-text format. One important point about using data encryption in communication with OSNs is that these systems and their providers should allow encrypted messages and data to be stored or transmitted. Moreover, data encryption should not affect OSNs' main functionalities such as search use cases.

Another beneficial feature toward real privacy for users is user-controlled or user-centered privacy. For example, Lockr, FaceCloak, and Scramble, allow users to define and control their preferred privacy mainly through access control lists.

As it is stated above, the centralized nature of OSNs in which all users' data is accessible by a single entity, i.e., OSN provider, encourages the researchers to change their mind about how to preserve users' data, which leads to a shift from client-server to a decentralized architecture coupled with encryption so that the users can protect their data. Diaspora [3] is an examples of such architecture for OSNs.

In decentralized P2P systems, connectivity and high availability are other issues that bring several other challenges to be discussed, along with other existing problems such as privacy. PeerSoN (short for "P2P Social Networking") [5], Safebook [28] and Porkut [20] are instances of decentralized OSNs that have tried to come up with solving some parts of these challenges. PeerSoN [5] tried to overcome connectivity and privacy limitations. The main properties of PeerSoN are encryption, decentralization, and direct data exchange. Safebook [28] is another system that tried to protect users, from potential privacy violations, against providers. It relies on the concept "peers", which points to the cooperation between users on the social network. Although Safebook has presented a decentralized structure, it still relies on central servers that keep pseudonyms of interacting nodes in the network. Also, there are criticisms of its privacy scheme. Porkut [20], as another example in this category, focuses mainly on data availability by replicating users' data on trusted friends' storages. Also, a privacy preserving indexing mechanism is introduced which facilitates content discovery among friends. The indexes are stored on a Distributed Hash Table (DHT) [27] in the form of $(key, value)$ pairs. As another different example, we can consider Cachet [21] which is an improvement of DECENT [11]. Cachet proposed a decentralized architecture to be used in OSNs, which protects confidentiality by an attribute-based encryption. It also provides integrity and availability by digital signature and gossip-based social caching algorithm, respectively.

However, all the discussed decentralized approaches rely on distributed data structures such as DHTs to enable the users to interact with each other and discover other users and resources. The nodes which construct the DHT network should be trusted to keep critical information about the users and the network topology. Another drawback of being relied on the DHT network is its need to a Proof-of-Work (PoW) protocol [19], which imposes considerable computational power on DHT nodes.

To summarize, in both centralized and decentralized architecture of discussed OSNs, we can still see unaddressed privacy, availability, and connectivity problems. Despite all efforts done to overcome these restrictive issues, proposed approaches seem superficial rather than beneficial, for our requirements. This matter leads us to think about lower layers of the system, where we are involved with the filesystem and its communication with applications in higher layers. If we can provide confidentiality, data integrity, and availability at the same level as the filesystem, then all applications running over that filesystem benefit from these properties.

4.2 File Systems

In most traditional filesystems, data integrity and availability is preferred over confidentiality and privacy. For several years, the concept of privacy was something beyond filesystems functionalities, and data writing and retrieval throughput was the most important feature. As an example, (ZFS) [4] is placed in the group of efficient widely adopted filesystems through its novel technique, Copy-on-Write (CoW). Thus, distributed filesystems were introduced with the main target of providing high availability along with the former feature. Examples of such filesystems are Coda [24], Ivy [18] and Ori [16].

Coda [24] is one of the inspiring distributed filesystems with the idea of shared data repositories. It retrieves data and resolves conflicts using the concept called accessible volume storage group (AVSG) as data replicas. Similar to Coda, Ivy [18], as a multi-user peer-to-peer filesystem, has focused on data availability with a different approach which relies on private snapshots from filesystem for each participant. Ivy stores logs from the state of the filesystem in a distributed hash table, called DHash [7]. A log constituted of the dedicated private snapshot for each user, contains all user's modifications to filesystem data and meta-data. Thus, we can find signs of user privacy in Ivy's approach, although confidentiality has not been stated as its main feature. We can find these features collected in Ori [16], plus its own data sharing mechanism, grafting, across user multiple devices. Synchronization, failures handling and data recovery, are expanded and emphasized in Ori more than two previous stated filesystems. Over time, filesystems and other sharing stores expanded their functionalities, such as content-addressing, based on new requirements in the community. As a modern filesystem, IPFS [2] synthesizes the key successful ideas behind systems such as DHTs [27], BitTorrent [6], Git [13], and SFS [17]. Moreover, IPFS deals with encrypted mutable objects to improve confidentiality.

Having inspired by discussed filesystems, we strongly believe that UPSS, as a cryptographic content-addressable filesystem can serve typical filesystem requirements associated with many of the modern requirements that are explained in Sect. 2. UPSS stores data in content-addressed fixed-length blocks and controls block accessibility through its sharing module that supports both peer-to-peer and client-server connections. The UPSS's APIs, discussed in the Sect. 3, provide a higher level of abstraction about the underlying storage model and enable a variety of applications to use the system without any assumption about the physical storage.

5   Conclusion

Distrustful information sharing is a common problem that is not well-addressed by the existing state of the art. In online social networks, sharing *any* information with friends requires sharing *all* information with a potentially-untrustworthy provider. Countermeasures to the all-seeing provider are brittle, ineffectual or else perform too poorly for general consumption. In the general social networking case, users lose control of how widely their data is shared; the stakes are even higher in censorship resistance scenarios. In environments with strong confidentiality properties, conversely, a lack of secure sharing techniques stifles collaboration, transparency and innovation. This is seen when organizations apply redaction with no linkability to original data or when health-care authorities silo patient information off from potentially-innovative applications.

One linkage among all four of these use cases is the need to share information *selectively* and *securely* among parties without requiring complete trust.

Any technique for enabling such sharing must not be strictly one-way: it must provide the possibility of reciprocation and collaboration. We have argued that all of these goals can be met by recasting the above problems in terms of a privacy-preserving filesystem. By decoupling storage from access control, a distributed user-centred filesystem can provide confidentiality, integrity and availability properties to support systems in all four of these use cases.

Using encrypted fixed-length blocks in a content-addressable store, information can be stored with untrusted providers, cached locally and/or distributed opportunistically via contact or peer-to-peer networks. Using convergent encryption and Merkle DAGs, file and directory structures can be stored as immutable DAGs in a manner that both preserves privacy and enables global deduplication. Higher-level mutable filesystem objects can be maintained using higher-level sharing protocols with application-specifiable authorization schemes. Finally, this filesystem can be exposed to users via direct embedding within applications, via local Web frontends or as a traditional filesystem within FUSE or a Unix VFS layer.

We are exploring these ideas in our prototype filesystem, *UPSS: the user-centred private sharing system*. We believe that the availability of such a filesystem will enable the development of applications and platforms that provide both strong user privacy and rich collaborative sharing. Designing such systems may yet demonstrate that sharing and security can go hand in hand.

References

1. Beato, F., Kohlweiss, M., Wouters, K.: Scramble! Your social network data. In: Fischer-Hübner, S., Hopper, N. (eds.) PETS 2011. LNCS, vol. 6794, pp. 211–225. Springer, Heidelberg (2011). https://doi.org/10.1007/978-3-642-22263-4_12
2. Benet, J.: IPFS-content addressed, versioned, P2P file system. arXiv preprint arXiv:1407.3561 (2014)
3. Bielenberg, A., Helm, L., Gentilucci, A., Stefanescu, D., Zhang, H.: The growth of diaspora-a decentralized online social network in the wild. In: 2012 Proceedings IEEE INFOCOM Workshops, pp. 13–18. IEEE (2012)
4. Bonwick, J., Ahrens, M., Henson, V., Maybee, M., Shellenbaum, M.: The zettabyte file system. In: Proceedings of the 2nd USENIX conference on File and Storage Technologies, vol. 215 (2003)
5. Buchegger, S., Schiöberg, D., Vu, L.H., Datta, A.: PeerSoN: P2P social networking: early experiences and insights. In: Proceedings of the Second ACM EuroSys Workshop on Social Network Systems, pp. 46–52. ACM (2009)
6. Cohen, B.: Incentives build robustness in BitTorrent. In: Workshop on Economics of Peer-to-Peer Systems, vol. 6, pp. 68–72 (2003)
7. Dabek, F., Kaashoek, M.F., Karger, D., Morris, R., Stoica, I.: Wide-area cooperative storage with CFS. In: ACM SIGOPS Operating Systems Review, vol. 35, pp. 202–215. ACM (2001)
8. Dennis, J.B., Van Horn, E.C.: Programming semantics for multiprogrammed computations. Commun. ACM **9**(3), 143–155 (1966)

9. Douceur, J.R., Adya, A., Bolosky, W.J., Simon, P., Theimer, M.: Reclaiming space from duplicate files in a serverless distributed file system. In: Proceedings 22nd International Conference on Distributed Computing Systems, pp. 617–624. IEEE (2002)

10. Guha, S., Tang, K., Francis, P.: NOYB: privacy in online social networks. In: Proceedings of the First Workshop on Online Social Networks, pp. 49–54. ACM (2008)

11. Jahid, S., Nilizadeh, S., Mittal, P., Borisov, N., Kapadia, A.: DECENT: a decentralized architecture for enforcing privacy in online social networks. In: 2012 IEEE International Conference on Pervasive Computing and Communications Workshops (PERCOM Workshops), pp. 326–332. IEEE (2012)

12. Kleppmann, M., Beresford, A.R.: A conflict-free replicated JSON datatype. IEEE Trans. Parallel Distrib. Syst. **28**(10), 2733–2746 (2017)

13. Loeliger, J., McCullough, M.: Version Control with Git: Powerful Tools and Techniques for Collaborative Software Development. O'Reilly Media Inc., Sebastopol (2012)

14. Lucas, M.M., Borisov, N.: FlyByNight: mitigating the privacy risks of social networking. In: Proceedings of the 7th ACM Workshop on Privacy in the Electronic Society, pp. 1–8. ACM (2008)

15. Luo, W., Xie, Q., Hengartner, U.: FaceCloak: an architecture for user privacy on social networking sites. In: International Conference on Computational Science and Engineering 2009, CSE 2009, vol. 3, pp. 26–33. IEEE (2009)

16. Mashtizadeh, A.J., Bittau, A., Huang, Y.F., Mazieres, D.: Replication, history, and grafting in the Ori file system. In: Proceedings of the Twenty-Fourth ACM Symposium on Operating Systems Principles, pp. 151–166. ACM (2013)

17. Mazieres, D., Kaashoek, M.F.: Escaping the evils of centralized control with self-certifying pathnames. In: Proceedings of the 8th ACM SIGOPS European Workshop on Support for Composing Distributed Applications, pp. 118–125. ACM (1998)

18. Muthitacharoen, A., Morris, R., Gil, T.M., Chen, B.: Ivy: a read/write peer-to-peer file system. ACM SIGOPS Oper. Syst. Rev. **36**(SI), 31–44 (2002)

19. Nakamoto, S.: Bitcoin: a peer-to-peer electronic cash system (2008)

20. Narendula, R., Papaioannou, T.G., Aberer, K.: Privacy-aware and highly-available OSN profiles. In: 2010 19th IEEE International Workshop on Enabling Technologies: Infrastructures for Collaborative Enterprises (WETICE), pp. 211–216. IEEE (2010)

21. Nilizadeh, S., Jahid, S., Mittal, P., Borisov, N., Kapadia, A.: Cachet: a decentralized architecture for privacy preserving social networking with caching. In: Proceedings of the 8th International Conference on Emerging Networking Experiments and Technologies, pp. 337–348. ACM (2012)

22. Raji, F., Miri, A., Jazi, M.D.: CP2: cryptographic privacy protection framework for online social networks. Comput. Electr. Eng. **39**(7), 2282–2298 (2013)

23. Rosenberg, J., Mahy, R., Matthews, P., Wing, D.: Session traversal utilities for NAT (STUN). Technical report (2008)

24. Satyanarayanan, M., Kistler, J.J., Kumar, P., Okasaki, M.E., Siegel, E.H., Steere, D.C.: Coda: a highly available file system for a distributed workstation environment. IEEE Trans. Comput. **39**(4), 447–459 (1990)

25. Shapiro, M., Preguiça, N., Baquero, C., Zawirski, M.: A comprehensive study of convergent and commutative replicated data types. Ph.D. thesis, Inria-Centre Paris-Rocquencourt; INRIA (2011)

26. Shapiro, M., Preguiça, N., Baquero, C., Zawirski, M.: Conflict-free replicated data types. In: Défago, X., Petit, F., Villain, V. (eds.) SSS 2011. LNCS, vol. 6976, pp. 386–400. Springer, Heidelberg (2011). https://doi.org/10.1007/978-3-642-24550-3_29

27. Stoica, I., Morris, R., Karger, D., Kaashoek, M.F., Balakrishnan, H.: Chord: a scalable peer-to-peer lookup service for internet applications. ACM SIGCOMM Comput. Commun. Rev. **31**(4), 149–160 (2001)

28. Strufe, T.: Safebook: a privacy-preserving online social network leveraging on real-life trust. IEEE Commun. Mag. **47**, 94–101 (2009)

29. Tootoonchian, A., Gollu, K.K., Saroiu, S., Ganjali, Y., Wolman, A.: Lockr: social access control for web 2.0. In: Proceedings of the First Workshop on Online Social Networks, pp. 43–48. ACM (2008)

Challenges in Designing a Distributed Cryptographic File System (Transcript of Discussion)

Arastoo Bozorgi[1(✉)], Mahya Soleimani Jadidi[2], and Jonathan Anderson[2]

[1] Department of Computer Science, Memorial University,
St. John's, NL A1B 3X9, Canada
ab1502@mun.ca

[2] Department of Electrical and Computer Engineering,
Memorial University, St. John's, NL, Canada
{msoleimanija,jonathan.anderson}@mun.ca

We are going to design a cryptographic file system, which has some cool features, which the current file system doesn't solve, like: file sharing, partial file sharing and also enable the users to collaborate with each other based on these shared files and also make this promise to users that their possible conflicts with your result in the file system level.

First, I will discuss some motivational use cases, and some problems that exist about these use cases and finally, I will introduce our system called UPSS or more easily to remember it, "Oops." So, you're going to trust a system called UPSS to store everything for you securely.

These cases are online social network, with untrusted service provider, a censorship resistant social network and a corporates file sharing with redaction integrity and finally, a healthcare data sharing, which provides some other things. So, we need a solution for all of them.

In the current online social networks, the users need to trust the provider to store their data and this is the main problem, because the providers use the user data for other purposes. So, instead we can store user data on untrusted storage accounts or on their storage devices and in this case we need to guarantee the confidentiality, availability and integrity of data and also we need to provide a frictionless and smooth file sharing between users and also keep the shared file consistent, different versions of the shared file.

Imagine that user data is stored somewhere on a cloud account or centrally on a server and some governments like my government applies some censorship to these accounts and the connection between the users and those storage accounts are blocked. In this case, we need to connect users directly, like in a peer to peer connection. But, the problem is that maybe the users are behind different firewalls and therefore we have some network partitions.

So, user data are stored on their storage devices on their own PCs for example and we need to increase the data availability when the user's offline. So we need to replicate data on for example users storage accounts. It brings with itself data inconsistency, because we have different versions of the data on different accounts.

© Springer Nature Switzerland AG 2020
J. Anderson et al. (Eds.): Security Protocols 2019, LNCS 12287, pp. 193–199, 2020.
https://doi.org/10.1007/978-3-030-57043-9_18

Also, imagine that we have an organisation that wants to partial share documents to different users and this document can be redacted. So the users shouldn't be aware of the redacted part of the document and also they need to be able to make some changes to the redacted document and this redacted document should be linkable, mergeable into the main document. So, again, we need partial file sharing and they should be editable and linkable to the original one and also here we may need to maintain a chain of custody.

There are a group of people that refers to us, and they say we have some drones, that they are capturing some videos from some companies or bad guys, that they are dumping some waste into the ocean. So we need to share some part of the video to some users like the police officers or the court and the other part to the others and we need a chain of custody. So as the result everything need to be presented to a court and definitely, we need to preserve integrity of everything here.

The other use case is, healthcare data sharing and other things. Here we have a central storage accounts, which stores some sensitive information about users. So we need to preserve the confidentiality, because health related information are stored on this storage and again we need the partial sharing.

For example, physician one needs to access some part of the patient one's record and the others to the other parts. And here another problem that need to be addressed is to audit the accesses to the files and documents. So, these audited accesses can be presented to some auditors, so based on these accesses they can identify the misbehaviour of the users. But these audits shouldn't reveal any information about the patients.

Until now, here is a summary of the problems that we have, and some of them are in the opposite direction of the others. Like in access auditing, we have central servers, and some things are important, but in the peer to peer one, we don't have any central thing.

We believe that, by having a cryptographic file system, which used the existing technologies and systems, we can address these problems. So we can combine research in the file systems and the security protocols like: the convergent encryption, immutable DAGs, content addressable storages and copy-on-write file modifications, to build up UPSS, which is a Usercentric Private Sharing System.

Here is a big picture of our layered structure of UPSS. We have encrypted data block layer, on top of that, immutable DAGs and mutable file system and on top of all of them, we have an API library, which provides some methods for other applications, in the higher layers.

So, as you can see one of the applications of UPSS can be a file system in user space or in kernel. Here we are storing everything, we are storing user data as fixed sized, immutable encrypted blocks. So they are immutable, which means we cannot modify the blocks and if any modification happens, we are creating new versions. And, for encrypting these immutable blocks, we use convergent encryptions. So this citation number is the same as the number in my references in the pre-proceedings.

We generate an encryption key from the hash of the plain text block and encrypt the block by this key and create a cryptographic hash of the ciphertext for the name of the block. The combination of this name and this key would be a block pointer, so we name everything in our system with these block pointers, and it is the content addressable storage, that we are building.

When we have a big file, we chunk it to smaller data blocks and inside each data block, we put the block pointer to the next block. By having these blocks, we are logically connecting the data blocks, and we are creating immutable DAGs. So the blocks are immutable, so the entire DAG is also immutable. And also, we've stored the decryption keys in the preceding block of each block. It means that by this, we don't need any central key manager server for storing our decryption keys. And also, by having the block pointer of for example, this root block, we can assess all the underlying blocks.

Fabio Massacci: So can you explain what's the reason you stored the key in the previous block, the preceding block. Right?

Reply: Yeah.

Fabio Massacci: Then everybody who has the block, can have the key, the decryption key. Is that right?

Reply: Yeah. So if you want to decrypt that block, you can access to the next block as well.

Fabio Massacci: So just need to trust only whoever has access to preceding blocks, has access to all the sub trees there. Right?

Reply: Yes.

Jonathan Anderson: Just pick a new file.

Bruce Christianson: how do you do the redaction?

Reply: Okay. I can explain it in the next slides. These blocks are related to a file. When you have the decryption key of the routes blocks, so you can decrypt all the blocks to create the file. So it is related to one file. And also, as we are creating everything from the cryptographic hash of their content, if two user or applications ... Question?

Vashek Matyas: What happens if the root block is corrupt?

Reply: Maybe, we can have some backups of the root block. But if the root block has been corrupted, so we cannot retrieve the file. So, if two different users or two different applications generate the same content, their cryptographic hash would be the same, and we are avoiding de-duplication of the blocks. And by defining everything as immutable, we are in fact reducing the data and inconsistency problem to a version control problem.

So, for example, here if you want to add something to the end of this file in fact, we are creating a new block, add the block pointer to this one and this file would be the new one. These blocks would be the new blocks. And in the root block of this file, we keep a pointer to the previous version of the file. So this is how the version control system somehow works.

Fabio Massacci: Sorry and I missed the immutable part. Because the block in the middle level has not been changed, it pointed to a different place and therefore is no longer immutable. You have changed the point, so the block is different.

Reply: Yes, exactly.

Fabio Massacci: So the root has been changed. Because now, it points to different next block and the previous one has been changed. So you have the entire thing has been changed up the root.

Reply: So, this is how we address exactly this problem. To address this specific problem, we use the copy-on-write file modification. As we mentioned before and based on your question, we said that everything is immutable. So, when we are adding a block pointer to this one, it means that we are changing the content of this one. We are not changing that block. We are creating a new block by having that block pointer and also we need to add the block pointer of this one in its parent one. So we update everything until the root one and this is the copy-on-write file notification.

Fabio Massacci: So then all the standards have been corrupt. But then you didn't answer the Bruce's question. So how do you do a redaction, because everyone changes something. Everybody from the root, know everything.

Reply: If two different users have two different versions of the file, they are changing their own versions, locally. In some point in time those changes need to be merged into the original one, like un-redacted one. In that case, we need to have some merge requests or updates, which need to be propagated to the main authority, which has the un-redacted version of the file. And, in both of them, we have a pointer to the previous version and we can access the full history of the changes, about the files and blocks.

Bruce Christianson: An alternative approach to redaction is to say, "If I'm giving you a block and it's got some pointers to other blocks and you can follow some of those pointers. But you can't follow other ones". Because-

Reply: Yes.

Bruce Christianson: ... You can't get to one of those other points.

Reply: Yeah.

Bruce Christianson: Did you make a deliberate decision, not to take that approach?

Reply: When I want to redact something for you, in fact, one possible solution can be creating sub blocks from that block, by creating new blocks and relate those blocks to each other and give the pointer of the roots, of the new thing to you and say, "Here's the thing that you can access." But in my system, I should also keep this thing, that this redacted thing is related to these main documents.

Bruce Christianson: Okay. So conceptually, they're separate documents.

Reply: Yeah.

Bruce Christianson: It's just then you know that they are related.

Reply: Until here, everything was immutable. So from this point on, we have some kind of mutability. So, per each file and directory, which are meaningful in classical file systems, we have some in-memory objects, which we call them FSObjects.

In this layer, we have a pointer inside these FSObjects to the root of the block, which is related to the file or directory. And when something is changed in these underlying layers, the only thing that needs be updated in this mutable, in-memory object, is the pointer to the most updated version of the block, or the file. The only thing that the higher level applications need to interact with UPSS, is a reference to these FSObjects. The modifications and also the file changes, the creation of the blocks and copy-on-write concepts are transparent from the higher level applications and just they have that reference of that FSObjects.

And here in this layer we can also define the local access time, creation time, and modification time. We separate these metadata from the original blocks. Because, these metadata are the things that are updating frequently. Therefore, if we add those metadata to those blocks, every time we need to do the copy-on-write file modification until the root. So we are separating them and put them inside this layer, inside the FSObjects.

Another cool thing about the FSObjects is that we can define some structures for files and directories in traditional file systems. So, one of them can be the CRDTs, that have been discussed recently and by having these CRDT data types inside the FSObjects, we can guarantee that the possible conflicts can be resolved. So here, the difference between this one from the traditional file system is that in traditional ones, we have just an array of bytes, but we can here define some structure for our files.

Also, on top of UPSS, (we can say it is a part of the entire UPSS project), is a private collaboration service. This service contains two primary sub modules, which are sharing control module or maybe, "Sharing" wouldn't not be a good word, Collaboration control module and the blocks store. This block store is responsible for retrieving something from the other storage accounts, those storage accounts can be a cloud account, a friend's account. So this one is responsible for reading or writing from/to those storages and also in share control module, we are defining the access rights for remote users, who can access a specific file, is controlled in this module.

Also, on top of UPSS as I mentioned in the beginning slides, we can have some VFS compatibility layers. So we can define a file system, which can be run in user space by FUSE or in kernel. By having this, we are trying to enable the applications to interact with UPSS, without modifying the application. In this case, if we have an UPSS system and UPSS is responsible for guaranteeing the data consistency between difference version of the file. So in this case, we don't need to modify the existing applications. So imagine that we have different copies of a word document and different users start working on word document and changing something inside the word document, then UPSS is responsible for solving any possible conflicts.

Fabio Massacci: Sorry. If I understand correctly, if you want to have a joint concurrent interaction with the same part of the document or the file, then this means you need the corporation of the guy, who has the root any time, and each time this concurrency happens. Because, if myself and Bruce, share a document, it will be one pointer from my block with the document and one pointer from Bruce's, a part of the document.

But then, when you do the concurrent end, because as you generate a new root, you have to go up the way to the root. So the guy with the root will have to agree with this each and every time. So you cannot have only the two of us participate into the protocol. You need everybody else up to the root to participate, to propagate the key up the root.

Reply: But everybody has its own local version of everything.

Bruce Christianson: We'll have different roots.

Reply: Yeah.

Fabio Massacci: It'd be for both of us, the root. But then I do the redaction.

Bruce Christianson: So the question then becomes, "How optimistic is your approach to concurrency? In what conceptual level do we have to commit our change? Can we just do that when we feel like it or does the system take a view about, when a change is committed?"

Reply: There should be a method or something provided that, whenever you want to merge your modifications, you need to do that explicitly.

Bruce Christianson: Okay, so explicitly.

Reply: For example, you say, "Okay I want to merge everything with the other guys." So you create a merge request and in that case UPSS is responsible to see all the previous versions, the history and based on those versions and based on the CRDT, merge everything into one document.

Benjamin Ylvisaker: I know this is up here. Just want to make clear I understand correctly, are you trying to make it so that regular unmodified applications ... I just think there's one copy of their data ... Can somehow be converged concurrent edits? I don't know. I don't see how that can happen.

Reply: Excuse me. I just don't get it.

Benjamin Ylvisaker: I mean, Microsoft Word and Microsoft Excel, whatever, they write their files in some format and if two people make concurrent changes, I don't see how you could hope to merge those, unless you had a deep understanding of those file formats.

Reply: So eventually, everything is a stored on the storage by some arrays of byte or whatever. So we can decide based on, for example, the first three bytes of the file is changed or the last five bytes of this file is changed. So UPSS looks at everything as these bytes. It doesn't matter what would be the format of the file.

Jonathan Anderson: If I could just add to that. I guess part of the goal is that the more semantic exposure you have, the more effective would we be. So, if you have a legacy application that's using the legacy compatibility layer, and it just sees an array of bytes, then the amount of merging it's going to be able to handle is going to be at a very low syntactic level. So you might not be able to get semantically, meaningful merging at a very high level there. But the goal is to be able to have some compatibility and then the more work you're willing to put into shifting to a different API, the more benefit you would get, in terms of the ability to have support from merging, based on a policy that's provided by the application.

Reply: The only thing that we need to enable a file system to run or interact with UPSS is, to keep a mapping from low level names, which are meaningful for file systems to these objects references. So this is the thing that we need and also, here, we are again separating some metadata, which are meaningful in file systems, like the uid, gid and permissions per each local user, and we need to somehow store these information in this layer. Because we think that these information are meaningless for UPSS. So the user data can be stored anywhere and uid, gid and permissions are meaningless. But these things are meaningful for a file system. So we can have two different users on a local system, different accounts that can interact with UPSS. Somehow we need to ask UPSS, when the file system is unmounted, to store these information somewhere inside the storage. And, that's it.

Is the Future Finally Arriving?

Zero-Knowledge User Authentication: An Old Idea Whose Time Has Come

Laurent Chuat[✉], Sarah Plocher, and Adrian Perrig

ETH Zurich, Zürich, Switzerland
laurent.chuat@inf.ethz.ch

Abstract. User authentication can rely on various factors (e.g., a password, a cryptographic key, and/or biometric data) but should not reveal any secret information held by the user. This seemingly paradoxical feat can be achieved through zero-knowledge proofs. Unfortunately, naive password-based approaches still prevail on the web. Multi-factor authentication schemes address some of the weaknesses of the traditional login process, but generally have deployability issues or degrade usability even further as they assume users do not possess adequate hardware. This assumption no longer holds: smartphones with biometric sensors, cameras, short-range communication capabilities, and unlimited data plans have become ubiquitous. In this paper, we show that, assuming the user has such a device, both security and usability can be drastically improved using an augmented password-authenticated key agreement (PAKE) protocol and message authentication codes.

1 Introduction

User authentication still typically involves transmitting a plaintext password to the web server, which is problematic for many reasons. First, an attacker could obtain the user's password using malware, a keystroke logger, phishing, or a man-in-the-middle attack. Second, the user might be using the same password on different websites, allowing a malicious server operator to impersonate the user. Third, if the website's database is breached, although passwords may be protected by a hash function, a brute-force attack could reveal low-entropy passwords. Fourth, as password-reuse and low-entropy passwords are problematic, users are constantly advised to pick new, long, complicated passwords. Finally, transmitting the password over a secure channel, storing it as a hash, and using a random salt as well as a strong cryptographic hash function are recommended measures, but they are impossible to enforce or even verify for the end user. The unsalted SHA-1-hashed passwords of millions of LinkedIn users were disclosed in 2012 [8] and hundreds of millions more were disclosed (with corresponding email addresses) in 2016 [5], for example.

Two-factor authentication (2FA) supposedly reinforces standard passwords. Typically on today's web, the time-based one-time password (TOTP) algorithm [10] is used to generate a new 6-digit code every 30 s, based on the current time and a secret shared between the server and the user's authentication device

© Springer Nature Switzerland AG 2020
J. Anderson et al. (Eds.): Security Protocols 2019, LNCS 12287, pp. 203–212, 2020.
https://doi.org/10.1007/978-3-030-57043-9_19

(i.e., either a dedicated token or a smartphone). Usually, the user must submit their one-time code after the traditional username/password step. For this reason, two-factor authentication is also referred to as "2-step verification" [6].

Although 2FA may protect users against certain attacks, it doesn't completely prevent them. Schneier [12] claims that it "doesn't solve anything". Indeed, an attacker could still obtain the password and a one-time code—or hijack the session—through a real-time attack [13]. The attacker could then "make any fraudulent transaction he wants", which includes changing the password and deactivating 2FA to gain long-term control over the user's online account. Passwords are still weak and typed on untrusted devices. Servers still receive plaintext passwords. Password re-use is still problematic. All secret values may still be known by the server. Finally, assuming that an attacker manages to uncover a large number of passwords, the entropy of a 6-digit code is too low to rule out a brute-force attack. Therefore, TOTP-based authentication alleviates neither website owners nor users from the consequences of password leaks.

Herein we challenge some of the assumptions underlying existing schemes. For example, should we still assume that authentication devices have no Internet access? Clearly, the fact that a smartphone may not have Internet access at all times should be taken into account, but such a situation has become the exception rather than the rule. Also, is it sufficient to supplement a weak form of authentication with a "second step"? We believe, on the contrary, that user authentication should be completely reassessed.

Besides security, usability is actually deteriorated by schemes based on the TOTP algorithm. Every time users want to log in, they must type an ever-changing code displayed on their device—in addition to their password. The scheme we present, ZeroTwo, on the other hand, would fit inside a streamlined process, where the user only enters a username or email address on the website and then approves the login/authorization request in a single step on their smartphone. ZeroTwo relies on an augmented PAKE[1] protocol and message authentication codes (MACs) to provide the server with a zero-knowledge password proof (ZKPP) and evidence that the legitimate user explicitly authorized critical actions.

Another problem that has been largely overlooked in previous work is that users share their credentials with friends and family [15]. This problem can be solved by moving critical parts of the authentication process to the user's smartphone, which allows them to remotely give someone they trust a restricted, temporary, and revokable access to their online account.

2   Protocol Overview

In this section, we provide an overview of how users can authenticate and explicitly authorize actions using ZeroTwo. We chose to base our scheme upon SRP [20] because mature implementations are available. We also borrowed concepts from

---

[1] Also referred to as *asymmetric* password-authenticated key establishment or aPAKE.

AugPAKE [14]. In principle, however, any PAKE protocol (e.g., OPAQUE [7]) could be used to develop a scheme similar to ours.

2.1 Notation

Table 1 shows the notation we use throughout the paper. The values n and g are agreed upon beforehand. All arithmetic is performed modulo n. H() and $H_K()$ denote a hash function and an HMAC, respectively.

Table 1. Notation summary

n	Large safe prime number, i.e., $n = 2q + 1$ where q is also prime
g	Primitive root modulo n
k	Multiplier parameter, $k = H(n, g)$
l	Public parameter, $l = (H(n)$ xor $H(g))$
I_u	User's identifier (username or email address)
I_s	Server's identifier (domain name)
P	Password and/or biometric input
p	Master secret (see Sect. 3)
x	Effective secret, discarded after the computation of the verifier, $x = H(I_u, I_s, p)$
v	Verifier, $v = g^x$
a, b	Ephemeral private keys
A, B	Corresponding public keys
u	Scrambling parameter, $u = H(A, B)$
S	Common exponential value
K	Session key
M	Authorization (evidence that K is known)
d	Duration of the session
o	Operation to authorize

2.2 Initialization

During sign up, the following operations must be performed:

1. The user chooses a unique identifier I_u and sends it to the server (from a browser).
2. The server replies with a QR code containing both the user identity I_u and the server identity I_s as well as the URL that the smartphone must use to send the initialization data.

3. The user scans the QR code; chooses a master secret p (see Sect. 3), if this has not been done before; and the app computes the following: ([2]As in Aug-PAKE [14] and other previous work [1], but unlike in SRP [20], using a salt is unnecessary here, as the effective secret is derived from unique identifiers.)

$$x = H(I_u, I_s, p)^2$$

$$v = g^x$$

4. The user's identity and the verifier are sent to the previously received URL.
5. The server stores the verifier permanently (if the identifier is valid and not already used) under the user's identifier. If the identifier is an email address, the server should first verify that the user has access to that address.

2.3   Authentication

The authentication process works as follows:

1. The user initiates a login attempt by sending their identifier I_u to the server (from a browser).
2. The server looks up the user's verifier v, generates a random ephemeral private key b, and computes the corresponding public key:

$$B = kv + g^b$$

3. The server sends its public key B as well as identifiers I_u and I_s to both the browser and smartphone. In the common case, the smartphone is connected to the Internet and receives B (with a notification), a fingerprint [4,17] of the public key is displayed on both the smartphone app and the browser, and the user is asked to make sure that the two fingerprints match. If the smartphone is not connected to the Internet, the user must select a method for transferring B from the browser to the app (see Sect. 2.6).
4. The user can accept the authentication request on their smartphone by entering a password P and/or using an embedded biometric sensor. The master secret p is then used to compute the session key K, and M, which constitutes evidence that the user authorized a session to be established for a time period d:

$$x = H(I_u, I_s, p)$$

$$a = \mathrm{random}()$$

$$A = g^a$$

$$u = H(A, B)$$

$$S = (B - kg^x)^{(a+ux)}$$

$$K = H(S)$$

$$M = H_K(l, I_u, I_s, A, B, d)$$

5. The user's identifier I_u, public key A, and proof M, as well as the authorized duration of the session d are transmitted to the server by the smartphone.
6. The server verifies M by computing its own session key:

$$S = (Av^u)^b$$

$$K = \mathrm{H}(S)$$

If the received data is correct, the server automatically redirects the client to the page that required authentication.

2.4 Explicit Authorization

Following the principle of least privilege and to mitigate session hijacking, web developers using ZeroTwo may choose to define a set of actions for which explicit authorization from the user is required. When such an action is requested by the client, the server generates a human-readable message o describing the action and sends it directly to the smartphone, with a notification and a random nonce c (for replay prevention). The smartphone then computes an authorization message M with the session key K:

$$M = \mathrm{H}_K(o, c)$$

and sends it to the server. This can also be performed through alternative channels, as described in Sect. 2.6.

This general concept is sometimes referred to as "transaction signing". In the context of this paper, however, because a shared key is established between the client and the server, symmetric cryptography is sufficient.

2.5 Session Management

The session key K is stored on the smartphone and considered valid by the server for as long as the session is valid (specified with d).

If the user wants to terminate the session before it expires automatically, then they can send an authenticated logout message M to the server:

$$M = \mathrm{H}_K(o), \quad \text{where } o = \texttt{logout}.$$

The user should also be able to logout in the usual way, i.e., from the web browser, but the above method allows the user (who forgot to logout or was prevented from doing so by an attacker, for example) to terminate the session from their smartphone.

2.6 Alternative Channels

A bidirectional communication channel between the smartphone and the server is needed during the authentication and authorization procedures. The server's public key B can simply be displayed as a QR code in the browser and scanned with the ZeroTwo app. Sending data back to the server from the smartphone is more challenging, because it may not be possible to establish a direct Internet connection. The WebRTC standard, through a collection of protocols and APIs, allows modern web browsers to access peripheral hardware, which provides several solutions to our problem:

- **Webcam:** A camera connected to or embedded in the terminal (e.g., laptop) is used to scan a QR code displayed on the smartphone.
- **Bluetooth:** A Bluetooth connection is established between the smartphone and the browser to transfer the authentication data.

The user may initiate the authentication process directly from a mobile browser. In that case, the above methods cannot be used. By definition, however, the smartphone would need an Internet connection to start the authentication procedure from the login page and thus an alternative channel would not be needed.

3   Nature of the Master Secret

One of the advantages of augmented PAKE protocols is that they provide a great deal of flexibility with regard to the nature of the secret they rely upon. In other words, the master secret (which we denote p), although it is traditionally assumed to be a password, can be arbitrary long and of any nature. And because of the zero-knowledge property of our protocol, no entity can learn anything about the secret aside from the one who created it. Therefore, the responsibility of developing a process for generating the master secret that is both secure and convenient for users lies entirely with the developers of compatible apps.

Our preferred approach consists in generating a random passphrase (e.g., composed of lowercase, hyphen-separated words). A passphrase has the advantage that it can be memorized and/or written on a piece of paper to be kept in a secure location. Moreover, a long passphrase generated at random from a large set of words has enough entropy to make brute-force and dictionary attacks infeasible. The passphrase can be re-used for several websites because the effective secret x is domain-dependent and the entropy of the master secret is high. The only disadvantage of a passphrase would be to type it at every login, but it can be stored on the smartphone.

One could also combine several secrets. Concatenating a key and a password, for example, would result in a multi-factor scheme. If the same combination is used on multiple websites, however, changing the password is inconvenient as all verifiers must be updated. Therefore, it is not clear whether the presumed security gain would be worth the decrease in usability. Instead, we propose to protect a high-entropy secret with another factor, as described in Sect. 4.

A single high-entropy secret is sufficient to protect multiple websites. However, to avoid a single point of failure, some users might choose to generate multiple secrets: one for personal websites and one for professional purposes, for example. Therefore, compatible apps should offer an option to manage multiple accounts.

4 Access Control, Storage, and Backup

If the master secret is stored on the smartphone, then the access to the ZeroTwo-compatible app and the storage of the secret should be protected. The two main options at our disposal are the following:

- **Biometric protection:** Fingerprint and facial scanners are becoming commonplace on high-end smartphones. Android and iOS both provide APIs for letting developers protect their app with embedded biometric sensors.
- **Password protection:** Although passwords do not allow for the same ease of use as biometrics, they offer another advantage: the master secret can be encrypted before a backup (in cloud storage, for example).

Although we favor the biometrics approach, a password can be used as a fallback in case the smartphone does not have a biometric sensor, or in case the biometric sensor produces a false negative. As for the backup strategy, assuming the master secret is a passphrase, users should be able to decide whether they want to only display the passphrase when it is first generated (to memorize it or write it down) or back it up using a protected cloud storage solution.

We note that a single-secret approach, as opposed to a naive password-based scheme, scales to an arbitrary number of websites without having to constantly remember/backup new secrets, which is particularly important should the user decide to use an offline backup solution.

5 Comparative Evaluation and Related Work

The last couple of decades has seen a plethora of proposals for user authentication. In general, existing schemes suffer from at least one of the following drawbacks: (a) they require a dedicated device, (b) they are proprietary, (c) they involve a shared secret, and/or (d) they still require a traditional password. Herein we only discuss a small subset of schemes and refer to the paper by Bonneau et al. [2] for an extensive evaluation of related work. Using their framework we evaluated ZeroTwo and present the results in Table 2.

Bonneau [1] had previously proposed a password-based authentication protocol, designed to avoid revealing the password to the server (using Javascript), which requires neither a software update on the client side nor a separate authentication device. Thomas et al. [19] similarly focused on restrictions imposed by legacy systems to address the issues of weak passwords.

Hardware tokens (such as YubiKey [21] or Pico [16]) have the advantage that they are shielded from remote attackers. Although they are particularly adapted to professional contexts, we believe that they are less suited to the general public as many users are unwilling to spend money for a dedicated device.

Cronto [11] is a phone-based scheme close to our proposal in terms of offered features, but it is a proprietary product whose exact design is not publicly known, which makes it hard to analyze and unlikely to be widely deployed outside of the banking industry. SQRL (pronounced "squirrel") or Secure Quick Reliable

Table 2. Comparative evaluation of ZeroTwo, assuming a single passphrase is used as the master secret. [1]*Best-case scenario:* The smartphone has a biometric sensor to protect the secret and Internet connectivity is available. [2]*Worst-case scenario:* The passphrase is protected with a password; the smartphone has no biometric sensor and no Internet connectivity.

Scheme	Usability								Deployability						Security										
	Memory-wise effortless	Scalable for users	Nothing to carry	Physically effortless	Easy to learn	Efficient to use	Infrequent errors	Easy recovery from loss	Accessible	Negligible cost per user	Server-compatible	Browser-compatible	Mature	Non-proprietary	Resilient to physical observation	Resilient to targeted impersonation	Resilient to throttled guessing	Resilient to unthrottled guessing	Resilient to internal observations	Resilient to leaks from other verifiers	Resilient to phishing	Resilient to theft	No trusted third party	Requiring explicit consent	Unlinkable
Passwords			●		●	●	○	●	●	●	●	●	●	●		○							●	●	●
ZeroTwo[1]	●	●	○	○	●	●	○	●	●	●	○		●	●	●	●	●	●	○	●	●	●	●	●	●
ZeroTwo[2]	●	○			●	○	○	●	○	○			●	●	●	●	●	●	○	●	●	●	●	●	●

● = offers the benefit; ○ = almost offers the benefit

Login [3] also offers a strong phone-based authentication solution, but it does not support transaction signing or explicit authorization.

Sound-Proof [9] is a recent system that relies on sound for the smartphone and browser to communicate. One of the main goals of Sound-Proof is to provide a seamless experience to users, i.e., the phone need not even be handled for the authentication process to complete. However, the user still has to type a password in the browser, which comes with the issues we discussed previously. Moreover, the complete seamlessness of Sound-Proof is not compatible with our view that certain actions should be explicitly authorized on a trusted device.

The FIDO Alliance has published a number of protocol, framework, and API specifications [18] for user authentication on the web, based on public-key cryptography. To the best our knowledge, none of these specifications rely on password-authenticated key establishment.

6   Conclusion

Many forms of user authentication on today's web suffer from severe drawbacks. Using public-key cryptography for authentication is not a novel idea. But whereas asymmetric cryptography is commonly used for server authentication on the web (through TLS), it is not a widespread approach for user authentication. There are several reasons for this: key management is difficult; users need a trusted device with storage, communication, and computation capabilities; and the authentication process must be fast and convenient. We believe, however, that the democratization of smartphones with embedded biometric sensors, unlimited cellular data plans, and new communication standards such as WebRTC now make asymmetric protocols a viable option for user authentication.

Acknowledgments. We gratefully thank Eduardo Solana for his valuable input in the early stages of this project, Daniel R. Thomas for his extensive feedback, and all the workshop attendees who participated in the discussion and helped improve this paper.

References

1. Bonneau, J.: Getting web authentication right: a best-case protocol for the remaining life of passwords. In: Proceedings of the 19th International Workshop on Security Protocols (2011)
2. Bonneau, J., Herley, C., van Oorschot, P.C., Stajano, F.: The quest to replace passwords: A framework for comparative evaluation of web authentication schemes. In: Proceedings of the 33rd IEEE Symposium on Security and Privacy (S&P) (2012)
3. Gibson Research Corporation: SQRL secure quick reliable login. https://www.grc.com/sqrl/sqrl.htm
4. Dechand, S., Schürmann, D., Busse, K., Acar, Y., Fahl, S., Smith, M.: An empirical study of textual key-fingerprint representations. In: Proceedings of the 25th USENIX Security Symposium (2016)
5. Franceschi-Bicchierai, L.: Another day, another hack: 117 million LinkedIn emails and passwords. Motherboard, May 2016. https://perma.cc/6MC6-EVHH
6. Google. 2-step verification. https://www.google.com/landing/2step
7. Jarecki, S., Krawczyk, H., Xu, J.: OPAQUE: an asymmetric PAKE protocol secure against pre-computation attacks. In: Proceedings of the 37th Annual International Conference on the Theory and Applications of Cryptographic Techniques (Eurocrypt) (2018)
8. Kamp, P.-H.: LinkedIn password leak: salt their hide. ACM Queue **10**(6), 20 (2012)
9. Karapanos, N., Marforio, C., Soriente, C., Capkun, S.: Sound-Proof: usable two-factor authentication based on ambient sound. In: Proceedings of the 24th USENIX Security Symposium (2015)
10. M'Raihi, D., Machani, S., Pei, M., Rydell, J.: TOTP: time-based one-time password algorithm. RFC 6238, May 2011
11. OneSpan: CRONTO mobile app. https://perma.cc/THZ6-3YFW
12. Schneier, B.: Two-factor authentication: too little, too late. Commun. ACM **48**(4), 136 (2005)
13. Schneier, B.: Real-time attacks against two-factor authentication. Schneier on Security, December 2018. https://perma.cc/FQ9R-USG6
14. Shin, S., Kobara, K.: Efficient augmented password-only authentication and key exchange for IKEv2. RFC 6628, June 2012

15. Singh, S., Cabraal, A., Demosthenous, C., Astbrink, G., Furlong, M.: Password sharing: implications for security design based on social practice. In: Proceedings of the SIGCHI Conference on Human Factors in Computing Systems (2007)

16. Stajano, F.: Pico: no more passwords!. In: Christianson, B., Crispo, B., Malcolm, J., Stajano, F. (eds.) Security Protocols 2011. LNCS, vol. 7114, pp. 49–81. Springer, Heidelberg (2011). https://doi.org/10.1007/978-3-642-25867-1_6

17. Tan, J., Bauer, L., Bonneau, J., Cranor, L.F., Thomas, J., Ur, B.: Can unicorns help users compare crypto key fingerprints? In: Proceedings of the SIGCHI Conference on Human Factors in Computing Systems (2017)

18. The FIDO Alliance: Specifications overview (FIDO2, WebAuthn, FIDO UAF, FIDO U2F). https://fidoalliance.org/specifications

19. Thomas, D.R., Beresford, A.R.: Better authentication: password revolution by evolution. In: Christianson, B., Malcolm, J., Matyáš, V., Švenda, P., Stajano, F., Anderson, J. (eds.) Security Protocols 2014. LNCS, vol. 8809, pp. 130–145. Springer, Cham (2014). https://doi.org/10.1007/978-3-319-12400-1_13

20. Wu, T.: SRP-6: improvements and refinements to the Secure Remote Password protocol. IEEE P1363 Working Group, October 2002

21. Yubico: YubiKey strong two factor authentication for business and individual use. https://www.yubico.com

Zero-Knowledge User Authentication: An Old Idea Whose Time Has Come (Transcript of Discussion)

Laurent Chuat[(✉)]

ETH Zurich, Zürich, Switzerland
laurent.chuat@inf.ethz.ch

So, user authentication on the web: I don't think it needs much introduction. Still, often, just a username and password, unfortunately. And I think it would be an understatement to say that this is suboptimal, both in terms of security and usability.

When the user, Alice, signs up, she chooses a password. She sends it to the server, which stores it, somehow. Then she sends the same password at login. I'm sure you're all familiar with potential attacks in this context, but just a brief recap: There's shoulder surfing (that's when the attacker tries to look over the user's shoulder). The machine may be infected. There may be an attacker on the line, either a passive eavesdropper, or an active man in the middle. The user may think that she's communicating with the server when, in fact, she's communicating directly with the attacker (that would be fishing or social engineering). Finally, and perhaps most importantly here, the server itself may be compromised, or even actively malicious. And even if it's not compromised and completely honest, we're still not sure that the server is not just storing the password in plain text.

That was for security. Now for usability. Because of all these problems, users are constantly advised to pick long and complicated passwords. The average user, although it's hard to get precise figures, probably has around 100 online accounts. I know that I have more than this on my password manager. So it's hard to expect that users will pick a different, hard-to-guess password for every website. Of course, if they have a password manager it makes it possible. But then there are other problems: the password manager database must be backed up, secured, and replicated. And still it doesn't solve many of our problems.

Now, supposedly, the solution to these security issues is to use two-factor authentication. This is one of the most common forms of it. A one-time code, typically a six-digit code, is generated every 30 s by a smartphone app. And the way it works is that the server just asks for this additional one-time code, in addition to the regular username and password. Clearly, the usability is even worse than it was before. Then for security, it actually doesn't really solve anything. The server may still know the password. In the protocol to generate these one-time codes and verify them, a shared key is required (the server needs to know the secret key the user knows). Then, if the machine is infected, the attacker could still steal the one-time code. If the attacker, in any way, is able to steal the password, then he's also able to obtain the one-time code.

© Springer Nature Switzerland AG 2020
J. Anderson et al. (Eds.): Security Protocols 2019, LNCS 12287, pp. 213–222, 2020.
https://doi.org/10.1007/978-3-030-57043-9_20

In the end, the only guarantee that we have is that the attacker must be fast. For any attack that was possible before, if the attacker is fast enough, if they can do this attack in less than 30 s, then the attack will succeed. The attacker can still steal session cookies, and do session hijacking. So it doesn't really solve anything.

Any objection to that statement?

Alastair Beresford: We know that users reuse passwords across many, many machines. So it does prevent passwords being used in these attacks.

Reply: Yes, that's a good point. That's one thing that it prevents. But you don't really need one-time codes to do that. You could also just pick different passwords. Let's be clear: I'm still using two-factor authentication for my online accounts. Because I think it makes me a little less vulnerable. But it's not so satisfying; it doesn't completely prevent any attack.

So where do we go from here? What are we aiming for? The first observation is that servers cannot be completely trusted with keeping secret data. Of course, passwords should be stored as hashes, with a secure, modern, cryptographic hash function, computed with a random salt. But many servers just don't do that. But servers cannot screw up if they don't get any private value to begin with. And that's possible with zero-knowledge protocols.

The next observation is that, because session hijacking is always possible, what we need is some kind of explicit authorization. Right now, by default, when the user logs in, he or she gets essentially a root shell to his/her online account. Typically users don't know exactly what they're authorising when they provide a password. We need a more fine-grained authorization.

Michael Millian: Could you just give an example of that?

Reply: Yes. That would be up to the server to choose what a critical action (one that requires an explicit authorization) means. But, for example, changing the main email address of an online account. Or changing the authentication procedure. Or anything that is security critical. Or transferring some amount of money, or something like that. That should be explicitly authorised by the user, who would receive a notification on the smartphone.

In the same train of thoughts, users should also be able to manage their session, and especially the duration of it. We know that some users share their online accounts with friends and family, and we cannot really prevent that. But maybe it would be less of a problem if a user could say, "Okay, I'm giving someone I know a session to my online account, but only for five minutes, or only for 24 h." And finally, although I just criticised multi-factor authentication, using multiple factors is still a sensible idea.

Here's an overview of an example of the protocol we are proposing. There are exactly two factors. The smartphone generates one master secret, and stores it. That is really one secret for all servers. Then, because it stores that secret, it must be protected somehow. So you need a second factor to either unlock the phone or unlock the app. Ideally, that second factor would be a biometric input. Then, with zero knowledge, you can prove the possession of that master secret to other servers.

So all you need here is what's called an augmented PAKE, an augmented password-authenticated key establishment protocol. SRP, which stands for secure remote password, is an example of such a protocol. And I'll go into the details of that protocol next. What this provides is every server has a different verifier. By "verifier" I mean a "verification value" that can be used to verify the knowledge of the secret.

Now, what I'm claiming here is that we have a whole family of protocols that can just solve this problem, and give us our desired properties. So why haven't we don't this before?

Well, first of all, as I said, ideally the smartphone will need a biometric sensor. And then you need communication between the smartphone and the server. So this is something you could not assume was possible a few years ago. But now most users have a smartphone, always in their pocket. And that smartphone has, most of the time, internet access. And even if it doesn't have an internet access, there are alternatives now, especially with the WebRTC framework.

This allows the browser to access peripherals like Bluetooth receivers and webcams. This could be used by the smartphone to communicate with the server, through the browser. For example, with a QR code displayed on the smartphone that's read by a webcam.

Fabio Massacci: Before you had at least two different pathways. But now if you go through the browser it's actually the same pathway. So as soon as you have compromised the browser, you have compromised everything. So you lost that really because you have a direct connection, not a separate path.

Reply: Not really, because the nice thing about such a protocol is that it's a zero-knowledge protocol. So anyone in between, in the middle, doesn't learn anything about the secret. It doesn't matter that there's a man in the middle, sort of, here.

Fabio Massacci: Zero knowledge is not so ... you can also counter it. You can do concurrent executions...

Reply: I'm going into the details of the protocol later on, but the idea is that even if there's someone in the middle, that shouldn't change anything, assuming that the protocol does what it's supposed to do.

Here's the protocol. This is during sign up. The user just sends an identifier, a username or email address, to the server through the browser. The server responds with its own identifier, a domain name, or URL. Then the user inputs, typically, a biometric input, to unlock the smartphone, or unlock the app. At this stage, the smartphone computes an effective secret x, which depends on both identities, and a master secret, p. And then the smartphone computes a verifier from that effective secret. Then the smartphone just sends, directly to the server, the username, and the verifier. And the server stores that verifier under the username.

That was during signup. Then during login, the user only sends the username. Nothing else, no password, just the username. The server looks up the corresponding verifier, and generates an ephemeral key pair. Then the public key, B, is sent to the smartphone, together with the two identifiers. Then, at this stage, the user unlocks the smartphone app with, again, typically a biometric input. And there's a bunch of computation, but essentially the smartphone computes a session key K, and a zero-knowledge evidence that the master secret is known. Then the smartphone sends this information to the server: the username, the ephemeral public key, evidence that the secret is known, and d is the duration of the session (an optional duration for the session). And the server verifies that information.

So the main advantages of this approach is, of course, the zero knowledge aspect. The master secret is proven to be known without revealing it. Then, because this is a PAKE, a key establishment protocol, the client and the server have a shared session key at the end of the protocol. And this key can be used—as we were discussing before—to authorise specific actions, like changing the main email address of the account, with a MAC, for example.

Sasa Radomirovic: Now that they have exchanged the key, does this mean that the transaction notification is given, even if the machine is compromised? So your laptop is compromised, you run your protocol, doesn't your laptop learn the key that will authorization that transaction?

Reply: No, the laptop, if it is in between, won't learn the key.

Sasa Radomirovic: So if you want to update your email address you have to run this protocol one more time?

Reply: Yes, the idea is that you would receive a notification on your smartphone saying "Do you really want to change your email address?" And you would accept it on your smartphone, with that session key.

Sasa Radomirovic: Right. So you've then run that protocol twice. Once for the login, and then another time to—

Reply: Well, for the second time, you don't run the same protocol. You just send a MAC, using the session key.

Sasa Radomirovic: Yes, but you have another communication through your smartphone?

Reply: Yes, exactly. Only for critical actions. It's just an option that the server has.

Jonathan Anderson: How does that session key expire?

Reply: The user specifies a duration, and then it's up to the server to say, at the end of the duration, that the session key is not valid any more.

Jonathan Anderson: Okay. But that needs to be specified specifically be the user?

Reply: Again, it's an option, but yes. If the user doesn't specify it, then it is as it currently is: just an infinite session.

Jonathan Anderson: I guess one thing that a compromised computer in the middle could do is to take advantage of the session that's already open. Not forwarding the message along that says "I'm logging out now", for example. If you're communicating through the compromised computer. Which doesn't allow you to authenticate new actions, perhaps. An explicit confirmation that you have logged out, for example, could be a useful addition.

Reply: You mean a compromised laptop who knows the session cookie could log out?

Jonathan Anderson: No, I mean that my intention is to log out, at which point I would expect the session to not have any value any more, but—

Reply: The laptop prevents you from doing that.

Jonathan Anderson: —yes, just forward that message along.

Reply: Yes, that's something the smartphone could send directly to the server. That would be another feature of such a smartphone app, to be able to kill any open session.

Jonathan Anderson: Okay. I just didn't see that protocol message anywhere.

Reply: Again, it's not a complicated protocol. It would be similar to authorising an action specifically, so just sending a MAC computed with the session key directly to the server.

I haven't talked yet about the nature of the master secret. The protocol is pretty agnostic to what the secret is. It could be anything. But, ideally, it should still have a high entropy. So what we suggest is just a long passphrase. Maybe a hyphen-separated, twenty-English-words passphrase. Something like that. And this would allow for an easy backup. The user could just write it on a piece of paper, put it in a safe.

Fabio Massacci: So I'm compromising the browser. Let's make the example, we went through the browser, and I'm compromising the browser and I run this ... and then I run it with LinkedIn and Google. So there's two servers. Can I now combine linearly your information at a certain point, to extract the g^p, and get it back?

Reply: You shouldn't be able to do that.

Fabio Massacci: Because I have two equations and I could just derive a combination between them, and then I can probably extract it.

Reply: You shouldn't be able to do that, because you ran two separate instances of the protocol, and there are different ephemeral key pairs in each instance of the protocol. And—

Fabio Massacci: No, when I do the first exchange, not after I found the MAC. But I mean between, so in the first round, when you start sending the feedback, together with g^p. I think that part will be possible through some different combination, if I am sitting in the middle.

Reply: It shouldn't be possible. Here we are not particularly interested in the intricacies of the cryptographic protocol. But if that kind of protocol, an augmented PAKE protocol, does what it's supposed to do, that shouldn't be possible.

Fabio Massacci: You have to check because, pardon me again, zero knowledge has not allowed to be primarily composed, unless you do certain tricks. So, if I sit in the browser, then I can grab part of the section, then I can probably infer something. You have to check what the equation actually does.

Reply: Okay, I'll look into that.

The last property is that, because each server stores a different verifier, then colluding servers cannot link their users, with just this authentication data, as they could if the user used the same password on different servers. So you have an unlinkability property.

We don't claim to have solved everything and have a definitive solution. Of course many solutions have been proposed in this space, and there is a lot of properties. I could not discuss all of these properties. We used this framework, which comes from one of Frank Stajano's papers, to evaluate this scheme. And it may not be one size fits all. Users may have different preferences, and there are many tradeoffs.

But I guess the main message is that our models and our assumptions should evolve, and that smartphones have become quite ideal identification devices. It's now common to have unlimited data plans, short-range communication capabilities, biometric sensors, and secure storage. It's fairly reasonable to expect that most users now have such a device in their pocket, most of the time.

The assumption behind TOTP-based two-factor authentication that users can only use a keyboard to input secrets no longer holds.

Benjamin Ylvisaker: Are you familiar with SQRL? It's a system that someone was trying to popularise that seems quite similar.

Reply: No, sorry, I'm not.

Sasa Radomirovic: I think SQRL will have the problem of only doing entity authentication. So the thing you have is transaction authentication on top of it, which I think SQRL doesn't have. But my question is, why is zero-knowledge important? If you look at, say, U2F, Universal 2nd Factor authentication, it would seem to cover much everything, as well. No... sorry, not transaction authentication. But the zero knowledge is not clear to me. Why is that so necessary?

Reply: There are different reasons. There are different properties, I think, in this table that come from the zero-knowledge aspect. You want an easy backup, for example. With our scheme, the user only has one passphrase. And you don't want the server to know that passphrase, otherwise you can link the users on different servers.

Sasa Radomirovic: If you were to generate different key pairs—

Reply: Then you don't have this backup property. The problem is key management, if you have a different key pairs.

Sasa Radomirovic: If you derive them from a long passphrase. Your private keys can be derived from one secret.

Reply: Yes, but it's not that different from what we're doing in the end. If you derived different key pairs from one passphrase, it goes back to this protocol, pretty much.

Chan Nam Ngo: I have a comment on the way that you have stopped your protocol. I think given the way you have obtained x, the only surprise factor for the attacker would be p, because I_u and I_s are not secret. Because they are the email address and the domain of the server. So I would say that depending on how you use the hash function here, that you can't satisfy the unlinkability. Because, for example, if you are using three generators g_1, g_2, g_3, and you raise up all of these values by different generators, and then if you then obtain x by just dividing the g_1 to I_u, g_2 to I_s, then you can easily obtain $(g_3)^p$. And then when all the verifiers do the same thing, they can easily see they are having the same $(g_3)^p$. So I think they can basically link you.

Reply: I'm not sure I follow exactly the attack.

Virgil Gligor: Is the value of p known? No.

Reply: No, it's secret.

Chan Nam Ngo: No, I'm talking only about little leaks. For example, if you choose three generators here, g_1, g_2, and g_3, right? And then you give them a hash function in the way that you raise g_1 to I_u, raise g_2 to I_s, and raise g_3 to p. Right? Then you can easily compute $(g_3)^p$, because you already know I_u and I_s.

Virgil Gligor: That doesn't work. Because of the hash function. p is unknown.

Chan Nam Ngo: I only want to say it depends on how you implement the hash function.

Reply: Yes, depending on how you implement it. But if you use, for example, SHA-3, I don't think that attack will work.

Virgil Gligor: I think that the problem is different, I think that you have to make sure that the value of the hash is from some Z_p or Z_q, right? Because that's a generator g, so x doesn't come from an arbitrary range.

Bruce Christianson: Could you say a little bit about your assumptions, for channels that you have during the signup process? During the signup, you must have some assumptions about integrity or something like that?

Reply: Not really.

Bruce Christianson: How do I know I've got the right server?

Reply: I mean, even if you don't, since you don't reveal the secret to the server afterwards, I'm not sure it matters.

Bruce Christianson: Okay. And I'm just assuming that the HTTPS is correct and not a domain that can lie to me?

Reply: HTTPS here is mostly for good measure. And because it requires some kind of API, and most APIs these days would use HTTPS. But we don't make a lot of assumptions on the channel that's established here. I'm not sure I see exactly what kind of attack you have in mind, but I don't think that it matters a lot.

Bruce Christianson: Well, you tell me the properties of the channel, and I'll tell you the attack.

Reply: Okay.

Diana Vasile: I might have misunderstood a little bit, but you protect the secret of the device with, say, a fingerprint, or face ID, right?

Reply: Right.

Diana Vasile: But that's not particularly secure, because there's a second side to the authentication. If someone stares at my phone, it will lock, unlock, and it will bring up the four-digit passcode. I don't understand how secure this secret actually is for you.

Reply: I'm not sure I get exactly the question.

Diana Vasile: Okay. In my case, if I want to authenticate, I would stare at my phone, log myself in to the device, and then authenticate. But my five-year-old son knows the passcode. So if he stares at my phone, his face is not recognised. So it brings up the digits. He punches in the digits, and then he's authenticated and he can go on to the forms. So then any user identification security that relies only on fingerprint, or not fingerprint, but face ID, or something.

Reply: For the protocol to work you need the passphrase that is stored by the app. And to unlock the app you need biometric input. And ...well, if those ...

Diana Vasile: So it's not one or the other, right? In order to get the passphrase you need to put in the biometric?

Reply: The passphrase really is the master secret. The only place where it is stored is in the app on the smartphone, and the smartphone is protected by the biometric input.

Alastair Beresford: I think, to summarise, Laurent is assuming that biometric is secure. And your contention is that it's not secure. Is that the point?

Diana Vasile: Okay, that's ...

Reply: Even if it's not secure, you still need the smartphone with the passphrase. But if both are compromised, of course, then it's over.

Diana Vasile: I guess my comment is that it could be easy to compromise.

Reply: Yes, but even if you do, you still need the right smartphone to compromise the account in the end.

Jonathan Anderson: So your toddler would have to be colluding with the malware in the browser, effectively. But toddlers collude, if they see just your phone would buzz, maybe they will pick it up.

Further to Bruce's point, looking at the protocol, if the computer didn't relay I_s faithfully, then that would just result in a verifier that can't be used to login on that server. So a malicious machine in that way would have to faithfully continue relaying the wrong I_s, at which point, given that's a pure name, if it's wrong, maybe that doesn't matter?

Reply: Sorry, your last sentence?

Jonathan Anderson: I was saying that, in the set up phase, if the machine relays the wrong I_s from the server to the smartphone, then you'll generate a verifier that only works with that I_s. Nothing will work, unless you faithfully continue sending the wrong I_s, at which point it's effectively the right I_s.

A Rest Stop on the Unending Road to Provable Security

Virgil D. Gligor[(✉)]

Carnegie Mellon University, Pittsburgh, USA
virgil.gligor@gmail.com

Abstract. During the past decade security research has offered persuasive arguments that the road to provable security is unending, and further that there's no *rest stop* on this road; e.g., there is no security property one can prove without making assumptions about other, often unproven, system properties. In this paper I suggest what a useful first rest stop might look like, and illustrate one possible place for it on the road to provable security. Specifically, I argue that a small and simple verifier can establish software *root of trust* (RoT) on an untrusted system *unconditionally*; i.e., without secrets, trusted hardware modules, or bounds on the adversary power; and the verifier's trustworthiness can be proven without dependencies of other unverified computations. The foundation for proving RoT establishment unconditionally already exists, and the proofs require only the availability of randomness in nature and correct specifications for the untrusted system. In this paper, I also illustrate why RoT establishment is useful for obtaining other basic properties unconditionally, such as *secure initial state* determination, *verifiable boot*, and *on-demand firmware verification* for I/O devices.

> There's no resting place on the road to
> perfection [1].

1 Introduction

A decade ago, Butler Lampson suggested that "security is fractal: Each part is as complex as the whole, and there are always more things to worry about [1]". That there is always more to worry about and the road to provable security is unending came as no surprise: we've known that new computing technologies and applications introduce new vulnerabilities that enable new adversary attacks [2]. Indeed, unending security concerns are axiomatic for commodity systems [3]. What was surprising is the assertion that *security is fractal*. If taken literally, Lampson's deliberately provocative metaphor would imply that a reductionist approach to secure system design becomes impractical. Recall that a reduction adds practical trustworthy defenses to a system, which enable system security to rely on components that *might be* less complex than the whole and thus easier to trust. However, if security is indeed fractal, we would have an immediate negative

© Springer Nature Switzerland AG 2020
J. Anderson et al. (Eds.): Security Protocols 2019, LNCS 12287, pp. 223–232, 2020.
https://doi.org/10.1007/978-3-030-57043-9_21

answer to a basic reduction question of secure systems: "Is it ever possible to add defenses and transform one system into another where the latter requires weaker assumptions about components being trusted [5]?"

Furthermore, if security is fractal, relocating trust by security reductions would offer no *rest stop* on the road to provable security. There would be no security property of the added defenses that can be proved unconditionally; e.g., without making assumptions about other, no less complex, system properties. This is a more sobering assessment than Schneider's already somber conjecture "Prove: Trust cannot be created, it can only be relocated [4], p. 48," which is consistent with Damgård's observation that reduction proofs only relate security to unproven conjectures [6], and with Gollmann's complaint that security reductions often assume "that something unknown cannot happen [7], p. 126." In effect, if security is fractal, *all proofs of security dangle*, as they depend on other properties that cannot be proved unconditionally in the real world [8].

Conversely, if a system transformation of the type suggested by Schneider's question above is possible, then security cannot be fractal. That is, trustworthy defenses could sometimes be added to a system that would make parts of the system less complex than the whole. However important in theory, this would be only a *rest stop* on the unending road to provable security. Even if not fractal, attaining provable security in commodity systems remains a very complex challenge [1,3,8,18].

In this paper I present a simple and efficient transformation of an untrusted system into another system comprising a small and simple local verifier that is connected to the untrusted system, whereby the verifier can establish some untrusted-system properties *unconditionally*. The verifier has an external source of true randomness [9,10] and the system specifications, and its trustworthiness can be established unconditionally; i.e., its proofs of correctness can be performed on binary code, *without* dependencies on other unverified computations.

The protocol between the trustworthy verifier and the untrusted system performs an unconditional reduction from a concrete space-time optimal computation to an untrusted-system state that contains all and only the contents chosen by the verifier. The proofs of the untrusted-system properties enabled by the unconditional reduction cannot be falsified in any realistic sense without ruling out correct specifications, and hence, *all* security and cryptography properties, or denying *all* physical laws underlying true random number generation; e.g., denying quantum effects [11]. The value of these proofs is basic: without them, no other subsequent security property can be proven regardless of how scientific the approach might be [18]. Conversely, even after the proofs of the untrusted system properties are done, the road to provable security for other properties remains unending. In effect, I provide the first *rest stop* on the road to provable security and illustrate one possible place for it.

A good candidate for the first rest stop is the software root of trust (RoT) establishment, which can be obtained unconditionally; i.e., without secrets, trusted hardware modules, or bounds on the adversary computing power. The foundation for proving RoT establishment unconditionally already exists [13].

I also briefly illustrate why software RoT establishment is required for determining whether an initial state is secure, performing verifiable boot, and verifying the firmware of I/O devices on demand.

2 Overview of Software RoT Establishment

Let a *system state* comprise the contents of all processor and I/O registers and primary memories of a chipset and peripheral device controllers at a particular time; e.g., before boot. A security property of interest is whether the device controllers contain malicious firmware. Another is whether the firmware of system management boards or of processors intended to be configured for virtual machine support contain malicious firmware. If so, these types of malware become persistent, as they survive power cycles, secure- and trusted-boot operations, and can infect the rest of a system's state.

As defined in previous work [12,13], root of trust (RoT) establishment on a system that might contain persistent malware ensures that the system's state comprises *all* and *only* content chosen by its user, and the user's code *begins execution* in that state. *All* implies that no content is missing, and *only* implies that no extra content exists. If a system state is initialized to content that satisfies security invariants and RoT establishment succeeds, a user's code begins execution in a *secure initial state*. Then trustworthy programs booted in a secure initial state can extend this state to include secondary storage. If RoT establishment fails, unaccounted content, such as malware, exists. Hence, RoT establishment is sufficient for assuring malware freedom and necessary for all access control models and cryptographic protocols, since all need secure initial states.

Establishing RoT makes all persistent malware ephemeral and forces the adversary to repeat malware-insertion attacks, perhaps a higher cost. Nevertheless repeated successful attacks in commodity systems and applications are always hard to deny. For example, only small and simple software components with rather limited function can be formally verified to counter all such attacks and *selectively maintain* the established RoT. This requires the verifiable boot of trustworthy micro-kernels, micro-hyprevisors, or separation kernels to isolated these components and limit their exposure to untrusted commodity OS code, other applications, and malicious I/O devices.

3 A Simple and Efficient Transformation

Let a small and simple *verifier* device be locally connected to an *untrusted* system. This transforms the untrusted system into a prover–verifier pair, where the verifier is easy to trust.

Unconditional Reduction. The simple and efficient RoT establishment protocol [13] between the trustworthy verifier and the untrusted system performs an unconditional reduction from a concrete space-time optimal computation to an untrusted-system state that contains all and only the contents chosen by the verifier. This implies the malware freedom of the untrusted system.

Untrusted System. Suppose that the untrusted system has a processor with register set R and a random access memory M, whose specifications are those of a real system. The registers have distinguished names and the memory comprises a finite sequence of words indexed by an integer. Operand addressing in memory is immediate, direct and indirect, and operands comprise words and bit fields. The system has *constant* word length and a *fixed* number of operands per instruction, typically up to two. It has a general ISA including as well as I/O instructions, special registers (e.g., for interrupt and device status), and an execution model that accounts for interrupts. For example, it includes all known register-to-register, register-to-memory, and branching instructions of real system ISAs, as well as all single-word integer, logic, and shift/rotate computation instructions.

A Simple Protocol. In a simple RoT establishment protocol, the verifier asks the untrusted system to initialize M and R to chosen content. Then the verifier sends a random *nonce*, which selects C_{nonce} from a family of computations $\mathbf{C_{m,t}}(M, R)$ with space and time bounds m and t, and challenges the system to execute computation C_{nonce} on input (M, R) in m words and time t. Suppose that $\mathbf{C_{m,t}}$ is space-time optimal, result $C_{nonce}(M, R)$ is unpredictable by an adversary, and C_{nonce} is non-interruptible. If $\mathbf{C_{m,t}}$ is also second pre-image free and the system outputs the correct result $C_{nonce}(M, R)$ in time t, then after accounting for the local communication delay, the verifier concludes that the system state (M, R) contains all and only the chosen content. When applied to multiple device controllers, the verifier's protocol must ensure that a controller cannot help another one to undetectably circumvent its bounds by executing some part of the latter's computation; e.g., act as an *on-board proxy.*

Let the untrusted system attempt to surreptitiously connect to a remote adversary of unbounded computation power, which can execute the result $C_{nonce}(M, R)$ in zero time; e.g., a *remote proxy* attack [14]. Recall that if M is large enough, the optimal time bound t of $C_{nonce}(M, R)$ can exceed the round trip time to an adversary's remote proxy computer, and thus the untrusted system could circumvent RoT establishment; i.e., the untrusted system would return the correct result in time without its state comprising the verifier's chosen content. To counter this attack, the verifier partitions the untrusted system's memory into n smaller space-time optimal computation segments $C_{nonce_1}(M_1, R) \ldots C_{nonce_n}(M_n, R)$ and invokes them sequentially in random selection $n \cdot log\, n$ times [13]. The size of segments M_i is small enough such that optimal evaluation time t_i is smaller than the round-trip time necessary to contact the remote proxy. Hence, any untrusted system attempt to enlist the help of a remote proxy and return the correct result without performing the computation of a segment $C_{nonce_i}(M_i, R)$ would cause the RoT protocol to fail the time check of the optimal t_i.

Trustworthy Verifier. The trustworthiness of the verifier code can be established unconditionally. First, the verifier constructs the *nonce* by selecting strings of random bits input from a true random number generator; e.g., a quantum RNG. It can do this off-line. No adversary can predict the RNG's next random bits after seeing past *nonces*, nor can it anticipate the verifier's selection of the next *nonce* until its system malware receives it. The adversary cannot access the verifier physically or otherwise without placing it in a conflict of interest. The verifier cannot communicate with the untrusted system except via the local bus interface; e.g., the verifier does not have a WiFi or Bluetooth interface to the untrusted system. Second, the verifier knows the correct result $C_{nonce}(M, R)$, and optimal time t and $m = |M| + |R|$. It can compute the correct result and time off-line on a simulator of the real system, or on a system that is *a priori* known not to contain malware. The verifier can do this since it knows the system specifications. Recall that without complete and correct system specifications security, cryptography, or reliability problems cannot be solved, in general, as the system becomes undefined.

The above two *no-leakage* properties can be verifiably established on the small and simple verifier by standard information flow tracing of verifier code; e.g., by taint analyses of the verifier's binary code. (Recall that the first formal information-flow analyses of much larger and more complex code were performed manually with the aid of simple Lisp programs [19]). Finally, the verifier can perform time measurements securely to determine the correct system response time. This is a provable property given that neither system malware nor a remote powerful adversary can circumvent the integrity of the control flow of the code initialized by the verifier on the system, as illustrated by the two properties below.

Why Does the Unconditional Reduction Work? Intuitively, the two properties presented below can jointly prevent an adversary from using fewer than m words or less time than t, or both, and hence from leaving unaccounted for content (e.g., malware) or undetectably executing arbitrary code in the system, including surreptitiously contacting a remote proxy.

1. *k-independent (almost) universal hash functions.* $C_{m,t}$ must be second pre-image free in a one-time evaluation. That is, no adversary can find memory or register words whose contents differ from the verifier's choice and pass its check, except with probability close to a random guess over *nonces*. Also, inputting the $C_{m,t}$ variables and *nonce* into an untrusted device must use a small constant amount of storage. k-independent (almost) universal hash functions based on polynomials satisfy both requirements. Such functions can be constructed with *randomized polynomials* for inputs of $d + 1$ *log* p-bit words independent of k; i.e., degree d polynomials over $\mathbf{Z_p}$ with k-independent, uniformly distributed coefficients [13].

2. *Optimal polynomial evaluation on a realistic model of computation.* $C_{m,t}$ must be concretely space-time optimal on a realistic model of computation. That is, no computation exists that can lower either the space or time bound, or both,

in a one-time evaluation on the model of computation of the untrusted system, except with probability close to a random guess over *nonces*. The non-asymptotic space-time optimality of randomized polynomials in adversary evaluation yields this property.

Why are these combined properties sufficient for RoT establishment? Randomized polynomials provably enable a verifier to check the *integrity of control flow* on the code it initializes on an untrusted device. In turn, this helps the verifier implement precise time measurements of randomized polynomial execution. They also assure bounds scalability, and lead to the establishment of malware-free states on a multi-device system [13].

4   Why Is Space-Time Optimality of Randomized Polynomial Evaluation Hard to Prove?

An immediate consequence of using a realistic model of computation (e.g., the constant word length and fixed number of operands per instruction) is that any instruction-complexity hierarchy based on variable circuit fan-in/fan-out and depth collapses. Hence, lower bounds established in computation models with variable word length and number of input operands (e.g., a general Word Random Access Machine and branching-program models) become irrelevant in any real system. For example, lower bounds for universal hash functions show the necessity of executing multiplication instructions. This result does not necessarily hold in a real system.

The Math Does Not Always Follow System Requirements. In security and cryptography, we often suggest that establishing system requirements is the hard part of a problem since the math always follows these. In the RoT establishment case this does not seem to hold, as the math did not follow the requirements established in *any* realistic model of computation [12] For example, since we use randomized polynomials to construct k-independent (almost) universal hash functions, we must prove their non-asymptotic optimality in the realistic model of a computer like the concrete Random Access Machine (cWRAM) model [13]. However, all non-asymptotic optimality results for polynomial evaluation are known *only* over infinite fields (e.g., the unique optimality of Horner's rule [15]) and the gap between these bounds and the lower bounds over finite fields (e.g., Z_p) is very large. Furthermore, optimality is obtained using only two operations (i.e., $+, \times$) and cannot hold in computation models with large instruction sets and real processors.

In recent work [13], we addressed these problems by adopting a complexity measure based on *function locality* [16], which enables us to distinguish between classes of computation instructions, and by providing an evaluation condition that extends the unique optimality of Horner's rule for polynomial evaluation to realistic models of computations. That is, we showed that Horner's rule is *uniquely optimal* in Z_p whenever the evaluation memory and time are simultaneously minimized.

Adversaries are Always Dishonest. Note that the unique optimality of Horner's rule holds only in *honest* execution. An execution is honest if the evaluation code is fixed before it reads any variables or input, and returns correct results for all inputs. Unfortunately, the optimality in honest execution does not necessarily hold in *adversary* execution since an adversary can change code both before and after its execution, or simply guess the evaluation result without executing any instructions. Moreover, a powerful adversary must be assumed to adapt its code to inputs at no cost.

An adversary can also take advantage of the optimal *code composition* with initialization and *I/O* programs. For instance, if the polynomial input (i.e., the polynomial coefficients and evaluation value) requires multiple packets, the adversary can pre-process input in early packet arrivals and circumvent the lower time and/or space bounds. Also, in a multi-device system, a device can perform part of the computation of another device and help the latter undetectably circumvent its optimal bounds. Naturally, the concrete space-time optimality of sequential execution on a single processor does not hold when additional processors and memories are available to an adversary. Note that these attacks must be provably countered in any evaluations of a verifier's initialized code (e.g., interrupt disable, clock-frequency setting code), not just for randomized polynomial evaluation.

5   Other Provable Properties

Secure Initial State. After the verifier establishes RoT, it can load a trustworthy program in the system's primary memory. That program sets the contents of all secondary storage to the verifier's choice of content; i.e., content that satisfies whatever security invariants are deemed necessary. This extends the notion of the *secure initial state* to all system objects.

The notion of the secure initial state is necessary for other useful properties; e.g., for *trusted recovery* after failure and for establishing the initial state in a variety of *access control* components. For example, the trustworthy program loaded in a secure initial state can be a micro-hypervisor [3]. In turn, the micro-hypervisor can initialize an isolated I/O kernel [21] and various stateful isolated applications to secure initial states. This allows RoT establishment to be maintained by the isolated system and application components despite the presence of an untrusted commodity OS.

Verifiable Boot. RoT establishment is also necessary for *verifiable boot* – a stronger notion than secure and trusted boot [20]. Verifiable boot states that either a verifier boots a program in a secure initial state or discovers the presence of unaccounted for content in that state (e.g., malware), unconditionally. Since an unbounded adversary could take over one's system at some later time, performing verifiable boot ensures that the verifier can play a version of the "*FlipIt* game" [17] and win by discovering the presence of malware on an untrusted system unconditionally – a goal not achieved to date.

On-Demand Verification of I/O Device Firmware. Modern architectures isolate security-sensitive applications from untrusted OS code and enable them to isolate their I/O transfers. In on-demand I/O, when an isolated application requires exclusive use of a device, an I/O kernel takes control of the device from the untrusted OS, verifies the device-controller firmware and register settings, and then allocates the device to the application. When the application is done with the device, the I/O kernel returns the device to the untrusted OS [21].

To verify the device-controller firmware, the I/O kernel establishes RoT on the device controller on demand. That is, the isolated I/O kernel encapsulates a trustworthy verifier and equips it with random numbers. Then, the verifier constructs the nonce, challenges the device controller to execute the randomized polynomial evaluation, measures its execution time, and compares the returned result and its timing with those it obtains from the simulated randomized-polynomial execution. To obtain the random numbers for the trustworthy verifier, the I/O kernel uses a private channel, which is created and by a micro-hypervisor or micro-kernel, with a statically allocated true random number generator (RNG) device. For example, in an Intel architecture, access to the RNG device can be protected by a PCIe Access Control Service, and its direct memory transfers can be protected by an IOMMU whose page table separates the I/O kernel memory from the untrusted OS. Similar protection mechanisms are available on other I/O architectures; e.g., ARM. However, if only *conditional* RoT establishment is deemed sufficient, the I/O kernel can be equipped with a *pseudo-random number generator*, and the private channel to the true RNG device becomes unnecessary.

6   Conclusions

In this paper I argue that, with a proper theory foundation, RoT establishment can be both provable *and* unconditional. A variety of other system security properties can also be established for selected system components unconditionally thereby offering a defender advantage over any adversary. A consequence of this is that it avoids the pitfalls inherent to *fractal security*, and offers a first rest stop on the road to provable security. I know of no other software security problem that has had such a solution, to date.

Acknowledgment. The application of RoT establishment to I/O device-firmware verification was supported in part by the Department of the Navy, Office of Naval Research under Grant No. N00014-18-1-2892.

References

1. Butler, W.: Lampson, usable security: how to get it. Commun. ACM **52**(11), 25–27 (2009)
2. Gligor, V.: On the evolution of adversary models in security protocols (or know your friend and foe alike). In: Christianson, B., Crispo, B., Malcolm, J.A., Roe, M. (eds.) Security Protocols 2005. LNCS, vol. 4631, pp. 276–283. Springer, Heidelberg (2007). https://doi.org/10.1007/978-3-540-77156-2_34

3. Gligor, V.: Security limitations of virtualization and how to overcome them. In: Christianson, B., Malcolm, J. (eds.) Security Protocols 2010. LNCS, vol. 7061, pp. 233–251. Springer, Heidelberg (2014). https://doi.org/10.1007/978-3-662-45921-8_34

4. Schneider, F.B.: Beyond hacking: an SOS! In: Keynote at the 32nd ACM/IEEE International Conference on Software Engineering (ICSE), Cape Town, South Africa, p. 48 (2010). http://www.sbs.co.za/icse2010/_DOWNLOADS/Fred%20Schneider.pdf. Accessed 4 Jan 2019

5. Schneider, F.B.: Blueprint for a science of cybersecurity. Next Wave 19(2), 47–57 (2012)

6. Damgård, I.: A "proof-reading" of some issues in cryptography. In: Arge, L., Cachin, C., Jurdziński, T., Tarlecki, A. (eds.) ICALP 2007. LNCS, vol. 4596, pp. 2–11. Springer, Heidelberg (2007). https://doi.org/10.1007/978-3-540-73420-8_2

7. Gollmann, D.: Commentary in transcript of discussion: Dancing with the adversary - a tale of wimps and giants. In: Proceedings of the 22nd International Workshop on Security Protocol (SPW-22). LNCS, vol. 8809, Cambridge, UK, March 2014, pp. 116–129. Springer. https://link.springer.com/chapter/10.1007%2F978-3-319-26096-9_8

8. Murray, T., Van Oorschot, P.: BP: formal proofs, the fine print and side effects. In: Proceedings of IEEE Cybersecurity Development Conference (SecDev), Cambridge, Mass, October 2018

9. Pironio, S., et al.: Random numbers certified by Bell's theorem. Nature 464, 1021–1024 (2010)

10. Herrero-Collantes, M., Garcia-Escartin, J.C.: Quantum random number generators. Rev. Mod. Phys. 89(1), 015004 (2017)

11. Campbell, H.: God does play dice with the universe (and the dice are fair). Science 2.0, July 2012

12. Gligor, V., Woo, M.: Requirements for root of trust establishment. In: Matyáš, V., Švenda, P., Stajano, F., Christianson, B., Anderson, J. (eds.) Security Protocols 2018. LNCS, vol. 11286, pp. 192–202. Springer, Cham (2018). https://doi.org/10.1007/978-3-030-03251-7_23

13. Gligor, V.D., Woo, M.S.L.: Establishing software root of trust unconditionally. In: Proceedings of the Network and Distributed Systems Symposium (NDSS), San Diego, CA, February 2019. Full paper: CMU - CyLab - Technical report 18–003, November 2018

14. Li, Y., McCune, J., Perrig, A.: VIPER: verifying the integrity of PERipherals' firmware. In: Proceedings of the 18th ACM CCS, Chicago, IL, pp. 3–16 (2011)

15. Borodin, A.: Horner's rule is uniquely optimal. In: Kohavi, Z., Paz, A. (eds.) Proceedings of the International Symposium on the Theory of Machines and Computations, pp. 47–57 (1971). Elsevier Inc

16. Miltersen, P.B.: Lower bounds for static dictionaries on RAMs with bit operations but no multiplication. In: Meyer, F., Monien, B. (eds.) ICALP 1996. LNCS, vol. 1099, pp. 442–453. Springer, Heidelberg (1996). https://doi.org/10.1007/3-540-61440-0_149

17. van Dijk, M., Juels, A., Oprea, A., Rivest, R.: FlipIt: the game of "stealthy takeover". J. Cryptol. 26(4), 655–713 (2013). https://doi.org/10.1007/s00145-012-9134-5

18. Herley, C., van Oorschot, P.C.: Science of security: combining theory and measurement to reflect the observable. IEEE Secur. Priv. 16(1), 12–22 (2018)

19. Tsai, C.-R., Gligor, V., Chandersekaran, C.S.: A formal method for the identification of covert storage channels in source code. In: Proceedings of the 1987 IEEE Symposium on Security and Privacy, pp. 74–87 (1987)
20. Parno, B., McCune, J., Perrig, A.: Bootstrapping Trust in Modern Computers. SpringerBriefs in Computer Science, vol. 10. Springer, New York (2011). https://doi.org/10.1007/978-1-4614-1460-5
21. Zhou, Z., Yu, M., Gligor, V.: Dancing with giants: wimpy kernels for on-demand isolated I/O. In: Proceedings of the IEEE Symposium on Security and Privacy, pp. 308–323 (2014)

A Rest Stop on the Unending Road to Provable Security (Transcript of Discussion)

Virgil D. Gligor$^{(\boxtimes)}$

Carnegie Mellon University, Pittsburgh, USA
virgil.gligor@gmail.com

The title of this paper is a spoof on Butler Lampson's assertion that there is no resting place on the road to perfection [1]. While I don't disagree with his assertion, the road to provable security is not exactly a road to perfection, so we can expect some rest stops. In this presentation I will first define what I mean by a *rest stop*, then I will argue that rest stops are hard to find, and finally will explain how to find one in one case.

Let's start with a question Fred Schneider asked in his blueprint for a science of security: "Is it ever possible to add defenses and transform one system into another, where the latter system requires weaker assumptions about the components being trusted?" [2] In essence, this question is about adding *trustworthy reductions* (i.e., defenses) to decrease the security liability of the trust assumptions required by a security property, or more. Let's suppose for the moment that the answer to this question is *"it's always possible."* Then, in principle, we could compose reductions repeatedly until we remove *all* trust assumptions. Thus, we could create trust *unconditionally*, or more accurately trustworthiness, for whatever security property we obtain at the end of the composition. (This exercise is hypothetical: Schneider's paper does not imply that trust creation is practical.)

A Hypothetical Example. Suppose that we define program partitions in an untrusted system. Then we remove the assumption that information does not flow between different partitions by adding a trustworthy *separation kernel*, which reduces a simple information-flow isolation model to a system with *isolated* partitions; see John Rushby's 1981 proposal [3]. Now if we connect this system to a network, we still have the remaining assumption that the network maintains flow isolation between network partitions. However, if the answer to the question above is *"it's always possible,"* then there *must be* a way to add another trustworthy reduction (or more) to this system and remove this remaining assumption. Suppose that we add another trustworthy reduction proposed by Rushby, namely a *red/black separation* [4]. For example, messages that originate from a red (classified) partition are split into two parts: the message data, which are encrypted in a separate partition, and the message header, which is sent to another separate partition to reduce the amount of information that can be leaked by header modulation (e.g., destination addresses, packet length, time between transmissions) to some acceptable level, possibly zero. Then a

© Springer Nature Switzerland AG 2020
J. Anderson et al. (Eds.): Security Protocols 2019, LNCS 12287, pp. 233–241, 2020.
https://doi.org/10.1007/978-3-030-57043-9_22

fourth partition combines the controlled header content with the ciphertext of the message data, and releases the resulting black (unclassified) message to the network. In effect, the four partitions and the unidirectional flows between them implement a red/black reduction which separates network flows between isolated partitions and removes the remaining trust assumption.

Conditional Reductions. Now recall Lampson's metaphor that "security is fractal: each part of it is as complex as the whole;" see the above-cited paper. Clearly, if this is true, neither of the previous two examples of reductions can be unconditional, as their trustworthiness *must be* conditioned on some other complex assumption. For example, to be trustworthy, the separation kernel must be formally verifiable, which implies that it must always be small and simple. However, this condition does not always hold in practice: in 2010, the Information Assurance Directorate of the NSA argued that high assurance for (i.e. formal verification of) separation kernels is inappropriate for *commodity* workstations due to their complexity [5]. Furthermore, the cryptographic library of the encryption partition used for the red/black separation reduction must also be formally verifiable. However, this is conditioned by hardness assumptions, specific bounds on the adversary computation power, and often hardware security modules. Since the trustworthiness of these reductions is conditional, it is impractical to create trust in network isolated partitions by composing them as in our hypothetical example.

If security is indeed fractal, the answer to Schneider's question above is always negative. His conjecture that "trust cannot be created, it can only be relocated," [6] supports this, and the composition example above illustrates the conjecture. First, we relocated trust from our system with isolated partitions to the first reduction, namely to the separation kernel, whose trustworthiness was assumed, since it is not always formally verifiable. Second, we relocated trust from the red/black separation network to the hardness assumptions made for the formal verification of the cryptographic libraries. The impracticality of creating trust unconditionally was also illustrated by an earlier paper where Ivan Damgård pointed out that, in cryptography, reduction proofs only relate security properties to unproven conjectures [7]. Finally, in his commentary to my talk at SPW-22, Dieter Gollmann came up with what I call the *Gollmann complaint* [8]: "reductions often assume that something unknown cannot happen" – a very succinct statement of the general problem.

Simon Foley: I guess the question I have is, what do you mean by reduction, because we're talking about information flow for security properties. If what we mean by reduction is, say, trace semantics of the system, then the reduction is the removal of certain traces. In that case, the composition is not going to preserve security properties because sometimes to achieve a security property we want to inject additional traces, or additional behaviours.

Reply: Yes, one can view my reduction examples as removals of certain traces. Note that I was careful to pick reductions that do compose [9]. That is, if one has isolated flow partitions, one can construct the red/black separation out of four partitions and unidirectional channels.

However, you're absolutely right that, in general, not all reductions can be composed to achieve a desired security property the way I did here.

Simon Foley: So a reduction is, in simple terms, removal of traces, and what you're producing in Fred Schneider's terms, is enforceable mechanisms or approximations of information-flow properties.

Reply: Certainly, one can view my example reductions this way.

Unconditional Reductions. The possibility of creating trust in a security property implies the existence of *unconditional* reductions. A reduction is unconditional if its efficient, trustworthy execution uses *no* secrets, *no* trusted hardware modules, and *no* bounds on the adversary power. For example, the trustworthy verifier implementing such a reduction would only need truly random bits and the specifications of a device's hardware. Finding truly random bits is not a major hurdle in practice. If the bandwidth of the random bit generator need not be very high (e.g., a bit per second), one can even build his/her own true random number generator by capturing simple quantum effects. Otherwise, one can purchase a commercially available quantum random number generator; e.g., from ID Quantique. The harder part is finding correct and complete device specifications. Note that this is *always* required: without such specifications, one cannot expect solutions to either security or cryptography problems. Instead, one can only expect surprises. Finally, the trustworthiness of the small and simple verifier must be proven and the proofs must not depend on any unverified computation.

What Is a Rest Stop? The existence of unconditional reductions is significant in security. Unconditional reductions imply that the security properties obtained have no dependency on conjectures whose veracity is unknown or on unknowable behaviours of individuals who install secrets in one's system. They offer provable advantage to a defender over any adversary, and outlive technology advances; e.g., they are useful post quantum computing. In effect, an unconditional reduction represents a practical *rest stop* on the unending road to provable security. Once we find a *rest stop* for a security property the property is unconditionally proved, and then we can move on to prove other security properties. I must admit that I do not know of any *rest stop* in software security or cryptography other than the one I describe in the following example.

A Rest Stop Example. Let a small and simple verifier machine be connected via a local bus to an external device that may contain *persistent malware*. The verifier wants to establish that the device contains all and only the content it initialized in the device (i.e., it establishes *root of trust*), and hence the device is malware free. The verifier knows the device's hardware specifications ranging from the ISA, register set (R) primary memory (M) caches, virtual memory,

TLB, pipelining, multiprocessors, etc. Furthermore, the verifier has a source of true random numbers. Then, the verifier initializes the device to a family of concrete space-time optimal computations $C_{m,t}$, and challenges the device to execute a program C_{nonce} in memory (M, R), whose optimal size m, and time t on a *nonce* constructed from the true random numbers. If $C_{m,t}$ is second pre-image free and the correct result $C_{nonce}(M, R)$, which is unpredictable, arrives in time t, the verifier concludes that the device is malware-free *efficiently*; i.e., in minutes [10]. Note that the adversary who controls the device malware has unbounded power but is remote. Thus it can only modify a device's software and firmware but not its hardware. Furthermore, it cannot access or foresee the true random numbers used by the verifier to construct the *nonce*.

Trustworthy Verification. The verifier has three trustworthy security properties. First, it leaks neither the random numbers to the device (malware) *before* it sends the *nonce* nor the result $C_{nonce}(M, R)$ and optimal t before it receives the untrusted-device response; e.g., it obtains and verifies the correct result $C_{nonce}(M, R)$ and optimal time t *after* the device returns its response to the verifier's *nonce*. These two *no-leakage* properties can be obtained by standard information flow tracing of verifier code; e.g., by taint analyses of binary code. Second, the verifier knows the device specifications and can either simulate this computation on a malware-free simulator or obtain the result and its timing from another similar device that is known to be malware-free. Third, the verifier can measure the device computation time in a provably correct manner; e.g., it can *verifiably* disable caches/TLBs, virtual memory, and *verifiably* set clock frequency.

In short, the verifier can be trusted to perform an unconditional reduction from the concrete space-time optimal computation to the device's root of trust property.

Jonathan Anderson: So the protocol is using the *overt* channels that the device is presenting to the verifier, but that doesn't necessarily prove that there is an absence of *covert* channels, right?

Reply: Yes. It must be proved that the verifier does not leak other information than the *nonce* to the device. Recall that to have a covert channel, one has to have Trojan horse, or a spy, code on the verifier that colludes with the receiver-device malware; i.e., it encodes information and sends it to the colluding device malware. There is no such thing on a *trusted* verifier.

Jonathan Anderson: But is that just because the random bits are never shared with the device?

Reply: Yes, but also because the verifier is trustworthy; e.g., one can prove that the random bits enter the local verifier, but not the device, and exit as the *nonce*, by information-flow tracing.

Jonathan Anderson: Right. So I guess one can prove that the device faithfully executes a function, but this doesn't necessarily prove what else the device is doing. There could be other behaviours.

Reply: The device cannot do anything else, since the computation is proven to be concretely space-time optimal on that device. And the device's hardware specifications are assumed to be correct.

Jonathan Anderson: Right. So, I guess this seems to put a lot of importance on having correct device specifications, but isn't the problem of verifying hardware devices even more challenging than the problem of verifying the correct result and its timing?

Reply: No, because the correct hardware specifications come from the manufacturer. And if they are incorrect, one cannot talk about either software security or cryptography solutions. One can only expect surprises.

Jonathan Anderson: That's true, but supply-chain attacks are possible, right?

Reply: Yes, but the protocol takes care of those, as I will show shortly.

Fabio Massacci: I have a question about $C_{m,t}$. This computation must use the full extent of the device memory. So if one uses only a subset of the memory, the computation is no longer going to be space-time optimal. Thus every time one executes $C_{m,t}$, one uses all available device memory. Right?

Reply: Exactly.

Martin Kleppmann: If you have the local verifier that's already sitting on the bus, why can't the verifier just read all of the memory of the machine and check that it has the expected state? Why do you need all of the complexity of these optimal $C_{m,t}$ algorithms?

Reply: One needs these computations because otherwise device malware can simulate the contents of the device memory and send them to the local verifier. Then the verifier will never know that it read the output of the malware simulator.

Martin Kleppmann: But you are, at the same time, assuming that your device specification accurately represents the speed at which the CPU can execute the algorithm, for example.

Reply: Correct. Accurate device specifications are always required.

The verifier also needs to use a space-time optimal computation because otherwise malware could hide in persistent memory and survive power cycles. Imagine that the device happens to be a controller (i.e., a disc controller, or a NIC controller, or a DMA controller, or a manageability engine controller), which has flash memory. That memory could contain malware that is inserted there by the *supply chain* [11,12]. For example, an on-line supplier-generated patch can be surreptitiously interdicted by an adversary who inserts malware into the controller's persistent (e.g., flash) memory. Running the space-time optimal computation either detects the presence of malware and other unaccounted content or returns a correct and timely result. In contrast, if the malware is in non-persistent (i.e., volatile) memory, all the verifier has to do is to turn off the device and the malware goes away.

Why is it hard to find such a rest stop? There are two reasons for this. First, complexity theory lacks examples of computations that are non-asymptotically space-time optimal in adversary execution on the device's instruction set architecture (ISA) rather than on abstract machines; e.g., on Turing Machines or algebraic computation models [13]. Second, even if such a computation is found, adversary malware can be powerful enough to violate any control flow integrity of the verifier-device protocol and exploit availability of multiple device controllers; e.g., space-time optimality in sequential execution does not necessarily hold when multiple concurrent device controllers execute different optimal computations.

For example, Horner's rule for a degree-d polynomial evaluation is known to be *uniquely optimal* in infinite fields using $2d$ operations: d multiplications and d additions. However, is is *not* optimal in finite fields or on any realistic ISA or when the device is controlled by an adversary. Furthermore, the verifier can send only a single input packet of $k << d$ words to represent a polynomial to the device regardless of how large d is. Otherwise, malware could pre-process the evaluation while additional inputs arrive and circumvent the evaluation bounds.

Even if the adversary cannot circumvent space-time optimality of polynomial evaluation on a specific device ISA and all attempts to use a powerful remote proxy (e.g., quantum) computer are detected, the adversary can post a future interrupt that violates the control flow integrity of the verifier-device protocol; i.e., it triggers after the optimal evaluation result is sent to the verifier and reboots a malware controlled OS image unbeknown to the verifier.

Furthermore, if the verifier is connected to multiple devices (e.g., peripheral controllers that have flash memory), each device must execute a different space-time optimal evaluation whose t scales independent of m. Otherwise, device evaluations cannot start and finish at roughly same times.

A Solution. A solution that satisfies all necessary requirements can use k-independent (almost) universal hash functions that are implemented by degree-d *randomized polynomials* using input v of $d + 1$ *log* p-bit words in length, independent of k. These polynomials, which we denote by $H(v)$, have degree d and k-independent, uniformly distributed coefficients in $\mathbf{Z_p}$. Each coefficient s_i is itself computed as a polynomial with k random coefficients and input variable $i + 1$. They are second pre-image free, so no adversary can find memory or register words whose contents differ from the verifier's choice and pass its check, except with probability close to a random guess. To input a $H(v)$ into a device, the verifier needs to send only $k + 1$ random numbers to the device.

Randomized polynomials have non-asymptotic optimal space-time bounds; in one-time evaluation on a concrete Word Random Access Machine (cWRAM); i.e., $m = k + 22$ and $t = (6k - 4)6d$, where t scales with d independent of m. These polynomials offer stronger collision freedom properties than ordinary universal hash functions. That is, no function and input exist in $\mathbf{Z_p}$ such that the function evaluation on the input matches a given randomized-polynomial evaluation result with more than a very small probability.

Randomized polynomials enable a verifier to check the *integrity of control flow* in the code it initializes on a cWRAM device. In turn, this helps implement *verifiable* time measurements by provably disabling asynchronous events, caches/TLBs, virtual memory and stateless peripheral controllers, and by setting clock frequency and the content of the special CPU state. They also assure *bounds scalability*, which enables the verifier to establish the existence of its chosen content on the initialized device. Finally, one can show that the space-time optimality of the randomized polynomials in cWRAM can be retained on a real device ISA, such as that of a x86 processor.

Fabio Massacci: I have a question about the instruction in memory *other* than those for calculating the randomized polynomial. How and when do you execute those? Of course, you need to have other instructions in memory; otherwise, you wouldn't have malware in the first place. Right?

Reply: Yes. Please notice what is in memory at this point: some initialization and input/output code, which doesn't have to be space-time optimal, the polynomial evaluation code, and lots of constants that fill the rest of the memory. However, I do *not* have any (e.g., OS, application) code I am really interested in executing now, but what I have helps me establish the content of the system state, with high probability. After this, I can load the instructions I really want to execute in my malware-free state; e.g., I can load the programme that establishes a secure initial state. In other words, it establishes the invariant that I want to set, such as the device is disconnected from the internet.

Fabio Massacci: So this means that first you run this code to make sure that the system state is clean.

Reply: Yes. After that, I can load any other instructions I want, because the system is in a malware-free initial state that is secure. This is when I start the system; e.g., I can perform a real boot now.

Jonathan Anderson: So, this is about proving that there's no malware in firmware on devices on your computer. What about things like microcode inside of CPUs?

Reply: If it's writable, it's already included in here; if it's not, it's hardware.

Jonathan Anderson: It's sort of writeable. One can't write arbitrary things to it; one can only write signed updates to it, for example.

Reply: That would be fine. These writable registers are part of the CPU state that is captured in the input v of the randomized polynomial, $H(v)$. This part of the CPU state can be pretty large [14] as it includes registers that indicate the disabling of asynchronous events, caches/TLBs, stateless devices, and setting clock frequencies. The initialization code sets all CPUs' states. The device may also include stateless components; e.g., the GPU is code-stateless, as it does not contain persistent *code*. So if one disables it, it can no longer contain any persistent malware.

Note that the input v includes all the CPU state, which can be pretty large, as noted. If any part of it changes, as for example when malware skips the disable or set register instructions, the correct input v is modified, so the end result will be different from the one expected by the verifier.

Jonathan Anderson: My concern is that, although we implicitly trust hardware currently, we're also all aware that it could be compromised. But in this circumstance, the thing I slightly worry about is that now you're going to make stronger assumptions about the trustworthiness of the device that you're running on, because you proved something based on an assumption that you have completely accurate device specifications. And that just makes me a little bit uncomfortable. Getting device specifications, like "tell me the proprietary details of your pipeline, please," seems impractical.

Reply: I'm not worried much about the hardware security itself. Why? If somebody finds security bugs (e.g., hardware Trojans) in an unscrupulous manufacturer's hardware, the manufacturer cannot patch/remove them online, unlike software/firmware. Eventually that manufacturer will go out of business. This suggests that the hardware security problem may not be as big as one thinks, because of business deterrence. However, I am concerned about the correctness of the (security-bug free) device specifications. This can be a major problem, as you noticed.

Who may be interested in providing correct device specifications today? Some device-controller, micro-controller, medical-device manufacturers, who have to know the specifications of their devices or else they won't sell them, for legal liability reasons. However, this is not necessarily true for laptop manufacturers, for example, where one can't even get to the bus for the purpose of attaching a verifier. Eventually one will get accurate device specifications and local bus connectivity for verification/testing purposes. A place to start is automotive engineering, where one can plug verification devices into the CAN bus and check almost everything connected to that bus. That's the kind of thing that we need to do, and for this to work we must have interfaces to plug in verifiers. We are not there yet, but we will be.

Alastair Beresford: All right, let's thank Virgil for his talk.

References

1. Lampson, B.W.: Usable security: how to get it. Commun. ACM **52**, 25–27 (2009)
2. Schneider, F.B.: Blueprint for a science of cybersecurity. Next Wave **19**(2), 47–57 (2012)
3. Rushby, J.: The design and verification of secure systems. In: 8th ACM Symposium on Operating System Principles, Asilomar, CA, pp. 12–21, December 1981. (ACM Operating Systems Review, Vol. 15, No. 5)
4. Rushby, J.: Separation and integration in MILS (The MILS Constitution). Technical report SRI-CSL-08-XX, February 2008
5. System and Network Analysis Center, Information Assurance Directorate, Separation Kernels on Commodity Workstations, NSA, 10 March 2010. https://www.niap-ccevs.org/announcements/Separation%20Kernels%20on%20Commodity%20Workstations.pdf
6. Schneider, F.B.: Beyond hacking: an SOS! In: Keynote at the 32nd ACM/IEEE International Conference on Software Engineering (ICSE), Cape Town, South Africa, p. 48 (2010). http://www.sbs.co.za/icse2010/_DOWNLOADS/Fred%20Schneider.pdf
7. Damgård, I.: A "proof-reading" of some issues in cryptography. In: Arge, L., Cachin, C., Jurdziński, T., Tarlecki, A. (eds.) ICALP 2007. LNCS, vol. 4596, pp. 2–11. Springer, Heidelberg (2007). https://doi.org/10.1007/978-3-540-73420-8_2
8. Gligor, V.: Dancing with the adversary: a tale of wimps and giants. In: Christianson, B., Malcolm, J., Matyáš, V., Švenda, P., Stajano, F., Anderson, J. (eds.) Security Protocols 2014. LNCS, vol. 8809, pp. 100–115. Springer, Cham (2014). https://doi.org/10.1007/978-3-319-12400-1_11
9. In separation and integration in MILS, Technical report SRI-CSL-08-XX, February 2008, Rushby illustrates how to approximate information-flow properties with various safety properties. Hence, their composition by trace removal becomes fairly straight forward
10. This protocol is similar to that presented in Gligor, V.D., Woo, M.S.L.: Establishing software root of trust unconditionally. In: Proceedings of the Network and Distributed Systems Symposium (NDSS), San Diego, CA, February 2019 (Full paper: CMU - CyLab - Technical Report 18–003, November 2018)
11. Constantin, L.: What is a supply chain attack? In: Motherboard, 29 September 2017. https://motherboard.vice.com/en_us/article/d3y48v/what-is-a-supply-chain-attack
12. Lee, M., Moltke, H.: Everybody does it: the messy truth about infiltrating computer supply chains. The Intercept, 24 January 2019. https://theintercept.com/2019/01/24/computer-supply-chain-attacks
13. Arora, S., Barak, B.: Computational Complexity - A Modern Approach. Cambridge University Press, Cambridge (2009)
14. E.g., Figure 6 of Gligor, V.D., Woo, M.S.L.: Establishing software root of trust unconditionally. In: CMU - CyLab - Technical report 18-003, November 2018

Evidence of Humans Behaving Badly

Ghost Trace on the Wire? Using Key Evidence for Informed Decisions

Diana A. Vasile$^{(\boxtimes)}$, Martin Kleppmann, Daniel R. Thomas,
and Alastair R. Beresford

Department of Computer Science and Technology,
University of Cambridge, Cambridge, UK
{Diana.Vasile,Martin.Kleppmann,
Daniel.Thomas,Alastair.Beresford}@cl.cam.ac.uk

Abstract. Modern smartphone messaging apps now use end-to-end encryption to provide authenticity, integrity and confidentiality. Consequently, the preferred strategy for wiretapping such apps is to insert a ghost user by compromising the platform's public key infrastructure. The use of warning messages alone is not a good defence against a ghost user attack since users change smartphones, and therefore keys, regularly, leading to a multitude of warning messages which are overwhelmingly false positives. Consequently, these false positives discourage users from viewing warning messages as evidence of a ghost user attack. To address this problem, we propose collecting evidence from a variety of sources, including direct communication between smartphones over local networks and CONIKS, to reduce the number of false positives and increase confidence in key validity. When there is enough confidence to suggest a ghost user attack has taken place, we can then supply the user with evidence to help them make a more informed decision.

Keywords: Trust establishment · Public key evidence · End-to-end encryption · Secure messaging · Security usability · Informed consent

1 Introduction

Modern messaging apps with end-to-end security, such as Signal, WhatsApp, and iMessage, are now regularly used by over 1 billion people [3, 21]. These apps use public-key cryptography to encrypt messages on the sending device such that it can only be decrypted by recipient devices; any server infrastructure used to store and forward such messages cannot read or modify message contents. However, modern messaging apps have a common weak point in their security model: knowing whether a user has the right public keys for their communication partners. In the case of Signal, WhatsApp, and iMessage, the discovery of public keys is performed using a *key server* or *key directory* operated by the app provider: when a device generates a keypair it sends its public key to the key server, and when a user wishes to communicate with a contact, the app looks up the public keys for the contact's devices using their phone number or email address.

© Springer Nature Switzerland AG 2020
J. Anderson et al. (Eds.): Security Protocols 2019, LNCS 12287, pp. 245–257, 2020.
https://doi.org/10.1007/978-3-030-57043-9_23

Key servers are an example of a *Public Key Infrastructure* (PKI). In this paper we compare them with *Certificate Authorities* (CAs), a more traditional form of PKI used e.g. in the context of TLS, to provide a mapping between DNS domain names and the public keys of TLS servers. Both key servers and CAs link human-readable names (email addresses, phone numbers, domain names) with public keys, and both require an element of trust in the PKI provider. Both forms of PKI remove the need for users to manually manage keys – a task that has repeatedly been shown to be challenging for users [7,17–19,22] – and effectively automate the security decision of whether to trust a particular public key.

Such automation of security decisions and key checking undoubtedly helps, and is one reason why the current generation of messaging apps with end-to-end security have seen widespread adoption, whereas PGP did not. Unfortunately, the security and privacy requirements of a user are not universal. For example, a human rights activist using a messaging app in a country with a repressive regime has a different threat model from a typical user communicating via social media in the United Kingdom. The effectiveness of specific attacks depends on how users behave, what they are trying to protect, and the degree to which they understand the security features of an app. In short, requirements and context matter. Consequently, an app cannot automate all security decisions; some decisions are necessarily deferred to the user.

Deferring security decisions to the user is hard to do safely because we cannot expect users to be cryptographers and security engineers: they do not have the knowledge to reason about and deal with security decisions appropriately.

Moreover, the PKI is a significant weak link in the end-to-end encryption ecosystem as deployed by messaging apps today: a compromised PKI allows an attacker to break end-to-end encryption by adding another "end" (sometimes called a *ghost user*) to the set of public keys that a user has registered with the PKI, allowing the ghost user to read all messages in a conversation. Neither user may be aware that this has happened. This approach has been proposed by GCHQ as the preferred way to provide law enforcement with access to end-to-end encrypted communication without inserting explicit back-doors into the actual encryption protocols [13].

To protect against this kind of attack, WhatsApp and Signal offer users the option of verifying public keys (a.k.a. *safety numbers*) for their contacts. Such verification can be performed manually by comparing long alphanumeric strings, or by scanning QR codes on each others' phones. However, such manual checks take a significant amount of time, and – in the case of the QR code at least – require both users to meet in person. Anecdotal evidence suggests that they are not used much in practice. Even if safety numbers have been checked, they have a tendency to change fairly often, due to a user replacing their device or reinstalling the app; since most changes to safety numbers are due to such benign causes, users are conditioned to treat a change in safety number as harmless, even though this is exactly what a ghost user attack would look like. Apple's iMessage does not even offer the option of checking keys manually.

Various approaches have been proposed to detect ghost user attacks and compromised PKIs, which we summarise in Sect. 2. However, these approaches are not perfect, and we discuss false positives and false negatives that can arise in the detection of such attacks in Sect. 3. We detail failure modes and user expectations in Sect. 4. Finally, in Sect. 5 we describe how incentivising users, understanding user context, and collecting and evaluating evidence for key changes could lead to better system designs.

2   Detecting Ghost Users and Key Mismatches

Older end-to-end encrypted communication tools such as PGP rely exclusively on manual key fingerprint checking and explicit key signing to build a graph of trusted keys (the *web of trust*). However, PGP has failed to gain traction partly because of the difficulty users faced in performing these operations [22].

PKIs (certificate authorities and key servers) replace these manual processes with a centralised authority; the challenge is then to ensure that this authority remains honest. To this end, Certificate Transparency [12] has introduced the use of public append-only logs. Here, certificate authorities are required to submit a record of all issued certificates to the log infrastructure, providing an externally auditable proof of their existence. While Certificate Transparency does not prevent certificates from being incorrectly issued, it makes it more likely that such behaviour is detected, and thus discourages it. For example, in September 2015 Symantec was found to have mis-issued thousands of certificates; this event was discovered through Certificate Transparency logs, and had consequences for Google Chrome's handling of Symantec-issued certificates [20].

CONIKS [15] and Key Transparency [11] apply the Certificate Transparency approach to key servers. They maintain an append-only log of all public keys submitted to the key server, together with the human-readable username (e.g. email address or phone number) associated with each key. When a client wishes to look up the public keys for a given username, the key server provides a cryptographic proof that its response is consistent with the audit log. CONIKS is able to achieve this while preserving the privacy of phone numbers and email addresses in the log.

In parallel work we propose an alternative solution: to use gossip protocols on local area networks to privately and automatically check the bindings between human-readable names and public keys between contacts without requiring any user intervention. Such a protocol can operate on a local Wi-Fi network with Multicast DNS [4], which enables two devices, such as smartphones, to discover each other and compare their links between human-readable names and public keys directly. If the link between names and keys are the same, this provides additional assurance that there is no ghost user; if the links are not the same, then the key server may have been compromised. Our protocol can also use Private Set Intersection [6] to allow two devices that meet on a local Wi-Fi network to check the links from names to keys of any contacts they both have in their respective address books, without revealing any contact details for individuals they do not share. The advantage of using gossiping over systems such as CONIKS is that different app PKIs do not need to collaborate and there is no need for the service provider to publish their key directory. Even if contacts only meet on the same Wi-Fi network once a month, this will still provide much better oversight than the current manual verification approach. Some contacts will meet much more frequently (colleagues or geographically close family or friends).

However, while these solutions automate the process of auditing the behaviour of PKIs, there are several cases that need to be resolved by user input. For instance, in CONIKS, users have to reason about errors relating to inconsistent key server summaries, which may be the result of benign clock synchronisation problems between the client and the server, or an actual malicious server publishing different views of its directory [14]. Furthermore, we expect key changes to be the most common errors that CONIKS users and automated gossiping users might have to reason about. While most key changes are caused by the user adding a new device or re-installing the app, it can also be the key server acting maliciously and modifying the user's set of keys.

Section 4 reasons about user perspectives and Sect. 5.3 explores different levels of evidence that can be used to reduce the number of false positive errors that often overwhelm the user and cause them to ignore security warnings.

3   The Imprecision of Key Change Errors

In an ideal world, a communication system would report an error (and refuse further communication) only in those situations where a genuine PKI compromise (e.g. a ghost user attack) by an adversary is taking place, and never otherwise. However, in practice, all PKIs have *false positives* (an error is reported even though no wiretap is taking place) and *false negatives* (a wiretap succeeds without the user being alerted).

User-facing errors related to public keys have been most extensively studied in the context of TLS. It has been shown that most users ignore TLS certificate errors [1,2]; this behaviour is rational, since almost all such errors are false positives (for example, the certificate presented by the server has expired, does not match the given domain name, or is not signed by a certificate authority trusted by the client). Most TLS errors are thus due to client or server misconfiguration rather than a true man-in-the-middle attack, and hence they can be safely ignored [10].

Our goal in designing communication systems should be to reduce the probabilities of both false positives and false negatives as far as possible. False negatives must be minimised because every false negative represents a failure to guarantee the system's required security properties. False positives must be minimised because unnecessary errors amount to "crying wolf", reducing users' confidence in the system, and making it more likely that users ignore true positive errors in the future [2,5,10].

3.1 Reducing False Negatives

With traditional PKIs, if the adversary is able to compromise the PKI (for example by stealing a certificate authority's secret key for signing certificates), it can perform interception without being detected by clients. Framed this way, we can see that CONIKS, Certificate Transparency, and Key Transparency are mechanisms for reducing false negatives: by employing a verifiable append-only log, they make it very difficult for a key server or CA to return different public keys to different clients depending on who is asking, without being detected.

Transparency logs address one particular weakness through which false negatives can occur, namely the compromise of a CA or key server, but they do not fully eliminate false negatives: for example, an adversary may be able to block communication between clients and the transparency log (thus preventing the log integrity from being checked), it may block OCSP requests (thus allowing an attacker to continue using a stolen private key with a revoked certificate), or it may tamper with NTP server responses (thus setting the client clock incorrectly). Adversary control over client clocks may allow interference with time-based actions, such as preventing a daily consistency check of keys from occurring by making the client believe that less than 24 h have elapsed since the last check. Further work is needed to address these additional sources of false negatives.

In Sect. 2 we described the use of gossip protocols to exchange public keys directly between clients on a local network; this approach also reduces false negatives, since it detects when two users have different public keys for the same contact, which may indicate that a wiretap key has been inserted for that contact. However, this approach also carries the risk of increasing false positives: if a client does not correctly follow the protocol, either by accident or by malice, it may report incorrect public keys for a contact and thus trigger warnings, even though no actual attack is taking place.

3.2 Reducing False Positives

A false positive occurs when a user is shown a warning or error that might indicate an attack, when in fact no attack is taking place. For example, the WhatsApp and Signal messaging apps show the user a warning message whenever the public key for one of their contacts changes (see Fig. 1), even though in the vast majority of cases the cause of this key change is benign (e.g. the user installed the app on a new device, or deleted and re-installed it on an existing device). The explanatory message rightly downplays the significance of this key change, so users are conditioned to ignore these warnings.

The most straightforward way of reducing false positives is to report fewer warnings and errors. For example, iMessage has no manual key verification feature and no transparency log, i.e. key server responses are assumed to be fully trusted, and it does not report key changes to users. This means that there are no key mismatch errors, reducing false positives; of course, this approach also increases false negatives, since a compromise of the key server remains undetected.

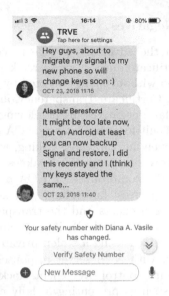

Fig. 1. Warning message displayed by Signal when a user's key changes.

Reducing false positives without increasing false negatives is also possible. For example, in the context of TLS, many false positive certificate errors are due to server misconfiguration (e.g. serving a certificate for the wrong hostname, or forgetting to renew a certificate before its expiry), client misconfiguration (e.g. client clock is set incorrectly, making the client believe it is outside of the certificate's validity period), or 'benign' network interference (e.g. antivirus software or captive portals on public Wi-Fi networks) [1].

Various measures can be taken to reduce these false positives: for example, about one third of HTTPS errors on Windows are due to misconfigured client clocks [1]; to reduce this source of errors, the use of authenticated time services has been proposed [8]. Key servers, such as those used by Signal and WhatsApp, are less susceptible to clock errors than certificate-based PKIs, since the key server's response is assumed to be valid immediately, and usually does not include an explicit validity period.[1] Also, smartphones typically sync to cellular network time (which is derived from GPS) and so (mostly) avoid clock synchronisation issues. Other devices may use NTP, but in all cases malicious action may cause problems.

3.3 Authenticating Key Changes

To reduce false positive warnings about key changes, systems could offer an authenticated key change: a user's old private key can be used to sign a statement

---

[1] Communication between client and key server occurs over TLS, with the key server usually authenticated with a certificate, so there is still some residual dependence on clocks in this case.

saying which public keys the user will be using henceforth, and other users will not be shown a warning if the key change is correctly authenticated in this way.[2] However, this approach is only possible if the old key is still accessible; if the user bought a new device because their old device was lost or irrecoverably destroyed, the user may need to recover their account without being able to access their old key.

For high-risk users it may be appropriate to disallow any unauthenticated key changes, requiring the user to back up their keys, and accepting that the user account would be irrecoverable if all keys are lost. However, for most users such a strict policy on lost keys is likely to be unacceptable: estimates indicate that approximately 20% of all Bitcoin ever mined, valued at billions of dollars, have been irretrievably lost due to the loss of the corresponding wallet private keys [16]. If so many keys with an immediate financial value are lost, we expect that keys for communication apps (with no direct financial value) are even more likely to be lost. From this statistic we conclude that for most users, a key change without signature from a previous key will sometimes be necessary.

Even if the system were restricted to only allow authenticated key changes, false negatives are possible: a malicious key server could return the attacker's public key the first time a key is requested for a user (for which there is no authentication, since there is no prior key), or withhold a key change to revoke a key that has been compromised. Detecting those attacks will still require either manual checking of public keys, a transparency log, or a gossip approach as discussed in Sect. 3.1.

4   Message Visibility and Key Changes

There are three main operations that will alter a user's set of keys:

Addition: a key is added to the set of current valid keys for a user;
Revocation: a key is revoked from the set of current valid keys for a user;
Replacement: an old key is replaced with a new key (revocation + addition).

Each one of these operations triggers warnings or errors in secure messaging apps, such as Signal and WhatsApp. For instance, a key replacement often happens when a user gets a new device or re-installs the app on their current device. While this is not an attack, it looks very similar to key server misbehaviour by changing the user's set of keys without authorisation because it triggers a key mismatch.

Most users, however, do not directly care about or understand key operations. Instead they care about the authenticity and confidentiality of the messages they send and receive.

---

[2] To avoid key changes, Signal allows the user to save a backup of the secret key on the old device, and restore it on the new device. However, this process is poorly documented and difficult to perform correctly. It requires the use of third-party apps to transfer and set up the backup before installing Signal on the new device.

For example, *read receipt* is a concept that serves the purpose of telling senders whether the intended user received their message and, if enabled, whether they read it or not. This could be further augmented by ensuring a full list of message readers is provided, for instance, if the recipient has two devices registered with the system, user-provided aliases may be used to identify to the sender that both the phone and the tablet received the message.

Message deletion can happen either at one client (deleting the messages only on one user's device) or, with application support, on all clients (deleting the messages from every communication participant). This is another important piece of information users would care about, but it may be difficult to explain the difference between the two to the average user until they experience someone deleting a message they had received.

Aside from the issues discussed above, end-to-end encrypted group messaging poses further difficulty. For instance, it is non-trivial to explain to users what happens to their messages when a new user joins their group, and different apps have taken different approaches. For instance, users may expect that a new joiner in the group would have access to the historical messages from the inception of the group, but this is not always the case.

5   Future Directions

We now explore possible solutions which ensure systems only display warning messages where necessary and that the content of such messages help users make informed decisions.

5.1   Incentivising Users

Anecdotal evidence suggests that a user treats a new app as a toy, exploring its features more in the first few sessions than later. This could be leveraged for the purpose of achieving better security.

For instance, an app can provide proactive manual checking as a feature, which can make it easier to detect if something has gone wrong. Users can be awarded points, levels, or badges to encourage such checks. The relative confidence in the correctness of the keys for a particular user can be displayed, e.g. with Bronze, Silver, Gold medals or a red-to-green scale with levels automatically assigned based on observed cryptographic evidence, as further explained in Sect. 5.3.

Such gamification is employed by many apps to incentivise user behaviour. However, gamification might incentivise users to spend more time on security than is rational given the benefits to them, so care is required to ensure the design is ethical.

5.2   User Context

Context matters and users have different threat models. Thus, allowing users to customise the display of key change notifications is important. This enables the system to vary what it displays based on the user's context, so a user who suspects they are of interest to an intelligence agency can be shown warnings which probably include false positives, while a more typical user would only be shown warnings more likely to be true positives. Alternatively, an initial setup phase to infer a user's threat model could then be used to customise defaults intelligently.

5.3   Evidence for Key Validity

To determine what notifications, if any, the messaging software should show to a user, we propose collecting evidence on the validity of a contact's keys. Rather than unconditionally trusting a signature from a PKI or a response from a key server, we can combine several types of evidence with prior expectations on the probability of a compromise to estimate the likelihood of a false-positive or a true-positive. This information can then, in turn, help users make an informed security decision.

To establish a binding between people (identified by a human-readable name, such as an email address or phone number) and the public keys of their devices, we propose collecting evidence in the following categories:

Trusted. The key for the user's currently in-use device is completely trusted.

Signed Trusted. A key can be signed by this device's key as being one of the user's keys on another device because, at some point in the past, they authorised it and optionally performed some mutual verification (QR-codes, local network gossiping, password authenticated key exchange [9]).

PKI Signature. This key-name mapping was supplied and signed by the PKI. So the PKI believed it to be correct at that time based on sending a text message/email or other verification process; this can also happen if the PKI is manipulating keys because of a warrant or a rogue employee.

Auditable PKI Signature. The signature on the key-name mapping by the PKI can be audited as it was published using CONIKS or Certificate Transparency. Therefore, the key-name mapping can be checked by the owner of the name and misbehaviour by the PKI will be detected.

Manually Verified. The user has verified the key-name mapping using QR-codes or some other out of band mechanism (confidence provided will vary with mechanism). This provides a strong guarantee that at a particular time the key-name mapping was correct.

Other Communication Channel. The user exchanged key material with the contact via a partially trusted communication channel, such as email, SMS, phone call, or another messaging app. Although this channel may not provide strong integrity or confidentiality guarantees, it may be difficult for the adversary to tamper with this communication.

Signed by a Key for the Same Name. Another key for the same name has signed this key-name mapping and it has its own evidence as to its validity. The evidence this provides depends recursively on the evidence for the validity of the signing key. In the context of the device for the key which did the signing this would be **signed trusted** but the evidence provided is lesser when this signature is from a key for a contact rather than your own device.

Gossiped Directly. The key-name mapping was directly gossiped with the device for that mapping and so was on the same network as the user's device at that time. Being able to display the location and time to the user provides greater confidence that either the key-name mapping is correct or the network they were on was compromised.

Gossiped Indirectly. The key-name mapping was gossiped via a mutual contact. Therefore the PKI has supplied the same key-name mapping to other contacts making detection of misbehaviour more likely.

Freshness from Gossiping. In the gossip protocol, devices use mDNS to publish advertisements proving that the device has control of the key at a particular point in time. These advertisements can be stored and provide evidence of the freshness of the key in a particular location. Since timestamps are chosen by the device producing the advertisement, the receiving device must verify it is within sensible bounds (advertisements time out).

Indirect Freshness. Mutual contacts can pass on advertisements they have observed for a key and so provide evidence of freshness during gossiping. Since timestamps cannot be verified by the device, this evidence is not absolute, but tampering requires collusion by the contact.

Revoked by Self. A message indicating that a key has been revoked, signed by the key being revoked, shows that someone in control of the key has tried to revoke it (not necessarily deliberately).

Revoked by a Signed Trusted Key. A key for the same name as the key being revoked has signed the revocation message and it was signed as trusted by the key being revoked. This means that a key on another device belonging to the user has been used to revoke the key (but it could have been compromised or this might be accidental).

Revoked by a Key for the Same Name. A key for the same name as the key being revoked has signed the revocation message and has some evidence as to its validity for that name.

Mutual Revocation. Two (or more) keys have mutually revoked each other (but not themselves) indicating that one of the keys has been compromised and which key under the control of the legitimate user is disputed. In this scenario relevant evidence for affected keys should be discarded and evidence built up again.

Expired. The key-name mapping has a validity period and the device's local time is outside of this period. This is probably accidental, as in the case of TLS certificates.

Most evidence is associated with a timestamp, such as the time manual verification occurred or the freshness timestamp in the gossip key-check message, and in most cases older evidence gives us less confidence than newer evidence. For example, we might have manually verified the key two years ago, which gave the user high confidence at the time, but the contact might have changed that device in the meantime. Hence, time-based discounting is required for the confidence derived from pieces of evidence. An exponential decay with a two-year half-life might be suitable as a conservative estimate of device replacement frequency. However, a contact maintaining the same key for an extended period of time gives greater confidence as a wiretap would have to have been maintained across the whole period to avoid detection. A log of gossip messages or timestamps when signed-session-keys for messaging were established could provide evidence of an extended period of continuous usage.

By leveraging such cryptographic evidence we can estimate confidence in key authenticity. This measurement can be used to decide whether to trigger a user warning, while also taking into account the user's notification settings as set up in Sect. 5.2.

6   Conclusions

Users of end-to-end encrypted messaging are not interested in key management: they are interested in who can read their messages and the authenticity and confidentiality of the messages they receive. The insertion of ghost users into end-to-end encrypted chats by unauthorised parties causes the same warning as a routine key change. Most of these warnings are false positives. After analysing existing approaches, we suggested how warning messages can be shown only when it is useful. We proposed deriving the prior probability of true positives from the user's context and combining it with evidence of key validity. In this way we aim to equip the user with the capacity to make informed decisions. We propose collecting this evidence from different sources, such as key directories, gossiping, or manual verification, and supplement this by incentivising the user to generate further evidence. Difficult trade-offs arise, as some measures to reduce false negatives may also increase false positives, or vice versa.

Acknowledgements. This work was supported by the Boeing Company and the Engineering and Physical Sciences Research Council (EPSRC) [grant numbers EP/M020320/1 and EP/M508007/1].

References

1. Acer, M.E., et al.: Where the wild warnings are: Root causes of Chrome HTTPS certificate errors. In: Proceedings of the ACM SIGSAC Conference on Computer and Communications Security, pp. 1407–1420. CCS 2017. ACM (2017). https://doi.org/10.1145/3133956.3134007
2. Akhawe, D., Amann, B., Vallentin, M., Sommer, R.: Here's my cert, so trust me, maybe?: understanding TLS errors on the Web. In: Proceedings of the 22nd International Conference on World Wide Web, pp. 59–70. WWW 2013. ACM (2013). https://doi.org/10.1145/2488388.2488395

3. Apple Inc.: Apple reports first quarter results, February 2018. https://www.apple.com/newsroom/2018/02/apple-reports-first-quarter-results, https://perma.cc/M6WV-Q4HK

4. Cheshire, S., Krochmal, M.: Multicast DNS. IETF RFC **6762**, 11 (2013)

5. Clark, J., van Oorschot, P.C.: SoK: SSL and HTTPS: revisiting past challenges and evaluating certificate trust model enhancements. In: IEEE Symposium on Security and Privacy, pp. 511–525 (2013). https://doi.org/10.1109/SP.2013.41

6. De Cristofaro, E., Tsudik, G.: Practical private set intersection protocols with linear computational and bandwidth complexity. IACR Cryptology ePrint Archive 2009/491 (2009)

7. Garfinkel, S.L., Miller, R.C.: Johnny 2: a user test of Key Continuity Management with S/MIME and Outlook Express. In: Proceedings of the Symposium on Usable Privacy and Security, pp. 13–24. SOUPS 2005, ACM (2005). https://doi.org/10.1145/1073001.1073003

8. Google Inc: Roughtime (2016). https://roughtime.googlesource.com/roughtime, https://perma.cc/C7TX-5ZK7

9. Hao, F., Ryan, P.Y.A.: Password authenticated key exchange by juggling. In: Christianson, B., Malcolm, J.A., Matyas, V., Roe, M. (eds.) Security Protocols 2008. LNCS, vol. 6615, pp. 159–171. Springer, Heidelberg (2011). https://doi.org/10.1007/978-3-642-22137-8_23

10. Herley, C.: So long, and no thanks for the externalities: the rational rejection of security advice by users. In: Proceedings of the New Security Paradigms Workshop, pp. 133–144. NSPW, ACM (2009).https://doi.org/10.1145/1719030.1719050

11. Hurst, R., Belvin, G.: Security through transparency, January 2017. https://security.googleblog.com/2017/01/security-through-transparency.html, https://perma.cc/ZJ33-NHH9

12. Laurie, B.: Certificate transparency. ACM Queue **12**(8), 10 (2014). https://doi.org/10.1145/2668152.2668154

13. Levy, I., Robinson, C.: Principles for a more informed exceptional access debate, November 2018. https://www.lawfareblog.com/principles-more-informed-exceptional-access-debate, https://perma.cc/7RJK-FM32

14. Melara, M.: Why making Johnny's key management transparent is so challenging, March 2016). https://freedom-to-tinker.com/2016/03/31/why-making-johnnys-key-management-transparent-is-so-challenging/, https://perma.cc/RX2S-MZQH

15. Melara, M.S., Blankstein, A., Bonneau, J., Felten, E.W., Freedman, M.J.: CONIKS: bringing key transparency to end users. In: USENIX Security Symposium, pp. 383–398 (2015)

16. Roberts, J.J., Rapp, N.: Nearly 4 million Bitcoins lost forever, new study says , November 2017. http://fortune.com/2017/11/25/lost-bitcoins/

17. Ruoti, S., Andersen, J., Zappala, D., Seamons, K.: Why Johnny still, still can't encrypt: evaluating the usability of a modern PGP client. arXiv (2015). http://arxiv.org/abs/1510.08555

18. Ruoti, S., Kim, N., Burgon, B., van der Horst, T., Seamons, K.: Confused Johnny: when automatic encryption leads to confusion and mistakes. In: Proceedings of the Ninth Symposium on Usable Privacy and Security, SOUPS 2013, pp. 5:1–5:12. ACM (2013). https://doi.org/10.1145/2501604.2501609

19. Sheng, S., Broderick, L., Hyland, J.J., Koranda, C.A.: Why Johnny still can't encrypt: evaluating the usability of email encryption software. In: Symposium On Usable Privacy and Security (SOUPS), pp. 3–4 (2006)

20. Sleevi, R.: Sustaining digital certificate security, October 2015. https://security.googleblog.com/2015/10/sustaining-digital-certificate-security.html, https://perma.cc/DV9F-8GUD

21. WhatsApp Inc.: Connecting one billion users every day, July 2017. https://blog.whatsapp.com/10000631/Connecting-One-Billion-Users-Every-Day, https://perma.cc/8WZJ-Y5UT

22. Whitten, A., Tygar, J.D.: Why Johnny can't encrypt: a usability evaluation of PGP 5.0. In: USENIX Security Symposium, pp. 169–184 (1999)

Ghost Trace on the Wire? Using Key Evidence for Informed Decisions (Transcript of Discussion)

Diana A. Vasile(✉)

Department of Computer Science and Technology, University of Cambridge,
Cambridge, UK
diana.vasile@cl.cam.ac.uk

Martin Ukrop: If there's an error shown that the secret has changed, when I'm alerted, because I'm an aware user, I message Alice on her phone and I find out that she hasn't got anything reinstalled, hasn't done anything new, hasn't reset her phone so it's probably a ghost being entered into the conversation. Can I then do something within the WhatsApp conversation to, let's say, renew the keys and kick the ghost out again?

Reply: Unfortunately, not at the moment, but the goal is to get people to notice these things, and then hopefully apps like WhatsApp and Signal would allow you to trigger a new key change or, alternatively, being yourself, you can just change to Signal, or change to something that's not being listened to.

Fabio Massacci: Can I opt out of telling the user that I have received on three devices? I have different levels of people that receive WhatsApp messages. Maybe I want my wife to know that I have several devices or maybe I don't really have several devices. But if I have a business partner that sends me a message, "I'm late," and I don't want them to know each time I've received a message, whether it's to all three devices, four devices, or one device ... can I opt out?

Reply: I'll talk a bit later about a few other things we can do to actually increase the certainty of whether a key change is actually something benign or something malicious. So in your case, you could customise it. You would not necessarily need to show that, if this is your privacy setting.

Frank Stajano: Triggered by Fabio's question, I just want to check that I understand things correctly. When you were saying, "I'm notifying the guy that this is being received by three recipients" , does three recipients mean three devices? Does it mean three different public keys? Because I expect that if I had seven devices, they'd all have the same public key, correct? And so then I thought that in that case it was received by Frank, and I don't care where.

Reply: Unfortunately, they don't have the same public key, or you don't necessarily need to have the same public key. It's down to whatever app and the way they implement it.

© Springer Nature Switzerland AG 2020
J. Anderson et al. (Eds.): Security Protocols 2019, LNCS 12287, pp. 258–263, 2020.
https://doi.org/10.1007/978-3-030-57043-9_24

Frank Stajano: I don't have many of the things that you have an icon for on your presentation, but I do have the Apple one, iMessage. So when my wife sends me an iMessage, she doesn't say "send it to Frank's phone or Frank's watch". She sends it to Frank. And then I get it on all of them. That's why I believed that the public key was of Frank, not the public key of the device.

Reply: It's actually particularly hard to know exactly what happens in iMessage and the Apple infrastructure but, having looked at it greatly, I believe that you get a public/private key pair for every device you own, especially given that you have to acknowledge them. When you get a new phone and you set it up and sign into iCloud with Frank's iCloud email address. Then a series of your devices get asked, "Is this authorised? Are you happy for this new device to use the iCloud email address?" which makes you think that they identify the device as its own, so you get a series of keys that link to a series of devices, and they all get drawn into Frank's bubble of trusted devices.

Frank Stajano: When you say send to three... Do you mean three phones, or do you mean three people?

Reply: So currently if you're in a group message, you can see the people. You can see how many people received or read your message. But if you're on a one-to-one, all you get is one of these options: sent, received, or read. What we're saying is you can go a level further and say sent to three devices that Frank owns.

Frank Stajano: Then for the purpose of identifying malicious, GCHQ listeners in, I would have thought in a naive way that they would appear as a different user. But is it possible technically that they would appear as another phone of mine? I think that that would require more hacking than just hacking into the central server.

Reply: So, yeah, it would require more hacking. The problem is, you see, when the key server sends your set of public keys for your devices, it will have to include all of the devices that are meant to be receiving that particular message. So they would appear as a different device, unless they eliminate one of your devices and put their own key in. But there are different ways that we'll talk about in a bit, of how you detect such attacks.

Frank Stajano: I don't know if I can cover that. I have no more questions.
(Presentation continues, describing the proposal in Sect. 5 from the paper.)

Jovan Powar: If you have a trusted key for Bob, why are you telling Alice that there might be something wrong with Bob's keys? Why don't you tell Bob? Because it might be more complicated to tell everyone else in the conversation that, "Hey, there's something fishy about Bob's keys." But if you have a trusted key for Bob, why don't you just tell all of the ones you trust on Bob's side that, "Hey, there's something wrong your key chain"? And then that requires less burden on users?

Reply: That's actually a really good idea. I don't think we've considered it. Thank you, yeah, we'll look into it.

Sasa Radomirovic: But the GCHQ will say "no, it's all fine" and then the ghost would say "no, it's all fine". You're telling Bob, who receives now on two devices that message.

Jovan Powar: But then this is assuming that you've got the untrusted one right.

Sasa Radomirovic: Well, what's also the problem is that the device will stop trusting Bob's key, because Charlie says that Bob's key is bad. Then you've left yourself open to all sorts of denial-of-service attacks who've listened to your behaviour. It may provide an interesting PhD thesis but it might be difficult to actually implement. There's one thing that strikes me the most; it's that your focus seems to be entirely on keys rather than on sessions. Now if you're using video chat, and if you trust the source code of the app enough to believe that you can physically see the face of or a screen for every party on the call. Then, provided you discount the possibility of real-time interference with video speed, the existence of a video call actually gives you a higher degree of confidence in the keys. Is that something that you're considering?

Reply: Actually, it's something I've chatted about last week when I was on a spring school. Someone has mentioned their usability researchers looking into fairly close area to mine, and they have run some user studies to try and improve manual verification. And their users have actually come back with saying they would trust it more if it was based on a series of exchanges of photographs or videos, short videos, rather than just a series of numbers. So that will be work I'll be looking into further. Thank you.

Frank Stajano: I like the suggestion of video as an extra validator, but as a regular user, I really have found so many instances where the sound is so broken up that it would mask the cases where something's gone bad because it just goes all the time anyway and sometime it goes back because someone is doing an attack. So I would not consider it as a very trustworthy indicator.

Reply: Unless you use it as a video recording, but then that raises other concerns.

Jovan Powar: A short one, I promise. Just to check, where exactly is the verification? Who is warning who the key in WhatsApp, is untrustworthy? Which entity? Is it everyone else in the conversation who warns the person that it looks like it? Or is it all of the user devices? Or is it the key server?

Reply: Everyone in the conversation gets notified that the key has changed.

Jovan Powar: And then each of them follows their own assessment of whether that's a trustworthy change or not?

Reply: Yes, based on their user contexts.

Martin Ukrop: Does the ghost have to be associated with either of the sides in the end-to-end encrypted communication, if I get it correctly, so there can be a third-

Reply: Yes, there can be a man-in-the middle, it's just not our scenario.

Martin Ukrop: You've been talking about notifying that there's a ghost on the other side of the conversation. But I would like to know that there's a ghost on my side of the conversation. "Oh, this conversation is being sent to your phone that you are on right now, your desktop, and your smartwatch". And then at some point if it says, "Oh, you've just added a second smartwatch," or "it's being sent to all four of your devices" where I only ever have three of my devices, that's one fishy thing for me. And I'm the one to judge better than the other side because the other side doesn't know how many smartwatches do I have. I want to know if you've considered informing the user of their own devices that are getting the copies of the message that they have just sent?

Reply: I guess that's down to the message visibility proposal we have. We can, given the privacy concerns that have been raised. It would make more sense, I guess, to move the visibility to the own user's devices and say, "I'm currently communicating off of these three devices" so yeah, it's definitely a possibility.

Michael Dodson: We've gotten into the conversation about what's actually being displayed on the screen. And I think that you haven't gotten to this yet, but several of the solutions that you talk about are actually offline solutions, right? They're peer-to-peer, so it's two people who know some third person having a conversation, gossiping keys. They're not actually in an active conversation where the person whose key is suspect-

Reply: This part of the discussion has been referring to active conversation.

Michael Dodson: Sure, but I mean ... in the actual key verification portion of it, you may not actually be in a conversation with the person, so it's two other people, potentially, who are the ones who discover that they have a mismatch of some kind, and so keys become suspect.

Reply: Yes, I'm getting to that now.
(Presentation continues, discussing the solutions to detect ghost user attacks from Sect. 2 in the paper.)

Ross Anderson: Well, using such mechanisms to fortify things like CONIKS is great. But it strikes me as another usability aspect, which is perhaps salient to me because my phone died last weekend, and so I had to survive a weekend in London on a 20th century basis. I also use Uber and so on. It strikes me that nowadays the loss of a phone is a major life event. It is appallingly disruptive. You're going to have to go and reboot all your services on a new phone, or in my case on an old phone that I've actually got. And so rather than using purely technical mechanisms, where you see a phone apparently being revoked you should demand from the counterparty an absolutely major social explanation of why his phone was lost. When did it die? How many hours was he unable to use Uber? How much did he pay for his new phone? Please tell us those people in the audience all about your new phone. Because the real life replacement of a telephone is not something that happens with a click as a glitch in the wire. And truly having it built in is an excellent means of fortifying protocols like this.

Reply: That's a very good point, thank you. The user is indeed the centre of it all.

Fabio Massacci: So I have a question on the gossip. I'm not so sure that going around on wifi improves their privacy even if using zero knowledge protocols, because you need to broadcast your location wherever you go. So this means if they get onto the wifi and your phone advertises every half an hour, telling your location to a lot of different things besides that. So broadcasting your location may be good for this particular protocol, but it would tell your location to lots of other people, so you have to look at the consequences of that.

Reply: I'm not sure I understand. We are proposing to gossip on the local network in this scenario, so you're not really telling your locations to other people. Plus you're always telling your location to other people when you connect to a wifi anyway.

Daniel Thomas: So, in this protocol, what you publish into the multicast DNS is completely opaque to anyone who doesn't know your key. So you need to know the key of the participant to be able to work out whether or not you know that person at all. So there's nothing identifying you that published on multicast DNS that's not already present because you've got your MAC address on. So it's true that if you normally turn your wifi off and don't connect to wifi for much, then you wouldn't benefit from this. And if you turn your wifi on to use this protocol, you've already lost the privacy protections because you've got the MAC being broadcast on the network. But there's nothing in this protocol that means more information is available about you than it would already be available just because you were online.

Reply: Thanks very much for clarifying. This is a key name graph we propose to gossip the bindings for because we expect that people actually have more phone numbers and email addresses identifying them and also more devices. The gossiping can actually gossip all of these bindings on the network. We do understand that people have certain contacts they do not often co-locate with. So in order to maintain the window of vulnerability for particular contacts as small as possible, we also see the possibility of performing the gossip over alternative channels, especially if the time threshold is met without the gossip between two contacts. If the right APIs existed, you could, for instance, gossip the keys WhatsApp uses over Signal and the other way around. Or you can use Dat for gossiping on the internet. This is work in progress, so we're currently looking into this possibility.

Martin Ukrop: I just realised that as I was checking my mail contacts, I have something like 1,500 contacts in my contacts list. So if we talk about the cost of this in terms of energy, if I have to start gossiping and synchronising all the data with all my contacts, because I need to keep broadcasting every time, right, if I want to keep the things updated? So we'll have to have a constant stream of synchronisation from my phone, probably end up with my phone without a battery, which as Ross said, is a major life event. And just to keep my key synchronised for a very rare event may not be the right mechanism. Do you want to have something that actually pushes the update rather than keep going all the time.

Reply: Thank you for the question. So, the thing with push for notification, it makes it manual again. We're hoping for automatic because of users not really understanding the importance of it all. But your point about consumption of battery is really good. There are certain mechanisms you can put in place such that batteries do not get completely drained. We're implementing a prototype to experiment with certain thresholds, say, you can perform the gossiping whenever you jump onto a new network, or you can perform the gossiping after a certain period of time. The multicast DNS actually has an advantage that it will store the entries in its table for 75 min. So that gives you about an hour and a bit of you not having to re-advertise yourself on the network. There's certain things we're experimenting with to arrive to the right solution.

I wanted finish by pointing out that gossiping is not necessarily restricted only to public keys. In the key directory example, we can see how this would be extended to gossiping app binaries, so that we can improve the binary transparency for similar reasons as we've displayed here. Thank you.

Warnings

Evolution of SSL/TLS Indicators and Warnings in Web Browsers

Lydia Kraus[1]([✉]), Martin Ukrop[1][iD], Vashek Matyas[1], and Tobias Fiebig[2][iD]

[1] Masaryk University, Brno, Czech Republic
{lydia.kraus,mukrop}@mail.muni.cz, matyas@fi.muni.cz
[2] TU Delft, Delft, Netherlands
T.Fiebig@tudelft.nl

Abstract. The creation of the World Wide Web (WWW) in the early 1990's finally made the Internet accessible to a wider part of the population. With this increase in users, security became more important. To address confidentiality and integrity requirements on the web, Netscape—by then a major web browser vendor—presented the Secure Socket Layer (SSL), later versions of which were renamed to Transport Layer Security (TLS). In turn, this necessitated the introduction of both security indicators in browsers to inform users about the TLS connection state and also of warnings to inform users about potential errors in the TLS connection to a website. Looking at the evolution of indicators and warnings, we find that the qualitative data on security indicators and warnings, i.e., screen shots of different browsers over time is inconsistent. Hence, in this paper we outline our methodology for collecting a comprehensive data set of web browser security indicators and warnings, which will enable researchers to better understand how security indicators and TLS warnings in web browsers evolved over time.

1 Introduction

The emergence of the World Wide Web (WWW) and the development of the first browser in the beginning of the 90's made the Internet accessible to the wider public. Today, web browsers are the major interface for users to engage with the Internet. However, availability of Internet access to the wide public also led to the average end-user being a common target of attacks. The common way on the web to ensure confidentiality, integrity, and ideally even identity is TLS (formerly SSL). In the case of web browsers, security indicators and warnings communicate TLS information to end-users, so these can take necessary action, e.g., not visit a site. However, communicating the current TLS security state and implications of TLS errors to end-users in the web browser user interface (UI), enabling them to make the right decisions and take the right actions is a still ongoing challenge.

While usability and user experience are drivers of UI design in consumer-oriented products, they are only one among several influencing factors in the context of security protocol related UIs. Security protocols evolve over time, in

J. Anderson et al. (Eds.): Security Protocols 2019, LNCS 12287, pp. 267–280, 2020.
https://doi.org/10.1007/978-3-030-57043-9_25

a complex process that is not only driven by market demands (including usability needs), but also by the interests of diverse actors (e.g., industry, academia, standardization bodies, etc.) [2] and changing security requirements [2,16].

For web browsers, this has natural implications for their user interface design, specifically for how they inform users about errors and the state of TLS-enabled (and plain text) connections. To better understand today's security and usability challenges, it is important to understand how these indicators and warnings evolved over time and how research, industry, and the practical reality of the Internet influenced this process.

However, until now, there is no consistent historical data set of browsers' ways of reporting SSL/TLS states via indicators and warnings. In practice, the qualitative data, i.e., screen shots of different browsers over time, is inconsistent. Figures found in the literature are temporarily and spatially limited, and online resources are not sufficiently uniform for a consistent comparison. To build a systematic overview of web browsers' communication of TLS states and error conditions in the UI, we need a data set that contains the evolution of TLS security indicators and warnings in web browsers over time. Hence, in this work we make the following contributions towards an open data set of browser UIs—currently focusing only on desktop browsers—in the context of TLS security:

- As the literature does not provide sufficient detail and consistent information on the evolution of browser security indicators and warnings, we propose to build an open data set to enable an in-depth analysis of the evolution.
- To set the ground for us and others to contribute to and to use such a data set, we outline the requirements for a browser TLS UI data set in terms of browsers, browser versions, and TLS errors and states.
- We describe the expected practical challenges in collecting this data in terms of data quality and comparability, including the visual representation of collected screen shots.

The remainder of this paper is structured as follows: In Sect. 2, we outline the technical background on TLS. In Sect. 3, we then revisit web browsers, and TLS information display and errors over time. We continue by providing data set requirements, outlining a data collection procedure and discussing its limitations and challenges in Sect. 4. Here, we address and discuss challenges like the impact of screen resolution and size on the visibility of indicators, and the limited availability of older software versions. Finally, we summarize our results and conclude in Sect. 5.

2   History and Functionality of SSL/TLS

2.1   History of SSL/TLS

SSL (Secure Socket Layer) 1.0 was first introduced by Netscape Communications in 1994, followed by versions 2.0 in 1995 and 3.0 in 1996 [43]. The protocol was further developed within the IETF, where its successor protocol was renamed to

TLS (Transport Layer Security) [11]. Since then, newer versions regularly appear, with TLS 1.1 in 2006 [12], TLS 1.2 in 2008 [13], and TLS 1.3 in 2018 [31]. While the development of new versions was initially driven by features, especially TLS 1.3 introduces new security mechanics and defenses against recently discovered attacks [31,35] and the discontinuation of by-now insecure algorithms and key-sizes [34]. In addition, existing attacks against TLS [35] led to the deprecation of SSL 2.0 [44] and SSL 3.0 [4] by the IETF. Similarly, TLS 1.0 is no longer an option for systems handling credit card data [29].

High-Level Functionality. In general, a TLS session follows four major steps while being established [11–13,31]:

1. **Session initiation:** Client and server exchange their capabilities (supported ciphers, etc.)
2. **(Mutual) authentication:** The server authenticates to the client by default. Optionally, the client may also authenticate to the server. Usually, this is done by using the local trust store found on most devices.
3. **Key establishment:** Server and client establish a shared secret, usually using public key cryptography.
4. **Symmetrically encrypted session:** Finally, the established key is used for a session using a symmetric cipher.

2.2 X.509 Certificates, PKI and CAs

An essential part of TLS is the authentication of at least the server by the client. For this purpose, TLS relies on a PKI system where Certificate Author-ities (CAs) issue X.509 certificates to parties operating a host with a specific DNS [25] name. Certificates are usually signed by intermediate CAs. Clients, e.g., web browsers then have a vendor-supplied (local/OS-wide) trust-store that contains the root certificates of CAs used to sign those intermediate certificates. Therefore, validating a certificate is also called validating the trust chain.

The process of a CA assuring that an entity is authorized to receive a certifi-cate for a name (has authority over the name) is called validation. Traditionally, there are Domain Validation (DV), Organization Validation (OV), and Extended Validation (EV) [10]. DV usually just requires the certificate requesting party to demonstrate authority over a proxy, e.g., being able to host content on the web-site a domain points to, or being able to access a mail address associated with a domain [5]. OV requires the issuing CA to verify an organization, while EV requires the CA to follow an extensive guide to verify the requesting entity [10]. Hence, in theory, EV certificates should significantly reduce phishing attacks [21].

2.3 Deployment on the Web

While SSL and TLS adoption has been traditionally slow, recent changes to the PKI ecosystem have led to a surge of TLS enabled websites. The introduction of

Let's Encrypt lead to a significant rise in websites using TLS [24] as it removed traditional—mostly cost—barriers to certificate deployment [1]. Similarly, various large browser vendors [19] and the payment card industry [29] increased requirements for TLS.

3 SSL/TLS in Web Browsers in the Present and Past

3.1 Web Browsers

Web browsers are the standard tool to browse the web. As of December 2018, there are at least 30 browsers from different vendors and organizations, with an even richer history of different versions [40]. Among those browsers are desktop and mobile versions of which some are bound to specific operating systems or devices. Mobile browsers became popular with the wider spread of mobile computing devices at the end of the last decade. As the scope of this work are desktop browsers, we use 'browser' and 'desktop browser' interchangeably in the remainder of this work.

From the mid 1990's up to the early years of the new millennium, the browser market used to be dominated first by Netscape Navigator and later by Microsoft Internet Explorer (IE) [26]. In 2004, Mozilla Firefox (FF) was officially released [28] and soon received constant growth, leading to a decreased market share of IE [40]. Soon after the release of the Chrome browser by Google in 2008, the browser landscape changed again significantly with Chrome becoming the most popular browser, see Table 1.

While the set of popular browsers did not change in the last decade, there was a significant change in popularity, with both FF and IE—as well as Edge as its successor—having lost popularity, while Chrome now accounts for nearly $\frac{3}{4}$ of the market, see Table 1. As of December 2018, the most popular browsers are Google's Chrome, followed by Mozilla's Firefox, Microsoft's Internet Explorer, Apple's Safari, Microsoft's Edge, and Opera's Opera.

3.2 Web Browser TLS User Interface Standards

Table 1. Market share of most popular web browsers in Jan. 2009 and Dec. 2018 according to statcounter.com [40]

Browser	Jan. 2009	Dec. 2018
Internet Explorer (IE)	65.41%	5.31%
Edge	N/A	4.03%
Firefox (FF)	27.30%	10.15%
Chrome	1.38%	71.29%
Safari	2.57%	5.09%
Opera	2.92%	2.18%

In 2010, the World Wide Web Consortium (W3C) has published user interface guidelines for the web security context [32]. These guidelines describe the TLS information that should be communicated to end-users in web user agents (such as web browsers) and provides recommendations on how this information has to be presented.

The guidelines differentiate between the *primary user interface* that is the part of the user interfaces that is directly accessible by the user, and the *secondary interface* that is not directly accessible, e.g., extended settings after clicking an 'options' button. The guidelines require a security indicator, either in the primary or in the secondary user interface in a consistent position, which can not be obscured by web content. They also require the presence of identity information, either in the primary or the secondary user interface. Again, the position must be consistent and the information must only be derived from the validated certificate. In addition, the guidelines explicitly require warnings for self-signed, untrusted root, expired, and revoked certificate errors, or if "TLS negotiation otherwise fails" [32]. While the guidelines provide a high-level set of requirements and definitions, the actual appearance of indicators and warnings is subject to the decisions of individual browser vendors.

3.3   Web Browser SSL/TLS User Interfaces in Practice

Traditionally, SSL/TLS information has been displayed by means of security indicators and warnings in the *primary UI*. Indicators are passive security signals that inform the user of the TLS security state, including TLS errors. They change their visual appearance based on TLS states (including error states). Major TLS errors are further accompanied by warnings in the UI. Warnings are active security signals: in contrast to indicators, they require users to actively take an action.

Indicator and Warning UI States. Current publications on browser security indicators and warnings distinguish five UI states [8,15]: HTTP (i.e., no HTTPS), HTTPS (including DV and OV certificates), HTTPS with EV certificate, HTTPS with minor errors, and HTTPS with major errors. In addition, Felt et al. also consider non-TLS related issues, e.g., if a website is blacklisted for hosting malware [15]. While these definitions provide an overview of the different UI states that indicators and warnings can take in concurrent browsers, the question is whether all browsers translate the (technical) TLS and error states equally to the respective UI states.

When looking at a fine-grained overview of (technical) TLS errors, as, for instance, provided on badssl.com [22], there seems to be an agreement on how browsers translate the majority of TLS states and errors to the UI. For instance, standard server-side certificate issues (self-signed, expired, unknown issuer, domain name mismatch) result in major errors and subsequent warnings in Edge 42, Chrome 71, and Firefox 64. However, as of December 2018, for some errors there are differences in how browsers translate them to the UI states. For instance, a revoked certificate (a major error) is displayed with a warning in Edge 42 and Chrome 71 (though without the option to add an exception), but Firefox 64 does not allow the connection and shows a "Secure connection failed" page.

There have been also differences in translating the error states to the UI in the past. For instance, whereas Firefox had a dedicated indicator for HTTPS with minor errors, most other browsers treated this state like HTTP [15].

Indicator Position. The position of indicators differed significantly among the different versions of the same browser and among different browsers in the past. For instance, Internet Explorer showed the indicator on the lower right of the browser, within the status bar (IE 5–6), whereas later versions (IE 7–9) showed it on the right side of the URL bar [7]. Similarly, Firefox has seen indicator position changes over time within the primary UI [7]. In contrast, today's major browsers, see Table 1, all show the security indicator on the left side of the URL bar [8].

Visual Appearance of Indicators. Indicators have mostly used symbols (e.g., padlocks, shields, or triangles), color (e.g., grey, yellow, green, red) and text strings (such as "not secure") to indicate different TLS and error states. For instance, a closed padlock has traditionally signaled in many – and even in early browsers such as Netscape Navigator [38] – a valid SSL/TLS connection (HTTPS): the data is encrypted in transit and the certificate chain validated

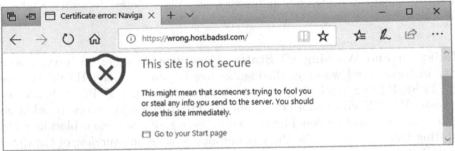

(a) Warning displayed due to an unmatching host.

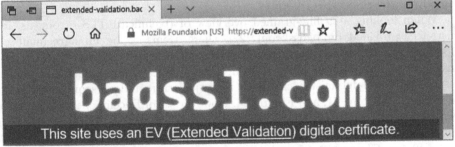

(b) Website with an extended validation certificate.

Fig. 1. Display and location of a) website with an error, and b) website with an extended validation certificate in Microsoft Edge 41.

correctly. Padlocks were used to indicate *HTTPS with major errors* in earlier Chrome versions, signaling the more risky state with red color or a crossed-out padlock [15]. Nowadays, they have been replaced with a red triangle that includes an exclamation mark (Chrome 71). Not all browsers have a dedicated indicator for major TLS errors (additionally to the warning): as of December 2018, the Firefox 64 indicator for *HTTPS with major errors* features a grey circle with an 'i' inside. Besides symbols, some browsers (e.g., IE 7) further used color-highlighted URL bars to distinguish different TLS and error states [21]. The URL bar also often holds the EV certificate state. An example of contemporary indicator placement is shown in Fig. 1.

Visual Appearance of Warnings. In case of *HTTPS with major errors*, browsers show a warning. Initially, as for example in Firefox 2 [41], warnings were presented as a pop-up dialog featuring a heading ("Website Certified by an Unknown Authority") and an additional description. Users received interaction options, for example, accepting the certificate permanently, temporarily (default), or not connecting to the website. Among other things, issues with this warning were that its appearance was similar to other uncritical dialogs and that it contained technical jargon [41].

Nowadays, the warnings in the five major browsers cover the full content window. All of them contain a heading, explanatory text, different interaction options (e.g. proceed or go back to previous page), and an image. This image may be a red shield with an exclamation mark (Chrome 70, Edge 42), a red-crossed padlock (Firefox 63), or just a padlock (Safari) [30, 39].

3.4 Examples for UI Evolution

The premise for our work is that indicators and warnings evolved over time and that research, industry, and the practical reality of the Internet influenced each other in this process. In this subsection, we will briefly go over examples for such use cases, which can be further investigated using our proposed data set.

HTTP Considered Insecure. HTTP works only with the plain-text communication, and is thus insecure by default. As such, researchers suggested indicating this [15]. While in the past many browsers did not feature a dedicated HTTP indicator [15], recent developments induced a shift in how the HTTP connection state is communicated to users. Starting from Chrome 56 and Firefox 51, the so far neutral HTTP indicator got accompanied with either text ("not secure", Chrome) or a symbol (Firefox), signaling an insecure state for HTTP pages which contain password and credit card fields [33, 46]. At the same time, the Chrome team announced future plans to further transit the HTTP state towards being shown as insecure by using the same indicator for this state as for the *HTTPS with major error* state [42]. The changes were motivated by the increase in HTTPS deployment in the Internet and the aim to further promote the use of TLS [33, 46]. They can thus be seen as an example of how the practical reality of the Internet (see also Sect. 2.3) influences indicator design.

Development of EV Certificates. The increase in phishing attacks led browser developers to collaborate on improving phishing defenses, among other things through means of EV certificates [17,37]. Eventually, the CA/Browser Forum, a standardization body of mainly certificate authorities and browser vendors, was founded [47] and issued later on the EV certificate guidelines in 2007 [9]. In the meantime, the Internet Explorer team was the first to come up with a proposal for indicating the *HTTPS with EV* state in their browser UI [17] and other browser vendors later on followed in designing a dedicated indicator [27]. However, as of 2009, usable security researchers criticized that indicators still differed considerably among browsers [36]. As of December 2018, the visual appearances of the HTTPS with EV state has harmonized: Major browsers show website identity information next to the padlock (by showing the company name and sometimes the company location) for EV certificates.

The introduction of EV certificates is an interesting example that shows how developments in the ecosystem led to observable changes in the user interface and usability improvements of the UI over time. However, some researchers claim that the end-users do not understand the different assurances provided by EV certificates as opposed to OV certificates. This leads to varying adoption of the extended verification since the extra burden may have only marginal benefit [20].

Treatment of Mixed Content. Mixed content occurs if parts of a web page are loaded via HTTPS while others are still loaded via HTTP. This used to trigger a warning pop-up dialog in IE 7 and IE 8 [6], necessitating a user interaction. IE 9 then started to automatically block insecure content [23], and changed indicator state by removing the padlock. Firefox traditionally used the padlock plus an additional indicator (a shield) to notify for mixed content. In 2015, they decided to remove the shield and to add additional cues to the padlock (e.g. a crossed padlock or a triangle with exclamation mark) [45]. Chrome used to have an *HTTPS with minor error* indicator for mixed content, but decided in 2015 to use the HTTP indicator for this state instead [18]. As the treatment of mixed content does not seem to be harmonized between browsers, it may be considered as an example of an ongoing indicator evolution in the UI.

4   Browser's Security Indicator Open-Data Set

In the previous section, we provided examples of how research, industry, and the practical reality of the Internet influence the evolution of indicators and warnings. To work towards a better understanding of how browser vendors adopt security technology from each other, and to correlate this with the browser version history and the general time-line of developments in the ecosystem, we need a qualitative data set of web browser UIs for TLS handling. Hence, we propose an open data repository of primary browser UI screen shots, and describe the requirements and challenges of creating such a repository. Thus, the focus of this paper is on the methodological framework.

4.1   Requirements

Security Warnings and Indicators Coverage. To get a complete picture of the developments around browsers' security indicators and warnings, a data set should test for all issues listed in Table 2. Please note that depending on specific research questions, this list might have to be extended or may be confined. For example, for research focusing on the evolution of indicator and warning usability it may be sufficient to look at the indicator and warning UI states, as outlined in

Table 2. Overview of relevant error scenarios, the content issues follow badssl.com [22].

Certificate Validation	Wrong Host
	Selfsigned
	Revoked
	Expired
	HSTS Violation
	No Common Name
	No Subject
	Untrusted Root
	No Certificate Transparency
	SNI Support
Content and Connection Type	HTTP Only
	HTTP Text Area
	HTTP Password
	HTTP Credit Card (+Autofill)
	Mixed Content
	Mixed Script
	HTTP Favicon
Protocols and Ciphers in Certificates, Chain, and Connection	Key Exchange Algorithms
	Digest
	Ciphers and Cipher Modes
	TLS Versions
	Attack Indicators (e.g. DH small subgroup)

Sect. 3.2. For research focusing on differences between browsers in the translation of TLS and error states to the UI, the full list should be considered.

In addition, non-security related work might also benefit from our data set. As such, we strive to keep an open mind towards additional cases that can be added to the data set. This includes cipher choices and TLS versions and various content issues, as well as straight-forward validation issues. Due to the ongoing nature of cipher discontinuation, we suggest to test against all ciphers from all supported SSL/TLS versions of the currently tested browser version (see below). Screen shots will only be recorded for combinations that divert from the happy flow (i.e. a website successfully validating). If an SSL/TLS version is no longer supported by a browser, it is sufficient to test against any non-supported SSL version to record a screen shot of browser behavior in this case.

Furthermore, as data collection is an ongoing process for the future, so far unsupported technology should be tested as soon as it becomes available in the first browser. Examples include DNSSEC validation of the target name zone [3], and TLSA record validation [14]. While both are available via plugins already, the focus of this work is on out-of-the-box UIs.

In addition, other relevant TLS mechanics, like SNI, might be worth evaluating in this context, if the data set is collected anyway. Finally, the happy flow should be captured for DV, OV, and EV certificates, including any warnings that might occur.[1] Depending on the time-line, the happy flow will require a dedicated setup with settings that might be considered insecure at a later point

[1] For example, early versions of Internet Explore displayed a warning when a *non* plain-text website was visited.

in time, e.g., SSLv3 support. Note that we do not make a distinction between major and minor errors, as this notion changes over time. For example, while a missing Certificate Transparency log entry may be acceptable for certificates issued before 2016, it may be a critical error for a certificate issued by Symantec in 2018 [19].

Comparable Visual Presentation. Creating screen shots in a manner that they are comparable is difficult. Furthermore, browsers may change their behavior if the window size decreases. For example, Microsoft Edge as in Fig. 1 removes the EV indicator if the window becomes too small. In addition, DPI (Dots Per Inch) settings may further influence the visibility or attention towards security indicators. Similarly, OS decorations may distract from indicators. The most common desktop screen resolutions and DPI settings, as well as aspect ratios (4:3/16:10/16:9) underwent changes over time as well.

Hence, we suggest to evaluate the 4 most common combinations of resolution and screen size per year. To cover the potential impact of OS decorations, we suggest to create screen shots of a default-full-screen browser, including decorations and other desktop elements like taskbars etc.

Browser Coverage. To build a data set that is as complete as possible, we suggest to evaluate all browsers, starting from 1994, focusing on all browsers that have been among the five most popular for any year since 1995, support SSL/TLS and have a graphical user interface. If a browser is discontinued, e.g., like Netscape Navigator, testing should presume up until the year the latest available version was released.

Platform Coverage. The underlying operating system may influence the appearance of browsers and how security indicators are recognized. We acknowledge that the large number of available platforms is an even more difficult issue than the issue of which browsers to test. To make this project feasible, we suggest the following selection:

- For the Windows platform, the most recent version as well as the most used one for each year.
- For the Linux platform Ubuntu (before then Debian) using the default desktop environment of default installation with a desktop environment. For the distribution we use the most recent stable (Debian) or Long Term Support (Ubuntu) version for the corresponding year.

We acknowledge that evaluating Safari Mac OS X (and Mac OS 9 before then) might yield interesting results. However, due the strong hardware dependence of Apple software, and the strict update regime making earlier versions hardly available (see below), we will leave Apple products out of scope for now.

Time Scale. The time scale with which we can evaluate browsers is heavily dependent on the availability of verified browser versions we can test. Hence, our time resolution will follow the software versions to which we can obtain access.

4.2 Challenges

Obtaining Correct Software Versions. Obtaining old software versions is a challenge. There is no consistent repository for outdated browser versions. While there usually are archive mirrors for, e.g., Linux, additional research is necessary to first compile such a software repository.

Creating a Reasonable Server-Side Test Environment. With the addition of a timescale, we will also have to provide a time-adjusted server-side. A 2018 TLS implementation is usually no longer interoperable with browsers using SSL implementation from the pre-TLS time. As with the client side software selection, this is an issue, especially as we will have to also simulate our own CA for this purpose. As this infrastructure can be created using open-source components, we will be able to utilize archive repositories.

Running Outdated Systems. In addition to getting access to the right software in terms of operating systems and web browsers, we also have to get access to hardware supported by this software. While virtualization may be feasible for many newer software versions, there will be limitations for Mac OS X and early Windows versions. In addition, the (automatic) update functionality of— especially more modern—software may prevent us from running older software versions.

Limitations, Open Data and Crowdsourcing. Building a *complete* data set certainly exceeds the capabilities of an individual research group. Therefore, we will focus on initially producing a data set that is complete in terms of error types (denied connection, major (with interaction), minor (without interaction), HTTP, HTTPS, HTTPS with EV [8,15]) for the most commonly used browsers today and ten years ago, see Table 1. We plan to integrate our screen shots in an open data setup, where researchers (and possibly crowd-sourcers) can assist us in collecting further data to build a complete list.

5 Conclusion

In this paper, we present our methodology for collecting an open data set of web browser UIs related to SSL/TLS over time. Rooted in a literature study and timeline of SSL and TLS development, we outline the basic requirements for such a data set and describe the necessary test cases. Furthermore, we identify several challenges, including the comparability of web browser screen shots due to changing conventions of screen resolution and size combinations, issues in operating outdated software, and hardware dependence of outdated software. We plan to collect the data in an automated and replicable manner, keeping it open for research collaboration.

Acknowledgements. We would like to thank Petr Švenda, Matúš Nemec, Marek Sýs and Adam Janovský for their comments during the paper writing and the participants of the 2019 Security Protocols Workshop for the lively discussion and the useful hints for our research and the paper. Furthermore, we would like to acknowledge the help of Richard Pánek and Filip Gontko with the collection of TLS warning screen shots.

This work has been partly funded by the European Union's Horizon 2020 research and innovation programme under grant agreements No. 830929 (CyberSec4Europe), and No. 825225 (Safe-DEED). The content herein reflects only the authors' view, and not that of the involved funding bodies.

References

1. Aertsen, M., Korczyński, M., Moura, G., Tajalizadehkhoob, S., van den Berg, J.: No domain left behind: is let's encrypt democratizing encryption? In: Proceedings of the Applied Networking Research Workshop, pp. 48–54. ACM (2017)
2. Anderson, R., Baqer, K.: Reconciling multiple objectives – politics or markets?. In: Stajano, F., Anderson, J., Christianson, B., Matyáš, V. (eds.) Security Protocols XXV. Security Protocols 2017. LNCS, vol. 10476, pp. 144–156 Springer, Cham (2017). https://doi.org/10.1007/978-3-319-71075-4_17
3. Arends, R., Austein, R., Larson, M., Massey, D., Rose, S.: DNS Security Introduction and Requirements. RFC 4033, IETF (March 2005). http://tools.ietf.org/rfc/rfc4033.txt
4. Barnes, R., Thomson, M., Pironti, A., Langley, A.: Deprecating Secure Sockets Layer Version 3.0. RFC 7568, IETF (June 2015). http://tools.ietf.org/rfc/rfc7568.txt
5. Borgolte, K., Fiebig, T., Hao, S., Kruegel, C., Vigna, G.: Cloud strife: mitigating the security risks of domain-validated certificates. In: Proceedings of 2018 Internet Society Symposium on Network and Distributed System Security (NDSS). The Internet Society (2018)
6. BrentgMS: Mixed content and Internet Explorer 8.0 (2009). https://blogs.msdn.microsoft.com/askie/2009/05/14/mixed-content-and-internet-explorer-8-0/
7. Burzstein, E.: Evolution of the https lock icon (infographic) (2011). https://elie.net/blog/security/evolution-of-the-https-lock-icon-infographic
8. CA Security Council: Browser UI security indicators (2017). https://casecurity.org/browser-ui-security-indicators/
9. CA/Browser Forum: Guidelines for the issuance and management of extended validation certificates (2007). https://cabforum.org/wp-content/uploads/EV-Certificate_Guidelines.pdf
10. Delignat-Lavaud, A., Abadi, M., Birrell, A., Mironov, I., Wobber, T., Xie, Y.: Web PKI: closing the gap between guidelines and practices. In: Proceedings of the 2014 Internet Society Symposium on Network and Distributed System Security (NDSS). The Internet Society (2014)
11. Dierks, T., Allen, C.: The TLS Protocol Version 1.0. RFC 2246, IETF (January 1999). http://tools.ietf.org/rfc/rfc2246.txt

12. Dierks, T., Rescorla, E.: The Transport Layer Security (TLS) Protocol Version 1.1. RFC 4346, IETF (April 2006). http://tools.ietf.org/rfc/rfc4346.txt
13. Dierks, T., Rescorla, E.: The Transport Layer Security (TLS) Protocol Version 1.2. RFC 5246, IETF (August 2008). http://tools.ietf.org/rfc/rfc5246.txt
14. Dukhovni, V., Hardaker, W.: The DNS-Based Authentication of Named Entities (DANE) Protocol: Updates and Operational Guidance. RFC 7671, IETF (October 2015). http://tools.ietf.org/rfc/rfc7671.txt
15. Felt, A.P., et al.: Rethinking connection security indicators. In: Proceedings of the 2016 Symposium on Usable Privacy and Security (SOUPS), pp. 1–14. USENIX Association (2016)
16. Fiebig, T., et al.: Learning from the past: designing secure network protocols. In: Bartsch, M., Frey, S. (eds.) Cybersecurity Best Practices, pp. 585–613. Springer, Wiesbaden (2018). https://doi.org/10.1007/978-3-658-21655-9_41
17. Franco, R.: Better website identification and extended validation certificates in IE7 and other browsers (2005). https://blogs.msdn.microsoft.com/ie/2005/11/21/better-website-identification-and-extended-validation-certificates-in-ie7-and-other-browsers/
18. Garron, L., Palmer, C.: Simplifying the page security icon in Chrome (2015). https://security.googleblog.com/2015/10/simplifying-page-security-icon-in-chrome.html
19. Gustafsson, J., Overier, G., Arlitt, M., Carlsson, N.: A first look at the CT landscape: certificate transparency logs in practice. In: Kaafar, M.A., Uhlig, S., Amann, J. (eds.) PAM 2017. LNCS, vol. 10176, pp. 87–99. Springer, Cham (2017). https://doi.org/10.1007/978-3-319-54328-4_7
20. Hunt, T.: Extended validation certificates are dead (2018). https://www.troyhunt.com/extended-validation-certificates-are-dead/
21. Jackson, C., Simon, D.R., Tan, D.S., Barth, A.: An evaluation of extended validation and picture-in-picture phishing attacks. In: Dietrich, S., Dhamija, R. (eds.) FC 2007. LNCS, vol. 4886, pp. 281–293. Springer, Heidelberg (2007). https://doi.org/10.1007/978-3-540-77366-5_27
22. King, A., Garron, L., Thompson, C.: Memorable site for testing clients against bad SSL configs (2018). https://badssl.com
23. Lawrence, E.: Mixed content and Internet Explorer 8.0 (2011). https://blogs.msdn.microsoft.com/ie/2011/06/23/internet-explorer-9-security-part-4-protecting-consumers-from-malicious-mixed-content/
24. Manousis, A., Ragsdale, R., Draffin, B., Agrawal, A., Sekar, V.: Shedding light on the adoption of Let's Encrypt. Computing Research Repository abs/1611.00469 (2016). http://arxiv.org/abs/1611.00469
25. Mockapetris, P.: Domain names - concepts and facilities. RFC 1034, IETF (November 1987). http://tools.ietf.org/rfc/rfc1034.txt
26. Naughton, J.: Netscape: the web browser that came back to haunt microsoft (2015). https://www.theguardian.com/global/2015/mar/22/web-browser-came-back-haunt-microsoft
27. Nightingale, J.: Will Firefox have a green bar? (2007). http://blog.johnath.com/2007/06/04/will-firefox-have-a-green-bar/
28. Orgera, S.: The history of Mozilla's Firefox web browser (2018). https://www.lifewire.com/the-history-of-firefox-446233
29. PCI Security standards council: payment card industry data security standards. Technical report, v3.2.1 (2018)

30. Reeder, R.W., Felt, A.P., Consolvo, S., Malkin, N., Thompson, C., Egelman, S.: An experience sampling study of user reactions to browser warnings in the field. In: Proceedings of the 2018 CHI Conference on Human Factors in Computing Systems, p. 512. ACM (2018)

31. Rescorla, E.: The Transport Layer Security (TLS) Protocol Version 1.3. RFC 8446, IETF (August 2018). http://tools.ietf.org/rfc/rfc8446.txt

32. Roessler, T., Saldhana, A.: Web security context: user interface guidelines. W3C recommendation, W3C (2010). https://www.w3.org/TR/wsc-ui/

33. Schechter, E.: Moving towards a more secure web (2016). https://security. googleblog.com/2016/09/moving-towards-more-secure-web.html

34. Sheffer, Y., Holz, R., Saint-Andre, P.: Recommendations for Secure Use of Transport Layer Security (TLS) and Datagram Transport Layer Security (DTLS). RFC 7525, IETF (May 2015). http://tools.ietf.org/rfc/rfc7525.txt

35. Sheffer, Y., Holz, R., Saint-Andre, P.: Summarizing Known Attacks on Transport Layer Security (TLS) and Datagram TLS (DTLS). RFC 7457, IETF (February 2015). http://tools.ietf.org/rfc/rfc7457.txt

36. Sobey, J., Van Oorschot, P.C., Patrick, A.S.: Browser interfaces and EV-SSL certificates: Confusion, inconsistencies and HCI challenges. Technical report, TR-09-02, Carleton University School of Computer Science, Canada (2009)

37. Staikos, G.: Web browser developers work together on security (2005). https:// dot.kde.org/2005/11/22/web-browser-developers-work-together-security

38. Stallings, W.: SSL: foundation for web security. Int. Protoc. J. **1**(1), 20–29 (1998)

39. Stark, E., et al.: Does certificate transparency break the web? Measuring adoption and error rate. In: Proceedings of the 2019 IEEE Symposium on Security and Privacy (S&P) (2019, to appear)

40. Statcounter GlobalStats: Browser market share worldwide (2018). http://gs. statcounter.com/browser-market-share/desktop/worldwide

41. Sunshine, J., Egelman, S., Almuhimedi, H., Atri, N., Cranor, L.F.: Crying wolf: an empirical study of SSL warning effectiveness. In: Proceedings of the 2009 USENIX Security Symposium, pp. 399–416. USENIX Association (2009)

42. The Chromium projects: Marking HTTP as non-secure (2016). https://www. chromium.org/Home/chromium-security/marking-http-as-non-secure

43. Thomas, S.A.: SSL and TLS Essentials: Securing the Web. Wiley, New York, NY, USA (2000)

44. Turner, S., Polk, T.: Prohibiting Secure Sockets Layer (SSL) Version 2.0. RFC 6176, IETF (March 2011). http://tools.ietf.org/rfc/rfc6176.txt

45. Vyas, T.: Updated Firefox security indicators (2015). https://blog.mozilla.org/ security/2015/11/03/updated-firefox-security-indicators-2/

46. Vyas, T., Dolanjski, P.: Communicating the dangers of non-secure HTTP (2017). https://blog.mozilla.org/security/2017/01/20/communicating-the-dangers-of-non-secure-http/

47. Yiu, K.: Improving SSL: extended validation (EV) SSL certificates coming in January (2006). https://blogs.msdn.microsoft.com/ie/2006/11/07/improving-ssl-extended-validation-ev-ssl-certificates-coming-in-january/

Evolution of SSL/TLS Indicators
and Warnings in Web Browsers
(Transcript of Discussion)

Lydia Kraus[✉]

Faculty of Informatics, Masaryk University, Brno, Czech Republic
lydia.kraus@fi.muni.cz

I would like to start my talk with a short thought experiment. Let's put aside, only for one minute, our interest in computing and imagine that we were archaeologists. As archaeologists, we would be interested in understanding the challenges that our ancestors faced hundreds of thousands years ago.

Unfortunately, we cannot just talk to them and ask them to give us some information, but they left behind some artefacts, which we could use to make sense of that question. So you can see some stone tools here, and we can see from the picture that their complexity increased over time. This is the time axis, and this is complexity. And we can also see that at certain points in time, namely here, here, here, and here, there was a conceptual change in the tools.

However, we cannot say (or maybe archaeologists could say) whether this was because somebody just had a good idea, or maybe there were some changes in the environment that forced the people to adapt. In summary, we can use the tools to understand the challenges that our ancestors faced in an ever-changing environment. So let's come back to the present and end the thought experiment here.

The theme of this year's workshop is: Security Protocols and Humans. I think that you'll agree if I say that security protocols are something inherently human. Why? They are designed by humans, they are implemented by humans, they are attacked by humans, and used by humans.

How does this relate to the stone tools that I have shown you on the slide before? Our idea is that we want to use the same approach as you can see for the stone tools—like looking at the evolution of artefacts; and, in our case, we are mostly interested in protocol-related artefacts—to see the challenges in protocol design and implementation and the resulting implications for security and usability in an ever-changing environment.

Our starting point is the TLS protocol, and its predecessor, SSL. It's a protocol which has a history of almost two decades, so the likelihood that we will find something is high. We are looking at the implementation in Web browsers, and we take Firefox, Opera, Chrome, Internet Explorer, and Edge as a starting point. And we are interested to see what are the implications of usability and usable security as a starting point, and there can be more interesting questions.

The artefacts that we intend to collect (we haven't started the data collection yet) are screenshots of the graphical user interfaces of browsers, namely of the

© Springer Nature Switzerland AG 2020
J. Anderson et al. (Eds.): Security Protocols 2019, LNCS 12287, pp. 281–288, 2020.
https://doi.org/10.1007/978-3-030-57043-9_26

primary user interface. There we can see TLS indicators and warnings and that can give us some information about protocol-related issues.

The research methodology that we suggest is to first define relevant scenarios for data collection, and we also would like to discuss it with you here at the workshop. Then the idea would be to install old browser versions and operating systems so we can reproduce the screenshots. And then we would start to collect the data: ideally, automatically. The data which we would collect would be screenshots or html-page content and potentially more, depending on whether you see some ideas that would be worth pursuing. Our goal is, in the end, to make the data collection tool and the data itself accessible to the research community.

In terms of scenarios we have thought about the SSL and TLS states and errors; and, from the usability perspective, potentially interesting candidates would be looking at the validation, which is okay, and considering different kinds of certificates, like DV, OV, and EV certificates. Then looking at certificate-validation errors, wrong host, self-signed, untrusted root, expired, and revoked certificates, and also looking at content like "mixed content" or "mixed script" and "HTTP only" or HTTP with password or credit card fields.

The reason why we selected those five scenarios from the usability perspective is that the first group, basically those two, also translate to the HTTPS indicator that you can see next to the URL bar. The EV certificates have an indicator on their own, and the certificate validation errors mostly result in major errors, where you can see these warning pages.

For the content, it's interesting to look at it because, for example mixed content or mixed script, they have some minor error indicators. They are different on the user interface than the rest. HTTP sometimes has its own indicator, sometimes hasn't. Basically, there were some interesting developments in the ecosystem, also.

Frank Stajano: In the previous slide you had something about installing old browser versions and OSes.

Now I am not sure if I understand the statement of the methodology correctly but this, I presume, means that some people would then browse today's web using the old browser versions and OSes in order to collect this data. Now, if this is what you are proposing to do, is it fair on them? Because those old browsers would have vulnerabilities that by now we know about; and these browsers were kind of okay in 2016 but by now the websites do other things that, on these old browsers, half the time don't work; and why should they be entering their passwords and credentials into those now-vulnerable browsers?

Reply: Okay, yeah the idea is not to make it available to end users. Basically this is only for data collection. We would install the old browsers and we would collect the screenshots and then we would make the screenshots available.

Frank Stajano: What I'm asking is: is the methodology just running an old browser and seeing its start up screen, or is it seeing it in action? In the latter case, you need to have some interaction; I mean, someone needs to use the old browser. Even if it's for research.

Reply: Well, for now, the idea's just to collect the primary user interface, basically only what you can see on the start screen when you start the browser. I think you can do it automatically. We already started, more or less, with a script that automatically installs an older version then runs the browser connecting to a certain website, and then takes the screenshot and does it all over again.

So basically for the primary user interface, it can be done automatically, though there are some challenges.

Fabio Massacci: Several of these validation errors depend on what is in your root repository of the different certificates.

If you start, and remove some certificates from the root of trust, then we get all kinds of errors even from normal websites. Did you try to consider giving them not only the old OS but, just saying, let's take the Chinese root of trust out, or take the Austrian root of trust out; have you considered this? Because that's the way you'll get a lot of wrong auth, self-sign or untrusted root errors, really get a lot, even from unsuspecting websites.

Reply: Yeah, that's an interesting point. We haven't considered it but I think probably it would be interesting to look at which certificates are pre-installed. Just yesterday we had a short discussion with Ross about the topic and, yeah, maybe this could be a research question we could also look at, like which certificates are pre-installed.

If we are only looking at the user interface, I think we would need to use a preset server side test environment where we produce specific errors, and maybe in that case we wouldn't look at which condition produces which error, but definitely that (like looking at which condition produces which error) is also an interesting research question that we could consider.

Fabio Massacci: No no, I wanted to say that you may not get only the obvious error. If you remove a root of trust, you may not get only the wrong error, that is "this certificate is the wrong root of trust". You may get even usability differences. So if you use UniCredit, depending upon the certificates as a root of trust that you have, you'll get a different website, you'll get a website with no pictures.

You'll really get a different thing because the credential that signs the picture, and the content delivery method, is different than the credential that signed the website. So you'll really see two different websites, one with pictures, one without, depending on the credentials that you have in the root of trust. I will show you if you want.

Reply: Ah, interesting. Okay, thanks!

Jonathan Anderson: I can see how you might build a self contained test apparatus with normal web servers and various kinds of certificates, et cetera. One thing that would be more difficult to take into account in a self contained system like that is how the user interface represents information about certificate transparency failures. Because in that case you have a kind of live system; I mean, unless you're going to re-build something that mocks up the CT, which maybe is possible. I mean, you can pre-build a library that fakes various CT errors; that would be a thing to think about.

The second thing I was going to mention is mixed content, mixed scripts and stuff. I guess mixed content could cover content from this provider, using this CA, and content using that CA. But also it would be useful to think about the way that the algorithms that people used over time; because at some point browsers started giving warnings about MD5 and then started giving warnings about SHA1, etc; so that might be another dimension that you might like to vary.

Reply: Okay. From the security perspective there would be other interesting examples that we have identified and we would be very happy, if more things come to your mind, if you pointed us in the relevant directions.

Daniel Thomas: Another app is perhaps different antivirus products. Some of them interfere with your SSL connections and make complaints about them, that the client doesn't. So, for example, Avast antivirus is complaining about the TLS certificate on my personal email server on Windows. On Thunderbird, it's perfectly happy to connect to it, but Avast doesn't like it and so even different browser versions might not be enough because there might be other bits of software that also would have caused strange messages for users who are using those browsers at that time, when you're thinking about it from an archeological perspective.

Reply: Yeah, thanks.

Jim Blythe: Are you also looking at other papers about usability of certificates? Because it seems to me that people have been writing about that since certificates first came out and they have given lots of screenshots for the different states at that time. They're cherry-picked, of course. But they are with the contemporary web, so you don't have these issues that are just responding to the things that the browser actually can't handle, which is now very common.

Another point that might be interesting is, I don't know if you know Jean Camp and her team made a survey of certificates. They attempted to download all of their certificates from the web a few years ago now, I don't know if she's still doing it, in which case there'd be this temporal data point, and she discovered some interesting patterns that would be worth looking at. One is that all the small banks in the US, a lot of them, like Bank of Indianapolis, had a web certificate that was from the company that made all its websites. So it wasn't the Bank's certificate but it didn't mean that it was a fraudulent site. I found that interesting at that time, but it's probably been fixed.

Reply: Okay, thanks for the hints. On your first point, originally the idea was to do a literature study, but then it turned out that the screenshots that are available in the papers are just not fine-grained enough and often it is not described like which browser version was it exactly and under which conditions was the screenshot taken and so on. So basically, yeah, it was our starting point and I guess we will report at some other point in time also on the literature survey and so now we try to collect first hand data.

Simon Foley: One question about the actual study itself. Do you have participants evaluating?

Reply: No, at the moment we don't plan to have participants evaluating. We collect the screenshots and then we would look at them and try (this is more or less what you can see on the picture with the stones) to figure out some developments that happened. Like for the stones, it is very hard to say what happened; but for SSL or TLS we have some developments in the ecosystem that we can track. We can then relate to them and try to make sense of the changes that we see.

Simon Foley: Would you consider how archaeologists conduct studies?

We had a paper at the Security Paradigm's Workshop in 2017 and related story work and again we were proposing this notion of security and archaeology, which is looking at artefacts from past, different versions of software (like what you're doing here) and developing theories about what the people were developing and how they were working; and, through those theories, trying to get insights into the good things that they were doing and the bad things they were doing and trying to prevent in the future.

Reply: Thanks. Any more questions at this point?

Ross Anderson: I suppose you, following on from what Simon said, could look to try and see whether particular incidents (such as the DigiNotar hack) stick out from the data as inflection points or points of change. Because it appears anecdotally that after the DigiNotar hack there was a huge flight to what we might call "quality", namely Verisign and Comodo. Although by that time I had already personally disabled Comodo in one of my browsers because they too had been hacked by the Iranians. That's one thing to look at.

Another possible thing to look at might be a text mining approach. If you were to collect the online talk about security over the past twenty-five years (which in itself is probably an MPhil project for somebody and will change from things like Usenet twenty-five years ago to the major security blogs now), that would also be a useful and complementary asset because people could then use NLP tools to identify those times at which people were getting worked up about HTTP issues; and whether these, in turn, correlate with any inflections in what you see as deployment.

Reply: Thanks.

Okay, here's some example of how the research could look like in the end. For example, on the indicator evolution we can see here screenshots from the late 90's. At that time, there was only the padlock down here at the bottom, on the right side of the browser; by the way, this is Internet Explorer and this is Netscape.

Or here on the bottom, on the left side. So, basically, it looks like there were only binary indicators, but I'm not hundred percent sure about it yet. And then some things evolved and at some point in time: the EV certificates were introduced because of an increase in phishing. So, basically, some change in the environment and then, as you can see here on the top, the EV certificate indicators of three different browsers.

And here the normal HTTPS certificate indicator. What is interesting is that those screenshots are from 2011, and between the browsers they looked quite different. I think this is also an interesting point that Sasa has made on Wednesday: there are inconsistencies also in the signage and between the browsers that are obvious here, but okay, they are not here nowadays anymore.

For example, here's the padlock on the right side and here there isn't a padlock at all. This is from Firefox and in that version the padlock has been on the bottom. Later on, here you can see the HTTP indicator from Chrome from earlier versions and now it looks like this, so there's a "not secure" phrase. They decided at one moment in time that they would consider HTTP insecure because of the increase of HTTPS connections on the whole web; it was a reasonable step to do it.

We intend to start with the five browsers that you can see here. Ideally for the full data set we would go with the top five browsers per year, starting from 1995, but, okay, as we need to start somewhere, we have decided for those five. And, excluding Safari because it is difficult to get the old hardware and the old versions and so on. And, we have decided for this group of browsers because they have more or less been the most popular ones in the last ten years. Sometimes one was on top and sometimes the other, but more or less the list of browsers was the same for the last ten years. And for the platforms...

Ross Anderson: Brave? There's other browsers, Brave, for example. There were more browsers than that. I'm just curious that that's the only list that we have.

Reply: Yeah, it's the only list that we have so far. The list will be longer and it will hopefully follow this rule that we will look at the top five browsers per year.

Sasa Radomirovic: Sorry, when you say Firefox I assume you mean Mozilla and Netscape as its predecessors as well.

Reply: Ideally we start from 1995. For Firefox we would only go back to 2004 because that's when it was released. But more or less we are interested in all browsers that existed starting from 1995, and we'd be looking at the top five for each year. Looking at which of the browsers were most popular in each year and then making the list and collecting the screenshots. This is the plan, but we would need to see which versions are available and what we can get. So, ideally, we would try to collect a data set that is as exhaustive as possible.

Sasa Radomirovic: So that includes hardware and so, not virtualizing necessarily.

Reply: It might be that we need to use old hardware.

Michael Millian: When you're looking at the top five browsers per year, is that browser *versions* per year? If I said that IE 7 and IE 8 were the top two, would in that case Internet Explorer take up two of your five slots?

Reply: Oh no, we would go per browser and take the most popular version of that year. For example for Internet Explorer the most popular version of that year, and so on.

Simon Foley: I guess it's not just the browser, because you'd also be looking at the descriptions of SSL and TLS and how it evolved as well. And bugs like the null-prefix bug for the certificates that was discussed yesterday; those types of errors.

It is part of the archaeology of studying these things that there were technical flaws that got fixed. What's the relationship between that and the interface that people are seeing?

Reply: Yes, that would be the idea: we look at all kinds of developments in the ecosystem like all certificate bugs, standardisation, whatever like happened and look how it relates with what can observe in the user interface. But, by the way, I think we could also collect other data than the screenshots. Does anybody have an idea of what would be interesting? Maybe default settings? Or the stored certificates in the browser? Any more suggestions?

Jonathan Anderson: Certainly if you had too many dimensions then the combinatorial explosion would become unmanageable, especially if you have things that require a lot of manual intervention. I could see how you could maybe write a script that will launch a browser that visits a URL then takes a screenshot and then kills the browser. But I think you have to get very manually involved in figuring out what are the default settings and that kind of thing; and the problem is the way to represent some of those things consistently across browsers and versions. But certainly a list of included defaults and certificates should translate fairly well across all of them, although some browsers might just default to whatever the OS set at the time.

Reply: Thanks.

The platforms we would look at are Windows and Linux. For the visual representation we would also try to collect screenshots with different resolution and screen size because there may be changes in the user interface or the position where the indicators are shown. And we would go for the four most common combinations per year of resolution and screen size.

I have already talked about our vision for data collection: our goal would be to collect the data in a replicable and automated way. And make our tool open source, and the data set as well. Do you see any developments in the SSL, TLS or browser ecosystem that you think are observable in the screenshots?

Vijay Kothari: I don't think this really gets to the question but I'm wondering. if there's any evolution that's in reverse because of other concerns? You might show us a prediction because it gets in the way of other usability concerns and you have someone swapping from this browser to another just because of security concerns. Did you notice that?

Reply: Just to make sure I understood it correctly: you think that there are maybe changes in the user interface towards showing more information and at some moment maybe showing less information again to the users?

Vijay Kothari: Just going from more security information they could connect with the interface, to less information being conveyed through the interface. Did you notice that?

Reply; As we haven't yet collected the full data set, I'm not sure; but I think it might have happened. Because it's a process of finding the right balance. We will see.

Jonathan Anderson: One thing to capture besides just the initial page loading screenshot (which unfortunately may be difficult to capture in an automated way) is what the click through messages look like when you would say "Yeah I know there's a problem but I really want to visit the page anyway". The language around that has changed very dramatically. But unfortunately you probably can't get that very easily.

Ilia Shumailov: This summer I got lucky to work with some people in Berkeley where we look at the underground forums and how the supply chain commoditization happens in those forums. One of the things that became apparent from the chains that they were building there is that the security policies which were introduced by companies change the way the underground markets work; and they changed them completely. Even if you introduce two-factor authentication, suddenly most of the market is actually looking for ways to disrupt it. And the price for just login passwords drops significantly. So do you see yourself trying to merge the works? And actually trying to estimate the benefits of the improved TLS notifications by building some sort of correlation analysis with the underground forums and the crime data that appears there?

Reply: We haven't considered that so far. I think I would need to think about that first before I can give you like a yes-no answer. But it's an interesting point, thanks for pointing us towards it.

Thanks to everybody!

Snitches Get Stitches: On the Difficulty of Whistleblowing

Mansoor Ahmed-Rengers[1(✉)], Ross Anderson[1], Darija Halatova[2], and Ilia Shumailov[1]

[1] Computer Laboratory, University of Cambridge, Cambridge, UK
mansoor.ahmed@cl.cam.ac.uk
[2] Department of Economics, University of Cambridge, Cambridge, UK

Abstract. One of the most critical security protocol problems for humans is when you are betraying a trust, perhaps for some higher purpose, and the world can turn against you if you're caught. In this short paper, we report on efforts to enable whistleblowers to leak sensitive documents to journalists more safely. Following a survey of cases where whistleblowers were discovered due to operational or technological issues, we propose a game-theoretic model capturing the power dynamics involved in whistleblowing. We find that the whistleblower is often at the mercy of motivations and abilities of others. We identify specific areas where technology may be used to mitigate the whistleblower's risk. However we warn against technical solutionism: the main constraints are often institutional.

1 Introduction

Whistleblowing is the act of exposing information relating to activities within an organization that are unethical, illegal or "wrong". Many believe that it is necessary for a healthy society that there be means by which a whistleblower can expose wrongdoing. The whistleblowing sections of government department websites reveal an interesting dissonance: they acknowledge the necessity of leaking [8,13,18], and some go as far as to offer rewards to whistleblowers [7]. Many organizations have dedicated departments for receiving complaints, as well as policies for whistleblower protection; this extends to private firms as well.

However, time and again such internal protection mechanisms have been found lacking. A systemic failure is unsurprising, because managers do not want their failings exposed, or even to know uncomfortable facts.

Thus, as a practical matter, whistleblowers may have to leak information to external agencies such as industry regulators, the police or news organizations if they want to force reform. Telling recent examples include the Chinese medics who tried to warn the world of the COVID-19 epidemic while the political leadership was still in denial, and the many women challenging sexual harrassment in workplaces from Hollywood to Silicon Valley. A more controversial change maker was Edward Snowden. After years in which internal complaints about unlawful surveillance fell on deaf ears within the NSA and even resulted in FBI

J. Anderson et al. (Eds.): Security Protocols 2019, LNCS 12287, pp. 289–303, 2020.
https://doi.org/10.1007/978-3-030-57043-9_27

action against complainants such as Bill Binney, Ed Snowden released classified information to the world media to prove that senior officials had lied to Congress about the legality of the NSA's operations. This resulted in President Obama setting up the NSA review group, leading to reforms in how the US intelligence community operates.

Following his disclosures, many media organisations set up supposedly secure means of making contact, using mechanisms such as PGP, Signal and Secure Drop. But do they actually work? We reviewed the advice given by a number of newspapers to potential users of their private contact mechanisms and found them to be lacking – indeed hazardous. We set out to find a better technological solution, but soon realised we were missing the forest for the trees. Technology plays a small part in a much larger game. A review of case studies taught us that whistleblowing is really about power dynamics. In this paper, we explain what these dynamics look like and present a game-theoretic model of the relevant power relations. This leads us to present some ideas for future research.

2   Case Studies

Although we looked at a wide range of case studies, we'd like to highlight a selection here to succinctly illustrate a range of scenarios. In the following section we will analyse them and see how they fit into a security game. Then we estimate weights for the different power relations and arrive at an equilibrium for each of the case studies.

2.1   Soft and Hard Power

First, a note about the taxonomy of power. Power is commonly seen as either soft power and hard power. Hard power is the ability to coerce, and can be based on one or more of a variety of tools: legal, financial, military, even physical intimidation. Soft power is the ability to co-opt and persuade, and its mechanisms are largely social including the credibility of a person, institution or country, public support for ideas more generally, prejudices such as sexism and racism, and even cults of personality [16]. We will use these terms as we discuss power dynamics in the following sections.

2.2   Edward Snowden

Edward Snowden was a contractor working for the NSA who blew the whistle on the NSA's mass data collection programs after Director of National Intelligence James Clapper lied to Congress about unlawful intelligence collection against US citizens. As an NSA (and former CIA) insider, Snowden understood the technologies that would be needed to communicate securely with a journalist at a distance. He first got in touch with the journalist Glenn Greenwald, but Greenwald found encrypted email too annoying to use. This led Snowden to contact another journalist, Laura Poitras, who got Greenwald on board.

The Snowden case is interesting because it pits the whistleblower against one of the strongest adversaries, and because Snowden's knowledge of surveillance enabled him to disclose his identity on his own terms. But interesting as this case is, it represents a tiny minority of whistleblowing situations. Usually the adversary is not the NSA but a medium-sized business or a public-sector body such as a hospital; the whistleblower is not an expert in anonymity; and, crucially, the anonymity set (the number of people who could feasibly be the whistleblower) is not the tens of thousands of NSA technical staff, but a handful of people who knew what was going on.

2.3   The PCAW Case Studies

To get a better sense of what a "typical" whistleblowing event looks like we went through the case studies published by Public Concern At Work (PCAW) [19], a UK-based whistleblowing charity. Their website lists a large number of cases where employees exposed wrongdoing by their employers. In most such cases the anonymity set – the set of people who knew the information – was small; sometimes it was just one person. In such cases, anonymity technologies aren't going to be much help.

PCAW's advice in these cases generally revolves around finding the right authorities to talk to. Rarely do they recommend broadcasting the information to the public at large or anonymously leaking documents to a journalist. Where there are competent authorities that can keep the wrongdoer in check, this approach can make sense. A bank that's ripping off its customers can be reported to the regulator, and junior medics could deal with an incompetent surgeon in the same way. However, this often doesn't work out in practice. In the case of UK banks, the mis-selling of payment protection insurance grew into a major abuse before regulators stepped in, leading to compensation in the multiple billions; and one incompetent breast surgeon subjected more than 1,000 patients to unnecessary and damaging operations over 14 years before he was stopped [4].

PCAW's advice ignores the *soft power* that the adversary may have or be able to enlist. The whistleblower may face social ostracism, difficulties in continuing work in a sector or intimidation by colluding actors. These repercussions are hard to predict and can have a severe impact. And the adverse reaction does not have to come from line managers; low-level employees can also pick on whistleblowers if they believe they have management's tacit support. In one employment tribunal case, a female employee of a Scottish government department was found gagged and tied up after complaining about sexism [5]. It can also be industry-wide. For example, the UK construction industry kept a secret blacklist of over 3,000 'undesirables' including union activists, whistleblowers and people who had raised health and safety concerns; over 40 firms paid £3,000 a year each to subscribe to the service. It was raided by the UK authorities and its operator prosecuted. It later turned out to have the covert support of the Security Service [23].

2.4 Harvey Weinstein

Another case where the effects of soft power are apparent is that of Harvey Weinstein, a Hollywood director who gained notoriety in 2017 when dozens of women accused him of pedatory sexual behaviour, indecent assault and rape [24]. These accusations kicked off the #MeToo movement in which a number of other rich or powerful men were publicly accused of sexual misconduct.

For years, there had been rumours about Weinstein's inappropriate behaviour, with some celebrities advising women in Hollywood to not go to his private parties [2]. But Weinstein's victims rarely spoke out. This involved a mixture of hard power (fear exclusion from work in Hollywood, fear of legal costs) and soft power (the social stigma attaching to survivors of sexual assault). In 2017 the New York Times broke the story that he'd paid off at least eight women after some thirty years of allegations of sexual harassment [11]. This opened the floodgates. Dozens more women felt legally and socially safe enough to come out and make allegations of rape or indecent assault against Weinstein; and hundreds more came forward to make allegations against a range of public figures including Prince Andrew and President Donald Trump. The key to whistleblowing on misogyny and sexual abuse in the workplace was not a new encryption technology. It was a shift in soft power that gave victims and witnesses the confidence to tell their stories in the knowledge that they had some chance of being taken seriously rather than being crushed or just ignored.

3   Related Work

There is no shortage of whistleblowing laws, organizational guidelines, and internal complaints procedures. Most of them appear aimed at damage limitation. The formal complaints procedure at the typical company will lead to the human resources department, which exists to protect the company. The usual outcome, as in Weinstein's career up to October 2017, is that complainants are intimidated into leaving and perhaps paid off.

We leave consideration of such laws and procedures to one side for now, until we have a better understanding of the power dynamics and the possible solutions. For now we focus on whistleblowing to news agencies by individuals who thereby place themselves at risk of being sued or prosecuted.

3.1   Academic Work

Academic work on whistleblowing in the security community has focused on the usability of encryption software products [25], the design of secure messaging systems [6] and so on. These tools can significantly cut the risk of leaking documents where the leaker is in a large anonymity set and the opponent is technically capable. However our focus is on how to minimise the overall risk rather on the specifics of the tools used.

3.2   Journalistic Resources

Dozens of news organisations have web pages with guides on how to leak documents to them; see for example the New York Times [17] and WikiLeaks [26]. However, they focus more on describing what makes a particular tip good and listing the acceptable communications channels, rather than on how to avoid catastrophic mistakes. For example, such pages do not provide adequate explanations of how information can leak through side channels, how to transfer physical evidence safely into digital formats, or more generally the capabilities of potential adversaries. None of them appears to help potential whistleblowers figure out what their anonymity set is and how they might expand that.

To illustrate these shortcomings, consider the guidelines published by the New York Times. Their web page has links to Instructions and Security, and suggests four channels: WhatsApp, Signal, physical post and email.

The web page mentions that WhatsApp keeps 'records of the phone numbers involved in the exchange and the users' metadata, including timestamps on messages', but does not explain what metadata is, or how it can allow the FBI to track the leaker. For Signal, the web page mentions that Signal saves only the phone number and the time of last activity and states that no metadata about the communication gets saved. This web page also fails to explain metadata and how Signal has been compromised in the past. The new user is just not told that the anonymity set of WhatsApp is much larger than that of Signal due to its greater number of users, or how to work out whether this matters. It does not spell out, for example 'If you're one of only six people with access to this document it might not be wise to use Signal if none of the other five ever do'. It would also have been prudent to explain that smartphone apps such as Signal and Whatsapp may link the leak to a specific phone number, and that changing your SIM card may not help if this is flagged as suspicious (whether by your social circle or by a network adversary).

The New York Times alternatively suggests sending documents through email, using PGP via the Mailvelope plug-in for Chrome and Firefox. The process for encryption here exhibits similar properties to those that confused most users in the canonical paper of security usability, 'Why Johnny Can't Encrypt' [25]. Furthermore, DNS is widely monitored to detect malware and botnets, so DNS access to a commonly-used plug-in for information leakage can flag up a machine as suspicious, especially just after accessing The New York Times.

Finally, the last option proposed by the New York Times is to use physical post. It recommends using a public mailbox, rather than a post office. It might be a good idea to explain why: the US government scans all snail mail and records sender and destination [9,14], and some letter destinations are more closely monitored than others – presumably including the New York Times [15]. Other risks associated with sending documents through the mail might also be discussed, including new methods for non-invasive content extraction [20]. Lastly, printers themselves represent a vulnerability due identifying watermarks left on documents [21] as well as difficult to clear on-device storage.

Another option mentioned fairly regularly on news organizations is Secure-Drop, an application designed specifically for leaking documents. We performed a cognitive walkthrough of this application and identified several usability issues. We believe it would be challenging for a novice user to install the Tor browser, navigate to onion links, and securely store the passphrase that SecureDrop requires them to remember. In fact, using Tor itself can severely reduce a leaker's anonymity set against any adversary that can monitor their network activity.

4   Whistleblowing Game

This review taught us that there is no formal model of whistleblowing. In the security literature, well-established "games" help shape the mental models of researchers and system designers; all computer science students become familiar with Alice, Bob and Eve playing games with encryption and authentication, and with the Byzantine Generals' Problem for consensus algorithms.

Perhaps the closest to a whistleblowing game is Simmons' model for covert communications [22], where Alice and Bob are in jail, and wish to plan an escape; all their communications are monitored by the warden Willie, who will put them in solitary confinement if he can find any evidence of covert communications. The object of the game for Alice and Bob is to communicate in a way that leaves no evidence of its existence, while for Willie it's to prevent this [1].

In this section, we propose a whistleblowing game that models a more realistic range of actors.

4.1   The Actors

The whistleblowing scenario is more elaborate than the covert communications game:

1. **Alice** is the whistleblower;
2. **Duncan** is the reporter;
3. **Max** is the boss whose wrongdoing Alice wishes to expose;
4. **Tom** is an ally of Max;
5. **Harry** is an ally of Alice.

Our final stakeholder is "the World", a final arbiter to which the documents may be released. Let us look at the goals for each of these entities:

- Alice wants to broadcast information about Max to the World;
- Duncan wants to know that Alice is genuine and, if so, broadcast information to the World;
- Max wants to stop Duncan from broadcasting this information;
- Alice wants to plausibly deny her involvement for as long as possible;
- Max wants to know who Alice is;
- Tom is an intimidator who can support Max with hard power;
- Harry is a regulator with hard power who wants to support Alice.

We suggest that a model of this size may be large enough to reflect real-world tensions while being small enough to be tractable. It is clear what the flow of information in this game looks like, and Fig. 1 illustrates it.

The more complex interaction is that of power. Let us see what the flows of power might look like.

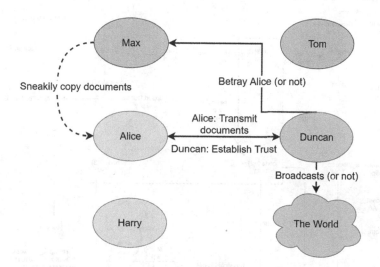

Fig. 1. Information flow in the whistleblowing sequence. Entities in red are trying to blow the whistle, entities in blue are their adversaries while the purple entities are ambivalent. (Color figure online)

5   Flows of Power

Some insights become obvious once we start thinking of power imbalances. A successful leak is only possible if Duncan, the reporter, can stand up to the miscreant Max; if Duncan can be coerced the leak will not get out to the World, and Alice's cover may be blown too – if Duncan knows who she is and can be forced to betray her. A second factor is the relative power of Tom and Harry. In a state governed by the rule of law, we would expect that Harry, the regulator, would be much more powerful than Tom, Max's thug, at least in the long run; while in a corrupt state the dictator's henchmen may be able to treat Harry with contempt. So, in a rule-of-law state, the leak may have some intrinsic soft or hard power on its side. If the story is seen as "just" or its disclosure "legal" then it could be harder for Max to coerce either Alice or Duncan. However, even in wealthy developed countries, an injustice may persist for many years before it catches the public's attention. So any decision by Max as to whether to set his thug Tom on Duncan, or on Alice directly, is likely to involve a calculation of likely consequences.

Let's look at this more closely with a game-theoretic model.

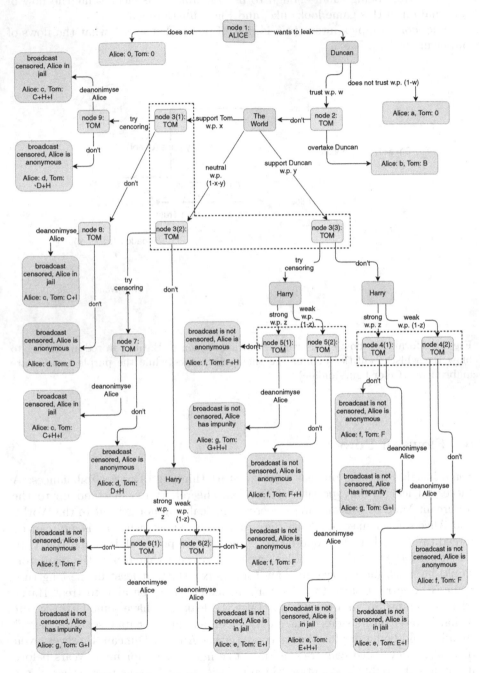

Fig. 2. Sequential-move two-player whistleblowing game

Figure 2 presents an extensive form of a stylised whistleblowing game. The game has two players – Alice and Tom – and three agents whose strategies are known in advance – Duncan, the World and Harry. In this setup, Tom is a combination of Tom and Max from the previous section.

Alice moves first and has to decide whether she wants to leak the information she has. If she does not, the game ends with both players getting a payoff of 0. If she decides to leak, Alice goes to Duncan, who decides whether or not to trust her. Duncan trusts Alice with a probability w known in advance to both Alice and Tom. If he does not trust Alice, the game ends, again with corresponding payoffs. If he does trust Alice, he broadcasts the information.

What happens next depends on how the World behaves. There are three possibilities: (1) the world supports Tom with probability x, or (2) it supports Duncan with probability y, or (3) it is neutral with probability $1 - x - y$. Tom does not know in advance which course the World will take. We consider these three cases in turn.

(1) The World supports Tom. In this case, the broadcast is in effect censored, regardless of whether Tom spends resources to attempt censoring or not. Subsequently, Tom needs to decide whether to spend resources to de-anonymise Alice. If he does, Alice ends up in jail, and otherwise she remains anonymous. Overall, there are four possible outcomes here, as shown in the figure.

(2) The world supports Duncan. If the world supports Duncan, then the broadcast is not censored, regardless of whether Tom spends resources to attempt censorship. Then Harry comes into the picture and may protect Alice. With probability z, Harry's protection is strong , so that Alice ends up with impunity, even if Tom tries to de-anonymise her. With probability $(1 - z)$ his protection is weak. In this case, if Tom goes after Alice, she ends up in jail. If Tom doesn't try, she remains free. Overall, there are eight possible outcomes here, each with its respective payoffs for both players.

(3) The world is neutral. If the world is neutral, then the broadcast will be censored if Tom spends resources to censor it, and not otherwise. If the broadcast is censored, then Tom has to decide, as in (1), whether he wants to go after Alice. If it is not censored, then Harry comes into the picture, as in (2), and we see six possible outcomes as shown in the figure.

This game is solved by backward induction. Payoffs are weighted by relevant probabilities to calculate expected payoffs for both players. Ultimately, Alice decides whether she wants to leak, based on whether the expected payoff of the leak for her is positive or not. The solution turns out to be straightforward if the players are risk-neutral, but it can also be solved assuming both risk-aversion and risk-seeking.

5.1   Subgame-Perfect Equilibrium

First, let us specify what are the payoffs of outcomes for Tom and Alice, who are the only two players of this game. These are as follows:

- Alice does not attempt to leak. both get 0;
- Duncan does not trust Alice. Alice gets a, Tom gets 0;
- If Duncan goes to Max for fact checking, then perhaps Max gets Tom to censor Duncan before the broadcast goes out. Here Alice gets b, Tom gets B;
- Duncan sends out a broadcast but it is quickly censored and Alice ends up in jail. Alice gets c, Tom gets C;
- Broadcast is censored but Alice remains anonymous. Alice gets d, Tom gets D;
- Broadcast is not censored and Alice remains anonymous. Alice gets e, Tom gets E;
- Broadcast is not censored and Alice has impunity. Alice gets f, Tom gets F;
- broadcast is not censored, but Alice ends up in jail. Alice gets g, Tom gets G.

Throughout the game, Tom has an opportunity to try to censor the broadcast and/or de-anonymise Alice. Tom is uncertain whether these attempts will be successful, since the outcome depends on The World and Harry. Yet Tom knows how much both attempts will cost him. In particular:

- An attempt at censorship costs Tom H;
- An attempt de-anonymise Alice costs him I.

Now, to the solution. For simplicity, assume risk-neutrality. Start with the very last decision that Tom has to make – i.e. whether to de-anonymise Alice. Assume that he will always try to do this if the expected utility is at least as large as that of not doing so. Then, at nodes 7–9, he will try to de-anonymise Alice if

$$C + I \geq D$$

Next, nodes 4–6 involve uncertainty over Harry, who can be either support Alice or not with a known probability. Here, Tom will only attempt to de-anonymise Alice if

$$zG + (1 - z)E + I \geq F.$$

For both types of nodes, determine the preferred action for Tom and label the corresponding expected utilities as $\mathbb{E}(U_n), n \in [4, 9]$.

Move one step above, to node 3, where Tom has to decide whether he wants to try to censor the broadcast. Again, he will attempt to do so if the expected utility of censorship is at least as large as that of not doing so – i.e.

$$x\mathbb{E}(U_9) + (1 - x - y)\mathbb{E}(U_7) + z\mathbb{E}(U_5) \geq x\mathbb{E}(U_8) + (1 - x - y)\mathbb{E}(U_6) + z\mathbb{E}(U_4).$$

Determine the preferred action for Tom, and record the expected value of this action as $\mathbb{E}(U_3)$.

Now move one step above to node 2. Tom will block Duncan if

$$B \geq \mathbb{E}(U_3).$$

Determine Tom's preferred action and label it as $\mathbb{E}(U_2)$.

Finally, at node 1, Alice will compare her expected payoff of trying to leak the information with the payoff of not attempting to leak, which we normalise to 0. She expects that with probability $1 - w$ Duncan will not trust her, in which case she will receive a payoff of a; with probability w he will trust her, in which case her payoff is determined by the actions of Tom as described above. She will only try to leak if her expected payoff of leaking

$$(1 - w)a + w * \mathbb{E} \text{ [as determined by Tom's actions]}$$

is positive.

Notice that this model can easily accommodate a case where Duncan goes directly to Harry without first trying to broadcast with the support of the World. Assuming that the broadcast will not be censored, if Harry is involved and the World is not, this requires one to set the probability that the World will support Duncan $y = 1$. Doing this essentially removes nodes 3(1) and 3(2) from the picture as well as all subsequent nodes. A slightly more complex situation is where Alice goes directly to Harry, ignoring both Duncan and the World. This case requires a slight modification in the model in the following way. First, set the probability that Duncan trusts Alice as $w = 1$. Next, Tom's payoff when attempting to overwhelm Duncan should be set to $-\infty$. Finally, as in the previous modification, we set $y = 1$. This will essentially remove Duncan and the World from the setup entirely, and eliminate node (2) from the picture as well as nodes 3(1), 3(2) and all subsequent nodes. The solution method for these two modified cases remain exactly the same as above – start from the final nodes and go up the tree, at each node determining the preferred action for Alice/Tom.

5.2 Revisiting Case Studies

Let's look at the case studies from Sect. 2 again through the lens of this model. In the case of Snowden, we see that the World acted more or less in a neutral fashion. (People in government mostly saw Snowden as a traitor while people in the tech industry mostly saw him as a whistleblower.) Snowden's adversary had the power to de-anonymize him, but his Duncan had impunity thanks to the US constitution and his Harry, the Russian government, was politically and militarily strong enough to provide Snowden with personal impunity in the form of asylum. We therefore end up with payoffs of g and G_I for Snowden and Tom respectively as shown in Fig. 2.

We see the World acting in favour of Alice in the Weinstein case, after the New York Times article triggered a shift in public opinion which changed sex abuse by powerful men from being normal to being unacceptable. Then regardless of the presence of a Tom, we would expect the information not to be censored. However, before the World changed its opinion, Tom (in the form of the rich abuser's lawyers) could censor the information with threats of actions for defamation and bills for legal costs. This is exactly what we saw happen in this case.

6   Recommendations and Future Work

This analysis suggests that if we wish to help whistleblowers, there are three ways in which technology might be able to help:

1. Reducing time-to-publish to zero;
2. Increasing the cost of de-anonymising Alice;
3. Facilitating trust establishment between Alice and Duncan.

Variants of reducing the time-to-publish include reducing Duncan's cost-to-publish to zero, increasing his cost-to-betray, and eliminating Duncan completely. Which version you pick may depend on how you characterise "the World". When you write a tweet, are you publishing directly to the world or is Twitter now your Duncan? But then there's a further complicating factor, namely the amount of influence you have and thus the likelihood that your tweet will go viral.

Improving Alice's anonymity has been the usual technical approach. As our game shows, increasing her anonymity results in a higher cost for Tom to interfere and thus increases the chances of a successful leak. Moreover, having a reliable means to leak that is well known and easily available could foster a culture of increased transparency [10]. This has the second-order effect of increasing Tom's costs in general.

But designers of media websites must be cognisant of the tiny anonymity sets in which most whistleblowers find themselves. This means that bespoke whistleblowing systems may be of suspect utility. Physical intimidation and confiscation of devices are a real possibility, and the mere existence of a leaking app on a person's device may be damning. After all, anonymity loves company, and it may be more effective anyway to teach potential sources to use existing communications tools with more effective operational security. If a newspaper wants sources to use special software to leak, it should be embedded in every single copy of the newspaper's app.

Operationally, the most under-researched avenue of the three mentioned above is the establishment of trust between Duncan and Alice. Not all leaks are bona fide; in a world of increasingly authoritarian governments, news editors must beware of bogus leakers, set up to discredit them. How is a reporter to tell Alice from Malice? What sort of technology might help Duncan establish Alice's good faith without blowing her cover? In the traditional world, trust could be established through mutual friends, or by showing organisational ID, or by disclosing paper documents that would be hard to forge. Electronic equivalents exist but often leave Duncan with digital evidence that might later be seized. Careful use of existing resources can mitigate these risks. For example, Alice might send a photo of her military ID to Duncan by Signal and set the message to disappear after five minutes; that's a decent online equivalent of meeting him in a pub and showing him the real thing. However we see no discussion of such issues on any of the web pages set up to encourage confidential sources to leak to newspapers.

Finally, every introductory lecture on the Prisoners' Dilemma points out that if you don't like the game you find yourself playing, you should try to change it into a different one. Make the dilemma a multi-round game, and you can play tit-for-tat. Can we change the game here?

A relevant case of whistleblowing in the computer industry is the disclosure of software vulnerabilities. Until about 2004–5 this was a Prisoners' Dilemma. If a researcher took a vulnerability to a vendor they might just be threatened with an expensive lawsuit and end up having to promise to keep quiet. The bug meanwhile remained unfixed. So if you wanted to get bugs fixed, you had to take the whistleblowing route and just publish bugs anonymously on bugtraq. That was a lose-lose outcome for everyone, as you didn't get the glory, and the vendor then had to scramble to fix its product, which could get hacked meanwhile. The solution was to change the game to responsible disclosure, whereby the discloser gives the vendor a period of time to patch the vulnerability. Research in security economics suggested this to be the best compromise [1].

Our own experience of reporting vulnerabilities is that responsible disclosure to non-tech companies can still result in legal threats, and so our standard procedure when we discover a vulnerability in a payment system is no longer to report it to the banks directly but rather to the banking regulators (the Fed, the European Central Bank and the UK Financial Conduct Authority). This was done for example with the vulnerabilities described in [12] and [3]. It removes the threat of legal action against the security researcher, pushes the industry to fix the problem, and with luck embeds compliance tests to ensure that it stays fixed.

If Alice can go directly to Harry, then Duncan becomes redundant. And where Harry's incentives are strong, we often find workable mechanisms. For example, many countries' tax authorities have mechanisms for company staff to blow the whistle on tax avoidance and in many cases to claim quite substantial rewards. However not all industries are regulated well or at all, and even regulated industries have abuses in which their regulators take no interest. So it might be of interest to study which of the world's thousands of regulatory bodies have serviceable whistleblowing mechanisms; this might give useful insights into whether they are serious, or whether they see their real role as protecting the industry they're tasked to supervise. In the context of healthcare, to whom should a concerned medic turn? March 2020 has seen large numbers of medics writing to the press about issues such as the availability of personal protective equipment because of lack of trust in the usual chain of command.

In short, whistleblowing is not just a problem of cryptographic protocol design, or even of usability engineering. It's a complex and fascinating problem in security economics which deserves study in its real-world context.

References

1. Anderson, R.: Security Engineering - A Guide to Building Dependable Distributed Systems. Wiley, Hoboken (2008)
2. CBS Los Angeles. Courtney love warns about harvey weinstein in 2005 video. https://www.youtube.com/watch?v=mDh4xeI-4KQ
3. Bond, M., Choudary, O., Murdoch, S., Skorobogatov, S., Anderson, R.: Chip and Skim: cloning EMV cards with the pre-play attack. In: IEEE Symposium on Security and Privacy (2014)
4. Campbell, D., Topping, A.: Ian paterson inquiry: more than 1,000 patients had needless operations. The Guardian, 4 February 2020
5. Daly, M.: Whistleblower taped to chair and gagged. BBC News, 23 May 2018. https://www.bbc.com/news/uk-scotland-44222575
6. Danezis, G., Dingledine, R., Mathewson, N.: Mixminion: design of a type iii anonymous remailer protocol. In: Proceedings of the 2003 IEEE Symposium on Security and Privacy, SP '03, p. 2, USA. IEEE Computer Society (2003)
7. FCA: Financial incentives for whistleblowers (2014). https://www.fca.org.uk/publication/financial-incentives-for-whistleblowers.pdf
8. GOV.UK: Whistleblowing for employees. https://www.gov.uk/whistleblowing
9. Kashmir Hill: The U.S. Government tracks all the snail mail you send too (2013). https://www.forbes.com/sites/kashmirhill/2013/07/03/the-u-s-government-tracks-all-the-snail-mail-you-send-too/
10. Transparency International: Corruption and whistleblowing. https://www.transparency.org/topic/detail/whistleblowing
11. Kantor, J., Twohey, M.: Harvey Weinstein paid off sexual harassment accusers for decades. New York Times, 5 October 2017
12. Murdoch, S., Drimer, S., Anderson, R., Bond, M.: Chip and pin is broken. In: IEEE Symposium on Security and Privacy (2010)
13. nidirect: Blowing the whistle on workplace wrongdoing. https://www.nidirect.gov.uk/articles/blowing-whistle-workplace-wrongdoing
14. Nixon, R.: Postal Service confirms photographing all U.S. mail (2013). http://www.nytimes.com/2013/08/03/us/postal-service-confirms-photographing-all-us-mail.html
15. Nixon, R.: U.S. Postal Service logging all mail for law enforcement (2013). http://www.nytimes.com/2013/07/04/us/monitoring-of-snail-mail.html
16. Nye, J.: Bound to Lead: The Changing Nature of American Power. Basic Books (1990)
17. NYTimes: Tips (2016). https://www.nytimes.com/newsgraphics/2016/news-tips/
18. Bank of England: Whistleblowing and the bank of England (2019). https://www.bankofengland.co.uk/whistleblowing
19. PCAW: Protect: Speak up, stop harm. https://protect-advice.org.uk/case-studies/
20. Redo-Sanchez, A., et al.: Tearahertz time-gated spectral imaging for content extraction through layered structures. Nat. Commun. **7**, 12665 (2016)
21. Errata Security: How the intercept outed reality winner (2017)
22. Simmons, G.J.: The Prisoners' Problem and the Subliminal Channel, pp. 51–67. Springer, Boston (1984). https://doi.org/10.1007/978-1-4684-4730-9_5
23. Smith, D., Chamberlain, P.: On the blacklist: how did the UK's top building firms get secret information on their workers? The Guardian, 27 February 2015

24. New York Times: Harvey Weinstein paid off sexual harassment accusers for decades. https://www.nytimes.com/2017/10/05/us/harvey-weinstein-harassment-allegations.html
25. Whitten, A., Tygar, D.: Why Johnny can't encrypt: a usability evaluation of PGP 5.0. In: 8th Usenix Security Symposium (1999)
26. WikiLeaks: Wikileaks tips. https://wikileaks.org/#submit_help_tips

Snitches Get Stitches: On the Difficulty of Whistleblowing (Transcript of Discussion)

Mansoor Ahmed-Rengers[(✉)], Ross Anderson, Darija Halatova, and Ilia Shumailov

Computer Laboratory, University of Cambridge, Cambridge, UK
mansoor.ahmed@cl.cam.ac.uk

I should first comment on the title. We wrote this a long time before the events of yesterday. We do not consider Julian Assange a snitch, and we sincerely hope he doesn't get stitches. So let's ignore the first part. Another thing we can ignore is the grace period. Please feel free to interrupt me, starting now.

Yesterday (Assange's arrest at the Ecuadorian embassy) has reminded us that whistle-blowing is a risky business. It's probably one of the most risky security protocols that human beings encounter – maybe next to nuclear command and control. But I hope that it also reminds us that whistle-blowing is necessary. It is often the last line of defence in a corrupt system. It helps us see information that powerful entities would rather us not see. For those who do not know, this is a screenshot from the Wikileaks video, Collateral Murder. And lastly, whistle-blowing is very interesting, because a whistle-blower is a traditional insider threat, except that in traditional security models, we want to curtail this insider threat. Here, we're trying to help the insider threat. This makes for a very interesting dynamic.

So, when we looked at this, we thought that this is an interesting area to work in. We started off by comparing technologies and looking for technological solutions. But as soon as we started looking into case studies we realised that we were being very short-sighted. We were missing the forest for the trees. In a broad variety of whistle-blowing cases, collected very conveniently by PCaW.org.uk, which is a charity organisation, technology wouldn't have helped. The anonymity set might be too small. The whistle-blower might be too susceptible to social pressure, or they might have already used some sort of internal complaints mechanism, which would have led them to be highly suspect in case a report came out.

In these cases, no matter how much encryption we used, we couldn't have saved the whistle-blower. Their anonymity, their plausible deniability, was blown from the start. And as we kept looking into these case studies, we started realising that whistle-blowing is really not about technology. It is about power dynamics. What can we say about these power dynamics? Can we be more specific?

We can start by dividing power. Power can be classified as either hard power or soft power. Hard power is very concrete. There's military, there's financial power, there's physical intimidation. All the Russian gangs that Ilia has been

J. Anderson et al. (Eds.): Security Protocols 2019, LNCS 12287, pp. 304–312, 2020.
https://doi.org/10.1007/978-3-030-57043-9_28

talking about recently; those are all examples of hard power. Soft power is more or less cultural context. They might be things like prejudice. If a black person complained about police brutality before ubiquitous video, they would not be taken seriously, because there was a prejudice against black people. Soft power can also include things like public support for ideas. If a leak is seen as just, then there's support that the whistle-blower can potentially get.

Now, when we start thinking of power in this way, and when we start thinking of it as hard versus soft, a couple of intuitions come to mind. One of them is that a successful leak is only possible if the recipient can challenge the power of the miscreant. If the recipient can be coerced, then either the leak will not be effective, in the sense that it might never be broadcast, or the whistle-blower's cover will be blown. If the reporter can be tortured for the identity of the whistle-blower, there's a very good chance of that. Another intuition that we immediately came up with is that the leak itself has a higher chance of being published if it has soft or hard power on its side. There might even be judicial protections or other hard-power protections afforded to the whistle-blower.

Let's look at a case study. Edward Snowden is the one we are probably most familiar with. Snowden was clearly up against the hard power of the NSA. But he had the soft power of public support by his side, for a little while at least. But as the years have gone on, we can see that public opinion of Edward Snowden has gone down, which leads us to believe that power is a fickle thing, especially soft power. This fickleness can work in our favour sometimes. If you look at the Me Too movement, there were industry jokes about Harvey Weinstein being a sexual predator for years, but no one had the courage to come out against him because there wasn't enough public support. Yet when there was this shift, this massive cultural movement of Me Too, many people felt emboldened enough to come out and accuse him of all these sexual misconducts. So soft power's fickleness can sometimes work in the favour of a whistle-blower.

So now we have a sense of the kind of case studies that happen in the real world; we have an intuition for what things might be expected in a world divided by hard power and soft power. Let's see if we can formulate a security protocol out of this.

We have a few actors. Alice is our protagonist: the whistle-blower. She wants to send sensitive information about Max to Duncan, named after Duncan Campbell. And Duncan wants to know that Alice is genuine, and if she is, then he wants to broadcast this information to the world. Max wants to stop Duncan from broadcasting this information, because it affects him adversely, and Alice wants to plausibly deny her involvement for as long as possible. Whether that plausible deniability involves anonymity or not we'll discuss later. On the other hand, Max wants to know who the original source was. Tom is an additional actor that we introduce. This is the hard power equivalent of Max. He is an intimidator that supports Max, and Harry is an entity with hard power that supports Alice. Both Tom and Harry may or may not exist in a particular given case.

Jonathan Anderson: So, in the case of Max wanting to know who the original source was; it seems like that's maybe actually a secondary goal for Max; that Max's primary goal is really to dissuade future Alices from doing the same thing?

Reply: Yes

Jonathan Anderson: By raising the costs of whistle-blowing?

Reply: Yes

Jonathan Anderson: Although that is a secondary goal that's implied by the primary one, it seems like they have slightly different implications.

Reply: That is true, and we did consider that, and to make it a one-shot game, it was easier to frame it this way, than having a sort of circular loop, which feels like the next round of the game, and that's why we went with this.

The flow of information in this game is actually quite simple. The first step is done by Alice. She decides to sneakily copy documents from Max, and send the documents to Duncan. Duncan, using the same channel, has to establish trust with Alice, and then Duncan has a choice. He's neither blue team nor red team. He's in the purple team. He can either choose to follow Alice's wishes and broadcast the documents to the world, or he can choose to betray Alice and inform Max of the leak.

The tricky dimension in all of this is trust. In the case of Snowden, he needed Laura Poitras to convince Glenn Greenwald to take him seriously, before Greenwald would even look at his documents. And this is because anonymous sources tend to be viewed with suspicion, because reporters receive a lot of spam, a lot of plausibly true documents which are not really true, and therefore there seems to be an inherent trade-off between trustworthiness and the whistle-blower's anonymity. This what leads us to believe that there is no general, purely technical solution possible.

Any solution for whistle-blowing has to depend on the context in which it takes place. The flow of information might be simple, but the flow of power in this game is really complicated.

In this graph, the yellow lines represent hard power, and the blue lines represent soft power. As we can see, Max has some sort of alliance with Tom, which allows him to use Tom's hard power. I've used the word "overwhelm" as a catch-all to encompass things like physical intimidation, social pressure, et cetera. And Tom uses this to either stop Duncan from broadcasting things or to censor him from publishing things to the world. He could use his hard power to try to de-anonymise Alice, or to stop her from making the leak in the first place. As for Harry, it depends on how much pressure he feels from the world. So if this is a judiciary committee, then depending on how much moral support there is for Alice, may choose to support Alice, using his hard power; he may even choose to overwhelm Max with subpoenas and things like that.

The interesting thing in this graph is that we can see that neither Alice nor Duncan have any power over any other actors once they've decided to make the leaks. Alice's fate is completely dependent on the balance of power between Tom and Harry, and this is a very precarious situation. On the other hand, Duncan's motivation to leak is a clear trade-off between how much pressure he faces from Tom, and how much moral support he receives from the world.

These are two areas that we've identified where technology could possibly help. The first case where technology could help is where Alice doesn't have impunity, so anonymity or plausible deniability equals self-preservation. And the second place where technology can help is to reduce the links needed to broadcast to the world to zero.

If any Duncan can be censored, then you need a way to broadcast directly to the world. We started thinking about ways in which technology can help in these two scenarios, and we came up with a few ideas. The first one we thought of was ad hoc networking. In the olden days before digital devices, the best way to leak was to bump into a reporter at the bar. We could do a similar thing if we had some sort of an ad hoc network, which worked on local area networks. The problem with this is that, again, since this is fairly anonymous, the reporter has no reason to trust the data coming in.

We thought about using mixing networks to increase anonymity sets, but there is a problem here, and the problem is that if you are the only person using Tor in your office, and the leaks went via Tor, then you are the whistle-blower. And this is a general curse of bespoke technology in this field.

Another thing we thought about was using plausible deniability via dual purpose apps, embedding a secure messaging service within a news app, but again, there's a flood of information that this will open up to the reporters, and it is going to be really difficult for the reporters to find anything useful using such an arrangement. And lastly, we thought about reducing the time to publish to zero, by using throwaway twitter accounts: just paste everything to Pastebin, copy a link to twitter using an anonymous account, and submit it. But, who's even listening? Even if we do manage to get this done, and even if the NSA can't trace you back, would it ever have any impact, without the reputation that Duncan brings along with him?

Aside from all these problems with technologies, there are general technological bear-traps. One famous one is usability. If Johnny can't encrypt, then how can he leak? The second one is one that I have highlighted, is that special software means that there is no crowd to hide in. And the last thing is probably the most profound, and that is that as technologists, we try to find one-size-fits-all solutions, but what I'm positing here is that the power dynamics are structured in such a way that there is no way to have a one-size-fits-all solution.

The advice that you give to a potential whistle-blower has to be tailor-made to a particular situation.

Now that we have discussed technologies, an important question that we have to face is do we want anonymity, do we want deniability, or we do we want impunity? One interesting thing that we came across by looking at all these case studies is that very few whistle-blowers remain anonymous. When we looked at massive leaks in the past ten years, we could only find a handful, the most famous one being Panama Papers. Most tend to be known whistle-blowers, who either get arrested, or find some sort of impunity, either via the law or by escaping to a different jurisdiction.

The difference between anonymity and plausible deniability depends on where you are. When we looked at case studies from India, we realised that it really doesn't matter if you can plausibly deny that you were the whistle-blower, because you will get murdered in either case.

If you look at the Wikipedia list of all the whistle-blowers from India, you would see that in the last ten years, only two have survived.

In such a scenario, you don't want plausible deniability. You want to be as far away from the news as possible. The ideal Duncan, in our opinion, is someone with impunity; someone that Tom's overwhelming hard power can do nothing to, and this could be members of parliament, journalists, regulators, people whose job it is to investigate these matters.

And the last thing that we wanted to think about while discussing anonymity is what matters more. Does the anonymity set matter more, or does the usability pattern? So does it matter more that ten people went to the bar on the same night that you did, or the fact that you go to this bar every single night?

And the answer to that sort of depends on your adversary's surveillance power. If Max is the NSA or the Google … Yes?

Jonathan Anderson: So, some of these things you're talking about: impunity, almost as if it's like a binary thing, but I think in some of these cases, you talk about impunity in the sense of, well, here's a journalist, who isn't going to be able to be hounded, or shut down, or something, in a given country. A lot of them do get shut down for being a journalist, but you also included in that category, people who have to then ensure they only ever live in countries that don't have extraditionary alliances with the country itself. It's different, I guess that impunity and anonymity is, in this case, not like a binary: Are you safe or not? It's what is the cost? And is it a cost that you are willing to pay, or you are not willing to pay, based on how important you think the leak is?

Reply: Yes.

Jonathan Anderson: You have to go: You can never go home. There is a real cost to that, but on the other hand, it may be that cost is worth it to you. Maybe some whistle-blower will decide, "It's worth it to me to go to prison, because this is so important, even though I might spend the rest of my life in prison in Canada." Obviously getting murdered, is less good, not many people are perhaps willing to pay that cost, but … it's not strictly a binary thing.

Reply: Yeah, and when we structured this game, we don't frame it as a binary thing. I guess this is a limitation of words. We structured this as investment made by Tom in doing all these actions versus the effect that it has on Duncan, and there is an intrinsic motivation, which depends on the particular Duncan.

Jim Blythe: Thank you, sorry I may have missed this, I apologise. You mentioned that once the whistleblower gives up the information, they kind of have no power?

Reply: Yes.

Jim Blythe: But that means that it's not an atomic operation. It's very rarely atomic. Right, this whistleblower is going to say, "I've got something; what can you give me, before I do this?" I didn't notice that that was in your protocol?

Reply: No, it's not. That's a very good point. So you would say that this is a multi-round sort of a negotiation, where -

Jim Blythe: Yeah maybe try to capture that part of the protocol, where the whistle-blower tries to get some kind of guarantees, before they give up the power.

Reply: Okay, so there's a sort of a two-way trust establishment?. How ... Do you imagine this as them getting some collateral over the reporter?

Jim Blythe: Possibly. I don't know ... yeah, trying to establish some kind of guarantees from the reporter. While there's still some incentive for the reporter to do that.

Reply: Right. Yeah, makes sense.

Jim Blythe: In that case, a certain question I have is about the nature of the information that's being whistle-blown, because sometimes once the world gets this information, it's very easy to know whether it's true or not. Let's say this factory is unsafe, and somebody's going to go and say look at it right away and verify that that was in fact true information.

Reply: Yes.

Jim Blythe: But if it's something that happened, and there's very little evidence -

Reply: Like the Bloomberg story -

Jim Blythe: The World would like to know that there's some proof, or some guarantee, that the person who gave the information, both plausibly could have the information, and plausibly wouldn't have much incentive to lie about it. So, another interesting point for technology might be to see if you can provide those guarantees, and maintain some level of anonymity or impunity.

Reply: Right, yeah. You're right that there should be another link where the world tries to establish trust. Here we've modeled trust as something between Alice and Duncan. You're right. That is a little limitation of this model.

Jim Blythe: Something about the nature of this information's verifiability.

Reply: Yeah.

Simon Foley: Just a quick follow-up from that on the nature of trust; it reminded me of the Boston papers, where a researcher had interviewed a number of IRA terrorists, who had conducted activities in Northern Ireland and elsewhere, and had as part of the agreement, had a guaranteed anonymity, and went all the way to I am not sure which court in the US, and the researchers were told that you have to identify these people.

Reply: Okay, alright.

Simon Foley: Exactly

Reply: Hard power being fickle, yes.

Fabio Massacci: So how do you distinguish this flow of trust. Slander from whistle-blowing?

Reply: Slander from whistle-blowing? We don't.
   That just depends on your perspective, I guess. Are you talking about the veracity, the truthfulness, of the documents or the intention behind the documents?

Fabio Massacci: Yes, I want to leak documents that would put Max in a bad light. Max has done nothing, or he was actually against some particular event that happened. But Alice only leaked the document in which he was asked to do something, and not the reply.

Ross Anderson: Well, libel and slander laws are part of the power structures talked about here. In theory, truth may be a defense against libel. In practise it's a very expensive one, that Alice may not be able to deploy. But Duncan, if he works for The Guardian, may be able to use truth as a defence, because The Guardian has enough money to be able to go to the High Court.
   So the only salient thing here is the power structure, not the detail of whether the power structure consists of storming into the Ecuadorian embassy, or slapping you with a writ that costs you a million pounds to make go away.

Alexander Hicks: Alex, So on the topic of immunity, have you looked into the new EU directive for the protection of whistle-blowers.

Reply: How new are we talking?

Alexander Hicks: I think they voted on it on Tuesday.

Reply: Oh, no.

Alexander Hicks: So I think they had a Directive of some kind and took it to a vote. It's sketchy in parts, because it kind of assumes that they'll go through official communication channels, not necessarily reliable. There's also something in it about giving you immunity, if you go to the media, as long as there's some form of responsible disclosure. So might be something to look into. I don't think it's the best thing but maybe it's sometuhing.

Reply: Right, thanks. I mean, even if there is no hard power consequences to whistle-blowing, you always pay social consequences. If you whistle-blow on your employer, there's a very good chance that you will be shunned by your community in the workspace. So there are other reasons why you might want to remain anonymous.

Alexander Hicks: Yes, and there was that whistleblower on Brexit who then got attacked on the BBC and so on.

Reply: Any other questions?

Right, so if Max is the NSA or Google, then they have the ability to look back at last week's traffic data. Now we are talking in the digital realm. And do correlation attacks. When you are operating at that scale, it might be possible for you to just collect the traffic data for an entire nation, and then see who messaged whom at a given point of time. And just the correlation, of talking to a particular reporter at a particular time, is probably enough to get you caught.

On the other hand, if Max is a medium to large organisation, then he may have some logs, and he can use data leakage prevention systems within the corporation itself. And the invariant here is that the larger that Max is, the larger the set of Alices that he can surveil or intimidate, which feeds back into his own power.

Before we get into recommendations for whistle-blowing, I would like to have a huge list of caveats. The first one being that everything eventually breaks, including crypto. And new avenues for surveillance are unearthed all the time. There was a recent case in Germany where they used the HR tracking data of a suspect to convict him of murder, because they noticed that he was running up and down the stairs at 2 AM, and that was found to be evidence enough. Thirdly, rubber hoses are cheap. It's very easy to physically intimidate people in many jurisdictions. Usability is hard, especially in a protocol as complicated as this one. And a point that is often ignored is that Alice may want to reveal herself voluntarily for reasons not explained by power dynamics. Chelsea Manning has admitted that she would have voluntarily disclosed her identity in a couple of years, to save other people from being falsely accused of being the whistle-blower. And the last problem is that there are way too many ways for Max or Tom to do a denial of service on the information that is leaked.

With that said, I'd like to conclude with a few high-level recommendations.

One is: Try to hide within the mundane, rather than the crowd. If your behavioural pattern changes dramatically during the whistle-blowing period, then that is going to stick out, and that is going to get you caught much faster than using some bespoke technology. For researchers, one thing they can explore is ad hoc mesh networking with mixing, this gives you both the scale of a mixing network with the serendipity of ad hoc networking. Third recommendation would be that you should tailor your solutions to a given Max, rather than trying to find a one size fits all approach, and the last one is that technological solutionism is insidious. Throwing technology at problems can be helpful, but the fundamental problems here are economic and rooted in human nature. The tool is not the task.

Thank you.

Jeff Yan: Just a quick comment, actually as you said, everything breaks. It strikes me that in some circumstances, going publicly is the best defence. Basically, you could find it easier to get actual social support, and get picked up by media easier. If actually you are isolated and you're suspected as a whistle-blower, so you would end up with a helpless situation.

Reply: I think that might be true in a lot of situations, but as the case studies in India show, whistle-blowers do get lynched by mobs. And if you are up in a regime where there is a cult of personality, where even if what you are saying is just, but the public support leans heavily in favour of the great leader, you might not come out of that alive.

Simon Foley: Any more questions. Okay, so let's thank the speaker

Reply: Thank you.

Author Index

Printed in the United States
By Bookmasters